# THE RUSSIAN WAY

by

Garo Dorian

DORRANCE PUBLISHING CO., INC.
PITTSBURGH, PENNSYLVANIA 15222

# CONTENTS

| | | |
|---|---|---|
| Introduction | | ............iv |
| Chapter I | The Beginning | ............1 |
| Chapter II | The Early Rulers | ............9 |
| Chapter III | The Mongol Invasion and the Golden Horde | ............22 |
| Chapter IV | The Romanov Czars, Autocrats, and Emperors | ............29 |
| Chapter V | The Revolution | ............94 |
| Chapter VI | The Civil War | ............109 |
| Chapter VII | Emigres | ............129 |
| Chapter VIII | Transformation of Society | ............140 |
| Chapter IX | Vladimir Illich Lenin (Ulianov): 1870-1924 | ............149 |
| Chapter X | Josef Visarionovich Stalin (Djugashvilli): 1878-1953 | ............162 |
| Chapter XI | The Great Patriotic War | ............188 |
| Chapter XII | The Successors | ............215 |
| Chapter XIII | Dissolution of the USSR | ............236 |
| Chapter XIV | Arts & Sciences | ............244 |
| Chapter XV | Russia Redux | ............261 |

# INTRODUCTION

This book does not assume to be an official or detailed history of the Russians. It is, however, a summary of events as published and interpreted in history books about the origins of the Russians, their early rulers, Moscovy, Imperial, and Soviet periods. In researching history during the Imperial regime from books available among the emigres and Soviet books available worldwide—which western writers have assessed—I have found some periods and personalities somewhat biased. However, as is common in most histories, various points of view are expressed by Russian and western writers; some are in agreement, and some are not. Legend and mythology of the early period surround the beginnings and lineage of the Russians with the house of Rurik, the Swede. It is alleged that he died in 879 in Novgorod in northern Russia. It is, however, unclear by evidence other than circumstantial, that Rurik even existed. What is more—the Varangian origins and lineage of some early Russian rulers are based solely on Rurik's existence. Some western writers have alleged that Rurik was a vassal of the western Emperor Lothaire, who sent him to explore unoccupied lands in what is now northern Russia. Others state that "Rus" is derived from "Ruotsi," a Finnish word for Swedes.

In addition, various periods are interpreted quite differently, and in some cases conflict substantially by writers under Soviet regime, who doctored documents to suit their requirements. Under Stalin, conflicts arose about contributions of individual rulers and generally appear throughout the fabric and content of events in Soviet history. To him, some rulers became heroes based on class-consciousness, economic policies, and their destruction of the noble classes.

Since Stalin, Soviet writers have done some valuable work in clearing up dubious writings in both Imperial and particularly Soviet historiography. I have endeavored to isolate these conflicts wherever possible. It is also important to clarify the reasons for Russian acceptance of autocracy and dictatorship throughout their history.

Although there are some conflicting versions in both Russian and Western views, the fabric of historical evidence remains intact and does not change the character of the Russians or their history. History recognizes continuity of customs and traditions in nations through centuries and acts as a reflection of its people; the Russians are no exception. A great people, held back and isolated from contact with western nations—Russians have contributed immensely to civilization.

It is unfortunate that the most basic freedoms were denied them. They have been governed and bound by traditions left over from Mongol-Tatar conquests and the role of Byzantine emperors as head of church and state. Their leaders readily absorbed these traditions and governed arbitrarily as they pleased. Early

Asiatic domination and expansion of their territories by their rulers—which seems never to have been enough—resulted in apprehension and danger to the west. Geography also played a major part in forming the character of the Russians. No civilized people have had a more traumatic existence under autocratic rule than the Russians. Histories of other nations have unpleasant overtones, yet none equal the troubled history of the Russians. Some Russian scholars have recently acknowledged the communist experiment as a cataclysmic experience under Stalin and a nightmare under his successors. They attribute this experience of seventy-four years to immaturity of the Russian working class, illiteracy of the peasantry under the czars, and a Soviet dictatorship which exploited it. Most acknowledge that Kerenskiy's provisional government in 1917 never had a chance under utopian propaganda of the Bolsheviks, promising people everything, when they had had nothing before. Yet these same writers cling to outdated economic and social structures, without true consideration for the "rights of men." The present Russian Parliament's lower chamber, the DUMA, doesn't have its own house in order to benefit their people, particularly in its economic and political structure. They are paranoid about the involvement by Western governments and businesses which would swamp the country with a brand of democracy and the free enterprise system.

Yet in order to survive, it is precisely what is needed for the twenty-first century. Interest centering on Russia has soared to remarkable proportions since the dissolution of the USSR in 1991. Prior to this event, most people were aware of the sinister character of the Soviet Union as an evil empire and superpower, which caused untold problems for the world, yet so many have not clearly understood the basis of that evil.

My life as a youth in the Soviet Union, an émigré in Manchuria, and an adult in America perhaps permits a more personal and balanced view of the Russians and what they call their "soul." This particular brand of soul is a difficult term to describe in view of its religious overtones mixed with destiny. After my own experiences, analyzing and reviewing numerous books (Russian and Western publications), and my own notes of several years, I gave serious thought to writing. Many people, including those attending my lectures, urged me to write on the subject in view of the great interest generated by the fall of the Soviet Union. It is precisely for general readers to whom this book is addressed. I have eliminated a considerable amount of minutia to maintain interest and emphasized critical events in endeavoring to condense the book. For the reader who wishes detailed knowledge, I recommend readings by scholars on particular subjects for further reference. It is hoped this book fulfills the request of many people who have encouraged me to write. I also wish to thank my many students, from whom I have learned a great deal. The opinions expressed in this book are strictly my own, and I am solely responsible for them.

Garo Dorian

# CHAPTER I
# THE BEGINNING

The eastern Slavic tribes about the third century occupied lands between the Baltic Sea, the Don River, the Black Sea, and the lower Danube River. Later, around A.D. 800, it is said that the Norsemen united them, coming down from the Baltic. It is after this period which the Russians consider the date of the founding of their state, in A.D. 879. It is relatively difficult to ascertain this chronological event to be the actual case, since no other available evidence exists. Ancient implements have shed some light on the subject, but insufficient for a definite conclusion. We should accept it as a tradition, since Russian historians prefer to allude to it. Ancient Greek records indicate that Scythians, a warlike people who spoke an Iranian language, inhabited the area of the lower Don and the Black Sea, around the seventh century B.C. Some of the artifacts made by Greek colonists on the northern shores of the Black Sea for Scythian kings are displayed at the Hermitage Museum in St. Petersburg, Russia. In the fourth century, Sarmatians—another Iranian-speaking people displaced the Scythians—by the end of the second century B.C. had settled on the Black Sea coast. Some Alans in the area began dominating several eastern Slavic tribes and eventually these tribes adopted some Alanic names and customs. To associate themselves with the Alans, the Russians accept this tradition as the basis of their origins. Although this appears to be more of a tradition than fact, we have no substantiated reasons to dispute it.

Sometime in the latter part of the third century of our era, the Sarmatians were displaced by Germanic Goths, coming in from the north, along the Dniester, Bug, and Dnieper rivers, and settled in the southern Russian steppe. By the middle of the fourth century, they became a military power under the leadership of Ermenrich, who subdued the Slavs. However, the Slavs were saved at the end of the century due to a most terrible invasion by the Huns, a Turco-Mongol tribe. Led by Attila the Hun, a militaristic aristocrat who overran the enclaves of the Alans, another Slavic tribe, the Huns made them slaves by vanquishing Ermenrich, which caused him to commit suicide. Subsequently, the Goths set out for western Europe with Attila in pursuit. Attila rested in Pannonia, present-day Hungary, while the Goths conquered most of Europe. The history of the Goths, Visigoths, and Ostrogoths later became indelibly intertwined with that of western Europe and became an integral part of Christendom and western Civilization. There was no useful purpose in pursuing the Gothic tribes to western Europe after they left the Russian steppe. We should now turn to the Russians to determine their progression to nationhood.

The origins of Russian extraction are somewhat obscured and muddled by distinguishing the early Swedes and Norwegians, whose descendants they claim they are from the early Varangians and Norsemen. After the Goths and Attila passed through to the west, several studies allude to the "Rus" from the north country. This tribe of Norsemen, headed by Rurik, settled in the area around the lake country in northern Russia, at Novgorod. Some studies claim Rurik was an adventurer, pirate, and vassal of western Emperor Lothaire. When Rurik died, his successor Oleg, a Norwegian, shifted south from Novgorod, overwhelmed some Rus tribes, and settled in the Kiev area, the present Ukraine. There he created a domain known as the "Kievan Rus." Some scholars attribute Slavic origins to the Galician Marshes around the area of the Pripet River. This confusion evolves from excavations in the Dnieper River basin and from revelations of pre-revolutionary Russian (and some Western) scholars. As of this writing, researchers have established that centuries before the Rus, earlier settlers from the East, after Barbarian passing, migrated into the area in Ukraine, Crimea, Caucasus, and even further west. The pre-revolutionary historian Kluichevsky claims the basis of Kievan Rus was due to Rurik and Oleg. This assumption is challenged by another historian, B.D. Grekov, who wrote in *Ancient Rus* that, "a state is not formed by one or two heroes, but is based on a study of history of a people rather than individuals," Other documents, such as the the recently translated Russian "Primary Chronicle," substantiated by Byzantine and Arabic scholars, state that local oral traditions, songs, tales, and archaeological evidence support the theory of the beginnings of a state in existence. Furthermore, Kiev's contacts and chronicles of the Byzantine Empire and Arab Mideast, along with their proximity and culture—mixed as it was—appear to have had a major and undeniable impact on the Kievan enclave, both socially and economically. It is therefore reasonable to assume that throughout early history, feudal societies were based on socioeconomic conditions in order to survive. Various groups fought and competed among each other for identity and trade, thus eventually creating a state. Whether Rurik existed or is a legend is now academic. The critical part was relocation south by Oleg the Norseman to the Kiev area after 879. Most likely he was a tribal chief or warlord of a clan who held the area as a fiefdom. His successor, Igor, was the last of the Norsemen, to serve as Prince of Kiev, and after his death in 945, all claimants thereafter were Slavs, who ruled over an existing entity in the Kievan enclave. B.D. Grekov conjectures that the Russian princely line started after Igor's death with Sviatoslav and Vladimir, who were Slavs. Again, no fundamental proof of the princely line exists, though we could assume the successors were really chiefs or warlords of tribes.

Byzantine records indicate substantial relations with the Kievans in trade, plunder, and wars. Through constant wars of succession, each with his own interests among the heirs of Igor, Kiev was no longer capable of trading effectively by controlling the flow of tribute. Additionally, the Crusades enhanced the creation of towns along the Mediterranean Sea and the Rhine River in Germany, thus bypassing the Kievan enclave. The trade routes between western Europe and

Byzantium were then routed through Venice by sea, and Bohemia by land, thus adversely affecting Byzantium and Kievan Rus. Disintegration began, and the enclave crumbled approximately in 1200.

The sack of Constantinople in 1204 by the Fourth Crusade, apparently secretly fostered by the pope, seriously weakened the power of Byzantium both economically and militarily. Later, attacks by Bulgars and Turcaic peoples on Kiev presaged the downfall of the already-weakening Byzantium. Thereafter, Kiev was surpassed in trade, principally by Novgorod in the north, who traded in the Baltic region as a member of the Hanseatic League. Vladimir, in the northeast, also became an important trading center, although later its own fratricidal problems caused its collapse. Thereafter, the center of Russian trade and gathering began moving west and north from Kiev. Paradoxically, the Norsemen first settled in the north at Novgorod, then travelled south to Kiev, and returned north again as Slavs.

In these few hundred years, Russian identity and religion gradually became established. Subsequently, sensing weakness of the Byzantine regime, Russians began a mighty effort to establish the beginnings of an independent Orthodox patriarchate in Moscow and eventually attained it in 1453 when Constantinople fell to the Ottoman Turks. Before this period, however, various conquering nomadic peoples from the east and south fought over the Russian steppe. Turco-Mongols and other Ural-Altai peoples—as well as the Alans, Goths, Sarmatians, Scythians, and several other nomadic tribes—claimed and fought over the land. History confirms that Attila the Hun conquered the area and moved his center of power to Pannonia, the western extremity of the Eurasian steppe (Puszta). By 680 or so, the Slavs also penetrated to the east of the Elbe River in Germany. Subsequently, when other tribes passed through to the west or settled in the steppe, they could not sustain sufficient military power to stop the Slavic people moving north to the forested areas, between the Volga, the Don, and northern Caucasus. The Slavic tribes organized into major groups and fought off all other nomadic peoples coming through. Through constant nomadic wars to repel others, they gained identity and tribal unity. Thus commenced the new settlements of the domains of the tribe of "Rus," which centuries later, became the basis of national identity of the Russians.

As we have seen, the early Russians were basically Slavs and belong to the greater Slavonic peoples of Indo-European family. Subsequently, they absorbed elements of different races and nationalities during their western and eastern conquests. Like all Slavic languages, the Russian language has its roots in the Aryan language, with three distinct geographic locations: in the east, Russian, Ukrainian, and Belorussian; in the south, Balkan Serbs, Slavonians (also referred to as Wends), Croatians, and Bosnians; in the west, the Czechs, Slovaks, and Poles. After the Crusades, but before the Ottoman conquests, Russians encountered the Byzantine Empire to the south for trade and plunder. This contact later flowered into a close relationship, with the Russians adopting the Cyrillic alphabet and Eastern Christian Rite.

Although the movement south and west by other Slavic peoples from the steppe was slower, some of these too adopted both the Eastern Christian Rite and the Cyrillic alphabet. Some Balkan Slavs, the Croatians, and Slovenians, came under the influence of the Holy Roman and later Austria-Hungarian empires in due time, and adopted Latin writing and Catholic Rite. Later, those coming under the influence of the Ottoman Empire as Bosnians adopted Islam. The western Czechs came under the influence of western Europe, and adopted the Latin alphabet, Catholicism, and Protestant religion after the Reformation. Their close brethren, the Slovaks, came under early Orthodox Christianity but use the Latin alphabet. All Slavs use the same basic Slavonic language with variations in their particular regions, as do most other language groups. The Poles, however, use Slavonic as their language but adopted western influence and came under the Catholic Rite and the western alphabet. Slavic Orthodox churches use Ancient Slavonic Liturgy, much like the Armenian church uses Ancient Krapar, and the Coptic Church with its own Liturgical Hamitic, as a basis of its own orthodox origin. With few exceptions, the Slavonic language subdivision holds true to this day.

The Russian lands, from a physical and political point of view, are considered today to be part of the continuum of Eurasian continental mass. In the years 1780-1825, German and Russian geographers divided Russia in two parts—Russia in Europe and Russia in Asia—with the Urals as the dividing line. While this exercise has some validity socially—due to diverse population of various racial and language groups in the eastern part—it has no validity in objective reality, considering that Hungarians, Finns, and some Estonians, who are of Mongol-Ugraic origins, are settled in Europe. Present-day geographers consider the limits of Europe to be the Ural Mountain range. From the Ural Mountains east, the country is considered to be part of Asia, although physically on either side of the Urals exist the same characteristics—tundra, forest, and steppe. Since these same characteristics spill over to Siberia, they helped in developmental stages of Russian territorial expansion. The fact that Russia expanded east to the Pacific Ocean areas with no serious physical or socio-political barriers and claimed it as its hegemony is reason enough to consider this as a Eurasian continental mass rather than a political subdivision. It is of course true that the Ural range is a partial physical barrier but not any more than any barrier on a single continental mass. A glance at a map would confirm this fact. The physical characteristics of this landmass begin at the North and stretch along the Arctic Ocean from west to east, spanning both sides of the Ural Mountain range, a band which is a barren tundra and untillable. The entire landmass is mostly flat, with most rivers constrained by limited flow to the seas. This problem and severe climate have constraining consequences in populating the area and exploiting the massive natural resources of northern Siberia. Although lately, with technological advances, progress has been made in exploiting gas, oil, and mineral resources. Geographers identify the land along the Arctic shores as the most useless landmass, where even the Russians don't live.

During Stalin's regime and thereafter—until rehabilitated years later—slave labor camps were located along this stretch. Even today still-frozen bodies occasionally surface. Further inland and south of this band stretches a massive forested area, and while still in a cold climate zone, it is somewhat industrialized and productive, with deposits of untold natural and mineral resources. Below this zone stretches the steppe from Siberia to Russia in the west, while farther south in the Siberian landmass, the desert stretches to Russia, though recedes substantially. These vast lands have been explored and occupied by the Russians for centuries, without claiming them as their own until the mid-1700s. Geopoliticians claim that the eastward expansion is imperialism, similar to western European powers with their colonial empires. Since no major country claimed or fought for it, the Russians subdued the local tribes. The scattered tribes and clans of Siberia, having had no organized power, fell under Russian domination when they arrived on the eastern Pacific shores and claimed the entire land area.

Moving south from Siberia, they approached the Dzungarian Basin and Altai Mountain range in central Asia, adjoining China and Mongolia, respectively. Later in 1689, by the Treaty of Nerchinsk, China ceded territory to Russia and territory north of the Amur River and the Pacific Maritime coast, adjoining the Sea of Japan. China had recently disputed some territory along the Manchurian border and Khingan Mountain range, which also ceded this territory to Russia by the Treaty of Nerchinsk. Three years later the Russians occupied the Kamchatka Peninsula, thus completing the occupation of the northern Eurasian land mass and the boundaries of their empire in the east.

From their early beginnings in Novgorod, down to the Kievan enclave and back north to the Moscow area and east to the Pacific shores, the Russians have traveled for centuries to stake their claim as a nation-state. Political scientists and historians claim that the land and the climate forged a nation of hardy but isolated people, allowing their rulers the freedom to exercise their autocratic powers. From the physical and socio-political conditions, it is reasonable to assume that Russia, acquiring huge territories with sparsely populated areas, could absorb at least another 250,000,000 people, if they had enough to feed them.

All established societies were clans originally and were based upon kinship of common interests, customs, traditions, and certain acceptable norms; these eventually evolved into larger groups called nationalities. The Russians, as most other nations, are also a part of that symbiotic process of evolution into nationhood. However, some societies record their extraction and existence in a form derived from recognizable origins and can be traced back by a historical process and thus are relatively easy to define. In the case of the Russians, in view of their beginnings, some of their records are dependent on certain assumptions made by historians.

The reader should bear in mind that Russian archival records, at least during the formation of the state, were quite loose, and most recorded documents were kept by the church when it affected its interests. Otherwise, "history" was passed down through tales and folklore and written down later by Russian historians. This is not a novel idea since it was also practiced in western Europe, India, China, and other civilizations, although generally backed by some evidence. Some Russian dates may be approximate, therefore their accuracy might be more interpretive rather than actual. In 1450s, the grand dukes of Moscovy annexed almost all independent cities and principalities of northern Russia, including the important cities of Novgorod and Tver. The Duchy of Moscovy—so named due to the enlarged area around Moscow—became a powerful military state by extending its influence into Islamic lands as far down as Afghanistan. Sometime in the 1450s the "Golden Horde" of Mongols, failed to maintain its alliance with the Crimean and Kazan Tatars and found itself confronted by the Moscovy state. Kazimov Tatars, on the other hand, remained faithful to Moscovy, and with their assistance, Ivan the Terrible defeated the Kazan Tatars and annexed the Kazan area to Moscow in 1552 and the Astrakhan area (on the northern shores of the Caspian Sea) in 1556. However, by 1554 Siberia was already reconnoitered and explored and sparsely occupied by Yermak, the Cossack leader. Since Moscovy's rulers claim to be descendants of Vladimir the Saint, who possessed western Russian lands, they occupied land from the Lithanians as their heritage. The struggle to reclaim them took considerable lives and substantial time and fortune. The union of Poland and Lithuania was based on an alliance which later formed a single nation and was accomplished in 1569. By 1791 Lithuania disappeared as an independent political entity. Subsequently, it was annexed by Russia in the third partition of Poland. Lithuania regained its independence in 1918, only to lose it again to the USSR in 1939. Meanwhile, Ivan the Terrible was at war not only with Lithuania, but also with other Baltic states, which interfered with Russian connections to Europe. This conflict involved Sweden in a war with Russia. Several years later, the Poles, under the leadership of Stepan Batory, defeated Ivan the Terrible and forced him to give up the lands and sign a humiliating treaty with Poland and Sweden. Russian historians like to describe the period before the Mongols as the time of principals of political authority—as democratic, aristocratic, and monarchical.

While the monarchical principal existed in Moscow, it was aristocratic in Poland-Lithuania. As regards democratic principals, they state it existed in northwest Russia in Novgorod and Pskov and was known as the *vieche*. It is further claimed that the *vieche* existed between the twelfth and the end of the fifteenth centuries. Moreover, we know that by the end of the fifteenth and beginning of the sixteenth centuries, Ivan IV (the Terrible) annexed these two cities and imposed autocracy. Additionally, to prove democratic principals existed, they and the Tatars of south Russia, around 1450—during the weakening Mongo-Tatar rule—in the intervening time between the Russians and Mongols, were governed by democratic principals. Also, those Russians and Tatars who tried to escape autocratic rule practiced democracy. It is explained that these two groups were Cossacks—Turcaic for frontiersman—who settled in southwest Russia in the 1550s. The group in the southwest was called the Host of the Don, while those in the southeast were the Host of Zaporog.

Originally, these Cossacks were robbers and marauders of trade caravans, which connected Russian lands and the Golden Horde. The basis of their authority was vested in the chiefs, Ataman and Hetman, both elected by their respective Hosts. Once elected, each had absolute dictatorial power when in war (and they were always at war) while the womenfolk did the fishing, hunting, and farming. In addition, Ataman and Hetman, having had unlimited power, could sentence a person to death by drowning. The judicial power rested with the *Rada*, (the Popular Council)—its practice was similar to Stalin, who ordered the executions but blamed the executioners. A reasonable analysis of existing documents and tales from the past show a complete lack of any elementary principals of democracy. Consider the conditions of land ownership which belonged to the Host and was commonly owned as a classless society. It is unquestionably correct in the first two principals. However, it is difficult to justify the third principal of democracy since not a scintilla of evidence exists for democratic rule after the expiration of Kievan Rus and other independent city-states. The intent in this case was to justify autocracy as the preferred method of governing people with absolute authoritarianism rather than democracy.

In forming their state, the Russians occupied lands belonging to other nationalities, clans, and tribes by imposing Russification and mixed marriages with Mongolians, Tatars, and other non-Slavic groups in the Siberian hinterlands. Their intent was to homogenize, and this resulted in Russian political domination. On their western borders they occupied portions of Poland, all of Lithuania, and the Baltic states; thus they created a multi-national state and called it "All-Russian." It is then reasonable to assume that the purity of the Russians is tempered by conquests and assimilation, as with most other racial groups, and it is generally considered no longer purely Slavic, at least in Siberian hinterlands and northern Caucasus. Furthermore, in the second half of the sixteenth century, when serfdom appeared, many Russians escaped to Cossack lands and profusely intermarried with the local population. In the seventeenth century, the Don Cossacks became vassals of Moscow but in return received arms and grain for the struggle against the Turks. In Russian territories, which subsequently became part of the Grand Duchy of Lithuania and the Kingdom of Poland, an aristocratic society evolved at the end of the fifteenth century. The power of the grand dukes there was restrained by an aristocratic council of boyars, the hereditary rulers of large feudal estates. They retained most government positions, commanded the troops, kept the monarchical seal, and controlled the purse—similar to western European lords and barons of their estates. Beside the Upper Council, there was also the *Seim* (assembly), made up of nobles, landowners, and some wealthy townspeople who had primary influence. The social structure of the state was defined in the "Code of Laws," known as Lithuanian Statutes. These statutes were drawn up around 1550 and were subsequently revised and adopted into a Russian version by 1588. The statutes reveal a high degree of judicial development, as well as human rights. Like most eastern European states with similar political structures, they were written primarily for the upper classes rather than for the entire population. By late sixteenth and early seventeenth centuries, Moscovy developed a system of political order, which became the standard of governance in the eighteenth and nineteenth centuries. As mentioned before, the absolute power of the Mongols, combined with Ceasaro-Papism of the Byzantine rulers, had a powerful influence on the Russian rulers in their relations among church, state-power, and people.

The reader may readily conclude from the above that the formation of the Russian state was born on territorial expansion, conquest, and assemblage of foreign people into their domains. Continual and unending wars of conquest, Russification, and the Byzantine emperors' authority as heads of church and state, and the absolute rule of the Mongols help explain the autocratic political development of governance, as a long standing tradition among the Russians. This concatenation of events in Russia continued throughout the fabric of its evolution until it developed into a recognizable entity, as a legacy and destiny of the nation. The reader may find this rather tedious and perhaps confusing, bearing in mind his own ethnic identity and political system. However, without an elementary understanding of the nature of Russian political evolution, the reader is left to wonder who the Russians are and how their rulers acquired autocratic and subsequently dictatorial power over their people. With this background in mind, the subsequent chapters outline the autocratic behavioral conditioning imposed by their rulers and accepted by the people. Russian history books of the Imperial and Soviet period make no mention of dissent against arbitrary autocratic and dictatorial rule imposed on their people.


**Recommended Reading**

Dukes, Paul. *A History of Russia.* New York: McGraw-Hill, 1974.
Grekov, B.D. *Kiev Rus.* Moscow: Foreign Languages Publishing House, New York; Macmillan, 1949.
Kluichevsky, V.O. *History of Russia.* 4 vol, E.P. Dutton & Co. 1911-1926.
Paszkiewicz, Henryk. *The Making of the Russian Nation.* London: Allen & Unwin, 1963.
Vernadsky, George. *A History of Russia.* rev. Yale University Press, 1948.
Vernadsky, George. *Kievan Russia.* Yale University Press, 1948.
Vernadsky, George. *Medieval Russian Laws.* Yale University Press, 1947.
Vernadsky, George. *The Origins of Russia.* Clarendon Press, Oxford, 1959.

# Chapter II
# The Early Rulers

Little is known about the early rulers of Kiev and the city-states of Rus regarding accuracy of dates or titles, except what was recorded in church chronicles. The chronicles and records were subject to interpretations and corrections at various periods by consecutive church fathers and are further marred by arbitrary confiscation and rewriting by subsequent rulers. Nevertheless, these records are of immense value for their identification of events. Probably more reliable accounts of early history are confirmed by other participants with or against the early Russians. The battle on icy Lake Peipus where Alexander Nevskiy and his allies, the Poles and Lithuanians, fought and vanquished German Teutonic knights in 1242 on the Neva River is one example. The records confirm his great victory over the knights in their attempt to invade Russian lands. The church fathers honored his name with an honorific, "Nevskiy," after the battle and acknowledged him prince. The date given in church chronicles, however, may not be strictly accurate nor is his princely status, although Polish-Lithuanian sources confirm the battle and date.

Another example is Dmitriy Donskoy. Although he was outnumbered at first, he unexpectedly repelled the Mongols at Kulikovo on the River Don in 1380. This victory helped to reduce the burden of taxation. He was also awarded an honorific, "Donskoy," after the battle on the Don. This record is preserved in whole by church chronicles; it does however show subsequent conflicting dates. Other instances of questionable dates due to Mongol-Tatar incursions into Moscow resulted in the burning and pillaging of churches and the Kremlin which destroyed valuable records. Subsequently, these records were resurrected from memory. They should be considered enhanced by church authorities as well as by other rulers to suit themselves. However, commencing with the rule of Ivan I in Moscovy, dates are more or less contemporary with events. We should acknowledge the Russian habit of using historic names and deeds more importantly than dates and accept it at face value as they come down to us. It is not surprising that dates don't always match, in view of the conflicts among Russian rulers themselves and their habits of continually and arbitrarily revising events, dates, and records. Even some Russian writers show confusion by conflicting dates and titles. The reader will also have to contend with published Soviet textbooks under Stalin and his successors who subtly doctored facts and figures to suit the records. Soviet reliance on church documents was minimal since emphasis was placed on personalities and events, which were judged important by their class-conscienceness and economic outlook. After Stalin, Soviet writers have become more objective and scholarly.

As the history of the Russians progresses in these pages, the reader could conclude that some of the events described are either doctored or discarded by appropriate bodies. The reader should also bear in mind that the chronological order outlined below is subject to various conflicting interpretations by both Russian and Western historians. Also the relatively sealed Russian borders prevented foreign nations from learning much about them, unless they had direct contact with Russians either in war or in trade relations. To delve deeply into early historical names and dates of the Russian rulers prior to Ivan I would confuse the reader and derail the intent of this book, since early rulers could be considered warlords or tribal chiefs—regardless of their lineage or titles—and would confine the reader to a narrow scope and cause pondering of distracting ambiguities. Suffice it to point out briefly in the chronological order that after Rurik and his Nordic successors, the rule passed on to the Slavs throughout various enclaves of early Rus. Russian writers are inclined to magnify titles and importance of many early rulers to establish continuity of their origins and lineage and connect them to uninterrupted process of direct historical sequence. The author's experience in schools was constantly challenged by contradictions of various teachers in exile, as well as Soviet propagandists regarding the status of rulers—whether warlords, tribal chiefs, or from the princely line. As the authority of the grand dukes of Moscovy increased over the land, they absorbed more territory; thus dates and titles became more accurate and reasonably well-documented. This portion of the chapter is involved only with identification of early rulers prior to the grand dukes of Moscovy, with subsequent assumption of the throne by the Romanov czars.

Rulers of Kiev and City-states of Rus[*]

Rurik of Novgorod . . . . . . . . . . . . . . . . . . . . . . . . . . . . . . . .862-79

Oleg of Kiev . . . . . . . . . . . . . . . . . . . . . . . . . . . . . . . . . . . .879-912

Igor . . . . . . . . . . . . . . . . . . . . . . . . . . . . . . . . . . . . . . . . . . .912-45

Olga . . . . . . . . . . . . . . . . . . . . . . . . . . . . . . . . . . . . . . . . . . .945-57

Sviatoslav . . . . . . . . . . . . . . . . . . . . . . . . . . . . . . . . . . . . . .957-72

Yaropolk . . . . . . . . . . . . . . . . . . . . . . . . . . . . . . . . . . . . . . .972-80

St. Vladimir . . . . . . . . . . . . . . . . . . . . . . . . . . . . . . . . . . . .980-1015

Svyatapolk . . . . . . . . . . . . . . . . . . . . . . . . . . . . . . . . . . . .1015-19

Yaroslav . . . . . . . . . . . . . . . . . . . . . . . . . . . . . . . . . . . . . . 1019-54

Mstislav . . . . . . . . . . . . . . . . . . . . . . . . . . . . . . . . . . . . died-1036

Izyaslav . . . . . . . . . . . . . . . . . . . . . . . . . . . . . . . . . . . . . . 1054-78

Sviatoslav (Chernigov) . . . . . . . . . . . . . . . . . . . . . . . . . . . 1073-76

Vsevolod (Pereyaslav) . . . . . . . . . . . . . . . . . . . . . . . . . . . 1078-93

Yaroslav (Galicia) . . . . . . . . . . . . . . . . . . . . . . . . . . . . . 1093-1187

Svyatopolk . . . . . . . . . . . . . . . . . . . . . . . . . . . . . . . . . . 1093-1113

Vladimir Monomakh . . . . . . . . . . . . . . . . . . . . . . . . . . . . 1113-25

Mstislav . . . . . . . . . . . . . . . . . . . . . . . . . . . . . . . . . . . . . . 1125-32

Yaropolk . . . . . . . . . . . . . . . . . . . . . . . . . . . . . . . . . . . . . 1132-39

Yuriy Dolgorukiy . . . . . . . . . . . . . . . . . . . . . . . . . . . . . died-1157

Andrey Bogoliubskiy . . . . . . . . . . . . . . . . . . . . . . . . . . . 1157-74

Vsevolod . . . . . . . . . . . . . . . . . . . . . . . . . . . . . . . . . . . . 1176-1212

Mikhail . . . . . . . . . . . . . . . . . . . . . . . . . . . . . . . . . . . . . . 1174-76

Vsevolod . . . . . . . . . . . . . . . . . . . . . . . . . . . . . . . . . . . . 1176-1212

Constantin . . . . . . . . . . . . . . . . . . . . . . . . . . . . . . . . . . . 1212-19

Yuriy . . . . . . . . . . . . . . . . . . . . . . . . . . . . . . . . . . . . . . . 1219-36

Yaroslav . . . . . . . . . . . . . . . . . . . . . . . . . . . . . . . . . . . . . 1236-46

Svyatoslav . . . . . . . . . . . . . . . . . . . . . . . . . . . . . . . . . . . 1246-48

Alexander Nevskiy[**] . . . . . . . . . . . . . . . . . . . . . . . . . . . . 1252-63

Yaroslav . . . . . . . . . . . . . . . . . . . . . . . . . . . . . . . . . . . . . 1263-73

Dmitriy . . . . . . . . . . . . . . . . . . . . . . . . . . . . . . . . . . . . . . 1274-94

Andrey . . . . . . . . . . . . . . . . . . . . . . . . . . . . . . . . . . . . . . . . . .1294-1304

Daniel . . . . . . . . . . . . . . . . . . . . . . . . . . . . . . . . . . . . . . . . . .1276-1303

Mikhail . . . . . . . . . . . . . . . . . . . . . . . . . . . . . . . . . . . . . . . . .1304-19

Yuriy . . . . . . . . . . . . . . . . . . . . . . . . . . . . . . . . . . . . . . . . . .1303-24

* Dates are not necessarily accurate   ** First identified prince

## The Grand Dukes of Moscovy*

Ivan I, Kalita . . . . . . . . . . . . . . . . . . . . . . . . . . . . . . . . . . . .1328-40

Seaymon the Proud . . . . . . . . . . . . . . . . . . . . . . . . . . . . . .1341-53

Ivan II . . . . . . . . . . . . . . . . . . . . . . . . . . . . . . . . . . . . . . . . .1341-59

Dmitriy I, Donskoy . . . . . . . . . . . . . . . . . . . . . . . . . . . . . .1359-89

Vasiliy I . . . . . . . . . . . . . . . . . . . . . . . . . . . . . . . . . . . . . . .1389-1425

Vasiliy II . . . . . . . . . . . . . . . . . . . . . . . . . . . . . . . . . . . . . .1425-62

Ivan III (The Great) . . . . . . . . . . . . . . . . . . . . . . . . . . . . .1462-1505

Vasiliy III . . . . . . . . . . . . . . . . . . . . . . . . . . . . . . . . . . . . .1505-33

Ivan IV (The Terrible) . . . . . . . . . . . . . . . . . . . . . . . . . . .1533-84

Fyodor I . . . . . . . . . . . . . . . . . . . . . . . . . . . . . . . . . . . . . .1584-98

Boris Godunov . . . . . . . . . . . . . . . . . . . . . . . . . . . . . . . .1598-1605

Foyodor II* . . . . . . . . . . . . . . . . . . . . . . . . . . . . . . . murdered-1605

Vasiliy Shuyskiy . . . . . . . . . . . . . . . . . . . . . . . . . . . . . . .1606-10

Rule by Boyars . . . . . . . . . . . . . . . . . . . . . . . . . . . . . . . .1610-13

* Dates are mostly accurate   ** Based on rota system

## Early Rulers of Moscovy

**Ivan I: 1328-41 (also known as Kalita [moneybags])**

Little if anything is known of Ivan prior to 1320 when he visited Khan Uzbeg of the Golden Horde. He spent some two years there, trying to secure a princely position in Moscow and the ouster of his brother, Yuriy, who ruled there. He went on several expeditions with Khan Uzbeg's forces to Rostov and Yaroslavl. After the murder of Yuriy and the defeat of the city of Tver, the khan rewarded him with authority to collect taxes and tribute and the power to rule Moscow. In 1331 the khan made him grand prince of northeastern Rus. He was a shrewd manipulator, paying homage to the kahn while consolidating his position. In so doing, he was trusted by Uzbeg. He kept the Russians docile, the country stable and unified, while he held two positions as head of church and state. The southwest portions of Russia were originally under the old law of Kievan Rus and influenced first by Roman and later by Byzantine laws; they now became free from this rule. The princes under the khans eventually became grand dukes. As was customary under the khans of the Golden Horde, allegiance and tribute were paid at Sarai on the Volga River, the seat of the Mongols, whose rule lasted over 250 years. The khans would occasionally create alliances with some nearby European princes or incite trouble among them to keep the Russians under control. The one custom of Mongol rule, not interfering in religious matters, turned out to be beneficial for the Orthodox Church. The church kept close watch on the faithful and their rulers and greatly contributed to stability later in their history. The church canonized Kalita for his benevolence. The Moscow state under the grand dukes gradually grew as their customs spread until in encompassed most of the northeastern and southeast areas. The Russians henceforth adopted most of the elements of Mongol rule of unquestioned obedience to their rulers. All political and social customs, along with freedom of their religion, were absorbed into their culture. If this custom is juxtaposed to the system of rule within the Kievan enclave and other cities of pre-Mongolian period, which were somewhat democratic in structure, then it follows that it was the causative effect to justify the existence for such behavior. The Moscowite tendency to deny the boyars the opportunity to become an aristocratic clan competing with the grand dukes apparently helped the dukes of Moscow to subject their people to rules similar to the khans of the Golden Horde. After exhaustive research, the author concludes that no other causative reason exists to find a basis for autocratic a dictorial rule. The acceptance of this legacy gradually came into use and permeated into Moscovy. This opinion is further confirmed not only from research, but also after living under both the communist rule and among emigres in exile. Otherwise, no other reason for autocratic and dictatorial rule exists as a tradition among the Russians to this day.

**Seamyon the Proud: 1341-53**

Seamyon welcomed all immigrants into his domains and thus added to his population. He also acquired several villages and substantial acreage—Pereyeslav, Vladimir, Kostroma, Dimitrov, and Yuriev to name a few. Because of his vast domains, he called himself "Grand Duke and Prince of all Russia." He was also known as Seamyon the Proud. He died in 1353 without an heir and left all his possessions to his widow. Prior to his death, his relations with Ivan II, his brother, were strained and so Seamyon left him no personal possessions.

**Ivan II, Grand Prince: 1353-59**

One of the sons of Ivan I, after a quarrel with his brother Seamyon the Proud, ascended the throne as prince and later as grand duke of Moscow and ruled from 1341 to 1359. His rule was not in anyway distinguished nor hid he contribute to the stable conditions in Russia. Competing princes fought among themselves as before; however his tenancy remained solid, and he further consolidated his position in Moscow as the prime seat of power among other city-states. As the authority of the Moscow grand dukes gradually increased, they absorbed more territories and eventually became czars. Other cities, including Tver and Novgorod, made an effort to compete with Moscow. The khans, having influence over the grand dukes of Moscow as their primary source of income and control, supported Moscow as vassals, thereby enhancing the position of the grand dukes, which later proved to be crucial.

**Dmitriy I, Donskoy, Prince and Grand Duke: 1359-89**

Dmitriy, prince and grand duke of Moscow and son of Ivan II, oversaw Moscow's further rise to primacy among other city-states. During his reign, the Orthodox primate, Metropolitan Alexey, who assisted (if not reigned) during Dmitriy's tenure, saw the rise of the church and state almost as one. Conflicts with Lithuania, Poland, and the Golden Horde continued until a climactic battle ensued with the Tatars, another Turco-Mongol people, in 1380 at Kulikovo on the River Don, with the victory by the Russians. The power of the Golden Horde was weakening, with the Russians paying little heed to their demands for taxes and tribute. The khan, angered by their tardiness sought battle against Dmitriy and temporarily defeated the Russians. Gathering a larger army, Dmitriy defeated the Tatars again, gaining the honorific of "Dmitriy Donskoy." Later, though, the Horde avenged its defeat and reimposed its rule. However, by that time, Moscow's drive to unify all the Russians was further advanced.

**Vasiliy I, Grand Duke of Moscow: 1389-1425**

Vasiliy ascended to the title in 1389 and managed to secure permission from the Horde to rule as a vassal. He married a daughter of Grand Duke Vitovt of Lithuania, hoping to secure an alliance against the Horde. Through continued squabblings among the Lithuanians, the Horde, and the Russians, as well as changing alliances, nothing important took place until Toktamish, a vassal of Tamerlane, advanced from the east. Vasiliy requested Vitovt to protect his son and daughter and died shortly thereafter.

**Vasiliy II, Grand Duke of Moscow: 1425-62 (also known as the Blind)**

Vasiliy II made no general impact on Moscow's unification of Russia until

1450, when he was able to absorb some territory to Moscow. He had had trouble with his uncle, Yuriy, who claimed seniority, but Vasiliy finally succeeded in wrestling the title. One of Yuriy's sons, Dmitriy, wouldn't give up his claim to dukedom, and had his father blinded. Vasiliy was able to carry through with unification, despite the handicap, with the support of the khan and the church. Successfully leaving his domain intact for his successor, he died in 1462.

**Ivan III, The Great: 1462-1505**

The first acknowledged consolidator of power, Ivan the Great ruled Moscovy's domains from Moscow. Moscow became the political and religious capital of expanded Moscovy, having absorbed the city-states of Yaroslavl, Vereya, Vyatka, Perm, Tver, and Novgorod and incorporating them under the Moscovy duchy. By extracting heavy tribute from Novgorod, he became master of northeastern Russia, thus making Moscovy a major European power. However, in so doing he alienated Lithuania, Livonian knights, Sweden, and some Tatar khanates in the east and south. The Tatar dominance, for all practical reasons, was liberated, and Moscovy's political basis was taking shape. The Duma (lower house of Parliament) was created and became a supporting element rather than an advisory board and later was transformed into a supreme council, due to similar views of Ivan and the boyars. The council was further transformed into *zemskiy sobor* (land assembly). During Ivan the Great's reign, architectural achievements brought forth some outstanding examples of artistic awakening in church design. By encouraging the church in its endeavors, it took upon itself the education of the peasants—as elementary as it was—including the promulgation of clerical art and literature. The priceless *Trinity Chronicle* was written at that time, containing records of events from 1060-73 and additions to 1116. Unfortunately, the manuscript was destroyed by Napoleon in 1812 after leaving Moscow. A search to locate them failed. Two later versions of copies were prepared in 1377, the first copy covering the years 852-1293 and the second 852-1305. These copies are the only source of the history of Kievan Rus. Some scholars doubt the contents and authenticity of the copies, claiming some passages were uniquely tailored to suit tales and conditions influenced by governing authorities. Associated with the church were some outstanding architects and religious painters, including the Greek Theophanes and Andrey Rublev, the iconographer.

The last serious incursion by the Golden Horde against Moscow itself occurred in 1480; this effort failed, and it retreated to Sarai on the Volga. Only the khanate of Kazan remained a threat, and that was finally eliminated by Ivan in 1487. After the death of his first wife, he married a niece of the last Byzantine emperor, Princess Zoe, later renamed Sophia. Due to this marriage, Ivan brought many Greek and Italian artists, scholars, and engineers to Moscow—not to mention a multitude of books. In possessing these books, he was able to produce a code of laws in 1497, known as "Sudebnik." With this code he declared himself grand prince of all Rus, and subsequently, to meet equal status of Western sovereigns, he pronounced himself czar. He claimed his marriage to Sophia gave him the privilege of Roman and Byzantine caesars. He confirmed his rule as czar by adopting the double-headed eagle as the emblem of the Third Rome and added St. George's orb as his standard. The eagle and the orb subsequently became the standard of the Romanovs. Upon his death in 1505, he left his mighty domains and succession to his son, Vasiliy III.

## Vasiliy III: 1505-1533

Vasiliy extended Moscovy's power over northeastern principalities by capturing Smolensk, Pskov, and Ryazan between the Oka and Don rivers. He also absorbed some other small principalities and increased military and economic power of his domains, becoming one of the principal powers of eastern Europe. In 1510 a theoretical basis of the dominant religion of Eastern Orthodoxy was formulated by Filofey of the monastery in Pskov. In accordance with its doctrine, since Orthodoxy's place of origin was Constantinople and with its believers in the Balkans under the Ottoman yoke, the only natural sovereign domain left in Orthodoxy was now Moscow. It therefore follows that the rulers of Moscow were the natural successors of Orthodoxy in the world. Vasiliy took this mantle upon himself by building a new cathedral in the name of Archangel Mikhail in the Kremlin grounds and introduced splendor in his court. To further enhance his position among his people, he decreed that his will and therefore wherever he did was the will of God. With this decree, he claimed he was defending Orthodoxy against Catholicism and Islam. In so doing, he enraged the khanate of Kazan by refusing to pay any further tribute. A conflict commenced in 1521 when the khanate succeeded in re-entering Moscow, pillaging and murdering people and taking numerous prisoners to be slaves. They were eventually evicted. While this was a temporary setback for his military might and rule, as well as his theoretical declarations of head of Orthodoxy by the will of God, he was careful enough between 1514 and 1519 to cement his relations with the Holy Roman Empire, the Teutonic knights, and Denmark. He also opened a dialogue with the Medici popes, Leo X, and Clement VII. Subsequently, he opened discussions with Sultan Suleiman of the Ottoman Empire. These events helped Moscow enhance its position in Europe, which resulted in a massive flow of European traders to Moscovy. Having accomplished much, although conditions were still unsettled, he died in 1533.

## The Regency of Elena, wife of Vasiliy III: 1533-38

Vasiliy left his domains in unsettled conditions to his widow, Elena, and his two sons, Ivan and Yuriy. A regency was formed by the Moscow Metropolitan and a number of boyars hoping to retain their former privileges. A power struggle ensued between Elena the Regent—whose intent was to succeed her husband, Vasiliy, as an autocrat—and her relatives and boyars. She fought them off, one by one, until she suddenly died. The court circles suspected she was poisoned. Intrigue, murder, and usurpation continued for the crown. Since Vasiliy III's son Ivan, the heir, was only three years old at the time Vasiliy died, conspirators among the princes and boyars were active trying to secure their appointees to the crown and privileged positions for themselves. For two years after Elena's death, the Shuiyskiy family ruled over Moscovy domains, enriching themselves. Two years thereafter, the Belskiy and Glinskiy families (Elena's family) ran the country until 1542. Unbelievable chaos reigned; murder, disregard of laws, corruption, and extortion prevailed in Moscovy. The conditions in the court circles were so corrupt and dangerous that Ivan's tutors encouraged him in cruelty and deceit, which apparently affected his behavior upon assumption to the throne as a future czar.

**Ivan IV, The Terrible, Czar: 1538-84**

Shortly after he became czar, Ivan married Anastasia, daughter of a boyar, Roman Zakharov-Koshkin, and passed his time away in all its pleasures, while the Glinskiy and Koshkin families ran Moscovy as they saw fit. Taking his privilege shortly thereafter, he ordered the arrest and execution of Andrey Shuiysky, and in 1547 on his coronation, he assumed full autocratic powers and took the title czar. However, in 1547 when a catastrophic fire destroyed most of Moscow and burned down the Kremlin, enemies blamed Prince Glinskiy, the czar's uncle. Ivan ordered the execution of the entire family and cunningly left Moscow for a monastery, apparently knowing Moscow citizens desired peace and his return to the helm. Upon clamor for his return, he began his infamous reign by executing the supposed perpetrators and regained the reigns of power. Beginning his reforms in 1547, he chose new advisors as the so-called "Chosen Council." The council members were Sylvester, a priest; Adashev, a minor nobleman; Prince Kurbskiy; and Morozov, an extremely wealthy boyar. The council advised a meeting with the *zemskiy sobor* to institute reforms, and in 1550 it produced a new *sudebnik* (code of laws) of 100 articles. While the new *sudebnik* was just, it was equally severe and contained articles to restrict the authority of local officials. The *sudebnik* included guidelines for elimination of local administrative system, limited the collection of taxes by civil and religious officials without authorization, and limited boyar land holdings. In addition, the council elected elders to administer the court system, to check on arbitrary judges, make new rules for the purchase of freedom for the serfs, and increased the importance of the czar's agents throughout the country. Church reforms were decreed in 1551 to eliminate its abuses in the collection of dues. It also decreed a modification of monastic life and abuses of its property by reducing income from its money-lending practices and constricting the growth of monastic ownership of land. It also decreed the correction of church books and orders as well as the painting of icons. In the next ten years it established the czar's personal full-time permanent army, the *streltzy*, and a number of departments of central authority in Moscow.

Ivan IV further ordered a survey and inventory of all Moscovy. The hereditary nobles were to perform military service similar to the service nobility. He established a state trade monopoly in caviar, potash, grain, and hemp; prohibited the export of money, gold, and silver items; assessed new uniform taxes; and instituted a new monetary system. These were achievements of monumental proportions in Moscovy.

Having attained his objective in government reforms, he then pursued his military ambitions in re-arming his army, which occupied him for the better part of his remaining years. His military objectives were clearly laid out to subdue remaining areas adjoining Moscovy's lands to the east and southeast. He also went after trading along the Siberian routes, to the Caucasus, and the Caspian Sea and gained land areas to the west for trade with the Baltic lands. It took him five years to subdue the khanate of Kazan on the Volga and open the trade routes to Central Asia and the rest of Siberia. His reign as czar was a time of continual warfare and turmoil within his domains. He used *oprichina*, his personal guard (similar to the KGB), against his imagined enemies, along with his wars with western and eastern neighbors. He assumed upon himself the legacy of Genghis Khan and decreed absolute power over the lives of his subjects with unquestioned authority. He is infamous for blood baths, which were executed during his temporary illness and fear-of-dying period against all who demurred in recognizing his infant son as the next czar and his wife Anastasia as regent. It is now assumed that he was afflicted with paranoia. He even suspected his own son Ivan of treason, so he promptly murdered him and later became so melancholy that madness apparently overcame his rational thinking. He and his *oprichina* destroyed the country and ruined the aristocracy and the supposed Rurik dynasty. These conditions eventually lead to the "Time of Troubles," which marked instability in the country for fifteen years of both comic and tragic proportions. Ivan IV died in 1584, leaving a cataclysmic legacy to his second son, Fyodor I. In 1993 the Russian press reported that Kremlin pathologists exhumed Ivan's skeleton and determined that his disposition to madness and cruelty may have been caused by a curved backbone, which they believe was the reason for excessive pain the rest of his life.

**Fyodor I, Czar: 1584-98**

Fyodor I, the heir, was twenty-seven years old when he became czar. He was not by nature equal to his father in intelligence, temper, or autocratic character. He faced a bleak future, with previously cultivated land abandoned and fallow and his country devastated and terrorized. This caused the population to flee to borderlands in search of food and safety. It was apparent the burden placed on Fyodor was of monumental proportions, and he was incapable of coping with them. His eight-year-old brother, Dmitriy, was no where to be found and later was declared dead by his own hand—a declaration not even accepted by most Russian scholars. A serious vacuum in administering the destabilized state developed—a state Russia had to endure for fifteen years, resulting in the "Time of Troubles" for the succession to the throne.

**"The Time of Troubles"**

A regency council of five members was set up to administer the state, consisting of three princes and two boyars. These princes were descendants of the supposed Rurik, the founder of the ancient tribe of Rus, constituting direct lineage of succession. The two boyars, Nikita Romanov (the brother of Anastasia, the first wife of Ivan the Terrible) and Boris Godunov, (of the famed film and opera *Boris Godunov*). The three princes were Mstislavskiy, Belskiy, and Shuiyskiy.

At first the government was run by Nikita Romanov, who fell ill in 1584 and lost his membership. Godunov—ever so suspicious, cautious, and cunning—sensed his opportunity to grab the reigns of government. He exiled Maria, Ivan the Terrible's last wife, and her young son from Moscow for fear they would challenge his regency. He next took on the three princes. He sent one far out of town to Nizhniy-Novgorod; another he banished to a monastery to be a monk; and the third he deported with his entire family to unknown places. By 1584 be became full master of the regency, hated and feared—although a wealthy man, autocrat, and regent, he was not yet the czar. The only other challenger left was Fyodor's younger brother, Dmitriy, who died in 1587. rumors persisted that Godunov had him murdered. However, no proof of that accusation exists except for circumstantial evidence. Godunov was cleared of any wrongdoing by a board of inquiry, one of whose members was Prince Shuiyskiy, his enemy.

**Boris Godunov, Regent and Czar: 1584-1605**

Boris Godunov had been a boyar whose power was based on marriage connections of his sister Irina, who was married to Czar Fyodor I. As luck would have it, Czar Fyodor died in early 1598. To make sure things were going right for him, he exiled Dmitriy's mother, a descendent of the house of Rurik, clearing the way for him to attain his supreme goal as czar. An extraordinary session of *zemskiy sobor* was called, and Godunov was elected czar of Rus and Moscovy. Research by Russian and Western historians indicates that the foreign and domestic policies he pursued were both well-conceived and well-administered. He realized the serious errors created by Ivan the Terrible's rule, so he took the best parts and discarded the most egregious. He demanded and administered restoration of order and tranquility in his domains without execution by exiling his enemies to Siberia or monasteries, which constituted his normal type of punishment. In exiling his enemies, he confiscated their estates and rewarded his supporters with them. He annulled the taxes of service nobility in 1591 and later reduced their military obligations and lifted other restraints imposed by Ivan the Terrible. He selected his friend, the archbishop of Rostov, to be the new Metropolitan of Moscow and in 1588 made him patriarch. He continued Moscovy's expansion east and south, using his acquisitions as military outposts. These moves were intended to curb incursions by Tatars, and provide for trade opportunities and safe havens for the people of Central Asia who sought protection. He pursued trade and learning in Europe, with England, Holland, France, and the Holy Roman Empire.

In 1601 an unexpected three-year drought devastated the country with famine, disease, and general upheavals, with thousands dying. Within two years a series of uprisings took place by the peasants against the government, resulting in heavy casualties among them by Godunov's troops. In the interim the country was being destabilized by a false pretender to the throne. Godunov was surprised by the pretender, and he sent ambassadors to Poland to forestall an invasion; alas it was too late. Shortly thereafter Godunov suddenly died in April 1605. He was succeeded by his sixteen-year-old son Fyodor II, who lasted only a few weeks before being caught in the Kremlin and promptly murdered.

Some Russian historians credit Godunov with being a link between Ivan III and Peter the Great. Pre-revolutionary books cited this comparison, and the author's schooling confirmed it. This assumption may or may not be valid. The time frame between Ivan III and Peter the Great is too extensive to conclude that. Since Godunov's reign was the actual cause of the "Time of Troubles," it follows that it has no relative significance for any link. In fairness to Godunov, one must commend him for the great reforms he instituted and the leniency of punishment he meted out—a gesture not practiced at the time. He did institute cathartic reforms in several departments of government to benefit the poor after Ivan IV's disastrous years. Interestingly, a few writers claim Godunov couldn't read or write; if that is so, he must have been an unusual person, since people do not usually ascend to such heights without this knowledge, making the assertion dubious. Who was Boris Godunov? Russian records indicate he was a descendent of a Tatar servant to some of Moscow's princes. How did he get to be a senior counselor to Ivan the Terrible, regardless of the fact that he was the brother of Irina, Fydor's second wife; and wind up as regent and later the czar? Some writers have tried to decipher the mystery but without success. Even historians with access to Kremlin archives have conflicting opinions of him. In Russian emigre schools with pre-revolutionary history books, he is identified as an evil and devious character who shouldn't have been a regent or a czar; yet no clear explanation is given to justify the adverse text. The film and opera productions of *Boris Godunov*, while entertaining, shed no light and represent a point of view of the writers and the film and opera directors under the guidance of authorities. He thus remains an enigma to this day.

**Vasiliy Shuyskiy: 1606-10**

Shuyskiy was a prince whose family was descended from the Rurik dynasty. He was selected to be the investigator of the death of Dmitriy—brother of and heir to Czar Fyodor I, who ruled Russia from 1584-98. Shuyskiy organized a movement to murder Godunov's son Fyodor II. He at first rejected allegations about a false Dmitriy, but shortly thereafter, he reversed himself and accused the new czar of being an imposter. For this reversal, he was banished into exile. He returned, however, and he provoked a conflict with the aid of Sweden and was able to defeat the opposition. However, a second false Dmitriy appeared from Tushino, backed by Poland, but Shuyskiy was unable to defeat him when the Poles threatened an attack on Moscow. Shuyskiy tried an alliance with the neighboring Tatars, but they refused. At this point the people of Moscow rioted, and an assembly of the upper classes and commoners deposed Shuyskiy as czar. He was exiled for the second time in July 1610 to a monastery and forced to take monastic vows. Moscow, being in a vacuum, turned all power to the boyars, who engineered a rapprochement with Poland and turned over Shuyskiy to the Poles. He subsequently died there in prison.

After all the turbulence, sometime in January 1613 a special session of the *Zemskiy Sobor* convened to elect a new czar. Various names were proposed including foreigners, and in the end they unanimously selected Mikhail Romanov. Neither Poland-Lithuania nor Sweden recognized him as czar. By now the reader should be able to discern the troubles, exiles, betrayals, deceit, murder, fratricide, and corruption that occurred when someone aspired to czardom or leadership. A question difficult to decipher, yet it remains a crucial problem, since turmoil still continues to this day. From their beginnings before 879 in Novgorod, thence to Kiev, and finally in Moscow in 1613, a sort of legitimacy had been attained to select a Romanov as czar. The Romanov dynasty lasted 304 years until the overthrow of czardom in 1917 by a communist coup d'etat. In this connection, not only the "Time of Troubles," but also the entire history of the Russians until the selection of a Romanov czar has been analyzed by scholars; they have yet to decipher the real causes of more than seven hundred years of turmoil. Probable causes given by the Russian scholars most closely involved with the "Time of Troubles," give various reasons for the turmoil—striving for identity; evolution to nationhood, and dynastic troubles. Yet no one scholar has yet sufficiently explained the problems to this day. Western Europe has experienced its share of turmoils throughout its long history, yet not one of its nations experienced the problems of Russia. To the reader, Russia may remain an enigma until the causes of its violence are clearly deciphered.

**Recommended Reading**

Dmytryshyn Basil. *A History of Russia*. Englewood Cliffs, NJ: Prentice Hall, Inc.
Russian history books of pre-revolutionary and Soviet textbooks.
Vernadsky, George. *The History of Russia*. Yale University Press, 1948.

# CHAPTER III
# THE MONGOL INVASION AND THE GOLDEN HORDE

The reader is advised to review Russia's physical and political geography, which constitute one of the principal reasons for the character and development of the Russian people. The Mongol invasions temporarily caused a geographic and political split of eastern and western portions of Russian lands between the Mongols and the Lithuanians, respectively. The territorial distribution of the Russian population changed little, if any. Following the first Mongol invasion, the Russians in the middle Dnieper Basin moved to the upper Volga and Oka rivers to avoid them. This movement gradually slowed, and the balance of the population remained on the borders of the southern steppes. In the southwest about 1350, the Russians in the Grand Duchy of Lithuania reached the Black Sea between the Dniester and the lower reaches of the Bug rivers. Russians in the Moscow area moved down to the Volga and the Don in the southeast. Their penetration to the forested area in the north continued steadily. Many Russian merchants visited north Caucasus and Sarai area, the seat of the Mongols, and also moved farther north. Sometime during the early thirteenth century, the Mongols in the Eurasian landmass adjoining Siberia organized a military force under one of their aristocratic chieftains, Temujin, a visionary who decided to create a Mongolian empire. Born in 1155 into an aristocratic family, he was made the khan of his nation and renamed Genghis (Heavenly Emperor). A master of military organization, he created an army roughly composed of squadrons, battalions, and divisions with logistical support. These formations closely resembled a triangular division of WWII. Apparently the first such organization in military history, it was commanded by select aristocratic officers. Since the religion of these people was Altaic which implied autocratic control over the people, he commanded this organization and ruled it with iron discipline.

Historians state that it took him a little over three years to train his army, and upon completion, a *Kuriltai* of the elders was called into session with the intent of beginning a war and creating a Mongol empire. Genghis Khan started his first war in neighboring northern China. It took him a substantial period of time to subdue the northern Chinese. When he finally captured Peking in 1215, he learned administrative and governmental procedures from a Chinese scholar, Ye-Liu-Chu-Tsai, whom he promptly made chief civil and military administrator. This relationship lasted after Genghis Khan's death and his son's assumption as head of the Mongol nation. Some historians believe that both Genghis and Ye-Liu-Chu-Tsai were geniuses in their respective fields at the time. Having achieved his goal in the east, he paused to rest and re-fit the army, and then he turned his eyes west to Khoresm, a large area comprising present-day Iran, Afganistan, and Russian Turkestan. He desired trade relations with Khoresm in order to acquire certain supplies and reserves and sent his spies to facilitate the conquest of Khoresm itself later. In this connection, he sent forward his emissaries to negotiate. By now the shah of Khoresm had heard of Genghis Khan's methods and of his puissant army, so he killed the emissaries when they arrived. This act brought about an immediate war. The khan called a *Kuriltai* in early 1219 and late in the year captured Otrar, the capitol of Khoresm; he failed to capture the shah, who escaped. Orders were given for his capture, and enroute to reconnoiter the scene for future conquest, the Mongols passed by northern Iran to Caucasia and encountered some Georgians and Armenians, whom they disposed of in short order. They then passed on to the Don and the lands of the Cumans, a Turcaic people. The Russian princes came to help the Cumans, and a battle ensued on the Kalka River, resulting in the defeat of the Cumans and their Russian allies. The Mongols then turned on the tribe of Tanguts, who were also no match for the Mongols. These successful battles completed the first phase of the Mongol master plan of conquest. Ironically, at the height of the last battle, Genghis Khan died at age seventy-two, forcing most of the aristocratic chieftains back for a *Kuriltai* in Mongolia to pay homage at the burial of the great khan.

Ogadai, his son, was selected the successor to Genghis. It took eight years to prepare and complete the second phase of the conquest. Ye-Liu-Chu-Tsai became so important that when he offered to leave the service after the death of the great khan, he was appointed instead to a position similar to a prime minister and chief counsellor. At a *Kuriltai* held in Karakorum in 1235, it was determined that the Mongol armies should move in three directions: China, Persia, and Russia. The Russian invasion was to be headed by Batu Khan, nephew of Ogadai, grandson of Genghis Khan. The military commander was Sabutai, considered by some military historians as an early genius. He had under his command 120,000-150,000 cavalry troops, and early in 1237 he completed his concentrations on the Volga. His first objective were the Bulgarians on the Volga. He beat them quickly, crossed the Volga, and by the end of 1237 approached Riazan and Vladimir in Russia. When both towns refused to submit, he vanquished them in a short battle and moved west to within 100 km of Novgorod. Afraid of being bogged down by snow, he turned south and settled on the lower Don and the Volga for a rest. He then suddenly lunged farther west and conquered Kiev in 1240.

In the reorganization of the administrative and military spheres, as prescribed by Ye-Lui-Chu-Tsai, the military command became subservient to civilian control, apparently the first such organized instance in history. The Mongol army's use of cavalry for quick reconnaissance and surprise attacks with overwhelming mass, splitting the enemy into helpless groups, was a tactic used by German General Heinz Guderian's Panzers in WWII, with great success. After the occupation of Kiev, a new strategy was devised, similar to present day operations of dividing the army in two. One army was sent against Poland and defeated the Poles and the Germans (who had come to their aid), then turned south and invaded Hungary. The other army under Sabutai and Khan Batu attacked the Magyars of Hungary, a Mongol-Ugraic people, and defeated them, with the Hungarian king fleeing to the Adriatic. Batu sent a small contingent to track him down and dispatched him in short order. When Batu reached Klosterneuburg, near Vienna, disturbing news reached him—that Ogadai Khan had passed away. This intelligence stopped all operations and a retreat was ordered. Batu's presence was required in appointing a new khan. He returned to Mongolia by the Black Sea through Bulgaria and Moldavia. The campaign of 1237-1241 ended with his return to the Volga steppes. His conquests included the southern steppes, the northern forested areas, and the lower Danube—an area of unbelievable size. Hungary was under his domination for only one year, probably due to outstretching his supplies and communications with his army. He next moved south and captured Bulgaria and Moldavia, which remained in the Mongol Empire for a hundred years. About the same time, the eastern armies conquered northern China, and the southern army conquered TransCaucasia. There are no specific records of dates available of Sabutai's or Ye-Liu-Chu-Tsai's deaths, although Chinese records indicate that with the cousellor's death in Peking, he was mourned by Kublai Khan and his court.

The Mongol Empire by the mid-thirteenth century spanned from the Pacific Ocean to the Adriatic Sea, a feat rarely recorded in history. As happens in most family breakups, this empire split into *ulus*, (principalities), under the descendants of Genghis Khan. However, the Mongol emperor of China, Kublai Khan, who reigned for forty-one years (1257-1298) and his descendants were considered the leading khans in the line of Mongolian kingdoms.

Russia was ruled by Juichi Khan of the Golden Horde, which centered in Sarai in the lower Volga, between the Volga and the Don, and close to Russian principalities, not far from the Black Sea. Later, Juichi's descendants became independent rulers, and the enclave was known as the Golden Horde. The highest pinnacle of their rule was in the middle of the fourteenth century. Due to enforcement of submission to their authority, and to balance their international position, they succeeded in keeping the Russians in check. The Mongols maintained diplomatic relations with Egypt, Byzantium, and other European states. Their main concern was protecting trade and internal peace, which succeeded to an unusual degree, making the Golden Horde an extremely wealthy entity. In addition, they realized the convulsive state of religious conflicts in their territories in Russia and developed a curious toleration toward all religions. Relatives of the khan adopted various religions without prejudice. On the other hand, when it came to Russian princes and their governmental institutions, they were obliged to accept complete submission to the khan. To be crowned, they had to receive permission for their coronation and were forced to travel, at first to Sarai and later to Karakorum in Mongolia, on the condition that they could retain their power, and it be limited as official emissaries of the khan. Frequently, disputes among the chiefs or princes were settled by the khans, who judged the problem and issued appropriate decision. In some instances the death penalty was administered. Submission to Mongol authority and its rule meant that harsh means prevailed for collection of revenues and recruitment of troops. The Mongols had agents in all principal Russian towns. In some instances troops were used to quell any insubordination of princes or the general population, who protested against both revenue collection and recruitment. Most princes adhered to these methods and encouraged the population to do likewise.

This submission protected Moscow from Lithuanian attacks for some years to come since the Mongols undertook the struggle against Lithuanian-Russian army, an expatriate army. The princes were also afraid of encroachment by Swedes and Germans. Alexander Nevsky was one prince who encouraged cooperation with the Golden Horde to fight off western incursions. To be sure, there were some princes who cooperated with the West, unwilling to submit to Mongol rule. Receiving only encouragement but no military support from the Polish-Lithuanian side, these princes eventually submitted to Mongol rule. Thus Mongol power was established in both east and west Russia. Around 1350 the power of the Golden Horde began to wane due to internal strife and bickering among pretenders and to the religious differences in the localities they governed. The khan in China converted to Buddhism, and eventually the numerous Chinese absorbed the Mongols in their midst. The khan in Persia converted to Islam, and the Mongol kingdom became the Persian Empire. Though the khans extended their patronage and support to the Orthodox Church, they never accepted Christianity and turned to Islam. Apparently the Orthodox faith, with all its mysteries, was too complex for them to bother.

However, in this period the foundation of the Russian state centered in Moscow rather than Sarai, further enhancing the pre-eminence of the Moscovy duchy. Moscow gained strength and power under the Golden Horde in the eastern and northern Russian principalities, and by the end of the fourteenth century, it became pre-eminent among other Russian principalities. Concurrent with the pre-eminence, a Lithuanian state came into existence under their grand dukes. Taking advantage of the weakening of the Golden Horde, they occupied a substantial portion of western Russia. Those Russian princes who would not submit to the Mongol-Tartar rule joined with Olgerd, the Lithuanian grand duke. He invaded and occupied all Russian principalities west of the Dnieper, which helped to extend his rule to the Black Sea. While Lithuania was influenced by Russia, it was more strongly influenced by Poland, where the Lithuanian grand duke was offered the throne of Poland. He accepted the offer, and thus the Lithuanian conversion to Catholicism began. Some Russian nobles also converted. The unification of these two kingdoms in addition to help from Alexander Nevskiy's troops made possible the conquest of German Teutonic knights in the battle at Tannenberg, East Prussia. Dissension in the Golden Horde slackened somewhat when Mamai, a pretender, seized supreme power. By now, the power of the Moscow grand duke, Dmitriy, had grown substantially, and he challenged and defeated Mamai in a decisive battle on the upper Don. He received an honorific, "Dmitriy Donskoy," for this battle on the Don. While the victory was psychologically important, the losses sustained by the Russian forces were unusually high. There was still a possibility of another battle, this being a precursor of future Russian battle tactics. After losing the battle, Mamai was overthrown by another pretender, Tokhtamish. The new khan was a vassal of another military genius, Tamerlane, a Turco-Mongol. Tokhtamish, encouraged by Tamerlane, sought battle with Dmitriy. Realizing the exhaustion of the troops and meager treasury, Dmitriy decided to retreat to northern Russia, leaving Moscow to be pillaged and sacked in 1382, which forced Dmitriy again to submit to the Golden Horde. Moscow was ruled by the Golden Horde for some thirty to forty years more. This submission protected Moscow from the struggle in the west with the Lithuanian-Russian armies, when Tokhtamish delivered a smashing defeat to the latter in 1399. There is no compelling reason to pursue the career of Tamerlane, who died in 1405, for he played no historic role in Russia proper, though it is a fascinating history.

The Mongol state was built on the principle of submission of the individual to the tribe (and thence to the state), based on military discipline; this was later refined by administrative directives by Ye-Liu-Chu-Tsai. This principle was absorbed by the Russians, as a system of service to the state. Subsequently, the political theory was refined into structure, at first in the Moscow kingdom and subsequently in the Russian empire. The power of the khan, as defined by the Mongols, was absolute and autocratic. The grand dukes of Moscow assumed the same authority when the power of the khans was weakened. All lands of the grand dukes belonged to them, and everyone else who worked on it had only temporary tenure. Additionally, taxation, census, the postal system, and military structure were adopted from the Mongols. The Russian nobles served the prince and in turn were served by others, similar to the feudal system in western Europe, though with less power. Eventually, the primacy of the Moscow princes increased to the position of czars and emperors. Prior to Mongol occupation laws, the Russians were influenced by the Roman and Byzantine laws, which had entered Russia through Poland and Moldavia. The different Mongol civil law represented an Asiatic influence and was only gradually absorbed by the Russians.

The Mongol period in Russian history was of great importance to the Russian church, as the khans acted as patrons of the Orthodox Church. The Russian metropolitans (bishops) received their licenses from the khans—by which the rights and integrity of the church were guaranteed. During the Mongol period, the organization of the church remained practically unchanged. Eventually, the Moscow metropolinate became the principal seat of all the patriarchs of Russia. During the fourteenth and the fifteenth centuries, monasteries multiplied due to severity of Mongol rule which led to a widespread desire to leave the world and lead an acetic life, much like in the early middle ages in Europe. Laymen also looked to the monasteries for consolation and advice, which led to the creation of villages around monasteries. The monks colonized northeastern Russia and spread their culture. Some monasteries were wayside inns, schools, hospitals, or libraries. Others housed extensive libraries with depositories of immense amounts of information on religious, historical and legal questions, to which princes and civil servants turned for edification. However, during the eighteenth century, as the spiritual demands of the people diminished and the importance of the monasteries decreased, the Imperial government closed many monasteries. It was left to the Soviet government to close the ones still open. During the Mongol period the artistic painting of icons reached a high point, especially the paintings by the artists of Novgorod. Icon painting of the fourteenth through sixteenth centuries is considered a highly artistic expression, they are sought after by collectors and museums the world over.

By now the reader should perceive the Mongol-Tatar influence on the Russians and adjoining Slavs. At a time in history when the Slavs had not yet organized into identifiable national groups, it was made easier to bring them under submission, as compared to western Europe, which was already developed into national groups. So overwhelming was the Mongol political influence, which had been forced on the Russian way of life, that the princes and grand dukes of Moscovy (and subsequent czars and commissars), assumed the rule of the khans quite naturally. It is therefore reasonable to assume that this social influence is derived from the Eastern Oriental Asiatic heritage of Mongol-Tatars—similar to the western Oriental heritage of Western civilization, which was equally absorbed. Although Mongol-Tatar influence was forced politically, having no spiritual values, the spiritual value of the Russians assumed a complementary character when they voluntarily absorbed the eastern Greco Oriental Orthodox religious despotism of the Byzantine Emperors, who were heads of both state and church. In contrast, western Oriental heritage had been absorbed by the barbarians centuries before, though not imposed. The difference is substantial since Mongol-Tatar heritage was imposed by force with no inherent spiritual roots, while Hebraic traditions and Greek mythology flowed naturally with Christian ideals and were absorbed voluntarily, having deep, traditional, historical roots and values. When the Roman popes arbitrarily assumed both spiritual and temporal power as ceasaro-papists, western Europe was already reasonably well-developed into major national identity groups. Although the Mongols penetrated into central Europe as far as Hungary and Austria, their stay was too short to impose their will. One could assume Europe was fortunate due to deaths of both Genghis Khan and later Ogadai, which caused the Mongols to cease operations farther west and depart. Western Europe's Crusades had passed, and it was slowly emerging from its feudal system imposed by its kings and baronial estates, while the Russians were experiencing convulsions with Mongol hordes. Furthermore, Russia's relations with Byzantium—since before the Mongol invasion when the emperors were also heads of the church—had an added influence on their political and spiritual values. After the fall of the Byzantine Empire in 1453, Russia was isolated from western Europe and fully saddled with the tradition of autocracy with the czars and as heads of the church. This mantle of duality was passed on for centuries, and was accepted by the people *ipso factum*. Subsequently, though, there were schisms in the Orthodox Church due to political division of Russia during the Polish-Lithuanian wars in the sixteenth and seventeenth centuries. Orthodoxy eventually succeeded in regaining its authority over Catholicism, with the czars retaining their pre-eminence as heads of the church. The Orthodox Church felt bound by Byzantine duality of autocracy and spiritual leadership of the czars and actually encouraged its existence, which lasted until the overthrow of the monarchy in 1917. As one patriarch of Moscow said of Orthodoxy, after the fall of Byzantium, "First there was Rome, the second was Constantinople, and the third is Moscow, and there is no more."

The author would suggest that since the spiritual character of the Russians is of Byzantine origins, mixed as it was with Mongol-Tatar political-social influence, it doesn't necessarily follow that they are not a civilized or a great people. In fact, they are both civilized and great. There is a difference between Western and Eastern people, having different experiences and characteristics, and this contributes to the Western world's arrogance toward the Russians. One must also acknowledge that the purity of the Russian Slavs—as with other national and ethnic origins—has undergone a major change. While Russification was originally forced it has become rather commonplace throughout the empire. Assimilation and intermarriages among their national minorities multiplied to the extent that even nationalities not assimilated spoke Russian as their main language and changed their last names to sound Russian—like the Chechen and other minority people of the Caucasus. Assimilation occurred more frequently under the Soviet Union, with minority nationalities as part of the union, with orders emanating from Moscow. The author, having lived among Russians, finds them particularly warm-hearted and friendly, despite their historic hard times. There exists a wide gap between ordinary Russians and their political leaders.

# CHAPTER IV
# THE ROMANOV CZARS, AUTOCRATS AND EMPERORS

**Mihhail I, Romanov, Czar 1613-45**

Mikhail was the first in the line of the Romanovs to ascend the throne of Russia, and with his election, the Romanov dynasty began its 304-year rule of Russia. When *Zemskiy Sobor* elected him czar after Shuiskiy's banishment and death, Mikhail faced a multitude of problems, being wholly unprepared for the task. Moscovy was at war with Sweden and Polish-Lithuanian domains, which occupied some of Russia's territory. The economy was in shambles; his authority was manipulated; chaos prevailed with the Cossacks and peasants who ran rampant throughout his domains. Faced with these problems, and unprepared as he was, he depended on the advice of the *Zemskiy Sobor* and government bureaucracy, previously created by and left over from Ivan IV. Patriarch Filaret, his father, after being released from Polish imprisonment in 1619, guided the affairs of state until his death in 1633. Mikhail's authority as czar was not at first recognized by Sweden or Poland or by some of his countrymen. Various Cossack bands, false pretenders, and dissatisfied peasants rampaged against his authority. He eventually disposed of his internal problems by the end of 1614, however he still had disputes with Sweden and Poland-Lithuania to occupy his time. The Swedish problem was settled rather amicably with the help of an Englishman, John Merrick, in 1617. The treaty they signed was concluded by an exchange of territory, with Sweden retaining Finnish Karelia and Poland acquiring Ingria, at the mouth of the Neva River. In return, Mikhail got Novgorod and Staraya Rus. It turned out that both sides exchanged possessions from the other's territory.

Russia's relations with Poland-Lithuania were more difficult, however, in view of King Wladislaw's refusal to renounce his claim to the throne of Moscovy. After some two years of seesaw battles, a peace treaty was signed in 1619, with Poland-Lithuania keeping Smolensk and Severia but refusing to recognize Mikhail's election as czar. These treaties in themselves were not beneficial to Moscovy, but they helped Mikhail to undertake the task of adressing the economic problems which were ruinous. Taxation was at an alarming rate and was considered unjust to all segments of society. In 1620 Mikhail convened the *Zemskiy Sobor* to address more fairly the tax issue, excluding peasants, and by 1626 it was completed. Strapping the already poor peasants with tax burdens plagued the country throughout its history. The intent of taxation was to bolster the military budget at the expense of the peasants. Subsequently, the same taxation procedure was used by the Imperial regime, and under disguised means that burden was affecting both the peasants and the working class in the Soviet Union. Under these circumstances, the service class was rewarded and agriculture made great headway, though tying the peasants to the land more than ever. However, these matters finally attained a certain measure of stability in the country, again at the expense of the poor peasantry, but it did result in population increase and expansion of trade. This stability again resulted, in firmer control by the government over the daily lives of its citizens.

By 1631 upon expiration of the previous armistice with Poland-Lithuania, Mikhail resumed war to recapture territory lost in 1619. Being overconfident, Mikhail lost the war—in part because Wladislaw received help from the Crimean Tatars. Wladislaw recognized Mikhail as czar of Moscovy, and in return Moscovy relinquished Smolensk and Severia and paid a large indemnity. To guarantee future preparedness against the Tatars on his southern borders, Mikhail erected fortresses near the Sea of Azov and in the Crimean area. In 1642 *Zemskiy Sobor* — weary of another war, this time with the Ottoman Empire—advised the czar to refrain from any further wars. The severe problems of taxation, war preparations, uneasiness of his subjects, and an empty treasury, as well as other mounting problems, were sufficient reasons to refrain from any future wars. At this juncture of events, Moscovy's possessions became large enough to cause *Zemskiy Sobor* to declare the lands of the Romanovs henceforth shall be called Russia. Mikhail died in 1645 and left all the problems of Russia to his son, Alexey, a youth of sixteen.

**Alexey I, Czar: 1645-16**

Alexey, a young czar at the age of sixteen, was completely unprepared to govern. Morozov, an extremely wealthy boyar, was recommended as his tutor. Morozov arranged a marriage between Alexey and his wife's sister in 1648. Morozov was an intelligent man and highly ambitious, but he was also a manipulative and unscrupulous character. He lost no time in assuming the reigns of power and wealth of the country. When faced with the discovery that the treasury was empty, revenues down, and nobles and townspeople depressed with unbearable conditions, he introduced a system previously used by other rulers. In 1645-46 he tied the peasants to the land owned by the nobles and decreed laws appeasing the townspeople by stripping all land from the nobles and monasteries and distributing them to town communes. He implemented measures of strict government economy by discharging many Kremlin officials and decreasing the salaries of provincial officials and the *streltzy*. He further decreed that foreign officers be granted lands instead of salaries and established a government monopoly on salt and tobacco by levying heavy taxes on both products.

As a result of unbearable conditions, in June 1648 strong opposition suddenly surfaced against Morozov's measures, and the people petitioned the czar to lift these restrictions. At first the czar declined, but when informed that *streltzy* backed the people, he relented. Resentment took the form of vengeance when three of Morozov's assistants were killed and their homes plundered. To shield

Morozov, the czar sent him to a monastery, replaced him with a prince, and called reinforcements to Moscow. Subsequently, in 1648 the *Zemskiy Sobor* was called into session by the recommendation of the nobles and merchants to change existing statues and write a new code of laws.

In late 1648 *Zemskiy Sobor* reconvened to move on the new laws. It was an amalgam of bits and pieces of Lithuanian laws, Ivan IV's *Sudebnik*, and sections of church and Byzantine laws. The *Sobor* called it *Sobornoe Ulozheniye* (assembly statutes). Included in these new laws were provisions for total control by the government over church and monastery lands. It deprived the church of its legal privileges, forbade it and the nobles to relocate peasants in settlements near towns, and prevented fictitious transfer of land which had been commonly practiced. The townspeople were permitted to reclaim lands they had lost and remove people who were not part of those settlements. All foreign merchants and their trade were confined to Arkhangelsk on the White Sea. Various death penalty provisions were prescribed for intent to murder the czar, armed rebellion, and treason. After reviewing the *Ulozheniye*, the author finds the new laws manifestly self-serving and unfair, an overreaction to please a small segment of society at the expense of the many. This new code of laws caused many uprisings, lootings, and destruction in the midst of a drought and the spread of cholera. Subsequently, several sections of these decrees were abrogated in the nineteenth century. What good did it do for the starving common people, two hundred years before? The government also complied with its peace treaty with Sweden in 1617 and exported grain, which was in short supply. Discontentment and disturbances were spreading, and in the midst of these problems, the plague appeared, spreading panic and flight from the villages, with the government trying in vain to force the villagers back.

If this were not enough, a war commenced with Sweden and Poland for access to the Baltic Sea. Being short of silver coins, the government resorted to copper and declared it to have the same value as silver coins, yet they required taxpayers to pay in silver to finance the war. This created havoc, but the government weathered the storm. Thereafter, things quieted down somewhat, but thousands died of starvation. It didn't take long before a new rebellion commenced in 1622. The peasants escaped to the steppes in the Don region in search of food. There they were rebuffed by the Cossacks who had settled there previously. With no place to flee, they were forced to start over again. Meanwhile, inflation soared to monumental proportions, causing small merchants and the poor to petition the czar for relief. The reply came instantaneously in the form of an order—execute thousands for rebellion and increase the taxes. The peasants fled to the Volga basin and the Caspian Sea where they were organized, along with the Old Believers and *streltzy* by Stenka Ryazin, a Cossack. In 1667 Ryazin turned them into a band of marauders and attacked along the Volga and Ural rivers. A year later they looted to their hearts' content—pillaging, robbing, terrorizing Persian lands and amassing huge spoils; they returned by way of Astrakhan, to the Don Basin. His successes caused an influx of more malcontents to join his forces. By 1670 he decided to march against Moscovy's possessions. He re-entered

Astrakhan and took Tsaritsyn, Saratov, and Samara. Enroute he gathered more volunteers from the Chuvash, Mordva, Mari, and Tatars in the countryside. He seemed unstoppable. In 1671 the czar, not fully trusting his own army, employed foreign officers to lead Moscovy against Stenka Ryazin, The czar's army succeeded in defeating Ryazin who fled to the Don, wounded. There he was captured by Cossacks loyal to the government and turned over to Moscow where he was tortured and executed before a crowd of thousands in Red Square. Ryazin left a legacy to the poor of Russia, who to this day, sang "Stenka Ryazin," made famous by his exploits in defense of the poor.

While this was going on, the czar faced new problems from the church, which challenged his authority and affected his health. Meanwhile, a schism developed within the Orthodox Church for authority between church and state. It is not the intent of the author to delve deeply into the problem of the state versus the church. A brief discourse will suffice to illustrate the principal cause and effect on Moscow and subsequently on Russia itself. The czar appointed his friend Nikon to be patriarch of Moscow; Nikon originally supported the Old Believers in the purity of the church by banning foreigners with their corrupting influences—Catholic and Protestant beliefs—which tainted and corrupted true Orthodoxy. Later, when these believers went too far in proclaiming abstinence from alcohol and forbidding the performing arts, they were banned. The Old Believers exposed corruption by boyars and nobles at the expense of the poor, who backed them as their leaders. When the Old Believers went further in their demands, Nikon changed his mind and refused to side with them, reversing many of their doctrinal convictions instituting liberal conditions within the church. He took the position that the Old Believers wanted to create a theocratic monastic society. In the beginning the czar abstained from interfering in ecclesiastical affairs. However, when things got out of hand between Nikon and the Old Believers, with mounting disturbances creating a greater schism between the poor and the privileged, the czar sided with the Old Believers, having had enough problems on his hands. The czar consulted with other bishops and called for the church council to replace Nikon. After four years without a patriarch, the Orthodox Church Council selected another whom they could easily manipulate. However, most of Nikon's moderate changes were reinstated shortly thereafter. The czar's motives were clear; he sided with the service nobles and boyars, who were his mainstay, knowing full well they were corrupt, and had nothing to lose with the poor, who were customarily overwhelmed with taxes and misery. Nevertheless, he gained an advantage in being able to assume full control of the affairs of the church, as head of state and church under the old Byzantine Imperial tradition.

The presence of a substantial colony of foreigners in Moscow and some throughout Russia—consisting of military officers, merchants, and technical people—were a partial cause for later disturbances, and they were confined to *Nemetskaya Sloboda*, a derogatory term for "German quarters," in view of their preponderance as foreigners. While some of them left the country in disgust, others converted to Orthodoxy and settled on estates set aside for them. During his thirty-one-year reign, Alexey was faced with continual internal disturbances at home, a war with Sweden until 1658, and a war with the Polish-Lithuanian kingdom for possession of Belorussia and Ukraine, which lasted until 1667. If these wars were insufficient in themselves to exhaust the country, he commenced another war with the Ottoman Empire for access to the Black Sea. What would the people of Russia gain with access to the Black Sea? A pattern and tradition of aggrandizement—which took an unbelievable toll on human resources and material wealth. In the end it was the poor who paid in blood and with their meager possessions. After exhausting all possible patience and living under starvation and a heavy tax burden, they turned to violence to relieve their existence. Some scholars conclude that this violence was equal to the "Time of Troubles" in Russian history.

Czar Alexey died in 1676 of heart trouble, probably caused by events during his reign. He fathered sixteen children—thirteen by his first wife, Maria Miloslavskaya, and three by his second wife, Natalya Naryshkina. He was succeeded by his oldest son.

**Fyodor III: 1676-82**

When Fyodor became czar at age fifteen, he was well educated but in poor health. Before his father died, he had appointed Prince Yuriy Dolgorukiy, a personal friend, as his son's primary advisor. The question of succession became all too apparent soon when the first and second wife's progenitors clashed on succession to the throne. A boyar of the Naryshkin family, Matveev, Alexey's second wife's brother, tried with the help of *streltzy* to place his relative, four-year-old Peter (the future Peter the Great) on the throne and failed. The first wife's relatives banished the entire Naryshkin family from the capital and confiscated their estates. When Fyodor III got married in 1680, a new group of self-styled czar makers appeared with the family of his new wife. Before he died in 1682, he promulgated several measures—forbidding disfigurement and maiming people for crimes they committed and instituting banishment for life to Siberia, a practice perviously used by Godunov. He imposed the decision of the Orthodox Church Council for further additional restrictions on the Old Believers and decided to permit Moslem conversion to Orthodoxy. He also terminated his father's war with the Ottoman Empire by a treaty. In the last year of his reign, he abolished the long established *mestnichestvo*, an old code still on the books which governed the level and length of service to Moscovite aristocracy. His reign lasted only six years. It could be said that he passed away too young, and yet he displayed human kindness and compassion in a land of uncivilized and autocratic behavior in his short life as czar.

**Regency of Sofia: 1689-1696**

Fyodor's death brought about a conflict among relatives of his father's two wives. The first wife's family, the Miloslavskiys, and his second wife's family, the Naryshkins, feuded for succession through third parties. Through constant squabbles, murders, exiles to monasteries and Siberia, the use of *streltzy* and deceptions, it was eventually settled to have Sofia, the eldest daughter of

Miloslavskiys, to be regent. Under this agreement, one of the sons of Ivan V, Miloslavskiy or Peter of Narishkin, would ascend to the throne after attaining manhood. Sofia was a well-educated and intelligent young woman of twenty-four, and became regent for the heirs. She had her older brother, Ivan V, live in the Kremlin while her step-brother, Peter I, lived in a village nearby in a former boyar mansion. She selected her lover, Prince Galitzyn, as her advisor and Shalkhovitiy as commander of the *streltzy*. She made numerous changes and introduced new legal procedures used in Western legal codes. Generally, she is considered to have created a system of order in legal matters, diplomatic relations and conduct, and technology; she also requested military officers from Prussia to train her own officers. She made engineering contracts and created machinery, metallurgical and textile industries, and other technical support. She established diplomatic relations with Poland, Prussia, Holland, France, Spain, and England. She ordered land surveys and investigations of land titles and ownership in addition to taking a census of the peasants, which had never been done. She considered fugitive peasants and Old Believers as criminals, however, and when they were caught, they were promptly incarcerated or exiled to Siberia. She authorized an arrangement for peace with Poland against the Ottomans. For her efforts she secured from Poland the cities of Smolensk, Kiev, Chernigov, and Zaporozhye. In 1689 the Treaty of Nerchinsk with China was secured, and a fixed boundary was established, which lasted until the mid-nineteenth century.

With these accomplishments and successes, she began to act autocratically, forgetting her position as regent, annoying many, including the Narishkins. Rumors spread of her sympathy for Catholicism, which proved to be untrue, and of an immoral lifestyle. Eventually, her legitimacy as regent was questioned. To stop these rumors, she decided to be crowned czarina. This idea didn't sit too well with Peter Narishkin, in Preobrazhenskoye, who gathered her enemies and his friends to discuss the matter. In August 1689 Peter rebuffed Sofia in refusing to grant an audience to heroes of the Crimean campaign. Afraid of being kidnapped, Peter fled to a monastery where his supporters—the patriarch, and most regiments of the *streltzy* who had abandoned Sofia—and gathered to plot a strategy to unseat her. Faced with a fait-accompli, she abdicated as regent. Peter ordered her to retire to Novodevichiye Convent, not far from Moscow. She died there in 1704, at age forty-six.

Meantime, the elimination of the duality of succession was solved when Ivan V, Peter's half-brother, died in 1696. The throne was ready for Peter, who couldn't wait to get it and turn to western Europe, much like Sofia before him. The author is intrigued by Sofia's enlightened and forward-looking policies pursued in her youth in an age of wars, convulsions, murder, deceit, and turbulence. The logical conclusion is that she was a remarkable young woman with an inquisitive mind—an intelligent woman in her own right. Intrigued by advances made in western Europe and the backwardness of her own people, she was responsible for many innovations, some borrowed from western Europe and others from the best in her own land, and all for the benefit of her countrymen. She prepared Peter the Great's reign, who subsequently copied and enlarged on them. Unfortunately she was destined to be a regent instead of czarina. Her misfortune was being under two different mothers of two separate families who fought among themselves in the usual Russian style throughout their history. It would have been interesting to watch and record her reign had she been a czarina instead of a regent.

**Peter I, The Great, Czar Emperor: 1682-1725**

Peter was born to Alexey's second wife, Natalya Narishkina. Not until his half-brother Fyodor died was he installed as co-czar with Ivan V, his other half-brother, who was mentally and physically incapable. At the time, actual power was in the hands of his uncle and mother, having wrested the throne from Sophia. Only after his mother's and Ivan V's death in 1696 did Peter actually assume power and responsibility, at age twenty-four. Having no formal education, he ascended the throne and at first was guided by his uncle Matveev, an intelligent man who believed in foreign languages and had a broad knowledge of world affairs. This guidance made an important contribution to Peter's reign. After his uncle died, he was influenced by other Russian and foreign friends, all the while absorbing ideas of how to govern. Among his Russian friends were Alexander Menshikov, who attained high civil and military positions (though after Peter's death, he became a conspirator and manipulator); Boris Kurakin, an astute diplomat with dedicated service to Peter; Peter Apraksin, a military man, who attained high military and administrative posts; Prince Galitzyn, who rose to the rank of field marshal; Peter Shafirov, a cultural Jew, a most skillful diplomat and negotiator under adverse conditions; Pavel Yagushinskiy, president of the senate, who pushed through Peter's agenda. Among his foreign friends were Franz Timmermann, a Dutchman, who taught Peter arithmetic, geometry, and the building of forts; General Patrick Gordon, a Catholic Scot, who joined Russian military service in 1665 by Peter's invitation and subsequently became the mastermind of most of Peter's victories; and Francois Lefort, a Swiss adventurer who came to Russia in 1675 and became Peter's closest friend and advisor.

With his new friends and advisors, Peter changed Moscow's established order, outlook, and stature. As a result of his service as Russian czar and upon demand from his advisors, he was rewarded with the title of emperor, after similar titles of monarchs in Europe. Having high ideals for his nation, he created an imperium of Russia out of the former Moscovy. He abandoned Moscow, the former capital, and built a new one on the Baltic as a window to Europe and named it Sankt Peterbourg. By most accounts, he was a boor—uncouth and temperamentally violent—yet he was intelligently gifted, shrewd, stubborn, and determined. When his half-brother Fyodor died, he shared equal status as czar with his other half-brother, Ivan V. His half-sister, Regent Sofia, ruled until one of the brothers attained manhood and assumed the throne. With Sofia in exile in a convent, his uncle and mother ruled the country. Prior to ascending the throne, his mother arranged for him to marry Evdokia Lupokhina. It appears that he was disdainful of her and later acquired a paramour, Anna Mons, a German wine maker's daughter.

Only upon his mother's death did he realize his serious responsibilities as czar. Shortly thereafter, when in full control, he plunged the nation into perpetual wars, his lifetime occupation. He decided to clean house first and fought within his own national boundaries against the Crimean Tatars, who blocked his passage to the Black Sea and the Mediterranean. The Tatars were vassals of the Ottoman Turks, and Peter thought it would be rather easy to beat them. To avoid making Moscovy's errors by fighting for the entire Crimea, he attacked them in 1695 to capture Azov fortress only. His main military advisors discouraged this effort in view of his unpreparedness. He disregarded their advice and failed in the effort, sustaining heavy casualties. He learned a lesson from General Patrick Gordon not to attack without preparation and knowledge of the enemy's strength. Learning from foreign advisors, he became obsessed with military and naval science, an obsession that lasted to the day he died. In 1696 he armed himself with a river flotilla. Having had no ships in his first attempt against Azov, he now bypassed Azov and isolated it. With newly trained recruits and Don Cossacks, he captured Azov, thus breaking the sole possession of the Black Sea by the Ottomans. Not satisfied with this victory, he joined with the Holy Roman Empire, Venice, Poland, and the pope in fighting against the Ottomans. By changing the equation in southeastern Europe, he proclaimed himself defender of Orthodoxy and saddled Poland with a new king, Augustus II of Saxony. Peter placed no faith in religion, except when it suited his schemes, but he maintained his primacy as head of the Orthodox Church.

Thereafter, he left Moscow for Europe in 1697 to enlist England and France in the league against the Ottomans and to enlist European scientists and engineers; he also inspected their military, naval, and scientific institutions. On his way to Europe, he stopped in Riga, Konigsberg, and Berlin, where Frederick III, the Elector of Brandenburg, tried to enlist him in an anti-Swedish campaign, which he declined. He then left for Holland, where he spent four and a half months working in shipyards. He then spent four months in England to review the English lifestyle. He then proceeded to Vienna, where he tried to persuade the Holy Roman emperor to join him against the Ottomans, but the emperor declined. On his way to Venice, he was informed of the revolt by the *streltzys*. Enroute home in 1698 he stopped in Poland, where he concluded an alliance with his friend, Augustus, against Sweden. He was back in Moscow within a month, after spending eighteen months in western Europe.

His experiences in Europe were both successes and failures. His successes were his knowledge about western Europe's advancements in military technology, architecture, science, and schools of learning, which he used to enhance Russia when he returned home. He enlisted several scholars from Europe in various disciplines and arranged for Russians to attend their universities and schools. He admitted to his court that his European trip was the most satisfying experience of his life. His failures in Europe resulted from his general behavior, and he was abhorred by royalty and nobles. His uncontrollable temper, his uncouth personal habits, and surprisingly low behavior were disastrous in an age of refinement in European society. Some scholars attribute this unacceptable behavior to his inability to enlist any nations in his military adventures, either against Sweden or the Ottoman Turks. Louis XIV refused to see him after hearing of his crude manners and behavior.

The revolt of the *streltzy* was caused by several factors—war weariness, desire for normal life, transfer of some troops from Azov to the Baltic, high casualty rate, and absence from their families. To eliminate the problem quickly, he ordered General Patrick Gordon and his police chief to get rid of the problem forthwith. Although Gordon advised him to punish the few ringleaders, Peter disregarded his advice and opted to execute them. Most of the rebels were shot, and the rest were imprisoned for life, while those who took no part in the rebellion were disbanded and forbidden to be part of the military. The emperor personally took part in executions. The decision to execute and disband the *streltzy*, was a critical error in his subsequent military campaigns when serious shortage of trained troops developed, preventing Peter from exercising a tougher stand during peace negotiations between the Holy League and the Ottomans. He demanded the Ottomans turn over the entire Kerch Peninsula, the right of free passage through the straits past Constantinople to the Mediterranean, and the exclusive right to protect all Orthodox Christians within their empire. For obvious political reasons, no nation taking part in the negotiations agreed to these terms. In retaliation, Peter refused to sign the Treaty of Karlowitz, lacking the required troop strength to enforce it. In the Treaty of Constantinople, Peter could only secure Azov and an exemption of tribute to the Crimean Tatar khan.

Peter's hope of gaining a foothold in the Baltic in a war with Sweden came through only on paper treaties. Treaties between anti-Swedish allies were agreed to in 1697 and 1698; Treaties with Brandenburg-Prussia, Augustus II of Poland, and Russo-Danish and Russo-Saxon peoples were signed in 1699. The conflict with Sweden which began in 1700 lasted until 1721, and proved a disaster to Peter and his allies, again due to shortage of troops without the *streltzy*. With some British and Dutch naval assistance, Sweden succeeded in repelling all attacks and went on the offensive against Peter's allies, capturing Narva by overwhelming 30,000 Russian troops. Peter learned a lesson in logistics (among other things) at Narva, apparently better than Charles XII of Sweden. After the defeat of the Russians, Charles became overextended and overconfident. He withdrew his principal forces to Poland and Saxony. In the meantime, Peter commenced an annual draft of all eligible youth and replaced his cannon by melting down church bells. This effort took him four years to complete. Subsequently, in further skirmishes, he dislodged a small contingent of Swedish troops at the Noteborg fortress in 1702 and 1703. He compelled Charles to give up the mouth of the Neva river. Peter fortified this zone by building the Petropavlovsk fortress, which became the site of his new capital, Sankt Petersbourg. Other conditions out of Charles's control—as luck would have it—helped Peter. The Poles and Lithuanians, pressed hard by Swedish occupation of their territory, requested Peter to rescue them and invited him to enter Poland. Charles installed a new king on the throne of Poland-Lithuania, as they wanted. About the same time, the War of Spanish Succession commenced. This action forced the British and the

Dutch to withdraw their naval support from Charles. Facing a new unexpected situation without naval support and the failure of diplomatic efforts to solve the problem, Charles found himself outmaneuvered, and in order to extricate himself, he got deeper into Poland. Peter, unsure of his strength, petitioned the British and the French to help mediate the war, promising to give up all his gains in the Baltic, except the coast along the Neva River. Charles demanded all gains be returned to former status. To make sure it was complied with, he made preparations to march on Moscow with the head of the Ukrainian Cossack's, Hetman Ivan Mazepa.

Meanwhile Charles invaded Belorussia and defeated the Russian troops defending it. In this battle a new tactic was employed by Peter—by destroying everything in a scorched earth policy, denying the enemy any supplies, and ordering his troops to advance on Mazepa's territory in the Ukraine. Both the scorched earth policy and the advance to Ukraine proved successful. Some military scholars, in reviewing the battle, concluded that Peter took an extremely calculated risk in timing and could have lost the battle because Swedish ships were in the Baltic, a short distance from Poland and Swedish possessions, and only a small coastline left to the Russians on the Narva. His luck held because of the scorched earth policy and the absence of naval support from the British and the Dutch to Charles. On the other hand, they fault Charles for his foolhardy advance deep into Poland and Belorussia and for resting his forces in the Ukraine in winter, as well as his ambitious advance to Moscow, perhaps fifteen hundred miles east, without appropriate logistical train throughout his campaign against Peter. Subsequently, the battle was won by Peter in Poltava, Ukraine on 8 July 1709, hundreds of miles from Moscow. Overcome by success and in pursuit of Charles, he penetrated deep into Poland, intruding into Ottoman territory, which precipitated the Turkish-Russian war of 1710-1711, a conflict which turned against Peter with dire humiliating consequences. A major Turkish army surrounded Peter's forces, but a potential disaster was averted through skillful diplomatic negotiations conducted by Peter Shafirov, Peter's diplomatic magician. During negotiations, Shafirov agreed to give up Azov, permitting safe passage to Charles and the evacuation of all Poland. By getting this treaty, Shafirov opened the gates to the Baltic and the possibility of acquiring more territory.

In 1714 Peter occupied Finland (then a possession of Sweden), and later that year Peter's fleet defeated the Swedish navy at the Battle of Cape Cangut. Four years later Charles XII died. Subsequently, England, Hanover, Poland, and Prussia supported Russian actions, as well as later Russian landings near Stockholm, which caused Sweden to sue for peace. By the Treaty of Nystadt in 1721, Sweden gave up "for all time to come" Karelia, Ingria, Estonia, and Latvia in exchange for Russian withdrawal from Finland, cessation of interfering in internal affairs, and payment of Dutch currency. This treaty gave Peter what he had long-sought, an outlet to the Baltic. For his long sought victory his close associates honored him with the title "Emperor of all the Russias." Henceforth, Moscovy ceased to exist, and Russia became the name of the country.

After vanquishing the finest army in Europe, he sought further wars in Asia.

Between 1710 and 1721, he embarked on expeditions to Siberia in search of resources and routes to India and China. Along the way, he built the towns of Omsk and Semipalatinsk. Not satisfied with measly possessions and conquests, he simultaneously embarked south to the Caspian Sea and the Caucasus. In capturing those areas, he fought a war with Persia and gained Baku, Ashkhabad, and Derbend by 1723. His real intent in this direction was to outflank the Ottoman Empire. Flushed with these victories, Russia became a great world power.

It was, however, lagging in reforms long overdue, which dawned on him. His natural inclination for reforms fell in the military sphere since he had spent his entire reign in wartime activities. He introduced an annual recruiting system as cannon fodder for his wars by a quota tax-paying system along with recruits per household. All the nobles in major towns were to supply recruits for infantry and cavalry based on a quota of 50 and 100, respectively. Using this method he raised over 280,000 recruits each year. He created several industrial enterprises—including armament plants, foundries, shipyards, ferrous and non-ferrous industries, textiles, leather, lumber, paper, glass, tobacco, and other goods—which could be used for both war and civilian consumption. Government systems were also reformed to accommodate expanding industries, birthrate, and consumer requirements. The Duma was terminated and replaced by a private chancery, and in turn was replaced by a nine-member Governing Senate. New colleges for each military arm were established, along with colleges focusing on foreign service, justice, commerce, accounting, and state revenue, to name a few. Administrative divisions throughout the country were reorganized by provinces and sections within each. While all these reforms were instituted on paper, they didn't work too well in practice—confusion, duplication of efforts, and corruption reigned. He decided to employ his military machine to solve the problem, which in the end proved futile, making cheaters invent new methods to avoid surveillance. Nevertheless, in the end the military accumulated extensive arbitrary power and therefore became power brokers and makers of national leaders. In fact the nation became a military-administered camp, similar to a present-day dictatorship.

Peter also undertook to create an educational system, with some native but mostly foreign instructors and experts. Accordingly, he created the School of Mathematical and Navigational Sciences and the Naval Academy, learning from his previous sad lesson of shortage of naval support. He later established artillery and engineering schools, which had never existed before 1700. His crowning achievement was the establishment of the Academy of Sciences, the first of its kind in Europe. These improvements in the educational system were poor, primarily because of the illiteracy in the country. Peter was advancing the country forward, but it was not yet prepared for such changes. However, a beginning was made and proved to be a great national asset in the future.

His next effort was directed at the church, which he deprived of teaching the people, thus subjecting its spiritual power to his authority. Upon the death of the patriarch, he left the seat vacant, and within a year he deprived the church of its estates and monasteries, which were transferred to the Department of Monasteries, and the income became military subsidies. He later curtailed most functions of the ecclesiastical courts, and by 1711 all church-related matters were transferred to the newly created Senate in 1721. He thus abolished the seat of the patriarch and replaced it with the Holy Synod. To keep the church in line with his directives, he created a position of High Procurator in 1722 to administer all church matters. Peter also instituted a law requiring all Orthodox Christians to attend church services on Sundays, where his government laws were read, and made confession mandatory in order to extract information for future evidence. As mentioned previously his attitude toward the church was generally one of contempt, although he attended services regularly. The church-state revamping was a profound change which later affected the country and could be characterized as a police state religious environment.

Next he went after the nobles and then the peasants. Because of the perpetual wars he conducted, he forced the children of the nobles to enlist in the army, making their service mandatory. He created new laws depriving all heirs except the elder sons to succession and inheritance of the nobles; thus he curtailed the privilege of evading military service. Those ineligible for military service were drafted into the constantly expanding government bureaucracy, most particularly into the Economics Department. The decree of 1714 made school enrollment mandatory for all male children of the nobles aged ten to fifteen, to prepare them for lifetime military or civil service positions. He established a table of ranks for nobles and eligible commoners, regardless of rank or social position, for advancement in either of the branches of service. Any soldier who possessed leadership qualities was promoted to the lowest rank of officer. Any civil servant who reached a specified rank within the bureaucracy was rewarded with a hereditary position of nobility, funds, or landed estates. These reforms didn't appeal to many old-time nobles. The system, however, created a military-civil service bureaucratic class of professionals which still exists to this day. He also ordered men in cities to wear French, German, or Hungarian clothes; to shave their beards or pay a special tax; and he encouraged members of the new class to learn a foreign language.

Socially, Peter introduced an innovation in Russia, defying centuries-old traditions, by encouraging attendance of social functions for men and women, who were normally sequestered at home; he also prohibited arranged marriages. He changed the calendar, published the first newspaper, simplified the Slavonic alphabet, and caused the translation of foreign text for arithmetic, architecture, engineering, and navigational aides. In increasing the cultural aspect in urban areas, he supported the creation of a new theater, organized a library, and built a museum and stocked it with books, manuscripts, and paintings. In creating these monumental reforms in a backward country, he passed on to Russian society a dependence on the government from cradle to death from which it has never recovered. These severe and absolute reforms and his never-ending wars created and infused the Russians with military chauvinism, which he passed on to his successors, the czar-emperors, and eventually the people.

In assessing Peter's accomplishments with reforms, it should be acknowledged that he did lift Russia from backwardness by striving to attain western European standards. For his reforms in a backward country, he was considered to be the most enlightened, but also the most feared, leader in Europe.

The main goal of his reign was war, which never ceased, sacrificing thousands upon thousands of precious lives to attain glory for himself and Russia. To that end he overturned all directives of old Moscovy society and order, impacting Russia forever. He created a military, bureaucratic society in which the future czars exercised with the prerogative of autocratic privilege, which lasted until the overthrow of the Imperial regime and was subsequently carried out under soviet commissars with impunity to its penultimate end.

His personal life was a marital failure beset with misfortune—perhaps because of his involvement in wars and absence from home—causing him instability and sadness with his three wives and his son, the heir apparent. Peter was married off by his mother at sixteen to Yevdokia Lupokhina, who gave him three sons, and he confined her to a convent. He acquired a paramour, Anna Mons, a beautiful daughter of a German wine merchant, and their union lasted till 1703. After discovering she had been unfaithful, he threw her out. He then acquired another lover, Marta Skovronskaya, a peasant girl from Livonia, who became his consort in 1712. She gave birth to nine children—Peter was never sure if they were his—and most of whom didn't survive. In 1724 she was crowned Empress Yekaterina (Catherine). She, too, was apparently unfaithful, but Peter's sudden death in 1725 spared her from execution. He probably would have administered the extreme penalty himself, considering infidelity a grave insult. His relationships with his three sons were as sad as those with his wives and lovers. His eldest son, Alexey, born in 1690 to Lopukhina, was confined to a convent with her. Peter never bothered to see Alexey, yet he was the intended heir. The young man was rather receptive to European ideas but seemed to disagree with some harsh measures his father instituted, and scorned his father's infidelity. Alexey married a German princess in 1711 without permission from his father, thus increasing tensions between father and son. The princess died early in 1716 after giving birth to a son, Peter II, the future emperor. At this point Alexey informed his father that he did not desire to succeed to the throne and fled with a peasant mistress to Vienna and then to Naples. Promising to forgive his son, Peter convinced Alexey to return home. When father and son confronted each other, Peter placed conditions on the promise and demanded formal renunciation of his succession. Being suspicious of his son, he arrested him in 1718, charging him in a plot to overthrow him (obviously a ploy) with Austria's help. He was not permitted to defend or exonerate himself and was found guilty of treason; he was tortured to death in his father's presence. Is Alexey's murder—Peter's own flesh and blood—a result of a sane father or one gone mad? History's judgment on Peter's accomplishments in Russia would be kind, yet his cruel treatment of peasants and serfs and their plight—the only major source of his taxes and cannon fodder for wars and food supplies since everyone else was on the government payroll—should be considered cruel and unjust.

While Europe was in the throes of war, they began to acknowledge their peoples' dignity within royal absolutism. The people of Europe achieved a certain degree of freedom and freed the serfs, commencing an amity among the kings and his subjects. Peter traveled in Europe to learn the culture, industrial, naval development, and lifestyles, yet he never bothered to learn how European monarchs began treating their people. Peter left a legacy of progressive reforms under his iron rule, patterned after the Mongol-Tatar legacy, disregarding the dignity of his subjects. He thus further cemented and institutionalized a most autocratic regime. Russian history is filled with his glory, but it was at a high cost. How true are his early exploits in warfare since he was not a soldier and relied on foreign military talents to achieve the goals. Can a youth of sixteen a few centuries past be such a brilliant, intelligent, military wizard (and everything else attributed to him) or is it his advisors who worked over the diaries and archives? When he died, he left a powerful military nation—completely exhausted and without a leader.

**Catherine I, Empress: 1725-1727**

Under the law of succession drawn up by Peter in 1722, he assumed the right to name his successor. Since he died unexpectedly, it was understood that the law of progenitor would prevail, and Peter's grandson, Peter II, the son of Alexey, would assume the crown. Since Peter II was nine-year-old child, a regent would have to be selected until he reached manhood. A number of possible eligible candidates were proposed, too numerous to mention here. It was decided by Peter's closest advisors to continue his course. Come what may, Menshikov led the fight for Marta Skovronskaya, the Livonian peasant girl and Peter's paramour, and her appointment was pushed through by him. Her illegitimacy was conveniently bypassed—since Peter's wife was alive and in the convent. To secure her candidacy, Menshikov decided to force the issue by calling out *Preobrazhenskiy* and *Seamenov* guard regiments for intimidation. Her acceptance was easily won in the supreme privy council, despite strong protests from the old aristocracy and other advisors in the government.

Having achieved the quick goal of succession, she was named Catherine I, Empress. Her past was not especially glorious or respected. She had previously been married to a Swede, but when the Russians occupied Livonia, she became Menshikov's lover. In 1724 when Peter crowned her, he soon discovered she was unfaithful. She was illiterate, lecherous, addicted to alcohol, and subject to easy manipulation—which was Menshikov's intent. Her reign was quite brief and for practical purposes, she had no power. Power lay in the hands of Supreme Privy Council—in which Menshikov, Admiral Apraksin, Counts Golovkin and Tolstoy, the Duke of Holstein, Baron Osterman, and Prince Galitsyn were members. While the Council's tenure was brief, it had power over domestic and foreign policy, the appointment and dismissal of government officials, and jurisdiction over the courts. In its short existence, it completed the organization of the Academy of Sciences and sponsored a Kamchatka expedition, led by Danish Captain Bering. The Council established a High Commission for the preparation of new codes; for the gradual emancipation of nobility, giving them rights to control peasants' movements; and repealed the rights of serfs to join the armed forces without approval of their keepers.

Since the empress took no part in discussions of the Council, Menshikov arranged in early 1727 a future marriage of his daughter Maria to Peter's eleven-year-old grandson, the future emperor. Catherine died in May 1727, and the eleven-year-old boy was made emperor. It appears the boy was quickly engaged to Maria and lived in Menshikov's palace, where he was mistreated severely. In view of Menshikov's excessive power, rudeness, and mistreatment of the young future emperor as well as in his involvement in the death of Peter's son Alexey, his colleagues commenced conspiring to eliminate his power. Menshikov's opponents convinced the young emperor to sign an order for his arrest and deprived him of his immense wealth, deporting him and his daughter to Siberia, where they both died in 1729. Having got rid of Menshikov, a new leadership took over with Princes Dolgorukiy and Galitsyn taking charge. Their positions in the leadership were not definitely established, and it was unclear whether they were followers of Peter the Great or Old Liners. In 1727 while young Peter was still under Menshikov's control, a decision was made to transfer the court and some other government departments to Moscow. Records indicate the transfer but not the reasons for the move—perhaps they wanted the traditional depository in the old Moscow.

**Peter II, Emperor: 1727-30**

In April 1729 the security organs were abolished, with Prince Dolgorukiy assuming important positions in government. In November of the same year, an announcement was issued on the engagement of fourteen-year-old Peter II to seventeen-year-old Catherine Dolgorukiy. The young emperor, who had been in poor health, became seriously ill and died on the day of his wedding. His death marked the end of the male progeny of the Romanov dynasty.

**Anna, Empress: 1730-40**

Here again confusion and intrigue prevailed, with various female members of the Romanovs being proposed and rejected. Eventually, after extensive maneuvering, the Council chose Anna, the third daughter of Ivan V and the widow of the Latvian Duke of Courland. Her selection had several conditions attached to her exercise of power—similar to a constitutional monarchy. Though humbled by restrictions, she was aware of the possible extinction of the Romanov dynastic heritage on the throne and therefore accepted. She was fully aware of the humiliating conditions imposed on her; since she was a woman she would not have the privilege of autocracy. She agreed to attain the consent of the Supreme Privy Council before appointing her successor (or anyone to high rank), imposing taxes, marrying, declaring war or peace, depriving the nobles of their estates, and excessively spending state income. These conditions were primarily the work of Prince Dolgorukiy and Baron Osterman, who were the leaders of the Supreme Privy Council. While this stirred considerable debate in power circles, they were nevertheless submitted to her in Mittau, Courland. It was identified as the will of the Russian people. Opposition began to mount, and a delegation of Peter the Great's young guard arrived in Mittau ahead of Dolgorukiy and petitioned her to reject the offer. Upon reflection, she refused. It could be she refused not to reveal her intent. Anna fell ill early in 1740 and resolved that her successor should be her niece, Princess Anne of Mecklenburg, the only living offspring of Ivan V. While intrigues were going on, Princess Anne gave birth to a boy, whom the empress designated her successor, with Buhren as regent. Empress Anna died October 1744, leaving no heir. The infant son of Princess Anne of Mecklenburg emerged as Emperor Ivan VI.

**Elizabeth I, Empress: 1741-1762**

A few weeks after Anna's death, Buhren and Osterman were ousted in a palace coup and packed off to Siberia—all masterminded by Elizabeth, the only surviving daughter of Peter the Great. She took the heir under her care, sending his mother and her group to Siberia, and proclaimed herself Empress of Russia. She ascended the throne at age thirty-two. She acquired her beauty and personal charm from her mother, Catherine I: from her father, Peter the Great, she acquired an uncontrollable temper, physical prowess, unusual mental alertness, and a desire to humiliate people. Russian historians identify her with extraordinary sexual behavior, both superstitious and religious. Having lost her betrothed future husband, she indulged in an amorous life. She turned over the affairs of government to her trusted advisors when it suited her and pursued other interests. In her earlier days she kept in touch with her relatives, mindful of the unstable conditions of the country, and fearful for her life because of laws enacted and revoked. When she assumed the throne, she quickly surmised that a dangerous German-dominated group was in charge and promptly dismissed them all. She issued an amnesty for victims of former czars and deprived all her opponents of property and liberty. For her resplendent court, she introduced singers, balls, dancers, masquerades, and above all, her guardsmen.

She thought of reverting to her father's policies and repealing all decrees issued after his death. However, after various circumstances and prevailing conditions, which prevented her from exercising her intentions, she decided to elevate the Senate as the highest organ of government. An intelligent woman, she excluded the armed forces, police, national security organs, and foreign affairs from the jurisdiction of the Senate and transferred these agencies and their functions to her private chancery to have more personal control over them. Her internal policies, however, were dictated by the desire to resurrect restrains on the peasants and serfs. In this connection she decreed that peasants and serfs were not legitimate citizens of the country and, as such, were not required to pay allegiance to the ruler. Four years later the peasants were deprived of trading their or anyone else's produce. In early 1746 the nobility was given exclusive right to own land and serfs. Elizabeth issued another decree in 1747 granting the nobles the right to sell serfs. A further decree was passed, denying the serfs to volunteer in the army and later to deny them marriage. The decrees placed on peasants and serfs became unbearable, and this caused serious complications and ended in convulsions. The peasants and serfs evacuated government areas, seeking refuge in western Siberia, the Caucasus, Poland, Lithuania, and the Baltics. These ruthless suppressions prevailed in the eastern sections of the country and Siberian domains.

About the same time an influx of nobles, refugees, and other Slavic peoples escaped from Turkish dominated areas of the Balkans and entered Ukraine, causing serious complications with the new rules applied and effective in Russia proper. This mismanagement commenced in 1744 and lasted until 1756. Conquest and control of foreign peoples were two things the Russian government had no experience with, and thousands upon thousands of Russians lost their lives in the struggle for domination. Apparently they hadn't learned from the Mongol-Tatars how to dominate and control with tribute.

Religious intolerance prevailed because of her constant attendance in church services and the position taken by the Holy Synod, which had authority to censure books entering Russia. Church leaders assumed extraordinary powers with the intent to convert Old Believers and all other religious groups to Orthodoxy. As a result of this intolerance, the Armenian churches in Moscow and Sankt Peterbourg were closed, along with dozens of non-Orthodox churches. Foreign books were banned—even those imported by her father, Peter the Great. All these measures and decrees retarded the enlightenment and intellectual development of the country. Some enlightened individuals, most particularly Count Shuvalov and the eminent scientist Lomonosov, prevailed on the empress and the Holy Synod to establish the University of Moscow in 1757, and a university at the Academy of Sciences in Sankt Peterbourg in 1747, and an Academy of the Arts in 1757. Schools were re-established where foreign languages were taught, in view of the interest displayed by the court. The ballet, la Comedie Francaise, and other performing arts were popular at the court as well as in some noble palaces. For unknown reasons even books by Racine, Corneille, Moliere, and Voltaire appeared without censure.

Elizabeth's foreign policy was primarily a reaction to continual shifting balance of power in Europe. To stabilize and attain a semblance of order, Count Bestuzhev-Riumin, the foreign minister, believed in order to counteract Swedish, Turkish, and Polish unhappiness with Russia's recent successes, Russia's best interests in Europe from 1741 to 1758 would be served by cooperating with Austria, Saxony, and England. Meanwhile, King Frederick II of Prussia invaded Lower Silesia and succeeded in defeating Austria, which upset the balance of power in central Europe. Additionally, the heir to the throne, Grand Duke Peter, grandson of Peter the Great, didn't help much with his sniping. Other intrigues took place at the court, hampering the conduct of foreign affairs of Bestuzhev-Riumin. It took considerable skill and virtuosity on his part to untangle the mess, and he succeeded in re-negotiating a fifteen year treaty with England. He also ended a festering war with Sweden by the Treaty of Abo. This treaty was advantageous to Russia because Sweden granted more Finnish territory to Russia and recognized Russian gains in the Baltic. In 1746 Russia signed a treaty with Austria in which both powers agreed to support each other in case of an attack by a third power; obviously directed against Prussia. Again in 1747 two treaties were negotiated in which England would furnish £300,000 in annual subsidy in exchange for Russian pledge of two armies, consisting of 60,000 troops, to fight France. After completion of these treaties, Russia entered the War of Austrian Succession in late 1747. In accordance with the terms of the agreement with England, Russia advanced its army all the way to the Rhine. After eight years this peace collapsed, ending in another war in 1756-63 known as the Seven Years' War.

France was dissatisfied with its loss of influence in Europe. It had lost Lower Silesia to Prussia while Austria feared future aggressive moves. Diplomatic relations deteriorated between Prussia and Russia. However, astute maneuvering by Austria secured a treaty of alliance with France in 1756 at the time known as the Diplomatic Revolution. The combatants squared off with France, Austria, Russia, and later Saxony and Sweden against Prussia and England. The war started two months after the treaty's signing, and in 1756 Prussia invaded Saxony. In late December of the same year, Russia agreed to help France, and in January 1757 both nations agreed to furnish 80,000 troops to fight Prussia. Austria agreed to pay Russia 1,000,000 rubles and secretly agreed not to seek peace until Saxony was returned to Austria. Field Marshal Apraksin invaded East Prussia in June 1757 and defeated the Prussians at Gross-Jagersdorf. Cautious of being outflanked and possibly trapped, he delayed his moves farther into East Prussia until he was certain of victory. By delaying the advance, both he and Bestuzhev-Riumin were arrested and replaced. In January 1758 the offensive resumed, with Russians, Konigsberg, and all of eastern Prussia, and in August of the same year they defeated Frederick II at Zorndorf. The Russians then joined with the Austrians to defeat the Prussians again in Frankfurt-on-Oder. Early in 1760 Russian forces occupied Pomerania, and later in the year they captured and burned portions of Berlin. On 5 January, 1762 Elizabeth I suddenly died, and her nephew succeeded to the throne.

**Peter III, Emperor: 5 January-9 July 1762**

Peter III was Elizabeth's nephew and ascended the throne on 5 January 1762 without help from the palace guard, clique, or contradictory lineage. Born in Kiel, Holstein in February 1728, a son of Empress Anna (whose father was Peter the Great) and Charles Frederick, Duke of Holstein (who was a nephew of Charles XII, the king of Sweden). His mother died a few weeks after he was born, and his father died when he was thirteen. With impeccable royal credentials and no conflicting ancestral disputes, he was a rarity in eighteenth century Russia. After his father's death he was reared by his uncles and aunts in a strict Germanic Lutheran and military environment. Peter's aunt, Empress Elizabeth, brought him to Russia in early 1742, at age fourteen, to prepare him for succession and keep the throne in Peter the Great's progeny—and to avoid constant palace revolts. That same year in November he was baptized into Orthodoxy and officially proclaimed heir to the throne, and then returned to Holstein to await his turn. When his turn came, he arrived in Russia showing no interest in the country or its people, being smitten with Holstein and considering Russia nothing more than a huge barbarian emptiness. He was well educated and an intelligent youth but conveyed the impression of disinterest. He didn't get along with people in general or his aunt, the empress. It appears that these weaknesses left an indelible mark on his character as a future emperor.

Shortly after he returned to Russia, the empress selected Princess Sophia Frederica Augusta of Anhalt-Zerbst for his wife, whose name was changed to Catherine after arriving in Russia. From the beginning of their marriage, it was apparent that they were an incompatible pair. Peter refused to give up his Lutheran and Germanic upbringing and displayed instability in behavior. Paying no attention to or affection for his new wife, he preferred other ladies at the court. Although Catherine was German, she chose freely to be Russian and converted to Orthodoxy. She was highly intelligent and well educated, clever, a charming hostess, mature, calculating with a touch of deceit, displayed a desire for power and a nymphomaniac. Catherine gave birth to a boy, performing a great gift to the nation; he may not have been Peter's child. Later she gave birth to a daughter; Peter knew it wasn't his. Separation between them spread, and intrigues commenced. During Elizabeth's illness each constantly interfered in foreign policy affairs. He sided with Frederick II while she sided with Russia's allies. What's more, neither could get along with each other or the empress, and all this during the Seven Years' War. When Peter III ascended the throne at thirty-four after Elizabeth's death, Catherine was thirty-three and continually intriguing against the new emperor. Since Peter owed no allegiance to the palace guard, he disregarded them and forced on them German uniforms and methods. He and the palace guard hated each other. Since he came to power legally, he made no arrests, which was rather uncommon then in Russia.

Within a few days of his enthronement, he freed many who had ben exiled by previous rulers. In early February of the following year, he appealed to the Old Believers to return home and exercise their beliefs. He ordered all persons who were previously imprisoned to be released. In March 1762 he disbanded the security organs and issued orders that no persons should be arrested on political charges until investigated by the Senate. A month later he lifted all restraints on grain exports and other restrains which hampered trade and approved the construction of the canal between Volga and Neva. He then authorized establishment of a state bank. His next step was to release the nobles from compulsory state service in peacetime and permitted them to travel at any time out of the country. Other liberal orders followed, as practiced in western Europe; however in so doing, the orders alienated the serfs—who expected emancipation and subsequently erupted in a rebellion. By the end of April of the same year, he ordered additional restrains on the secularization of church property, which further aggravated church and state relations by transferring all church lands from the Holy Synod to the Economic College. He gave church peasants the land they worked on and replaced heavy taxes with payment of one ruble per year—part of which went to support the church, and the balance went to the state. Peter's contempt for the Orthodox Church was well known, as were his views of its theatrics and its powerful political influence on the state. Resentment among church people grew, which subsequently contributed to his downfall.

The reader should be aware of Peter's innovations in Russian society in political, social, economic, and religious affairs was significant in unshackling constraints placed by both the rulers and the church. Being a western European, Peter obviously believed in these changes and hoped to change Russian society into more liberal country, free from oppressive and arbitrary rules. For an emperor who had no special liking for the country, his accomplishments were truly astounding. All these changes occurred in a matter of months and were subsequently brought down in a few hours by edict.

On the other hand, his foreign policy should be considered biased, harmful and disrespectful to Russia and was probably more injurious than his drastic church reforms. On 19 February 1762 he ordered all operations against Frederick II to cease. Fascinated with Frederick II, Peter abrogated the treaty and ordered evacuation from all territory captured from Prussia by a new treaty in May 1762. A military alliance between them, drafted by Frederick, was signed and directed against Austria. The Seven Years' War ended with the Treaty of Hubertusburg on 15 February 1763, after Peter's death. The treaty saved Frederick from certain disaster, since his troops were encircled by the allies. In May he detached a contingent of 20,000 Russian troops to Frederick to fight against their former ally, Austria. The following July he signed a military agreement with Frederick against Denmark to protect his beloved Holstein. Meanwhile, Catherine gave birth to another illegitimate child, whereupon the emperor, in disgust, officially announced plans to dispose of Catherine. Two days after the announcement, Catherine's lover, Orlov, hatched a plot to dispose of Peter III. After her marriage to Peter, Catherine developed a close relationship with the palace guard, who were a powerful element in court circles. She was fully aware of their hatred toward the emperor, and acquiring lovers among them, she used every opportunity to defame him as being non-Russian. On 9 July 1762 she called out the palace guard, military, and naval contingents of Sankt Peterbourg, who swore allegiance to her as the future empress of Russia. Meantime, Peter fell under conflicting advice from his counselors, confused whether to leave Russia or rule jointly with Catherine. Catherine wasted no time and demanded his abdication on 9 July. He was arrested, stripped of his dignity, and murdered by Orlov's brother. Catherine attributed his death to an attack of colic. Peter could have been an enlightened emperor and could have bridged the gap between the past unworthy rulers and the commencement of a new era in Imperial succession and tranquillity. Intelligent as he was, he cared little for Russia, whose blood flowed in his veins. So died an emperor, confused with loyalty to his Germanic upbringing and birthplace and his legitimate right as the ruler of Russia.

**Catherine II, Empress: 1762-96**

Catherine, a princess of Germanic origins, became empress of Russia, on 9 July 9 1762 by action of few conspirators and the palace guard. She acquiesced in her husband's murder and appropriately rewarded all those who helped her become empress. Her only fear was Ivan VI and his supporters, who wanted him to be the rightful ruler of Russia. It is still unclear whether Ivan's supporters wanted to use his power on the throne or felt he was legitimately entitled to it. He was imprisoned for many years and eventually went insane. Catherine meted out severe punishment to his supporters in 1764, as well as to Ivan himself, after three attempts were discovered to free Ivan from prison. So desirous was she to be empress, she even disregarded her infant son, Paul, who should have been named emperor after attaining manhood. Being an ambitious woman, intelligent, cunning, and of strong character, she could not permit herself a demeaning second place. She reigned for some thirty-four long years, leaving an indelible mark on Russian history. Her career as empress, according to various Russian historians, was hypocritical, an enigma, an enlightened despot, a brilliant opportunist, dilettante, a reactionary, a writer of history, a lawgiver, and much else—indeed a controversial figure by Russian and western historians alike. She is, however, acknowledged as a German who made Russia a great and expansive power, even beyond the conquests of Peter the Great—whom she greatly admired—and as the most feared power in Europe. As empress she tried to justify her actions to appease influential people, both at home and in Europe.

A few days after the coup, she tried to enlist outstanding and influential philosophers and other scholars in the Age of Reason, which commenced in western Europe. Among the outstanding people were Diderot, whom she invited to transfer his suppressed publication, *Encyclopedie*, to Riga from France, but he refused. Later the same year she invited philosopher and mathematician d'Alambert to tutor her son, Paul, an offer he also declined. After being rebuffed, Catherine contacted Voltaire and gave him her version of the coup and showered him with gifts and money, inviting him to visit Russia. In addition she contacted several other influential people of letters and arts who agreed with her description of the events of the coup with and her policies and whom she used as spokesmen to promote her image abroad as the most enlightened monarch in all Europe. For reasons quite unclear, Voltaire was her great backer and apologist—perhaps he believed her too much—while d'Alambert was her greatest critic. Nevertheless, she seems to have appeased most critics at home and abroad.

Satisfied with her efforts in pursuit of scholars and critics, she then set about to govern Russia, despite her eighteen years in Russia as a meddler in the court and intriguer. She was confounded by the difficulties confronting her. It is inconceivable to Russian scholars how quickly she reviewed the reforms previously enacted by former rulers, most particularly those of Peter the Great, adopting most of his reforms with modifications. She streamlined his reforms and tightened control and overall supervision of the country. Accordingly, she introduced measures which seriously changed and affected the administrative structure of government and the empire. She first tackled the Senate, the highest administrative organ of the country, and introduced changes which quickly made governing the country more efficient. By placing six departments under the Senate—internal political policies, military, judicial, administrative, local justice, Ukrainian, and Baltic departments—she made the Senate a supervisorial agency. These changes lasted until the fall of the Imperial dynasty in the early twentieth century.

Probably her most ambitious reform, which was two years in the making, was in the project of the Legislative Committee, which included *nakaz* (instructions) and contained monarchical absolutism; the nature and forms of laws, industry, and trade; education; crime and punishment; social composition; freedom of religion; state administration; revenues; and expenditures. It was a document mainly modeled after the great philosophes of western Europe. Among them were Montesquieu's "The Spirit of Laws," Beccaria's "Essay on Crime and Punishment," and others from d'Alambert, Diderot, Quesnay, and other encyclopedists. Most historians agree that she deferred to these philosophes, though they had to be adjusted to applicable Russian conditions. In the end, when finally published and submitted to the Legislative Committee—in usual Russian deliberative sessions—nothing useful was accomplished, and it remained a document for the archives. Since the vast majority of the population was either peasant or serf and illiterate, their dreams of fair treatment under the nobles and merchants passed into oblivion.

With regard to her imperial principal of autocracy, she commenced Russification, first of Ukraine and later of the Bashkirs, Tatars, and other minority nationalities and tribes, who were pressured to convert to Orthodoxy. Due to failure of the Legislative Committee's enactment of the expected laws for peasants and serfs and the enforcement of Russification, things were beginning to get out of hand and resulted in rebellion, led by a Don Cossack, Emelyan Pugachev. The rebellion caused an excessive loss of life, destruction, and hunger, despite the seizure by the rebels of towns and enormous territory, which they subsequently surrendered or were killed trying to defend them. Pugachev was finally cornered and brought to Moscow in a cage; he was found guilty and beheaded in January 1775. When the Holy Synod stepped in, it anathematized him and his followers. She ordered a cleansing period by government troops which was more ferocious than the acts by the rebels, where thousands of peasants and serfs died like cattle. One would think that Catherine learned a lesson from this; on the contrary, she tightened the noose even more. This rebellion was the most serious of her reign and left an indelible mark of injustice and extreme cruelty during her reign.

She later decreed, in October 1775, the opening of rich lands on the Volga, the Don, and the so-called free Ukraine to all foreigners except Jews. In this connection, she opened an office for Foreign Settlement in mid-summer 1763 to attract foreigners and exempted them from taxes and any obligations for thirty years with the right of self-government. Within five years 12,000 Germans settled in the lower Volga and preserved their identity, language, and culture until exiled to concentration camps in Siberia by Stalin during WWII, and subsequently many returned to Germany after the fall of the USSR. New decrees in 1764 irrevocably secularized church property, along with one million peasants who belonged to the church, convents, and monasteries. She closed a multitude of convents and monasteries, and the small number which remained were allowed on the condition that they maintain themselves on alms. Her intellectual pursuits caused her to create various research and educational institutions which put Russia on a higher plane than ever before. These institutions of learning included the Academy of Letters to advance the learning of literature and languages, founded in 1763. The Academy of Arts, for girls of noble families, was founded in 1764.

The Economic Society was founded in 1765 and published several books and various economic theories. In addition to the above, she had previously established the Commission for Schools, which oversaw the creation of schools. She sent many young students for study and supported expeditions by Russian and non-Russian scientists. All the above institutions and their support lasted until the revolution, and some were reinstated under communism. These institutions subsequently bred amorphous intellectual brotherhood, which were not sponsored by the government, and exposed shortcomings in society, whose members later paid for it with exile or prison.

Her legacy to Imperial Russia was a decree in 1783 depriving the Jewish Autonomous Communities, the *kahals*, of all their power, except for fiscal matters and spiritual control. A further decree in 1792 established the Jewish Pale; its verdict in 1794 forced all Jews to register as merchants, and without a formal hearing of grievances, she doubled their taxes. When it came to foreign policy matters, she adopted Peter's alliance with Frederick II and proposed by her advisor, Count Panin, known as the Northern Accord. This treaty with Prussia pledged mutual military and financial support, in case Russia was attacked by Turkey, and Prussia by France or Austria. It also pledged to keep weak Sweden in power. The treaty included maintaining the status quo (civil war) in Poland, destabilizing its government by using force if necessary, but granting freedom of religion. On face value, it appeared to be a reasonable alliance between two countries; however it turned out to be against Poland and Sweden, which actually ended in the partition of Poland. This treaty was signed in 1764 in Sankt Peterbourg, permitting Russian occupation of Courland, a part of the Polish crown, and eventually resulted in the invasion of Poland. This guaranteed Count Poniatowski's, (her former lover) selection as king of Poland.

To insure Orthodoxy in Polish communities occupied by Russia, her troops overran Poland and occupied Warsaw on 7 September 1764 and later encroached to Cracow. The troops deported Catholic opposition leaders to Russia. Russia's heavy-handed behavior and Prussian's occupation of West Prussia caused an uprising, resulting in a massacre of Catholics, Uniates, and Jews. The Russo-Prussian action caused considerable disturbance and gained sympathy from France, Austria, Turkey, and Sweden. This action subsequently caused the Russian-Turkish War of 1768-74. Turkey started the war, afraid of being outflanked. The Russians wanted to get even and settle previous Polish incursions into Russia, once and for all. The Russians took the initiative by employing their Baltic squadron from the Baltic to the Mediterranean and managed to destroy the Turkish fleet at Scio and Chesme, occupying Azov, Izmail, Akkerman, Bucharest, and several other points in Crimea. The Russian victory was gained at an astounding loss of life, causing great anxiety in Europe about Russian designs on Turkish possessions there. Coupled with peasant uprisings in Russia, the combatants decided for their own reasons to commence peace negotiations in Kuchuk-Kainardzi in 1774. In negotiations Russia agreed to give up Bulgaria, Bessarabia, Wallachia, Moldavia, Georgia, and Mingrelia but retain Azov and Kerch, a portion of Kuban and Terek areas, and the land area between Dnieper and Bug rivers. In return, the Turks agreed to allow free and unfettered passage for Russian Orthodox Christians to Jerusalem and passage through the straits. In addition, the Turks were obliged to give access to Russia for commercial markets in Tripoli, Tunis, and Algeria. The treaty effectively made Russia a Black Sea power, and Turkey "The Sick Man of Europe." What Russia could not gain on the battlefield, it got at the peace table—and then some.

Frederick II and Austria got nervous over the unexpected gains in Russian territory. To allay their fears, Russia accepted a proposal of Frederick's to partition Poland, contrary to Poland's agreement with Russia. Early in February 1772 Austria, Prussia, and Russia, signed the first Partition of Poland, with each occupying their respective sectors. Again by signing this treaty, Russia gained Mogilev, Polotsk, Vitebsk, and a slice of Livonia (Latvia). Prussia gained West Prussia and Pomerania, while Austria annexed Galicia. If this were not enough compensation for Catherine, in 1778-89, she was asked to arbitrate in the War of Bavarian Succession between Prussia and Austria. This right gave Russia both prestige and power in Europe.

About the same time, her greatest ambition was the Greek Project, which envisioned the expulsion of the Turks from Europe, and the restoration of the Byzantine Empire under Russian hegemony, to create a new Kingdom of Dacia at the western edge of the Black Sea, (present-day Romania) with Prince Potemkin as its king. This scheme required the cooperation of Austria because of its geographic proximity. In this connection, she secured a treaty with Emperor Joseph II of Austria in May 1781. Joseph II agreed to the status-quo in Poland and also to partition the European area of the Ottoman Empire. Austria was to receive the western portion of the Balkans (roughly former Yugoslavia), with the balance going to Russia. In order to prepare for this historic event, she annexed Crimea in April 1783 in violation of her agreement with the Ottomans. This made western Europe apprehensive. That same year, she extended protection over Georgia, on its border with Turkey; on this occasion western Europe turned panicky. On her way to visit her new possessions in Crimea, she met Emperor Joseph and Poniatowski to coordinate their moves in the concept. The Turks demanded evacuation of Crimea; when Catherine refused, they declared war on Russia, which lasted from 1787 to 1791. In January 1788 in accordance with the treaty, Emperor Joseph declared war on the Turks. The Russian campaign was almost a similar version of the previous war in 1768-74. It included a Balkan uprising, a naval battle in the Mediterranean and the Black Sea, a land assault on the Caucasus, and joining with the Austrians on the Danube. At first the coordination of their plans became faulty because of squabbles among Russian generals and subsequently between them and the Austrians. Nevertheless they secured Khotin, Yassy, and Ochakov-Ochakov which caused unusually heavy casualties. Her plans were upset in July 1788 by Sweden's declaration of war against Russia, by land and naval attacks supported by England and Prussia. Frederick II was exceptionally angered by Catherine's betrayal. However, her plan for the Mediterranean and the Black Sea was upset in transferring troops to the Baltic to protect Sankt Peterbourg.

A few months later, in 1789, the French Revolution erupted, which helped the Russians in the Baltic campaign against Sweden because England detached its forces from Sweden to protect its interests in western Europe. Battles between the Russians and Swedes were won and lost, and in 1790 Catherine decided the war with Sweden was a waste of manpower and detracted from her main objective, so she signed a peace treaty with the Swedes. The treaty required Russian non-interference in Sweden's constitutional order. About this time, western Europe was erupting in various unexpected convulsions; in addition to the French Revolution, the Austrian Netherlands successfully rebelled and attained its independence. The Hungarian and Galician instability threatened the very existence of the Hapsburg monarchy. Meanwhile, Frederick II, alarmed by the might of the Austrians and Russians in southeastern Europe, concluded a defensive treaty with the Ottomans in January 1790 against Russian and Austrian alliance with Poland. In February 1790 Emperor Joseph II died and was succeeded by his brother, Leopold II.

The new emperor, seeing his opportunity to extricate Austria from this mess, promptly entered into peace negotiations with the Ottoman Turks and with Prussia. Abandoned by her Austrian ally, Catherine insisted on continuing the war by herself. In September 1790 the Russians captured the Izmail fortress on the Danube, crossed the river in 1791, and rejected all peaceful mediation efforts and threats from England and Prussia. She finally compelled the Turks to accept her terms in January 1792. The Turks agreed to Russian annexation of Kuban, Crimea, and territories between Dniester and the Bug rivers. Further, they agreed to stop their raids against Russian territories in northern Caucasus in exchange for captured territories of Wallachia, Moldavia, and Bessarabia. The end of the war with the Turks didn't realize her "Greek Project;" however it secured for her substantial areas of the Black Sea.

At the conclusion of Catherine's conflict with the Ottoman Empire, she re-entered her conflict of domination of Poland. Polish nationalistic expressions resurfaced again while she was busy with the Ottomans and Swedes. The Poles, being inspired by the French and American revolutions and assurances of Prussian and Austrian military help, adopted a constitution in 1791. This document rejected a single veto over any parliamentary measure as well as elective monarchy and the federation system, which Catherine had previously ordained. This act angered Catherine. Unfortunately for the Poles, Austria and Prussia got into a war with revolutionary France, which allowed Catherine to re-enter Poland by way of Ukraine, with 100,000 troops and revoke the Polish constitution. Catherine's action, in turn, angered Frederick of Prussia who demanded immediate reinstatement of his rights in Poland. In 1793 by the Treaty of Sankt Peterbourg, Poland was partitioned for the second time. In this partition Prussia received approximately 24,500 square miles of Polish territory, including the important port of Danzig, Poznan, and greater Poland, mostly inhabited by the Poles. Russia's share was substantially more—90,000 square miles—stretching along the Dvina to the Dniester rivers, and from there to Pinsk (which was inhabited by the Lithuanians, Belorussians, Ukrainians, Poles, and Jews), thus placing the balance of Polish lands under Russian control. The Poles were provoked by dismemberment and an uprising commenced in March 1794 under Thadeuz Kosciezko, who previously had taken part in the American revolution. The Poles were overwhelmed by superior forces, and the war ended with a Russian victory. The next year Austria and Prussia joined Russia in a final attempt to partition Poland for the third time, with no trace of its existence until after WWI.

Apparently feeling she had not enough territory, Catherine approved another grandiose plan, the Oriental Project. This dreamlike scheme by her young lover, Platon Zubov, called for the occupation of the Caucasus by attacking Persia to the east and thereafter the territories below Ottoman-occupied Turkey to secure Constantinople. Enroute, the Russians occupied Baku and Derbend. For reasons still unclear, whether the route itself was defined or even feasible, or whether it was a figment of Zubov's or Catherine's imagination, it was decided to abandon the harebrained idea. Catherine desired at least another venture for the glory of Russia. This plan envisaged an expedition to Siberia, securing the Chukchi Peninsula, occupying the Aleutian Islands, and laying claim to Alaska.

As busy as she was in her government reforms and foreign affairs, Catherine never failed in her avaricious appetite for sex. Retiring and rewarding her lovers—too many to outline here—she picked one, Grigoriy Potemkin, of "Potemkin Villages" fame, she made him a prince in 1776, as well as her male harem-keeper, who selected appropriate lovers for the next thirteen years. She made Platon Zubov, of the Oriental Project scheme, a prince for his personal services to her. Perhaps exerting herself too much, she died of a stroke on 17 November 1796, unattended by anyone. Every assignment she undertook was done with dispatch and intelligent determination, knowing well in advance the objectives she wanted to attain.

How does one qualify Catherine the Great, Empress of Russia, a German princess from a tiny principality of Zerbst, Germany, who came to Russia to marry a future emperor? If one measures her qualifications based on acquisition of lands for empire building, using territories of conquered nations, and attaching them as acquisition to Russia, one must inevitably conclude that she is great, at least in a historical sense in centuries past. Her far-reaching reforms in a feudal land even surpassed those of Peter the Great. History will have to judge her objectively. Present historians have varying opinions of her. Some generally agree that her treatment of the nobles at the expense of poor peasants, who carried the burden of taxation, and her treatment of serfs as rewards and gifts was fundamentally flawed, unjust, and cruel. Yet others defend her on grounds that she acted in the interest of Russia, regardless of actual conditions of the peasant and serfs—a custom of the time in Russia. They also apply to her the term "benevolent autocrat," common to Russian Imperial temperament at a time of unsavory monarchical social behavior in feudal Russian history, though western European monarchs had passed that period long before and shed their barbarism earlier. To the ordinary Russian she is the epitome of Russian greatness, as pre-revolutionary historians claim. Early Soviet historians treated her on the basis of class-consciousness and criticize her for being non-responsive to the plight of peasant and serf. The reader is left to form his own opinion, bearing in mind the conditions in the latter part of the eighteenth century in a feudal society.

**Paul I, 1796-1801**

Paul was born 1 October 1754, the son of Catherine the Great and an unknown father. He was an intelligent and educated person. His grandmother, Empress Elizabeth, took him away from his mother soon after his birth. He was brought up in isolation in the Imperial estate in Gachina, a few miles from Sankt Peterbourg, with his mother's acquiescence. Because of Paul's unknown parental origins, Catherine unofficially selected her first born son, Alexander, to succeed her. Before she could officially do so, however, she died without attaining her wish. Therefore, Paul ascended the throne of Russia upon his mother's death in 1796 at the age of forty-two. Having been isolated from events as a bastard, he hated his mother's governing of the country and resolved to change social and political conditions in the country she left him. Conditions in Russia after Catherine's death were an amalgam of contradictions—a vast multitude of illiterate hungry peasants and serfs and a small group of extremely wealthy nobles, who attended good schools and indulged in the political and literary ideas of western Europe.

He launched his changes immediately, which caused great confusion and resulted in disturbances among the nobles, poor peasants, and serfs. He issued orders prohibiting the use of such words, as "society," "revolution," and "citizen." He also introduced press censorship, forbade import of foreign literature, and recalled all Russians home from abroad. He also reopened several colleges that his grandfather, Peter the Great, had created. He introduced a system to reduce fifty provinces (*gubernias*) to forty-one and simplified the awkward judicial system. During his coronation he decreed a law making the crown hereditary to prevent surreptitious assumption of power and defined the order of succession. Socially, he decreed reduction of service by the serfs to the nobles, from six to three days a week, with no work on Sundays and holidays. However, he also decreed a confusing set of requirements which required the serfs to pledge allegiance to him and not the nobles, which caused the upper classes to protest his interference into their households. He canceled all drafting of recruits and restored corporal punishment and some other minor privileges of the nobles. These decrees appear to have been done for the concern of the lower classes and not to spite the nobles, yet rumors spread otherwise. Paul's confusing and contradictory decrees caused serious fear among the nobles while the lower classes had high expectations from him. As a result a conspiracy was planned against him in 1799.

During his short reign, he decided to undo some of the wrongs his mother had done in foreign affairs. Paul also concluded that Russia was completely exhausted from innumerable wars since 1756 which had impoverished both the peasants and serfs. He abandoned the Oriental Project, withdrew from the anti-French coalition with England and Austria, and recalled his troops home. Shortly after withdrawal from this coalition, and under great pressure from French loyalists exiled in Russia, he reversed himself. When he became aware of rumors of French intent to liberate Poland from the Tri-Partite partition and then heard of Napoleon's seizure of Malta enroute to his Egyptian campaign, Paul again changed his mind and abandoned his reversal. After Malta was liberated from the French, he was honored by Napoleon in being selected its grand master—a clever ruse. He then joined in a coalition of forces against France with England, Austria, Portugal, Turkey, and the kingdom of Naples in July 1798 and dispatched his Baltic Fleet to join with the British fleet off the coast of Holland; and later the same year he dispatched his Black Sea fleet to join the Turkish fleet to eject the French from Corfu, the Ionic Islands, Rome, and Naples. Concurrently, Russian Field Marshal Suvorov was advancing with the Austrians into northern Italy and Switzerland and began to occupy Milan and Turin. After capturing the two towns, Suvorov proceeded to join other Russian and Austrian troops in Switzerland who were waiting for him under command of another Russian general. Suvorov's movements were too slow, and they were beaten near Zurich.

Soon after, Anglo-Russian troops in Holland were also beaten, creating serious animosity and hostility between them. Meanwhile, in retaliation the British forces occupied Malta in September 1800, refusing to surrender it to Paul I, who was its grand master. Napoleon played a shrewdly decisive game, offering to cede the island back to Paul and recognize him as the grand master again. Napoleon had nothing to lose since the island was not his to give, having lost it previously to the British. To add further to Paul's ego, Napoleon unconditionally offered to release all Russian prisoners in France. Paul, not realizing the ruse, agreed to an anti-British alliance to invade India.

These grandiose plans never saw the light of day because Paul was murdered. With the consent of Grand Duke Alexander, Paul's son, and with support of high-ranking government officials, the conspirators decided to take action against him, on 23 March 1801. During the attempted coup, the emperor was killed. It is not clear whether the attempt was accidental or murder. Officially, Russian records indicate that his death was caused by an apoplectic stroke yet rumors persisted that he was strangled.

Alexander I, his son, assumed the throne and ordered the troops to cease the march to India. So ended the reign of a well-meaning, but naive emperor, whom the Russians call a "non-person." Paul was a victim of his mother's promiscuity and his grandmother's autocratic shield.

## Alexander I, 1801-25

Alexander was born 22 December 1777 and ascended the throne of Russia at age twenty-three. His education was entrusted by his grandmother, Catherine II, to General Saltikov, a tyrant, who installed in him autocracy. Later, however, his principal tutor was a staunch Swiss republican, Frederic LaHarpe, who taught Alexander humility, equality, reason, and justice as practiced by French philosophes, particularly a brand of Jean Jacques Rousseau. Unfortunately for the young man, neither one of his tutors taught him about his own country. This contradictory dose of education helped to confuse him and stopped only when he got married at age fifteen to Princess Elizabeth of Baden. He was exposed to further contradiction by the luxurious and corrupt court of Catherine II and his father's militarily austere environment at Gachina. He didn't like court life or government affairs, preferring the country life. Reflecting on acquiescence of his father's murder, he brooded deeply, which affected him the rest of his tragic life.

If anyone was unfit to govern the country, it was Alexander. The empire at home was in shambles with administrative chaos, a corrupt bureaucracy, an illiterate population, outdated social and political structure, indebtedness, and a demand by the nobles for a greater role in government affairs. In foreign affairs Russia was beset with problems in Central Asia and the Caucasus, the British challenge in the Baltic, and Napoleonic incursions in most of Europe. These problems would challenge the best efforts of a highly intelligent, even-tempered, and particularly conscious individual, but Alexander found it difficult to cope. In 1801-12, he was exceedingly cautious yet involved with three wars; from 1813 to 1825 he was embroiled in European affairs.

In the first six months of his reign, he assured all he would rule in accordance with his grandmother Catherine's laws. He immediately stopped the march to India, released all prisoners and exiles who had no court trials, warned the police not to overstep their authority, restored privileges of the nobility, and lifted all restrictions on exports and imports. Being more artistic by character, he financially helped writers, scholars, and educational institutions. He also terminated security organs and appointed a commission for the preparation of new codes of law. He earnestly desired to help the plight of the poor peasants and serfs. The liberal nobles agreed to release the serfs, while the conservative ones objected strenuously, cautioning him not to give in or rebellion would again result, undermining autocracy, similar to Pugachev's previous revolt. In confronting these problems, his decision was a vacillating and conflicting one. His decision to prohibit publication in the press of the sale of serfs without the land they worked on was conclusive, yet a few short years later, to appease the conservative nobles, he agreed to free them on condition the owners agree to release them. Few, if any, nobles agreed.

Prior to assuming the throne, he preferred a constitutional monarchical system; once he became emperor, he was a staunch supporter of autocracy. In 1803 he approved the creation of the Main Administration of Schools, with control over the entire grade school system and most universities. Each educational district was intended to have a university, though Russia didn't have enough capable teachers and university professors to staff them. By then, the University of Paris was already eight hundred years old. The nobles preferred not to send them to their schools with common children and either hired personal tutors or sent them abroad for study. Additionally, there were no funds available for universities; when added to Napoleon's wars in Europe, the country was almost bankrupt. The whole educational system became a paper exercise. In participating in the war of the Third Coalition with Britain and Austria, he drained his treasury to its limits.

He was also forced to confront domestic affairs because of agricultural failures. In despair he turned to his best friends for advice who suggested he employ the son of a village priest, Mikhail Speranskiy. Speranskiy was a highly educated person for a villager, a hard worker, and had the support of influential people. From reasonably careful study of that period, the author is convinced it was the most successful and truly diligent appointment of Alexander's entire reign. Speranskiy was probably the most astute organizational person in Russia in the nineteenth century. He introduced a curriculum in schools which included foreign languages, natural sciences, history, economics, and geography, along with uniform examinations for the bureaucracy, instead of patronage. Alexander was so impressed with Speranskiy's capabilities that he appointed him chief administrative secretary in 1807 and in 1809 made him principal advisor in all matters, except military—a prerogative of all czars and emperors of Russia. Had he made him principal civil advisor in military matters, Russia may have had fewer wars and less cannon fodder. Speranskiy's introduction of these reforms subsequently produced a product of superior quality in the bureaucracy. That was precisely what the nobles and the old bureaucracy disliked. They had to take examinations and reach the highest rank or they could lose their hereditary positions and rank.

To help alleviate the dire financial conditions in the country, he proposed various financial reforms; he terminated the use of paper currency and the floating of domestic loans, increased direct and indirect taxes, and instituted a progressive income tax. Subsequently, Speranskiy prepared a constitutional project with several social class changes within the population, as well as reorganizing of executive, legislative, and judicial branches. These monumental reforms, long overdue, were well accepted by progressive elements within the society and as always rejected by conservative elements who curiously called them "Jacobin Atheism," undermining autocracy. In the end only the State Council was approved, which conservative elements dominated.

Relations between Alexander and Speranskiy deteriorated because of unfavorable remarks about the emperor attributed to Speranskiy, probably floated by conservatives. Notwithstanding his service to the emperor, he was exiled by Alexander to Siberia in March 1812, just before Napoleon's invasion of Russia. His exile was approved by the conservative nobles. After the successful conclusion of the war against Napoleon, Speranskiy was recalled from exile to serve the emperor again as one of his advisors. Mikhail Speranskiy was a brilliant, selfless reformer whose service was mostly unappreciated.

Napoleon's invasion of Russia with 600,000 troops, as reported by Russian historians, (although French records indicate 500,000, of whom 300,000 were French), was a terrible blow to Alexander, who by then was thirty-five years old. Russian records indicate they only had 200,000 troops in the field. These figures are somewhat suspect by several military researchers, primarily because of the size of the Russian population, though acknowledged being less than Napoleon's. A battle at Smolensk on the way to Moscow was costly to both sides and proved indecisive, though Napoleon continued his advance on Moscow. Enroute, another battle erupted at Borodino with extremely heavy casualties on both sides.

The Russians retreated to Moscow, pursued by Napoleon. Prior to

Napoleon's entry to Moscow, a fire enveloped the entire town, leaving the old capital a charred ruin when Napoleon arrived there in triumph, waiting for Alexander to sign peace terms. Russian responses under adverse conditions of war have a history of their own. Nevertheless, Alexander disregarded the invitation. Russian retreats and evacuation of Moscow and their scorched earth policy caused Napoleon to evacuate his troops from the old city within five weeks. Running short of logistical support, Napoleon evacuated Moscow by the southern route but was blocked, forcing him to turn north, by the same route he first attacked. He was relentlessly pursued and sustained unusually heavy casualties, principally by Russian hit-and-run tactics, extremely cold weather, hunger, and frostbite. He finally extricated himself and retreated by way of Courland, pursued by the Russians, while his erstwhile former allies now turned and pounced on him. Eventually he arrived home with the remnants of his hungry and bedraggled 100,000-man army. The French defeat broke Napoleon's domination of the continent and raised Russia's prestige.

While Alexander's prestige was high, the cost of Russian victory was abominably high in manpower and ruinous to many towns and villages. Napoleon may have been beaten by the Russian winter and unfamiliar environment, but he was not down and out when retreating through Prussia. Meantime, flattered by Prussian and English diplomats who suggested he pursue Napoleon further, Alexander ordered his troops along with the Austrians and Prussians to finish off Napoleon for good. At the next battles at Lutzen, Bautzen, and Dresden, Napoleon vanquished his foes. However, further west at Leipzig in October 1813, with his veterans completely exhausted and outnumbered, he sustained more casualties than the allies, who forced him to retreat across the Rhine. After the battle of Leipzig, his grip on western Europe ceased. The allies entered Paris at the end of March 1814. Abandoned by his generals and his people, Napoleon abdicated and was subsequently exiled to the tiny island of Elba, off Italy.

While Napoleon was beaten by numbers against him, he developed a plan for a comeback battle while relaxing on Elba. At the Congress of Vienna in September 1814, principally engineered by the shrewd French diplomat Prince Telleyrand, a liberal treaty was signed. However, the allies fell into a squabble among themselves shortly thereafter, with various realigning cliques. These squabbles were the queue for Napoleon's return battle. On 8 March 1815 Napoleon escaped Elba, re-entered France, and fought his last battle at Waterloo, losing to Wellington and Field Marshal Blucher. This battle was lost by Napoleon with serious errors in timing committed by his generals and their inability to adjust to various conditions in battle. Napoleon was finished and exiled to Saint Helena.

Flushed with victory over Napoleon in September 1825, Alexander went on an inspection trip of his troops in preparation for an assault on the Turks to aid Greek co-religionists and "suddenly died" there in December 1825. His death, like some other monarchs, is classified in the records as unexplained. It would appear that too many monarchs die suddenly, perhaps poisoned by certain opposition elements.

There is some reason to believe that the emperor had been inclined to grant some reasonable freedom, at least on paper. In their pursuit and advance through Europe, Russian officers and troops encountered European peoples of several nationalities with higher lifestyles, clothing, food, housing, and freedom not available in Russia. Returning home, the victory generated Russian nationalism and chauvinism and also created expectations of radical social reforms by young officers and liberal elements. The conservative elements, fearing loss of autocracy and their privileged status, petitioned the emperor to act quickly to stem the tide. Alexander ordered General Count Arakcheev to oversee domestic affairs and repress the liberals. Arakcheev's principal policy was for the army to develop military colonies. It was intended to promise a decent lifestyle for soldiers and peasants, who were the vast majority of the army. In practice, however, it proved to be unpopular with liberal elements, while the nobles thought them to be economic competition with free labor. On the other hand, the army officers found the regimen too hard on discipline with brutal treatment. These military colonies lasted forty-five years, causing two unsuccessful rebellions. What's more, the educational system based on the secular system was abandoned and replaced with strict ecclesiastical control, which prohibited liberal thought, preached great Russian chauvinism, and suspended all desire for inquiry. These prohibitions made Russia the least educated society in Europe for years to come. The liberal elements and freethinkers in society, confronted with these strict rules, greatly contributed to the growth of the upcoming "Decembrist Revolt," which occurred shortly.

**Nicholas I, Emperor: 1825-55**

Alexander's sudden death at Taganrog at age forty-eight near the Sea of Azov found one of his brothers, Constantin, forty-six, in Warsaw, while his younger brother, Nicholas, twenty-eight, was in Sankt Peterbourg. Alexander's death caused confusion for three weeks over succession. Having no sons, under the Law of Succession of 1797, Constantin was the natural successor. However, since Constantin divorced his wife to marry a Polish countess, he renounced his right to succession. Therefore, Nicholas was the logical successor and heir. Alexander formally approved the law in 1823, signing a manifesto designating Nicholas the heir. Sealed copies of the contents were unknown to anyone, including his brothers, and deposited in the Holy Synod, the State Council, the Senate, and Uspenskiy Cathedral in Moscow. For some unknown reasons, copies of the manifesto were bypassed by the appropriate authorities, and Constantin was assumed to be the heir. When Nicholas took the oath of allegiance to Constantin, ordering it to be read throughout the coronation, Constantin refused to accept the crown. This caused confusion for a few days until Nicholas disclosed the contents, fearful of reports that a conspiracy was brewing among army officers. Discovering that he was the heir, he issued orders to have the oath administered to him on 25 December.

Nicholas was well educated, spoke several languages, and loved the performing arts, but he particularly disliked political science. His training in military engineering, parades, and drills instilled in him a certain discipline which he never abandoned upon becoming emperor. He married Princess Charlotte, daughter of King Frederick III of Prussia. It appears that, having no assignments under Alexander, he was cautious and hesitant to use his power at first. Subsequently, he turned out to be an extreme autocrat and severe chauvinist.

Shortly after assuming power, he was confronted with the rankling Decembrist Revolt. The Decembrists were patriotic and intelligent young aristocrats, mostly officers in the army, whose previous war sojourns in Europe acquainted them with huge differences between Russian and European standards. They were exposed to the ideas of the French Revolution and were equally exposed to social revolutionary thinkers in Europe in 1848. They quickly surmised that Napoleon was beaten by the overwhelming numbers of troops against him. The ideas of the French Revolution—freedom, equality, and brotherhood—attracted them for the simplicity and fairness to all citizens, not any specifically privileged group. Moreover, they discovered there were no serfs in Europe anymore; all the peasants worked for themselves. They also discovered that the Industrial Revolution in Europe was now in full swing, with workers having strike privileges and health and vacation privileges. Laws were being made by free men and not autocrats, and legislators were truly representatives of the people. Informed that the University of Paris was eight hundred years old, they went there to discover books written by Russians and heard European scholars and philosophers lecturing freely on various subjects without supervision of authorities.

Returning home they thought of implementing these ideas to help Russia modernize. Instead they found Russia a closed autocratic society, with arbitrary military colonies, poverty, and hunger—and generally behind European standards by a few centuries. In 1816 when some of them returned home (some stayed on and lived in Paris), they organized a secret society, the Union of Salvation. Its main objectives included constitutional government, judicial reforms, abolition of serfdom, and acceptance of foreign influences. By 1817 they reorganized to broaden their scope and renamed the society Union of Welfare. Its goals included humane treatment of serfs, maintaining hospitals, enacting prison reform, establishing homes for the aged, providing education for all youths, and eradicating corruption in government and civil affairs. It further wanted to advance agricultural sciences, industrial and commercial development. In addition, a substantial number pledged secretly for the destruction of monarchical system and serfdom.

The union was organized in two groups, the northern group and the southern group. The northern group in Sankt Peterburg and Moscow advocated a steady but gradual implementation of federalism, abolition of serfdom, freedom of speech and press, religious belief, and trial by jury; it was patterned after the American model but had some additions. The southern group advocated a radical approach to political, economic, and linguistic uniformity, freedom of religious belief, and trial by jury; it was patterned after both the English and American models; however, it advocated a reign of terror against the ruling class. They also believed they could convince Alexander I to adopt their program and were upset by his sudden death. Actually, the two groups had only minor differences in their ideas, yet they never could close the gap and compromise. Both groups suffered the same dangerous anxiety about infiltration by informers.

When Nicholas I assumed power, the northern group tried to incite a few formations not to take the oath of allegiance unless Nicholas accepted a constitutional form of government. On 25 December, the day of Nicholas's oath of allegiance, the northern group could gather fewer than three thousand troops to assemble at the Senate Square. When their troops refused to surrender, the ten thousand loyal troops surrounded them. Nicholas called for an artillery volley directly at the troops, to avoid civilian casualties. Documented casualties list eighty dead and the rest fleeing. The southern group had heard of the coming confrontation a few days earlier when some of its leaders were captured on 24 December. However one of their leaders escaped and gathered a force and captured a few small towns around Kiev and issued a number of unsuccessful appeals for support but was defeated in battle.

Nicholas appointed an investigative committee and personally investigated a few hundred conspirators, with most receiving light sentences for a "noble" cause. Since they were punished for a noble cause—seemingly acknowledged as a just cause—they became a symbol against autocratic rule, and subsequently the foundation for Russia's revolutionary movement. In Europe Nicholas was ordained "the detested gendarme of Europe." After disposing of the problem with Decembrists, taking note of their grievances, he removed some of his advisors. The reorganization included the establishment of the Council of Ministers, the State Council, and the Senate. However he still made use of his secret committees headed by trusted associates. Nevertheless, he kept for himself his autocratic authority, reserving the right to disregard any recommendations—which he often did.

He used the chancery, first established in 1812, which had reformed and reorganized it into six departments. The author thinks it wise to outline the departments, which had a critical effect on Nicholas's rule, as well as on the future emperors. The First Department served as his personal secretariat and later exercised jurisdiction over the bureaucracy. The Second Department, organized in 1826, served to codify Russia's laws and was placed under Speranskiy, though with some critical constraints from Nicholas. The reader should be aware that no previous or present bureaucrat could refuse service to the emperor; therefore Speranskiy was employed and discharged constantly, having no choice. The Third Department was in charge of security matters. The Fourth Department, organized in 1828, was in charge of administering educational and charitable institutions. The Fifth Department was organized in 1836 to be in charge of poor conditions of state peasants. The Sixth Department, organized in 1843, administered TransCaucasian affairs.

Since Speranskiy was in charge of the Second Department, the most useful work done was systematizing, arranging, and publishing more than fifty thousand decrees which spanned a period between 1649 and 1830 known as the *Complete Collection of Laws of the Russian Empire*. Subsequently, this department published a code of laws (living laws). However this code excluded any reference to constitutional constrains on power. While it omitted the most important part of power sharing, it served to standardize uniformity and administrative unification. It was a work of outstanding scholarship by Speranskiy which lasted with minor exceptions throughout the period of Imperial rule.

The work of the Fifth Department was commendable, although it never tackled the critical issues of state peasants and serfs. Its agenda for the peasants called for practical considerations of past and recent conditions, considering the magnitude of disturbances by the peasants. It was approved by Nicholas in 1838 and was long overdue. The whole peasant population at the time was about seventeen million people. The peasants organized themselves into village communes similar to the organization of Soviet collective farms—granting them authority to meet every three years to elect officials and judicial magistrates. They had permission to allocate and apportion land, levy the "soul" tax, enforce military conscription quotas and impose local taxes as they saw fit. All the above measures were executed under the Board of State Domains. The board introduced better farming techniques and set up schools, hospitals, and a welfare section, which eventually made for better conditions for state peasants.

However, when it came to the serfs, the strong opposition of the nobles to improving their lot was proclaimed from the very beginning. Every effort was made not to interfere with the interests of the nobles, although the emperor and his advisors agreed that serfdom was an evil. In 1833 the sale of serfs without the land they worked on was confirmed, and all sales to break up families were prohibited. By 1842 serfs were permitted to be transferred with land into an obligated chattel in return for agreed compensation. Two years later the nobles were permitted to emancipate their serfs without their land, and in 1848 serfs were given the right to purchase land with their masters' approval. Despite these transactions and laws, millions of serfs still remained in bondage.

The Third Department (the forerunner of the KGB) in Nicholas's chancery was intended from its inception in 1826 to be the eyes and ears of the regime. In the beginning it was placed under General Benkendorf with the responsibility for state security. It operated under the gendarmerie, secret informants, and spies, gathering information on religious sects, political unreliables, and other suspected elements of society which could threaten autocratic rule. Additionally, it controlled the movements of all foreigners, having the authority to detain and exile. It also had total authority of censorship in newspapers and literature, could subsidize propaganda, and actually supervised all facets of private and public life. Nicholas was kept constantly informed, by both Benkendorff and his successor, General Orlov, who formed a part of a personal circle of intimate friends, through which Nicholas ruled over the country and the empire.

The Fourth Department, having charge of charitable and educational institutions, did perform rather well under severely restrained conditions in education. While schools were generally good, they were inadequate for the size of the population. The school system was subdivided by a class system of tiers in ascending order. Church schools for lower classes of society also included serfs. County schools catered to the children of artisans, urban people, and merchants. The *gim-*

*nazia* was established for the children of the nobles and government officials. By 1843 there were six universities, open to qualified students of all classes, including emancipated serfs. The lucky few exceptionally bright students were sent to foreign universities and secretly observed throughout their stay. Nevertheless a foundation for education was being established, though inadequate, under the Imperial system of Russia. The government feared the spread of education, which might have the tendency to question autocracy. It is estimated by Russian scholars that the nation's population in 1825 was somewhere between 55 and 60 million. Unfortunately the lack of facilities of higher education prevailed and plagued the Imperial regime until its demise.

Meanwhile, about 1827 and thereafter, circles were being organized for discussion about the cause of Decembrists at Moscow University. These circles were penetrated by informers, and as soon as they sprang up, members were promptly arrested. In the early 1830s Alexander Herzen, a serious social and political thinker, and some of his associates established a circle for discussions on foreign political philosophers—Hegel, Fichte, and other German and French romantic writers. Another circle, organized in the late 1830s by Nikolai Stankevich, had the same broad objectives and included literary critics Belinskiy and Katkov; a journalist and future anarchist, Bakunin; and Slavophiles Aksakov and Samarin. In the 1840s, a minor official in the Ministry of Foreign Affairs organized another circle for the study of French socialist ideas which included the young writer Fyodor Dostoyevskiy.

Other groups were also organized and included Slavophiles and Westernizers who dealt with philosophical thoughts on Russia's future. Both groups agreed with one another on some issues but disagreed rather sharply on other issues. Their agreements were on the freedom of the press, abolition of serfdom, hope for Russia's future, the uniqueness of the Russian Orthodox Church, and the value of village communes. The Slavophiles stretched their thinking to value Russian folksongs as a Russian inheritance and opposed the "decadent West." This dislike of the West was based on rationalism, socialism, materialism, and Western parliamentary democracy. They abhorred Peter the Great's modernization and bureaucracy and advocated the supremacy of pan-Slavism; they also hated the non-Orthodox Slavs like the Poles. Most Slavophiles advocated Russification of non-Russian minorities. On the other hand, Westernizers were young Russian intellectuals, nobles and non-nobles, who organized in the 1840s, and whose platform was the Russian relationship to Europe. They too were inspired by German romanticism, a love for Russia, and a desire to be part of Western civilization. They were fully cognizant of the difference between Russia and Europe. To breech the gap they criticized past and present mistakes of Russian society, condemned serfdom, yearned to free themselves from religious mysticism, and desired to learn European technology and science. They also preached freedom of the press but opposed pan-Slavism and believed in European-style socialism. They defamed nationalism and considered themselves the avant-garde of Russian scientific and progressive elements of future society.

The Third Department (security service) along with the Fourth Department (education) kept a close watch on the Westernizers; many were harassed, and some were exiled. Because of this harassment, many social thinkers—Bakunin, Herzen, and Belinskiy, to name a few—escaped to Europe. The government's policy toward its non-Russian minorities was exceptionally harsh because of the threat to Russian security and nationalism. Non-Russians openly challenged the political, economic, social, and administrative systems, and the claims of the Romanovs as a dynasty and their rulers. They hated Russian overbearing nationalism, chauvinism, and Orthodox conversions under threat.

The patriotic feelings of non-Russians were completely different and opposed to the government's policies. Their feelings were inspired by the principals of the French Revolution and German romanticism and its idealistic philosophy. They aspired to termination of domination with an independent nationhood and identity of their own. The Poles were the first to rebel against repressive rule among non-Russians who opposed Russia's acquisition of Poland under the conditions of the Treaty of Vienna. Nicholas was the king of Poland, and his brother Constantin was the viceroy with a Polish countess as his wife. He tried to soften conditions, as promised; however Nicholas's rule was oppressive to the breaking point, and his brother could do nothing about it. This inevitably caused a revolt in November 1830. The Poles were the most cultured, educated, and the most politically conscious in the Russian Empire among non-Russians. They demanded independence, and when Nicholas refused, the Polish diet deposed Nicholas as king of Poland. Infuriated, Nicholas ordered fresh reinforcements to Poland, fully aware of the lack of leadership and solidarity among the Poles, causing thousands of them to flee abroad. Those caught in the country were exiled to Siberia, and their property was confiscated. Nicholas replaced the Organic Statute of February 1815 with the Constitution of 1815, making Poland an indivisible part of the Russian Empire.

After he disposed of the Polish question, Nicholas went after the other Western areas of his empire, pursuing identical policies and adding religion to his Russification policy in Lithuania, Belorussia, and Ukraine. In 1836 he established an Orthodox Bishopric in Riga, Latvia (a Protestant stronghold), exploiting anti-German feelings among Estonians and converting them to Orthodoxy by force. In the 1830s Russia replaced the Lithuanian Statute with its own legal code, reorganizing the school system and commencing Russification in all schools in western provinces which had previously been under direct Polish and Catholic control.

In addition to the above, one-and-a-half million Jews in the western provinces were selected for special treatment in the summer of 1827. A law was published to replace the traditional head tax with twenty-five years of compulsory military service for young Jews. In the application of these laws, great harassment and cruelties were perpetuated against them, expelling them from a number of villages and several urban areas and restricting their movements without authorization. Nicholas denied them employment of Christians as servants and forbade the use of Hebrew in conducting business in public. In 1842 all Jewish schools were placed under the Ministry of Education, closing all *kahals*, and brought them under the city government, the better to control their destinies. These measures under Nicholas made conditions of Russian Jews intolerable. Amazingly, he never thought of using them productively and utilizing a great collective talent in most disciplines for the benefit of his own Russian people. Many fields of endeavor—medicine, economics, business, law, and teaching professions—lay dormant because of these measures. He considered the Jewish question solved and left this legacy for future generation of emperors.

Effective in 1848, Russian intellectuals suffered in many cases worse than the Jews, being singled out for supporting revolutionary outbreaks in Europe. The regime displayed total ignorance in the rapid fall of European governments where democratic laws were being enacted, anti-Russian speeches given, and feelings of European revolutionaries encouraged. To combat such dangerous practices at home, a special committee was set up in 1848 to restrict dangerous publications and applied severe pressure on university professors and students in voicing their thoughts freely. The schools were forbidden any lectures in philosophy, constitutional law, and classics. The rule applied to university enrollments and went into effect immediately. Subsequently, they arrested some young intellectuals connected to a "circle," and after the trial, fifteen members of the group were sentenced to death. On the day of the execution, Nicholas commuted their death sentences to forced labor in Siberia. Among those exiled was the acclaimed author Fyodor Dostoyevskiy. The Censor Terror, as that period is known, ended only when Nicholas I died in 1855.

Having completed his clean-up in the western provinces, he turned his attention to the so-called eastern question (*vostochniy vopros*). He commenced thinking of the problem a few months after assuming the crown, revealed his plans to the chancery, and received full support for his scheme. His scheme included the capture of Constantinople, the destruction of the Ottoman Empire on European soil, and complete protection of Orthodox Christians under their empire. From mid-1840 to 1854 Nicholas caused enough problems with several wars involving Great Britain, France, Austria, Prussia, the Ottoman Empire, Denmark, and Sardinia, all due to his ambitions for territorial aggrandizement. He committed an enormous comedy of errors in changing alliances, aggravating religious clashes, double-dealing, blackmailing, turning diplomatic somersaults, and handling surreptitious cash payments. Not satisfied with his expansionist schemes, he turned his attention to the Caucasus in the summer of 1826 following the outbreak of the Russo-Persian war. The Persians, who had previously lost territory to Russia by the Treaty of Gullistan in 1813, began a conflict to regain their territories. At first they were successful apparently due to a surprise attack; later, however, with the Russian reinforcements the tide turned, and they were compelled to sign the Treaty of Turkmanchai in February 1828. The terms of the treaty were harsh on Persia, and they agreed to the occupation of northern Azerbaijan and Persian Armenia, with the frontier set at the Arax River. In addition Nicholas secured navigational rights in the Caspian Sea and a large indemnity.

In acquiring these territories, Russia faced a fiercely opposed population who had had full freedom under the Persians. A guerrilla war promptly commenced against the Russians with Moslem factions, including Chechens, Inguish,

Assetians, Abkhazians, Avars, and several other minor tribal peoples. In three campaigns beginning in 1838, in an effort to capture the leader of one tribe, Shamil, fifteen thousand Russian troops lost their lives. It took an additional force of 200,000 men and many years to pacify and incorporate them into the empire. Yet Nicholas had to win this war to protect "Holy Russia" from these tribesmen.

Why stop there, when there was more territorial prey in the southeast to conquer? On this occasion, he turned his eyes to Central Asia by fortifying the Kazakh steppes after 1830 and built new fortifications and Cossack settlements. By advancing further east, the Russians came in contact with Tatar Khanates of Kokand as well as Bokhara and Khiva of the Turkomans, who populated the eastern shores of the Caspian Sea. This contact created a conflict which resulted in conquest—except Khiva, whose turn came later. The Russians continued their drive, setting up military bases north of the Aral Sea in 1845, then on to Syr Darya River in 1853, and Alma-Ata a year later. As a result of these and other aggressions, more than half of Central Asia fell during Nicholas's reign. As if it were not enough territory that Nicholas had conquered, his map showed more land could be easily acquired, and he marched east and the sailed to the mouth of the Amur river, establishing a settlement called Nikolayevsk. This last step violated the Treaty of Nerchinsk with China previously signed with Russian explorers. The Ministry of Foreign Affairs advised strongly against it. Nicholas vetoed their advice by abruptly stating that "where once the Russian flag flies, it shall never be lowered again."

Nicholas instructed his people of the Russian-American Company in 1853 to occupy and administer Sakhalin Island off the mainland of Siberia and La Peruse Strait adjoining the Japanese island of Hokaido. In August of the same year, he sent an expedition to establish contact with Japan, perhaps hoping to occupy Japan and treat with it, as he did others in Siberia and elsewhere. The Japanese refused entry. Since his problem of the eastern question was not resolved, he made up for it a hundredfold with his new conquests in the south and east adjoining Russia proper. In acquiring these territories, he was not aware of their wealth of natural resources. Subsequent expeditions in 1858-60 accumulated more than 350,000 squares miles of territory rich in gold, platinum, precious stones, exotic minerals, and oil. The acquisitions by Nicholas were a further extension of aggrandizement by Russia, which has afflicted Russian leaders ever since. When the czars were exhausted from indigestion of acquiring foreign lands, they sold to the Unites States, and subsequently the commissars took over and acquired more. Viewed from a geopolitical perspective, these conquests covered the Eurasian continental mass, extending from the eastern portion of Poland, the Gulf of Finland, the Barents Sea, thence the length and breadth of Siberia, to the shores of the Pacific, across the Bering Sea to the Aleutian Islands and to Alaska. Russia became a territorial giant, covering one fifth of the world's mass, and became a power with which to be reckoned.

If this were not enough, Nicholas blundered into the Crimean War in June 1854. Completely unprepared for it, thinking his masses of Russian troops were sufficient to guarantee to beat any nation or combination of nations, he sacrificed

600,000 of his troops in this slaughter. The Crimean War should be considered historically a massive slaughter, in which only Florence Nightingale received great honors. Yet back home, where it mattered most, the vast majority of its people—the poor peasants and serfs and those who died for it—never gained a kopek for their sacrifices. Yet Nicholas, who caused the slaughter, died peacefully in bed and didn't live long enough to see its disastrous end. Nicholas I died 2 March 1855, leaving the country thoroughly in turmoil, exhausted, and in debt, with poor peasants and serfs starving; he left this legacy to his son, Alexander II. Apparently it was all for the glory of Holy Russia and not for its deprived people. The tragedy of Russia's ruling class in utterly disregarding the welfare of their people—the most precious commodity of any nation—plagued the country from its beginning to this day.

## Alexander II, Czar, Emperor: 1855-81

Alexander was born in 1818 and at age thirty-seven ascended the throne in March 1855. He was very well educated and brought up under humane tutors who taught him justice and fairness to the down-trodden. This tutoring affected him the rest of his life. When he assumed the powers of emperor, he was faced with crisis at home and abroad left for him by his father's capers, with terrible casualties sustained in the Crimean War and a losing war in Europe against several allied nations. The liberal elements demanded immediate constitutional reforms, the peasants were downcast and uneasy, and the nobles feared loss of power, privileges, and land. Crimean War, the wars in Europe, and the expansions in the east and south not only sapped the energy of the nation but actually bankrupted it.

During his father's reign, he had performed various services at his father's request, including a trip to Siberia, promising reforms and a period of peace. Shortly after ascending the throne, he addressed the nobles and informed them that he had no intention of abolishing serfdom, though he clearly stated to them that serfdom could not remain unchanged, and it was better to abolish serfdom at the top than when it was at the bottom, lest it destroy itself from below. This statement leaked out, which disappointed the liberal elements, peasants, and serfs, and confused the nobles. In 1839 he visited several countries in Europe and dropped in at Hesse-Darmstadt in Germany, where he met Princess Wilhelmina, his future wife.

In becoming emperor, his primary goals were to free the serfs and institute educational and judicial reforms. Like most rulers in Russia, he created a secret committee to study the problem of serfdom. The basic intent of emancipation—rooted in the evil it posed—was freeing the serfs in stages, lest convulsions occur precipitously and get out of hand. Since serfs were in the domains of the nobles, the intent to free them was based on the value of the land in various parts of the country. The more productive the land, the less acreage for the serfs; conversely, the least productive, the more acreage. Compensation for the land was based on redemption payments to former landowners, with the serfs obligated to serve the nobles until 1780, when landowners would have their inventory of land, its value, and a method of compensation. In most cases the nobles had to turn over the land to village communes which the government created. It was a complex and difficult undertaking, which became unsatisfactory from the start. Emancipation itself was closely related to measures which affected other peasant categories. The peasants in former Polish lands—since acquired by Russia—were given larger land allotments and lower rates of redemption payments as punishment to Poles for their support in 1863 against Russian rule. Also brought in to the equation was Ukrainian and Lithuanian support. Baltic and Caucasian emancipation came in 1870, though the terms were not as generous as others. Regardless of allotments, troubles were springing up in Russia, and troops were brought in to quell disturbances. These disturbances helped arouse protests among university students and intellectuals. Nobles too were dissatisfied, with some unable to adjust to the new realities, and many sold or rented out their estates. Other nobles, taking advantage of new business opportunities, technology, and professions, entered various fields, although already wealthy in their own right. Essentially neither the nobles nor the peasants were satisfied with miscellaneous solutions of emancipation and land ownership.

Emancipation, as unfair and complex as it was, unleashed other reforms concerning local government and judiciary. Governmental and judicial reform was considered important by both liberal and conservative nobles who called for local governments to be based on separation of powers, with emancipation in force. The nobles tried to regain their privileges with separation of powers. Alexander vetoed the request; however, in March 1859 he appointed a committee to review the matter, and after several modifications and regulations concerning provinces and county land institutions, it became law in January 1864. These laws were introduced in thirty-four provinces, with the exceptions of Siberia, the Caucasus, western portions of Ukraine, Belorussia, Lithuania, and Poland. Under the law county landholders were empowered to build local bridges and roads, to take care of education and public health, furnish food in emergencies, accelerate commerce and agriculture, and among other things, to collect local taxes for the government. The county assemblies met every three years to elect new officials. The assemblies had no official powers and were forced to rely on the central government representatives. They were always short of funds, partly due to the poverty of the area and partly due to the diversion of funds to maintain justices and extending relief to families of men killed in war. Surprisingly, it was one of the few enterprises to succeed, primarily because of minimum interference by government bodies and hard work with sacrifices by thousands, becoming a showpiece of the great reforms. What is not mentioned here in detail is the graft and corruption associated with many government agents who were not involved with the usual tax collections and who behaved as they pleased.

Municipal government reform was next. As with the judicial system, after going through with bureaucratic modifications, it was made into law in June 1870. The law was drafted by the Ministry of the Interior and included the division of town population into three groups—the large tax payers, the middle, and the small. The municipal governments were responsible for local administration, health and welfare, municipal services, public works, and requests to the central government for local needs. The Statute of Judiciary became law in December 1864. Various changes took place prior to the law's enactment which forbade use of the lash, branding of prisoners, running the gauntlet, and excessive abuses in the army. The Judicial Statutes established equality of men before the law, and class courts were abolished. For the first time courts were free from executive power, and this raised the standards of professionalism among the judges, making them permanent holders of office. It introduced a jury system of twelve jurors and twelve alternates, in addition to oral testimony, which was required to be public. However, the jury system was not law in Siberia, the Caucasus, western Ukraine, Belorussia, Lithuania, or Poland. Every effort was made by the author to research the reasons for denial of the jury system to those areas; unfortunately no reasonable answers were available in any references. One may suspect ulterior motives or perhaps those areas were not part of Russia proper.

The lowest courts were involved with minor cases and were tried by justices of the peace. The next higher courts were involved with appeals from the lower courts. The highest court was the Chamber of Justice, under the Senate, with the emperor acting as supreme arbitrator. A supreme court as such—traditional in most democratic countries—didn't exist, but recourse to the emperor as the supreme judge was sought. Many bureaucrats never bothered with the court system and acted arbitrarily on their own initiative as they pleased and encouraged corruption step by step. The revolutionary elements also disregarded the court system, as well as the existence of imperial edicts. In reviewing the court system as implemented, one would agree that the judicial system was an innovation in Russia and a rarity in justice. It was previously administered on the highest level either by the emperor or the nobles, as each saw fit. Substantial portions of rules for the courts were lifted verbatim from western European source codes, particularly German and French. The court system was at the initiative of Alexander himself. The Judiciary Statutes established equality of men before the law, giving a degree of human dignity never before experienced in Russia.

The revolutionary upheavals in 1848 in Europe, along with reprisals by Nicholas I at home, created a need for the educational system to be reactivated. Elementary schools, if any, hardly existed; secondary schools were somewhat better but still insufficient. The university system became a hotbed of revolutionary activity, with few professors in attendance. After four years of discussion and deliberations, in July 1864 the statutes declared elementary schools open to all classes of society, with the objective of strengthening the religious and moral standing of the people and the dissemination of essentials of useful knowledge. As a result reading, writing, arithmetic, and religion became mandatory. The ministry of Education and the clergy were empowered to supervise the moral and political views of teachers. As regards to secondary education, by the statute of December 1864, there were established two types of schools—classical schools, teaching a curricula which included Latin, Greek, and modern languages and a second type of school, *gymnazia*, which taught German, French, physics, chemistry, and sciences, with an emphasis on mathematics. With regards to the highest form of schooling the universities, though few in number, were intended to placate the students who were dissatisfied with the quality of the system, including housing. A new university statute was approved in June 1863, restoring autonomy, relaxing the power of the university rector, and removing most restrictions forced by Nicholas I. It also raised faculty salaries, fixed tuition fees, created university courts, and allowed the council of professors to elect the rector, deans, and professors. Women were forbidden to attend universities but were admitted to schools of medicine or were sent abroad to study in Europe at their own expense.

An unsuccessful attempt on Alexander's life was made by a student in 1866, which caused the cancellation of most of the liberal university statutes. The old rules, which made academic heads subject to cooperation with the police on investigation of student views and their activities, became effective immediately in *gymnazia* and universities. The additional new rules required the Ministry of Education to select teachers and school principals, among other restrictions. In considering these factors, the Russian population was estimated by then to be a little over 90 million people, yet there were only eight universities and some 235 *gymnazia*, with only a few church or other privately run schools. This system prevailed throughout the years of Imperial Russia and got substantially worse in surveillance under communism. Censorship was imposed in 1865, following reform changes, and this continued for another seventeen years. The ministry of the Interior had unprecedented authority in book, periodical, academic, and newspaper publishing and could impose with various restrictions (including fines), although permanent closures required the consent of the Senate.

In January 1874 military reform took place caused by several factors, including the catastrophic Crimean campaign. Outdated military weapons, illiteracy, inhuman treatment of recruits, incomprehension of command orders, and the poor quality of the officer corps, which contributed to their defeat in the Crimean War, were among the most serious problems. The War Ministry was overhauled, and some fundamental changes in the army were made. The War Ministry ordered advanced technological improvements by employing newly trained professional military engineers, ordered new artillery pieces from Skoda Works, Krupp Industries, and Schneider-Cruesot, and began to manufacture these and other weaponry under license. It changed recruiting methods by ordering all eligible men at age twenty to serve in the military, regardless of class; previously the nobles and merchant classes had been exempt. It lowered mandatory service to six years, down from twenty five, and upon completion placed men in reserve for nine years. It forbade corporal and inhumane punishment and eliminated hazing and the gauntlet. Exemptions from service were issued because of family reasons and other extenuating circumstances. Selected staff officers were retrained, and some were sent to Western military academies for intensive field and staff courses. Upon their return, they retrained their staff officers at home. These fundamental reforms in the army changed the status, efficiency, and educational background of the army, making it a professional institution.

Other changes implemented—mentioned previously—were equally profound and were approaching western European standards. Alexander II was not only the emancipator of the serfs, he was also the transformer of Russian society, culture, and economy after years of darkness. At first the liberal reforms produced an aura of freedom, however they subsequently became a rallying cry for rebellions, revolutionaries, and a demand for change by social intellectuals. Impatience and ill-timing apparently became common among intellectuals by disregarding the existing traditions of autocracy. The Poles misunderstood liberal reforms and assumed them to be the government's weakness, and struck out against Russian occupation. Although they had vocal support from Russian liberal circles and western Europeans, no effective support of any kind was offered, and the revolt was brutally put down by local commanders who took it upon themselves to mete out traditional brutal punishment. Exile to prison in Siberia or deprivation of liberty and various other restrictions were imposed within the occupied countries. Thereafter exiled radical thinkers Alexander Herzen and Nikolai Bakunin, the anarchist, implored their fellow Russian liberals to demand abolition of autocracy and help the Poles, but they received no response.

The critics in Ukraine called for restoration of their language in schools, literature, courts, books, and the stage. To silence the critics, Russian authorities cracked down severely with exile to Siberia and commenced Russification. Though Alexander had hoped for some sort of understanding in behalf of the Ukrainians, he received none, so he reluctantly signed them. Other minorities fared better or worse, depending on the status of their reaction. The Finns and Germans had good relations with the government, probably because of their economic enterprises, which helped the Russians. Jews in some cases were treated better, and in some cases rather inhumanely. Indiscriminate recruiting was abolished in 1856, and after 1859 wealthy Jewish merchants, doctors, professional people, and university students were permitted to live outside the Jewish Pale. However, for ordinary Jews there was no improvement, and they remained confined to the Pale.

Treatment of the Armenians and Georgians was fair, probably due to absence of revolutionary aspirations on the part of the Armenians, whose shelter they sought against the Ottoman Turks and their Christian religion. Georgia, being part of the Russian Empire and Orthodox Christian, fared well. As for the rest of the minorities throughout the empire, treatment was relatively decent, especially in Central Asia, Siberia, and TransCaucasus, where mostly Muslim peoples resided. They were left alone to fend for themselves and paid little heed to Russian sovereignty, though they traded and had good relations with the common Russians.

It was during Alexander's reign that revolutionary thinkers sprang into action; not only did they disagree with his autocracy, though sparingly used, they plotted his assassination and overthrow of the government. They were mainly a group of utopian social thinkers, militant revolutionaries, and plain people seeking justice for poor peasants. Alexander Herzen, a great humanitarian and social thinker, was in London in exile, publishing his paper "Kolokol" (The Bell), an influential bi-monthly, which attracted moderate people who believed the time was ripe for moderate change. Unfortunately, taking advice from other social thinkers to champion Poland's cause, he lost subscribers and moved to Geneva to commence his publication. His effort failed, and he subsequently died in Paris of despair.

Two radical social thinkers, Chernishevskiy and Dobroluibov, spread their theories in book reviews, attracting a substantial amount of interest among younger people. Chernishevskiy was accused of spreading dangerous propaganda and was exiled to Siberia for twenty-five years. In Siberia he wrote a novel—the typical Russian mode of expression or propaganda to avoid censure—*What Is To Be Done*, a highly popular edition, causing thousands to become radicals. While Herzen was a humanitarian, Cherrnishevskiy was a radical who preached freedom of equality for women, education for all, cooperatives, sacrifice and welfare, and division of profits for the common good. There were other radicals like Nechayev, the terrorist, who preached extreme radical measures, including assassination. Others preached basically the same doctrines, which caused creation of secret societies, and some even more radical student groups which called for the abolition of monarchy, seizure of power, and transforming Russia into a republic, with equal rights for minority nationalities. Bakunin published a newspaper in Geneva, "The People's Cause," and attracted other semi-extremists who preached terrorism as a political solution. A member of this radical group in 1866 made an effort to assassinate Alexander; failing to do so, he paid the extreme penalty for his effort. The reader should not conclude that the main objective in this period was assassination of the czar—it was fairness to the poor peasants and serfs by young nobles who preached socialism. These efforts failed, and when the police got wind of it, they exiled hundreds to Siberia. Another attempt was made in April 1879 to assassinate the czar, which failed again.

Therefore, a split occurred among revolutionary radicals—those in favor of assassination, and those opposed to it. The terrorists organized in June 1879 as the "People's Will;" those who opposed it were known as the "Black Partition;" they considered themselves socialists who hoped to restore power by political revolution. It was the "People's Will" which succeeded in assassinating Alexander II on 13 March 1881. The party was hounded down until most members were eliminated by the police. The assassination was not only unpopular; it in fact received no support throughout the country.

The "Black Partition," on the other hand, believed in agitation and revolution among the peasantry as a preliminary step in reforming Russian social-economic foundation, their basis being the so-called scientific socialism. They didn't believe political revolutions would secure economic or political freedom, but rather they urged the peasants to seize the land and the urban workers to appropriate factories. This group was also hounded by the police, and the leaders fled to Europe in 1883. There they created a new organization, the "Liberation of Labor," whose program included a democratic constitution; freedom of speech, press, and association; salaried public officials; and arming the people in lieu of a standing army. The new program abandoned its original support for agrarian communes and urban seizure of factories by substituting capitalism for its future objective of attaining socialism. In another sense it meant let the rich get rich first, then rob them later. Members were closely in touch with Marxist socialist thinkers in Europe. Subsequently, this party became the basis of the Russian Social Democratic Party, with complete freedom to debate within the organization. The principal organizers of this group were Plekhanov, Zasulich, and Axelrod. It was Plekhanov who subsequently confronted Lenin with democratic principals instead of dictatorship of the proletariat—as expounded by Lenin—while both were in exile in Europe.

About this time the foreign policy of Alexander was formed by local and treaty demands of his father. A Pan-Slavic movement developed among some Foreign Ministry officials, military officers, professors, and the church hierarchy for a Slavic Orthodox brotherhood within the Balkans. They considered Russia the big brother of the Slavs. While the group was vociferous, it enjoyed no official or popular national support. The intent was to defend the Slavs who lived under the Ottoman yoke, particularly Serbs and Montenegrans of the Balkans. In June 1875 the Serb population of Herzegovina rebelled against the oppressive Ottoman regime, and a few weeks later the rebellion spread to Bosnia. What's more, the Bulgarians also joined the rebellion against the Turks in early 1876. The sultan was unable to control the rebellion and committed suicide. In June of the same year, Muslim fanatics overcame the Bulgars in a ferocious battle, with no prisoners taken.

This aroused indignation in both the Balkans and western Europe, causing war to breakout between Turkey and Serbia and Montenegro. The Russian, Austro-Hungarian, and German governments opposed the war. However, the Pan-Slavs in Russia, incensed by atrocities committed by the Turks, besieged the government to aid the Slavs. Alexander agreed to raise volunteers under command of a Pan-Slav general and gave both financial and moral support. The Turks, however, defeated the Serbs, Montenegrans, and Russian volunteers but were prevented from exercising their excesses by diplomatic intervention of the League of Three Emperors.

In view of this condition, a new war broke out. A secret understanding between Russia and Austro-Hungary was formulated based on two alternatives: should the Turks defeat the Christians, the allies would intervene to stop massacres; and in the event the Turks lost, the allies would create a new order in the Balkans, making Constantinople a free city, with Russia taking outright possession of Bessarabia and some territory in Asia Minor. Regarding the Austro-Hungarians, they would receive Bosnia-Herzegovina. The balance of the Ottoman lands in Europe were to be allocated to Bulgaria, Greece, Albania, Serbia, Montenegro, and Rumania. The war in the Balkans, the Danube, and along the Caucasian fronts broke out in April 1877. The Turks mounted a strong defense; nevertheless, Kars, Ardakhan, and Bayazid occupied by Armenians in provinces of Turkey and Batum on the Black Sea of Georgia, and a few months later overran Bulgaria and faced Constantinople. The Russians and Turks, afraid of consequences from England and France—with the British fleet nearby—if Constantinople was captured, agreed to sign a peace treaty in March 1878, in San Stefano, Italy. The Russian victory was a source of apprehension to England,

France, and Austro-Hungary. Russian influence and possible possession of the Balkans probably could have caused a general European war. However, by then the Russians were exhausted and accepted intervention.

In view of Russia's capture of excessive territory, Britain, France, and Austro-Hungary became apprehensive and complained about the unbalanced map of Europe. Faced with these criticisms, Alexander submitted them to Bismark for his opinion. In Bismark's opinion, Russia—with few exceptions—got all the territory it had won. Alexander was displeased and stated that Germany was biased in favor of the Anglo-French and Austro-Hungarian side. This surprised the ever-cautious Bismark; he decided to meet secretly with the Austro-Hungarian emperor for an alliance, in case Russia attacked either country. This treaty was signed in August 1879.

Alexander II began his reforms in earnest and gave serious attention to the problems of his people, being the first emperor to accept liberal ideas, and eventually paid a heavy price for it as a reward for his genuine efforts. Liberal though he was, he maintained his veto power although it was sparingly used. The reforms he pursued gave rise to serious militant disruptions, terror, and further expanded Russia's violent revolutionary movements. In considering the balance between his father's and his own reign, the reader should by now conclude that under Alexander II, giant steps were undertaken by his reforms in social justice and the reduction in class discrimination, as compared to other rulers. Life became easier for more classes of society, with less dependence on the crown and thereby less support of the nobles. When comparing justice, education, laws, and fairness in pursuit of life, one should conclude Alexander II was a progressive ruler. He was socially conscious, civilized, and progressive.

Had he been given a chance for longer life by impatient revolutionaries and radical social philosophers to see his reforms completed, there could have possibly been a constitutional monarchy or at least a benevolent czardom during or after his reign. Unfortunately, since radical Russian revolutionaries were emotionally unstable and an amalgam of contradictions between dreamlike utopia and physical terror, one was forced to endure their experiments before their collapse—witness the Soviet Union and its dissolution. Although the French Revolution, with its Jacobin excesses, lasted only a few years and had less than 2,000 casualties, it wound up in a collapsed order as a monarchy. A Napoleonic imperium arose and subsequently converted to a truly constitutional democratic order under first a monarchical and finally a republican government.

The reader is urged to review the map of Russia and its independent states after the collapse of the Soviet Union to view the magnitude of the country itself and to locate where the Russians fought and colonized—in Central Asia, Siberia, the Pacific Ocean areas, as well as its acquisitions in China, Eastern Europe, the Baltics, Balkans, and the Caucasus. In China, Russia forced the Treaty of Aigun in order to protect its newly conquered territories next to the Manchurian provinces. It encouraged its settlers to occupy the lands without payment to the Russian government and sent along military detachments. There they built three towns—Vladivostok on the Pacific coast, Khabarovsk on the northeastern border of

Manchuria, and Blagoveschenk on its northwestern border—almost surrounding Manchuria in the north. Since China was weak, it conceded and subsequently repudiated the treaty, and later the communist Chinese government reconfirmed its repudiation to Khrushchev. Not content with these acquisitions, they crossed the north Pacific and occupied the Aleutian Islands and smaller islands on the way to Alaska, which they settled for exploitation. Since possession of Alaskan territories eventually proved to be an economic burden, they decided to sell it to the United States to support its own Siberian conquests with proceeds from the sale. The sale was consummated in March 1867, after the American Civil War. The American possession of Alaska proved to be a great economic and military asset in the north Pacific. The benevolent chapter of Russian history in the third quarter of the nineteenth century ended with the assassination of Alexander II.

**Alexander III, Emperor, 1881-94**

Alexander ascended the throne at age thirty-six, after his father's assassination. He was bent on revenge against his father's killers as well as against the liberal reformers. He replaced his father's liberal advisers with new ultra-conservatives—just the wrong thing to do given the great progress thus far attained. One may consider his reign one of an anti-reformist policy of vengeance. To punish the perpetrators, all those involved in the plot were hanged, despite pleas for leniency. Surprisingly no response was encountered from revolutionary circles. Alexander III commenced his new policies with a law in August 1881 providing the government with emergency measures when it considered the safety of public order. Excessive leeway was given to the bureaucracy, which could at its pleasure declare an emergency. New rules for the press were implemented under Measures Concerning the Periodical Press, which could indefinitely order the shut down of any publication.

Educational reforms were also implemented at elementary, secondary, and university levels. Church-sponsored parish schools flourished. Secondary education fees were raised to a point where children of lower classes couldn't afford to attend. To add further to humiliation, in 1884 secret orders were issued to prevent children of servants, cooks, and other similar classifications entry into the schools, lest they be tainted with too much knowledge. By August 1884 university rules prohibited belonging to student organizations and excessive gatherings of students in any place for discussions. The Education Ministry was given authority to rewrite the school curriculum, raise tuition, and implement arbitrary admission rules, which affected students of low income families, women, and politically unreliable Jews. The 1887 codicil restricted the number of students in secondary and university levels, both in the Jewish Pale and those outside.

A rule was also issued prohibiting Jews from living in St. Peterbourg, Moscow, and other major urban areas. The same year a further decree was issued for Russification of minority peoples, their conversion to Orthodoxy, and elimination of all their traditions. Russification affected various regions of the empire in different ways. The German Balts were subject to Russification in every way possible, including schools, children of mixed marriages, and administrative and judicial functions. These Germans lived in the Baltic regions for centuries before Russia acquired the territories by conquest, and they were instrumental in economy and political culture. Afraid of being evicted and restrained further, they sought protection from the German government but received no help. All Protestant churches could be built only with permission from the Holy Synod. These decrees had an extremely negative atmosphere among the German Balts of the Russian Empire, and Germany, which later resulted in dire consequences for both countries. The Ukraine suffered the same conditions in the empire, in which portions under Austrian control had relative freedom and rights. Muslims in the empire were treated badly and unacceptable means were used to convert them to Orthodoxy. The Georgians were mistreated by confiscation of their church properties, which deprived the church of any income except alms.

Poland was also treated badly; Russian language was mandatory in its schools and it was coordinated with administrative functions with the rest of the empire. The Polish population was substantially larger than any other minority nationality; the Russians found it difficult to control them and tried changing their identity in various ways, including the renaming of the area, calling it *Prievylianski Kray* (the land by the shores of the Vistula River). The Russians succeeded with strong arm methods in driving the Poles underground or forcing them to escape to the Austrian-controlled Polish lands. There they experienced—similar to the Ukrainians—freedoms and political rights. Those Poles who remained in Poland joined underground units to sabotage Russian enforcement. They also made Poland a successful economic and industrialized region.

Repressions were equally applied to the Old Believers and other religious denominations, including Buddhists. The new rules affected the Armenians by closing down all parish schools. The repressions were hard on the Jews, who were a docile population, but since Vera Zasulich took part in his Alexander II's assassination, the bureaucrats encouraged anti-semitic terror known as the pogroms. Rules became effective in 1883 which were known as the "Temporary Rules" which provided, among other things, that no Jew could own land or real estate. They were excluded from the legal professions, zemstvos, and municipal self-governing service. In the end something like twenty thousand were expelled from Moscow. To escape persecution and inhumane laws, many left the country while others joined the secret Jewish Bund, and those who considered themselves Russians joined revolutionary organizations. The laws against their own people concerned zemstvo assemblies, which comprised three class-segregated types—nobles, peasants, and ordinary people—subject to arbitrary rules by the Minister of the Interior.

The Ministry of Justice had authority over judges and some criminal cases without juries. These rules aroused criticisms and objections that the government backed down in behalf of the peasants. The terms of redemption payments were eased, making state lands easier to secure by opening a peasant bank to purchase land, encouraging them to migrate to Siberian lands, and rescinding the poll tax. Further reaction took place when criticism arose allowing children under twelve to work in industry; this and other rules were rescinded. These rule changes were forced on the government by an outcry of European and American labor and social groups. These amended rules, though beneficial to the country, were overshadowed by elimination of most of his father's reforms of 1860. Some Russian sources have recently stated that Maria Fyodorvna, Alexander III's wife, objected strenuously against excessive counter reforms applied by Alexander's advisors, stating that these measures would be counterproductive and create radicalism, but she had no influence over him or his advisors. If true, she would have been the most progressive and far-sighted person in that palace, especially unusual a young woman in that time.

With regard to foreign policy, it appears Alexander had no other territories to acquire, so the country was relatively peaceful except for skirmishes at Afghanistan's northern borders. Britain found it disturbing yet could do nothing about it, since Afghanistan was landlocked. Its military bases in India didn't have sufficient troops, what with its own colonial troops keeping India in check; it consequently decided to approach the matter diplomatically in 1887. The League of Three Emperors lay dormant after the Congress of Berlin but was revived for this occasion, to permit the three of them to agree on neutrality, in case one party found itself with a fourth great power which would also include the Ottoman Empire. It also called for conditions with the Russian solution for the closure of the Bosphorus Straits. The measure stipulated that any violation by the Ottoman Empire would be cause for war with the Turks. A separate agreement permitted Austro-Hungary to annex Bosnia and Herzegovina at any time. The agreement also included the eventual reunion of Bulgaria and eastern Rumelia, and lastly the powers were to cooperate in the Near and Middle East.

No sooner had the agreement been signed, than Russia created a crisis in Bulgaria. The Treaty of Berlin, signed in 1878, authorized the Russians to establish a legal and political order in Bulgaria. They enforced this mandate by selecting a Prussian officer, Prince Alexander of Battenberg, as the new ruler. Pompous Russian advisors acted as if it was a Russian dependency. The prince set aside the constitution, thus further aggravating the Bulgarians, who demanded its restoration. Alexander, feeling degraded, recalled his Russian advisors, hoping to collapse Bulgaria. Being free, the Bulgars did better for themselves, except for creating a crisis by annexing Eastern Rumelia, which was originally part of Bulgaria. The Russians denounced the seizure, although they were for annexation under the Treaty of Berlin. On the other hand, Britain had originally been against the annexation, but now it reversed itself, primarily because the Bulgars achieved it themselves. Bulgaria also had a larger shore on the Black Sea, denying Russia more access there.

As is typical of the Balkan boiling pot, the Bulgarians upset the Serbs, who declared war on Bulgaria in 1885 and quickly lost the war. Subsequently, the Russians kidnapped Prince Battenberg and set up a pro-Russian government, an action Austria-Hungary found upsetting and intimated to Russia that their entry to Bulgaria would be challenged. Bulgarians handled themselves rather well, upsetting Russian schemes in 1886 by selecting Prince Saxe-Coburg Gotha as their ruler. The Russians took offense at Vienna and refused to participate in the Three

Emperor's League. Afraid of being isolated and left out of diplomatic involvement, Russia arranged for a secret agreement with Germany in June 1887. This agreement was not effective against a war with Austria or a German war against France. In addition to other concessions, Germany agreed to Russia's seizure of Constantinople and the straits. Shortly thereafter, the treaty was denounced in Russia for failure of its policies in Bulgaria. Other conditions intervened to unbalance the treaty. Germany applied tariff increases on Russian grain imports as retaliation for imposition of Russification on Germans living in the Baltics and the refusal of German banks to lend money to Russia. When London banks refused similar loans, conditions began deteriorating daily. By then, only France remained as a creditor and made the loan of 400,000,000 francs and sold them French armaments.

Bismark's dismissal as Chancellor of Germany in March 1890, coupled with the decision not to renew the last treaty with Russia, caused Russia and France to make a compact, which later developed into an informal alliance in August 1891. The condition of the compact between them was based on possible German attack on either France or Russia, and each was to come to the aid of the other. Among other things, France pledged 1,300,000 troops against Germany, and the Russians pledged 700,000-800,000 thousand troops. Alexander ratified this compact into a treaty in December 1893, and France ratified it in January 1894. This decision was so profound that it is doubtful that they realized the consequences, which manifested themselves in excessive rearmament and line-up of opposing forces. These alliances eventually caused the greatest convulsion and upheaval in Europe in the beginning of the twentieth century, which resulted in World War I and changed the map of Europe, with some new nations appearing and some disappearing or cut down to their proper size.

The reader should bear in mind that until that time, alliances and wars were playthings of the czars and emperors of Europe. Without consulting their peoples they declared wars; their subjects had nothing to say but were conscripted into armies to await their destinies. Alexander III's reign should be characterized as reactionary, anti-liberal, regressive, and careless with his people. Had he drawn proper conclusions from his father's murder, been more tolerant, and less emotional, he could have set Russia on a progressive course with a consulting role for people's representatives. Afflicted with kidney problems, which had been kept secret, he died in 1894. In entering this alliance, he chose the wrong path and saddled his son and heir, Nicholas II, with critically unresolved problems from all the Romanovs since 1613.

**Nicholas II, Czar Emperor, 1894-1917**

Since Alexander III's first-born son died in infancy, Nicholas became the heir apparent. He was brought up austerely, though he liked the good life. His mother, the former Princess Dagmar of Denmark and now dowager empress, insisted he tour Europe and Asia and acquaint himself with the world beyond Russia. He had English, French, and German tutors and was fluent in all three languages. Although many Russian and European princesses wanted to marry him, he pre-

*Nicholas II, painted by Serov.*

ferred being loose and dated Mathilde Kshessinskaya, the world renowned Russian prima ballerina. Later he fell in love with Princess Alix of Hesse-Darmstadt of Germany, and chose her for his wife. By Russian custom, Princess Alix, a Lutheran, was consecrated into Orthodoxy. After the ceremony, Nicholas issued his first decree—that Princess Alix had become "a truly believing grand duchess, Alexandra Fyodorovna"—her father's first name, a patronym by Russian custom. A week after his father's death, Nicholas and Alexandra were married on 26 November 1894, his mother's birthday. It was a magnificent wedding, with most European royalty in attendance. Sometime after the wedding, the dowager czarina went to visit her family home in Copenhagen. In May 1896 the couple were crowned in Moscow. He later confided to his court marshals that he never wanted to be czar, but since he had no choice, he accepted the fact. As time went on, the empress gave birth to four daughters. Olga was born in 1895, Tatiana in 1897, Marie in 1899, and Anastasia in 1901, the grand duchess of the famed movie "Anastasia," with a myriad of pretenders. Three years later, to the delight of the nation, an heir was born in 1904. Unfortunately for the family and the nation, the boy was born a hemophiliac. At first it was unknown but was later confirmed that the czarina's grandmother, Queen Victoria of England, was a hemophilia carrier. Subsequently, the illness would cause serious consequences for the family and the nation.

Nicholas and Alexandra took a tour of western Europe and visited the children's grandparents in Denmark and dropped in for a visit with Queen Victoria. After leaving England, they spent time in France, visited Paris, and left for home. In the latter half of the nineteenth century, Russian royalty, princes, and nobility were considered the most opulent in all Europe. Their palaces, banquets, and lifestyles were lavish, and to be invited to their palaces was considered a great privilege for any nobility and a prize for any aspiring princess. After all, Russia was the fourth largest economy in Europe—after Britain, Germany, and France. The czar's court asked for and received all the required funds from the treasury for public functions, although not for personal use. The English, German, and Danish nobilities in particular enjoyed and received favors from the court. The granting of favors became a practice of the crown and gentry. They entertained and rewarded their guests lavishly upon departure.

In 1904 Nicholas II's cousin, German Kaiser Wilhelm II, who was some eight years older, induced Nicholas to fight for his Far Eastern expansion against Japan, the better to manage his own aggressive designs against Britain, France, and Austria without Russian involvement. Nicholas was not yet fully mature in the tricks of diplomacy at the time and took the bait. To the surprise of most military authorities, the war with Japan ended with the annihilation of the Russian navy. Reinforcements to the army were delayed and didn't reach Port Arthur (on the Kwantung/Liautung Peninsula in south Manchuria) on time. The port had been blockaded by the Japanese navy in a surprise attack, and at least one section of the TransSiberian Railway was still incomplete for delivery of reinforcements. The Russian army was forced to retreat to Mukden, farther north in southern Manchuria where the headquarters of the Russian command was located, and subsequently to their Maritime Provinces, along the eastern shores, opposite the Sea of Japan.

The battle was an uneven match from the start. Japan attacked without declaration of war, catching the Russians by surprise. The Russian Baltic Fleet and some minor elements of Far Eastern coastal ships, based in Maritime provinces, were tracked by Japanese spies. The commander of the Japanese navy, Admiral Togo, lured and maneuvered the Russian ships broadside—as on parade—into a trap between the Tsushima Strait and some smaller islands, between the Korean Peninsula and southernmost island of Kyushu. With no room to maneuver, all twenty-three Russian ships were sunk in a matter of hours. As a result, the Russian Baltic Fleet ceased to exist. The modern Russian Black Sea Fleet took no part in the battle, being bottled up for want of passage through the Straits at Constantinople. As for the Russian army, it was led by an incompetent commander, General Kuropatkin, primarily a garrison commander.

While it lost battles in Liautung Peninsula and the city of Mukden, it sustained two-and-a-half times fewer casualties than the Japanese troops with their banzai attacks. As a result of severe Japanese losses and exhaustion, Russia retained its hold on the Chinese Eastern Railway farther north in Manchuria. The railway had been built by Russia with a ninety-nine year lease with adjoining territory. The defeat, despite reasonable terms of the peace treaty, caused Russia a serious loss of prestige throughout the world and brought on disturbances in Russia itself. After the Russo-Japanese war, it seemed Nicholas matured remarkably; alas, it was too late.

The czar had continuous problems with his uncles, the grand dukes, Alexander III's brothers. Since Alexander III was a frugal and austere person, he doled out money to his brothers based on their minimum needs. His eldest uncle, Grand Duke Vladimir was a hunter, a gourmet, a patron of the arts, commander of the Imperial Guard, and president of the Academy of Fine Arts. Next in line was Grand Duke Alexis, who was grand admiral of the Navy, a bon vivant, and a charmer of ladies. Grand Duke Sergey, husband of Elizabeth of Hesse (Ella), was a reactionary and ultra-conservative governor of Moscow. Grand Duke Mikhail was commander of the Russian army and a professional soldier. Grand Duke Paul, the youngest uncle and Nicholas's favorite, was the only one with whom he consulted daily, who was subsequently arrested by Bolshevik thugs and executed.

Since Nicholas was utterly unprepared to assume the crown, he had to learn (among other things) about the upkeep of his palaces, the salaries of servants, giving to charities, and overseeing his properties. The czar's annual salary was equivalent to $12 million a year at the exchange rate in 1914 and $20 million from the extensive acres of farmland previously bought by Catherine the Great as a Romanov endowment. In addition to the upkeep of his palaces, he had to support the dowries of his daughters, hospitals, orphanages, and several other charities—all out of personal funds. By the end of the year, his funds were almost depleted, and he was obliged to take loans from the treasury and pay interest.

He was kindly but was of stubborn disposition. Unprepared as he was by his father, although not autocratic by nature he refused to give up autocracy lest he betray his father's will. Even during upheavals at home after the Russo-Japanese war, he was rather indecisive when they broke out and allowed the commanders in the field to make their own decisions. Nicholas's character was such that he couldn't stand unpleasantness and was exceedingly shy, a behavior which cost him dearly later. He hated to order troops to quell protest marches, forcing commanders to make decisions on the spot to disperse the crowds, with ensuing losses of life. Subsequently, his uncles warned him that since he lost his power of autocracy during the 1905 upheavals, he would be wise to heed the Duma's consensus instead of dissolving it. He didn't heed their advice and later paid for it with his and his family's life. The loss of the war with Japan was a personal blow for him, and he decided to call a conference of his ministers to address the problems. He felt that the Franco-Russian treaty—previously entered into by his father—in itself was not a guarantee of peace and stability in Europe or the Far East.

In view of his convictions on peace, he embarked upon a policy of both rearmament and abolition of war. To this end he declared to the world, "War does not solve any problems, but causes death, destruction, and bankruptcy to people and nations, creating animosity for winners and losers, and is immoral," quoting Ivan Bliokh, a Jewish railroad financier. Bliokh submitted a six-volume treatise on war, in which he outlined probabilities backed by statistics. In the treatise he spelled out casualties and costs of a future war as totally unacceptable to civilized nations. In reviewing the latest figures in industrial production in armaments alone, he concluded that among the four powers in Europe—Britain, Germany, France, and Austro-Hungary—there was enough to blow up all Europe. In a postscript to the treatise, he mentioned that sums expended on the future war would be more than adequate to create jobs and feed millions of poor Russians. The czarina vigorously backed Bliokh and added her own version of immorality. Nicholas himself was also instrumental in helping to create the international court of justice. European powers were staggered by such revelations in which semi-barbaric Russia could submit such dribble. Nicholas, in fact, pleaded with his cousin, Kaiser Wilhelm, to help him submit the Austrian-Serbian dispute to arbitration in the Hague in 1914. The kaiser rejected it out of hand, and the Prince of Wales called it "nonsense." At the time, war was considered chivalrous among major European powers. In advancing his proposals, he was deeply disappointed by rejection from western Europe, particularly Britain and Germany. Nevertheless a conference was held in the Hague on the rules of warfare and arbitration. Nicholas also strongly believed that Russia possessed an abundance of natural resources and deserved to be a great industrial power for peace at home and in Europe. Its export trade was continually expanding and with its industrial transformation in full swing, he found it natural for Russia to become a great industrial power for peace instead of war. Edmund Thery, the French economist, published a treatise in January 1914, "The Economic Transformation of Russia," listing data outlined below:

- Russian coal production increased by 79% between 1908 and 1912

- Iron production increased by 25%

- Steel and metal manufacturing increased by 46% between 1900 and 1913

- Heavy industrial output increased by 74%

- The rail network increased from 15,000 miles to 38,000 miles, projected for 1915

- The above figures reduced foreign investment in Russia from 50% to less than 12% by 1913

These figures permitted Russia to expand its markets and reduce its unfavorable balance of trade. While war fever increased almost daily, no serious measures were taken to increase armaments production. Yet *History of Russia*—by Stalin's order—states that foreign investment in 1914 in Russia was 47%. These statistics were an invention of Stalin's imagination. While these were salutary news for industrialization, other important problems were left unresolved in the agricultural sector and in the proposed constitution. The *History of Russia* mentions nothing about agricultural achievements—which were a disaster—nor the proposed constitution. When the time finally came for the constitution, it took several years and was known as the Stalin Constitution; one can imagine what it was. Sergei Witte's reforms after 1905, and subsequently Stolypin's reforms, were at last taking hold, which created a new social class of peasant farmers from lands bought by the government from wealthy landowners at reasonable prices. These reforms were not fully complete because of a backlog of pending applications which caused continual delays. Another far more serious problem was the internal political-social problem of the empire with the proposed constitution which was still not carried out. This delay affected both the Russian population and the national minorities by causing friction and dissension. While the economy was improving, the social problem kept festering along with no end in sight. In addition to the above, eastern Poland, Ukraine, Estonia, Latvia, and Lithuania were unsettled with native aspirations, and no effort was made to solve the problem. Though the National Assembly was aware of these problems and petitioned the czar to accept the first constitution to define the rights of minorities and peripheral countries under Russian domination, the czar delayed and finally turned it down. At the time, tensions in Europe were running high because of rearmament and diplomatic maneuvering among probable combatants. It would only take a spark to ignite hostilities, and this wasn't long in coming. Adequate notice was apparent when major European countries were aligned to undertake warlike measures at any time.

**The First World War**

Archduke Ferdinand, the heir to the Austrian throne, went on a visit to review his domains and was assassinated on 28 June 1914 by Gavrilo Princip, a Serb nationalist in Sarajevo, Bosnia-Herzegovina. The Hapsburg emperor, Franz Joseph, issued an ultimatum to Serbia on 23 July convinced the murder was sanctioned by the Serbian government. After receiving an unacceptable reply to the ultimatum, the emperor promptly declared war on Serbia on 28 July. The ultimatum was timed to be dispatched when the French president left for home after his state visit to Russia. On 29 July the German ambassador informed the Russian foreign minister, Sazonov, that even a partial mobilization of Russia's troops would automatically trigger total mobilization by Germany. Russian intelligence informed Nicholas that Germany ordered a full mobilization the same day. In view of these circumstances, Russia ordered a mobilization, too. The British prime minister called for negotiations to avoid war. Concurrent with his call the German ambassador informed Sazonov that Germany was at war with Russia, effective 1 August. The Duma was called into a special session and unanimously agreed with the course taken by the government. When Nicholas declared war on the Central Powers, it was the first time under the Imperial regime that the Duma and the entire country were united.

In case of war, the German objective was based on two principal strategic concepts: first, to hold the Russians at bay in the east until disposing of the French in the west, and then to turn on the Russians with a knockout blow to finish them off on the battlefield; second, to exploit Russia's internal weakness of national minority aspirations in the empire—precisely what its National Assembly was trying to reconcile, which Nicholas rejected. The most apparent weakness was Ukraine, in view of Galicia and Bukovina being a part of the Hapsburg domains, whose population was Slavic and directly related to its kin in Russian-occupied Ukraine. Neither the German or Austrian empires had such problems. Germany had no subjugated people, while the Austrians patronized their minorities and succeeded, at least in the beginning, by keeping its minorities reasonably docile, except for Bosnia-Herzegovina in 1908 because of a disagreement with Russia. In this respect Russia was at a serious disadvantage, having substantial problems with its minorities, yet nothing was done to alleviate the problem.

The Russian plan in the beginning of the conflict, was to free all Slavs from Austrian and Ottoman domination. Apart from that, no specifically detailed plans were outlined for the Russian general staff—which strenuously complained of the lack of detail—other than its treaty obligations to France to relieve pressure on the western front. The Russian obligations were intended to cause Germany to draw on their reserves and to engage them on the eastern front as soon as possible after Germany attacked France.

However, prior to these critical events, the prelude to WWI was set in the Balkans in 1912 when Serbia, Montenegro, Bulgaria, and Greece united in a war against the Ottomans to extricate themselves from the Turkish yoke. The Little Alliance—as it was then known—unexpectedly won the war. Shortly thereafter, they fell apart in a dispute on territorial gains. Serbia and Greece joined against Bulgaria the aggrieved party, with Rumania later joining them also. Bulgaria was defeated and found itself isolated. Looking for allies, it found them in the Austro-

Hungarian empire and Germany. Greece, Serbia, Montenegro, and later Rumania, joined the western alliance.

Russia made every effort to avoid war at all costs, being wholly unprepared. Nicholas was a pacifist and unrealistic about prevailing tensions during the Balkan war and procrastinated, instead of commencing rearmament. He sent cables hourly to Kaiser Wilhelm and Franz Josef for a compromise solution. To avoid precipitating Germany into a rash move, Nicholas ordered a partial mobilization in southern Russia, clearly intended for Austria and to pacify Germany. The Russian general staff objected and, after being exasperated, informed the czar of technical reasons of unpreparedness in mobilization in case of sudden attack by Germany, which could create a serious problem. One of his uncles, Grand Duke Nicholas, the commander of the army, eventually convinced him to act promptly. Nevertheless Russia was unprepared for the coming events. Unexpectedly, Germany launched a surprise attack against France by invading neutral Belgium in order to outflank heavy French fortifications at Sedan. Only when France was overrun was the German command prepared to take on Russia with all available strength. The German general staff calculated that the Russian campaign wouldn't take long and that the entire war would be a forgone conclusion.

The reader should bear in mind that the German general staff was a product of superb organization and training, previously tested in other campaigns and distinguishing itself in the War of 1870 against France. Its officer class was mainly derived from East Prussian domains of the aristocratic landowning families, who were originally in the service of the Elector of Brandenberg, with its capitol in Berlin. As the history of WWI unfolds, the reader is advised to review a short narrative of its operational qualities and the failure of Germany's national capabilities to sustain the war at least to a standstill. Hitler's meddling into its operational doctrines in WWII ruined its qualities and irreparably damaged the organization, which was dissolved after WWII.

The French plan of counter-attack called for instant invasion against Alsace-Lorraine, farther south, to draw German reserves from Sedan. It also called upon the Russians to concurrently mount an offensive to divert as many German troops as possible in order to equalize the forces on their front. The Russian command had previously promised to mount an offensive against Germany within sixteen days after Germany's attack. The Russians had sufficient manpower but lacked the necessary ammunition stocks, artillery, small arms, and logistical support to effectively mount and sustain offensive operations. The Russian offensive against East Prussia, under command of General Rennenkampf, commenced 17 August and another army, under command of General Samsonov, commenced an offensive in the area of Mazurian Lakes (swamps) on 21 August also in the direction of East Prussia. As stated above, both attacks were hastened by request of the French. Since haste was promised by the Russians, insufficient stocks to sustain the offensive became critical.

On the other hand, while the German army launched its offensive in the west, it intended to hold firm in the east against the Russians or even abandon East

Prussia and entrench behind the Vistula River. The abandonment of East Prussia was vetoed for social-political reasons. When the plan was revised, an army under General von Hundenburg and his chief of staff, Ludendorff, was organized on the northeastern front by withdrawing troops from the west to defend East Prussia. The decision by the German command to divert troops from the west made a profound influence on the future conduct of the war for Germany in the west. In that sense, Russia accomplished its goal immeasurably in helping the western allies. At the most critical time of the German offensive in the west, one cavalry and six infantry divisions were withdrawn for the eastern campaign, jeopardizing its offensive operations in the west. Ludendorff succeeded in trapping and destroying Samsonov's southern army in the Mazurian Lakes. At the loss of his army, Samsonov committed suicide. A few days later, with different operational tactics, Ludendorff also succeeded in destroying Rennenkampf's army at the Battle of Tannenberg, on 31 August—almost in the same area where Lithuanian, Polish, and Russian armies defeated the German Teutonic knights in 1410. As a result of these two battles, the Russian armies were ejected from East Prussia within a few weeks.

Subsequently, they succeeded against the Austrians under command of General Alexeyeev by capturing Galicia. In this operation, the Russian army captured 200,000 prisoners, half of whom were minority nationalities of the Austro-Hungarian domains. In view of German successes in East Prussia, Ludendorff succeeded in convincing his colleagues in the German high command and general staff to reverse direction of the front to the eastern area, to eliminate the Russian threat for good and thence to renew offensive operations in the west. This concept meant the abandonment of the original "von Shlieffen Plan" of operations. The von Shlieffen plan called for a knockout blow against the French, with a turning wheel movement at Sedan on the way to Paris. Though not fully reinforced, Ludendorff moved in the direction of Warsaw—then Russian-occupied—directly south of East Prussia, with insufficient and delayed forces, afraid of being seriously outnumbered. After a deadly battle lasting a month, he ordered a retreat on 27 October with the Russians holding the same positions. This battle was the high point of the Russian army's effort in WWI.

The allies again asked for Russian help in drawing German reserves from their front by attacking Poznan in Silesia—which they did in November 1914, without success—though it had no benefit for the joint war effort. Yet the Russian command yielded as always, although exhausted from previous battles with heavy casualties. In summing up the first three months of the war, it revealed severe manpower losses and equipment in Russian forces, which needed to rest, recuperate, and refurbish more than the allies. Following another allied request the Russians again attacked to probe German frontline positions with minimum light and heavy artillery support, with a shortage of appropriate ammunition and a constant supply problem. After their local probing operations in the west, a lull on the eastern front was broken in the spring of 1915 when the German command brought up thirteen new divisions to the southeastern front in Rumania to stretch out the Russian front. Under command of von Mackensen, the Germans launched an offensive against Russian positions with massed artillery techniques. It soon became apparent that the Russians couldn't stand the furious infantry and concentrated artillery attacks, primarily because of their depleted supplies and improper troop concentrations. They were forced to retreat, losing all the territory previously captured, as well as all of Poland, Lithuania, Courland on the Baltic, the western part of Ukraine, and some provinces of Belorussia. By autumn 1915, the German front stretched from Riga on the Baltic to Dvinsk and Tarnapol in western Ukraine.

The German advance halted due to overrunning their supply capabilities with extensive territorial gains. After the retreat the front was quiet, and supplies began to come in for Russian troops, but they were still insufficient. During the retreat, the allies made no effort to go on the offensive to relieve the pressure on Russian forces—most probably because they were afraid of sustaining severe casualties, considering the Anglo-French population was less than Russia's. Meanwhile, German strength on the Russian front amounted to 161 divisions in September 1915, with only 84 divisions on the western front. The Germans certainly succeeded in driving the Russians back, but they failed in their main objective: to destroy Russian military power.

The German operational plan against France was originally based on the von Molke formula, conceived after the German conquest of France in 1870, but was somewhat revised by General von Schlieffen, because of technological improvements and other refinements. When the German attack against Belgium began, it was somewhat slowed by unexpected Belgian resistance which delayed their advance and allowed the French to speed reinforcements from Alsace-Lorraine to the critical battle area at Sedan. The German attack wavered, and not to lose momentum, they penetrated aimlessly into France, abandoning the original objective. The French realized that the German movements were aimed at Sedan, and they concentrated their formations there by transporting their troops in taxis from Paris, which subsequently resulted in the Battle of the Marne. This second battle sprung up along the Marne River and resulted in German defeat and a stalemate in the west.

At first, the western allies concluded that the German disengagement was because of a direct Russian victory instead of a standoff. The Russian attack failed again, with insufficient preparation for softening German positions. It would seem that Russia went out of its way to accommodate its allies and couldn't say no or delay until it was ready. From the beginning of hostilities to the Silesian-Poznan failure, Russia suffered unacceptably severe losses. It was time to rest and equip the armies before undertaking any further offensive operations. A lull on the eastern front was broken by a German attack in the spring of 1915 when they transferred thirteen divisions from the western front for an offensive in the east. Unprecedented day and night artillery barrages were used to soften up Russian positions before German infantry demoralized poorly equipped Russian troops. The attack caused the lines to buckle, and a retreat was ordered, with more territory lost which the Russian army had previously occupied. The German attack halted unexpectedly because of its capture of vast territories, which caused serious logistical and manpower shortages in the German army. By mid-September, the German army's strength in the east was estimated to be over 161 fully equipped divisions, abundant artillery, motorcycles, truck convoys, and huge ammunition depots. However the German army's strength on the western front was down to eighty-five divisions.

In Russia, however, the loss of two successive battles and a standoff, with staggering losses caused serious repercussions at home. Many patriotic and charitable organizations supplied the troops with food and clothing. Failing to supply the army properly created hostility between the Duma and the government. By the end of 1916, most industrial workers were engaged in the production of military supplies. This hasty increase of supplies to the army caused serious shortages for home consumption as well as an increase in circulation of currency, which created inflation. Economic conditions began deteriorating with shortages of foodstuffs and goods. In March 1916 a fully equipped army corps launched an offensive operation in a thinly manned area of the front near Poland and promptly ground to a halt, again causing heavy casualties. In sustaining severe losses from the beginning of hostilities, the Russian command and troops were left with the impression that the German army was unbeatable—a dangerous attitude for a field army.

If this were not enough, on 4 June the Italian command requested a Russian offensive against the Austrians on the southwestern front to relieve pressure on their troops. Once again, Russia came to the aid of an ally and launched an offensive, which happily succeeded, netting 400,000 captured troops, more than half of whom were minority nationals of Austria. On this occasion, Austro-Hungarian armies were forced to draw on troops from other sectors to stem the Russian advance. When Rumania entered the war on the side of the allies and was defeated in short order by the Germans, it caused the extension of the Russian front south to the Black Sea. The German victories in the east against the Russians were rather impressive, yet they never succeeded in eliminating Russia from the war.

During the winter of 1916-17, the conflict between the czar and the Duma intensified to dangerous proportions. Nicholas, as commander-in-chief, bore full responsibility and moral authority, though he was advised not to assume this responsibility by the generals, his uncles, and close associates. Malicious rumors were spread about the empress and the pseudo-monk Rasputin and their influence on the war effort. A plot was hatched by three conspirators—Grand Duke Dmitriy, Puriskevich (a member of the Duma), and Prince Yusupov (husband of Irina, the grand duchess and daughter of Nicholas's older sister) to kill Rasputin. They poisoned and killed him on 30 December 1916. Informed of the murder, the czar knew the reasons, yet didn't change his policies. Rumors appeared to overthrow the czar and replace him with another member of the royal family; although this was said after the revolution, no evidence exists to support the claim. A spontaneous uprising took place, having no connection to any organized groups. This and other similar incidents later had profound effect on the war and great political consequences.

On the twelfth anniversary of the 1905 massacre, after the loss of the war with

Japan, on 9 January 1917, nearly three hundred thousand workers in Petrograd came out on strike. The capital was receiving only 21 freight cars of grain per day, instead of the normal 125. Bakeries were posting signs that no bread was available. Okhrana civil agents reported, "Every day the food question becomes acute. Never before has there been such cussing, argument, and scandal." The Okhrana, always on the alert for organized demonstrations, found it impossible to foretell spontaneous demonstrations. Surprisingly, the main demonstrations were sponsored by the liberal Cadets and Constitutional Democrats of the middle class, both supporters of the monarchy, and the Octobrists, representing rich farmers and factory owners in the halls of the Duma. All demanded real authority to address the food problem. The czar did so in 1905 to pacify that year's revolt. General Alexander Balk, the city governor, who had command of the Okhrana secret police and the gendarmerie, issued standing orders in case of disorders to shoot, as in 1905. On 10 February General Khabalov, commander of the Petrograd military district, issued orders prohibiting public meetings, reminding workers of the existence of martial law.

On 14 February some nine hundred workers of the huge Putilov armaments plants in Petrograd went on strike and demonstrated on Nevskiy Prospekt with banners reading "down with the war, down with the government," while singing "Marseillaise." Police reported army officers mingling with the crowds. The Duma finally stepped in and called for democratic reforms and immediate improvements in the food supply. Inflation ran rampant, with prices escalating daily. The transport system broke down and left thousands of freight cars snowbound and stranded. General Gurko, chief of the general staff, after presiding over an allied war conference, had an audience with the czar on 13 February imploring him to institute constitutional reforms before it was too late. Nicholas took it upon himself to assume the general was exaggerating, and ignored the situation. This disregard and many others which followed was a precursor of things to come. Workers at the Putilov armaments plants came out to demand a pay raise to keep up with inflation. On 22 February the general manager ordered the plant closed.

On the same day, Nicholas left for general staff headquarters at Mogilev, oblivious to events at home. The local communists, being out of touch with true conditions, were planning a strike in May, so they were warning workers not to strike, to refrain from any dangerous acts, and to maintain restraint. This advice was ignored by the strikers in the plants. The small Bolshevik organization played almost no part in any of the events. Nikolay Sukhanov, probably the most astute diarist of the revolution, was present at the time under an assumed false name of Nikolay Gimmer, equally unaware of the true conditions and assuming them to be one of many disturbances. More disturbances were mounted daily in Petrograd, with police unable to control strikers, who were becoming rowdy. Some police agents reported that the troops would only fire in the air. At this point, however, things were getting out of control, although the strikers had no organized leadership other than plant strike speakers.

Limonin, a police spy, attended a Bolshevik committee meeting and reported wallowing, the possibility of issuing leaflets, and the thought of erecting barricades the next Monday. Concurrently 300,000 strikers were erecting barricades as the Bolsheviks were outlining their plans. The Bolshevik committee was meeting on Sunday morning, 26 February, while the police, alerted by Limonin, surrounded the group and marched them away without resistance. Meanwhile, the garrison commander issued a warning that live ammunition would be used, after firing a warning volley with blank ammunition. Rodzianko, the chairman of the Duma, cabled the czar at Mogilev: "Situation serious, anarchy in the capital, government paralyzed, disorderly firing in the streets. Essential, immediately to order persons having confidence in the country to form a new government. Any delay deadly." When the cable arrived in the afternoon, the czar complained of being disturbed by panic mongers. "Once again, that fat Rodzianko has written me some kind of rubbish, which I am not going to answer," he is reported as saying. Some troops in the capital joined the strikers and fought both the police and training battalions. Subsequently the Preobrazhenskiy guards battalion was summoned and dispersed the mutineers. For a time it appeared the mutiny was over, and the czar was not informed. Prince Galitsyn, the prime minister, requested the czar to appoint General Belayev as overall commander in the capital. The general was looking forward to trying the revolutionaries and later hanging them. Finally, the government agreed to suspend the Duma, and the decree was sent to Rodzianko at his apartment.

The same evening, a gathering of socialists met at Kerenskiy's apartment. The most radical of them was Yurenev, who said there would be no revolution since the troops got the better of the strikers and mutineers. Shlyapnikov, the Bolshevik leader, rejected the idea of forming armed squads of workers, thinking it would irritate the hostile troops. The Okhrana agent, Limonin, thought otherwise and reported that if the troops sided with the workers, nothing could save the country. The troops did side with the workers, creating chaos in the capital. At this point the reader should bear in mind that the troops were mainly conscripts, rather than regular army formations. With the government in disarray, the cabinet not functioning, the Duma dissolved, and the czar in Mogilev, bands of workers and army conscripts ran wild and shot at anything that moved. With discipline gone, some members of the Duma assembled to create the Provisional Committee. The members were careful not to create an impression of an unlawful act in convening the assembly, which the cabinet had previously dissolved. In this connection a meeting was held in Alexander Kerenskiy's apartment, to all outward appearances to create a commission to restore discipline in the capital and appropriate measures to control disorder. Shortly beforehand, some disorganized troops asked for officers to lead them. Alexander Kerenskiy stepped forward and took charge, creating a provisional committee. Kerenskiy was thirty-six years old, a distinguished lawyer, a fiery speaker with theatrical mannerisms, and an effective leader. He was born in Simbirsk on the Volga, where his father was a principal of a school—one which Lenin attended and received a commendation as an excellent pupil, but one who was lacking in logic. Though Lenin was older, it seems they had never met in Simbirsk. They became enemies during the revolution.

Nikolay Sukhanov, present at most critical moments from the beginning of the revolution and through the civil war wrote a critical analysis entitled "Notes on the Revolution" before disappearing without a trace under the Bolsheviks. He summarized Stalin during the revolution and the civil war as "a grey blur." Writing an epitaph on 1917, he wrote of the Bolsheviks, "By virtue of their characteristic willpower and organizational ruthlessness, they constituted themselves the heirs of the revolutionary upsurge after it had spent itself." No better description has ever been written about the part the Bolsheviks, and particularly Stalin, played in raising and taking charge of the revolution. A few copies of these notes made their way to France, Germany, and Manchuria. Any reference subsequently claimed by Bolshevik propaganda under Stalin that they, and he particularly, stage-managed revolutionary upheavals should be considered a fantasy created by Stalin.

The czar's train was on its way ever slowly to Mogilev, the army's battle headquarters. As previously mentioned, he hated disorder, argument, and loss of autocratic power, and seemed indifferent to prevailing conditions in the country. He arrived at Mogilev in a dreamlike state and remained so to the day he tendered his abdication. After the loss of the war with Japan in 1905, he allowed the government to take appropriate action against the demonstrators, which resulted in a bloody crackdown and later acceded to the Duma for the restitution it deemed. His uncles warned him of the loss of autocracy in that incident and advised him to accommodate rather than confront the Duma on this occasion. He wouldn't accept the advice. Although the Duma acted under the government's authority, it actually reflected the conditions of the people in the country. In the middle of a war gone badly for the country on the battlefield, and at home with hunger, inflation, and rebellion, the Duma never failed in its patriotic duty to the people. It pleaded with the government and the czar to alter the course quickly, before it was too late. Neither the czar nor the government paid heed to its pleadings.

As a result of neglect by the government and czar, the revolutionary upheavals in Petrograd were accepted by the army and most of the people when Nicholas tendered his abdication on 15 March 1917, with the same nonchalant attitude as was befitting his character. Two members of the cabinet arrived to request his abdication, which he was pleased to tender, feeling relieved of the burden. He abdicated in favor of his son, but soon thereafter changed his mind, not wishing to be separated from his ill son and abdicated in favor of his younger brother, Mikhail. Grand Duke Mikhail refused to accept the honor unless the Constituent Assembly specifically asked him. With Mikhail's refusal, the 304-year rule of the Romanov dynasty ended forever. With Nicholas's abdication the traditionally accepted Russian princely rule of the Rurik lineage similarly expired. Not until the czar abdicated and his government evaporated, leaving the country in a state of anarchy, was some effort undertaken to put some semblance of order in place. In disregarding the advice of his uncles and the pleadings of the Duma to shed autocracy and to reflect the earnest and profound needs of his people.

The historical verdict on Nicholas II, as czar and emperor of Russia at the beginning of the twentieth century, cannot be kind or forgiving. His inept behavior toward his people condemned them and others to unsurpassed cruelty, which affected millions of other people throughout the world. He alone is responsible for the revolution and the turbulent years that befell the Russian people and the rest of the world in the twentieth century. He could have declined to accept the throne since he never wanted to be czar, yet of his own free will he chose to rule. After a reflection and analysis of three-quarters of a century on the subject, many sources agree that Nicholas II was unworthy of ruling his people as czar. The verdict on Nicholas is irreversible.

**Recommended Reading**

Cowles, Virginia. *The Romanovs*. Harper & Rowe, 1971.
Florinskiy, Michael T. *The End of the Russian Empire*. Yale University Press, 1931.
Kennan, George F. *Decision to Intervene*. Princeton University, 1958.
Kerenskiy, Alexander. *The Catastrophe*. New York: Appleton-Century-Crofts, 1929.
Lincoln, W. Bruce. *Romanovs*. New York: Dial Press, 1981.
Masie, Robert K. *Nicholas and Alexandra*. Atheneum, 1967.
Masie, Robert K. *The Romanovs, The Final Chapter*. New York: Random House, 1995.
Miluikov, Pavel. *History of Russia* (written in European exile after the revolution) 3 vols. Funk & Wagnalls, 1969.
Pares, Bernard. *The Fall of the Russian Monarchy*. New York: Alfred Knopf, 1939.
Seton-Watson, Hugh. *Russian Empire, 1801-1917*. Oxford: Clarendon Press, 1967.

# CHAPTER V
# THE REVOLUTION

**The Provisional Government**
Under normally accepted political and historical standards, there were two revolutions in Russia in 1917. The First Revolution occurred when Nicholas abdicated his throne in favor of the Provisional Government, making Russia a de-facto republic. The Second Revolution was on 7 November (New Style) or 25 October (Old Style) when Lenin illegally seized power from the Provisional Government, although he previously stated, to contradict the Provisional Government, that the revolutionary movement had already taken place before the Bolsheviks took over. It is therefore incorrect, as proclaimed by the Bolsheviks, that the revolution occurred on 7 November when the communists took over an existing republic before proclaiming a new government. It would be more correct to say that a new Bolshevik government took over on 7 November 1917.

Soviet interpretations are mostly different from recognized historical norms to suit their purposes. The revolutionary upheaval in Petrograd was accepted by the Duma, the Russian army, and most Russians when Nicholas II tendered his abdication in a railroad car in Mogilev on 15 March 1917 to two representatives of the Duma, Guchkov and Shulgin. At first Nicholas wished to abdicate in favor of his son, but quickly changed his mind because he couldn't bear to part with his ailing son and decided to abdicate in favor of his brother, Grand Duke Mikhail. The grand duke refused unless the Constituent Assembly requested it. The bureaucracy found itself bewildered and turned to the Duma for authority. After the abdication the administrative organs of power evaporated, and in its place a self-appointed revolutionary committee took over. It was an amalgam of Russians and non-Russians, who tried to maintain order, while many others robbed and disappeared during the confusion.

In this relatively short period, there began a disorderly breakup of all existing state institutions. There is no record of another nation having such convulsions in the twentieth century, not even in the French Revolution of 1789 or Germany after WWI. The most prominent and best-organized of the groups were the Petrograd Soviet (Council) of Workers' and Soldiers' Deputies and the Provisional Government. However, it became evident from the start that the Provisional Government lacked authority, in view of its self-appointment, so it had to share power with the Soviet. In fact, the first decree by the Provisional Government in March was mandated by the Soviet. This decree was so liberal in an autocratic country that it included a blanket amnesty for all political, military, and religious prisoners, freedom of the press and speech, and the right to strike. In addition, it abolished all social, religious, and national distinctions, convoked the National Assembly, created a people's militia replacing the police, and declared universal suffrage in elections. A note attached to the decree called for troops taking part in revolutionary activities in Petrograd to remain in place, without transfer to the front, and for soldiers not on active duty to have the same rights and privileges as civilians.

Since this decree was considered a compromise after an agreement with the Duma and the Provisional Government, the Soviet issued another decree, without informing the Government. The decree, named "Order No. 1"—as distinct from the first and to emphasize its intent not to compromise with the government—called for soldiers' committees to be chosen in each detachment, and each was to obey only the Soviet in its political decisions. As regard to the Duma, its orders were to be obeyed if not in conflict with the orders of the Soviet. This decree was the beginning of disintegration of the Russian army. All weapons were to be under the control of Soviet committees and not delivered to officers. To deprive the authority of the Army's supreme command, the order called for all weapons to be delivered to Soviet committees forthwith. In effect this order was intended to introduce political decisions into the army by any soldier and actually meant—without so stating—quit the battlefield and go home. The Provisional Government, realizing the consequences of this order, made every effort to overturn it but failed. The Soviet was careful and nervous about issuing the order, lest it give the impression that the authority of the Duma and the Provisional Government were being pre-empted. To correctly interpret these positions, one should conclude that the centers of both authorities had divergent degrees of power. The Duma and Provisional Government had political power, while the Soviet of Deputies had social power. Most writers agree with this assessment, including legislators present at the time who later confirmed it while in exile. On the other hand, the Bolshevik party disagreed with this opinion and flatly stated that it was the Soviet which had the power, since revolutionary movement had already taken place. They reasoned that until the National Assembly met, the Provisional Government hung on uselessly. This logic was based on Bolshevik convenience.

The Duma's main problem lay in its diversity of parties and their opinions, as well as conflicting conditions facing the country. The Provisional Government, too, found it almost impossible to run the country with intervention of the Soviet of Deputies in almost all facets of work. The Soviet of Deputies had their own problems, finding it difficult to represent two different parties—the Social Revolutionary party of the peasants and the Social Democratic party of labor. The Social Democrats had diverse views, and although the Bolsheviks in the party were a minority, they demanded cessation of the war. The Mensheviks were in the majority and supported the continuation of the war to honor its obligations to the allies and for full democracy. In this confusion most parties deliberated between themselves instead of acting in unison or compromising. Having had no basis for democratic origins upon which to compromise and heal their differences, they either yielded or disagreed. The reader should bear in mind that most members of the First Provisional Government belonged to the Constitutional Democratic party, somewhat similar to western European Parliamentary parties. To honor the previously drafted document for universal, equal, and secret balloting for the future Constituent Assembly—in view of the diverse opinions in the Duma, the Provisional Government, and the Soviet—they found it necessary to delay the election process until sometime in autumn 1917, a fatal error discovered too late. The Provisional Government wasn't capable of solving both military and political problems because of intransigence of the Executive Committee of the Petrograd Soviet and the Government's insistence on continuing the war.

However, the First Provisional Government did perform reasonably well in some instances where the Soviet and the Government agreed. It granted amnesty to political and religious prisoners, reformed an impossible prison system, eliminated restrictions on class, partially settled national minority questions, reformed the court system, eliminated capital punishment, and terminated all exile practices. It guaranteed freedom of speech, the press, and assembly. It also standardized an eight-hour work day, granting labor the right to strike. Finally, it prepared a basis for convoking the Constituent Assembly. In its short existence, saddled with confusing and deliberate provocations by the Soviet and the Bolsheviks, it is a wonder it did as much.

Nevertheless measures taken by the Central Executive Committee of the Petrograd Soviet brought about a crisis in the army when on 19 March the government in its official "Manifesto to the People of Russia" declared its intent "to bring the war to a successful conclusion." However a negative position was held on the declaration by the Central Executive Committee of the Soviet, though it had no official policy of its own. The Soviet did, however, use every means—including nationwide meetings and newspaper announcements—to denounce the continuation of the war in favor of "peace without annexations and indemnities." This appeal for peace was so effective that the government was forced to back down on its war declaration. On 8 April the government was forced to issue a new declaration to the people stating, "Russia favored the establishment of peace on the basis of self-determination of nations." Pavel Miluikov, the foreign minister, refused to assume responsibility for this formula and promptly resigned on 15 May. The position of the War Minister Guchkov was similar, and he had resigned a few days earlier.

In view of these resignations, the Government was forced to reorganize itself into a representative form with fifteen members. The majority in the new government were liberals, of whom six moderates were from the Central Executive Committee of the Soviet. The reader should be aware that Kerenskiy was vice-president of the Petrograd Soviet and had influence in coaxing the Soviet to take part in the government. The liberal members of the Soviet joined the government on condition of exploring peace, instituting democracy in the army, improving food and transport, untangling the land problem, and convening the Constituent Assembly. These liberals were subject to the dictates of the Central Executive

Committee of the Soviet. Reviewed from a historical point of view, the last condition meant the eventual downfall of the reorganized government. It opened the gates within the Petrograd Soviet to the radical wing of the Soviet, the Bolsheviks. In view of the government's liberal policies to free all political prisoners from domestic and foreign exile, a flood of exiles returned from the European part of Russia, Siberia, and Europe. Still faced with unresolved problems, the government postponed major decisions. Lacking consensus and administrative capability, it deferred it to the future Constituent Assembly, while the masses waited for answers and action.

Lenin, the leader of the Russian Social Democratic Workers party, arrived from Switzerland on 16 April with his group of revolutionaries. After his return he published his "April Theses" as a cure for all the ills in the country. He excoriated the war as imperialistic, criticizing all who defended it, and claiming that "If the state power was in the hands of the proletariat, annexations renounced, and capitalist influence severed, only then would the country solve all its problems. Until these conditions were met, propaganda should be used, particularly to sway the army." Additionally, he proclaimed, "We demand that all parties withdraw their support from the Provisional Government, and all power be transferred to the Soviet. The country should be a Soviet Republic, with no police, bureaucracy, or army." He further went on, "Nationalization of the land should be under the control of the Soviet, and all private land and property should be confiscated. Banking should be totally revised, and its assets placed under Soviet control." He also surprised his party members to rework the party's outdated program and change its name to the Communist party. If these proposals were not enough, he urged organizing the Communist International, to promote revolution abroad, and all under his leadership. At first, his own party members vetoed the "April Theses," but later in May most of the program was approved at a party conference. He proposed an immediate propaganda for peace—land to the peasants to expropriate from the expropriators to make headway with this program among the lower classes. Under the conditions and the temper in the country, the Provisional Government couldn't continue the war or make any headway in its political problems and waited for the convocation for the Constituent Assembly. This delay caused future complications.

To impress the allies that Russia was still at war with them, a new military offensive was ordered for 1 July. The government was aware of transportation, supply, and domestic upheavals, yet to bolster the morale of the population and entrench its control, it decided to go on the offensive against the advice of the Supreme Army Command, which hardly saw any chance of success. The army was forced to launch an attack on the Galician front against the Austro-Hungarian armies; they made some progress and took some prisoners, the majority of whom were minority nationals of Austria-Hungary. Heavy casualties were sustained on both sides, but the army couldn't break through to force a decision. On 19 July Austro-Hungarian armies—this time with nationals in the majority—along with some German army elements launched a counterattack, which resulted in a full scale panic among Russian troops. Fleeing in disorder, they inflicted unspeakable atrocities on the local population. As a result, the Russian army was no longer a disciplined organization.

To add to the country's further problems, self-determination of national minorities, as called for in the program of the Central Committee of the Petrograd Soviet, was another thorn in the flesh of the Provisional Government. Since the Committee's program had been announced, national minorities were taking advantage of the confusion by taking matters in their own hands. Some declared autonomy within the empire; a few desired autonomy with special rights in the new order within a restructured Russia: others wished to sever relations with Russia altogether. The Ukrainian problem was the toughest for the government, in view of Russian acceptance of the Ukrainians as little Russians who had become part of the Empire. The Government took the position that it assumed legitimate power as successor of the fallen regime and intended to hand over its powers to the Constituent Assembly or face the possibility of non-Russians disintegrating the country. Lacking powers of enforcement to prevent disintegration, it approved a constitution for Finland and freedom for Poland—at the time occupied by Germany—thereby using this method for other national minorities in preventing disintegration, all subject to approval of the Constituent Assembly. It was ingenious solution, yet it denied cessation to other nationalities. Ukraine's insistence on autonomy and its possible cessation was a total surprise to the government, yet it knew of its creation and public knowledge of the existence of their own revolutionary Rada (Assembly). They proceeded on the road to independence, which the Provisional Government wouldn't accept, yet it had no power to enforce. The Rada proclaimed full autonomy on 23 June. On 12 July Kerenskiy and some advisors left for Kiev to discuss autonomy and Ukraine's demands. Four Cadet party members of the Government refused to accept Ukraine's position and resigned, creating a crisis, which in turn caused the fall of the government. These events occurred concurrently with the Russian offensive and debacle on the Galician front, which would cause July upheavals.

Events took on a different character in July, when the Soviet threatened to take power, incited by the Bolsheviks with their propaganda, and made headway with the Petrograd garrison. This caused an uprising against the Provisional Government, which was put down 16-17 July by Petrograd Soviet itself. However, on 14 June (a month before), the First All-Russian Congress of Workers' and Soldiers' Deputies held its first conference in the capital. Stenographic records of the Congress show an attendance of 1,090 delegates, of whom 638 declared direct party affiliation; the Social Revolutionaries, the Mensheviks, the Bolsheviks, and a few splinter parties totaled 452. The Congress approved the policies of the Provisional Government by a vote of 545 to 125 with 52 abstentions. The vote clearly approved a coalition Provisional Government and was officially confirmed by the Socialist delegate Tseretelli, leader of the Socialists. The vote was challenged by Lenin, who announced that the Bolsheviks were ready to assume power at any minute. Records further indicate that Kerenskiy stood up to answer Lenin's challenge thus: "The task of Russian democracy is to consolidate its gains, so that comrade Lenin, who was abroad, may be able to continue to speak here and not have to go back to Switzerland. You are offering childish prescriptions to arrest—destroy and kill. What are you, socialists or the police of the old regime? You recommend that we follow the road of the French revolution of 1792 when by unintentionally reckless alliance with reaction, you would destroy our power and open the door for a real dictator." This response uttered by Kerenskiy was not only appropriate, but prophetic indeed. Prior to these events in July, Bolshevik influence was minimal at best, yet their propaganda machine and slogans were better organized among all other parties, workers, and the Petrograd garrison. The defeat of the uprising in the capital didn't solve the problem by the Cadets' resignation, and the balance of the Government agreed to support the socialist program on agrarian matters. The All-Russian Soviet of Peasants' Deputies demanded the government be guided by resolutions of these bodies. Prince Lvov, the prime minister, couldn't support this action without bringing it up before the Constituent Assembly for approval, and he promptly resigned, finding it unacceptable to submit an accomplished fact to higher authority.

**The Second Provisional Government**

The void created by Prince Lvov's resignation was filled by Kerenskiy, who became prime minister in the Second Provisional Government. The Cadet effort to join the government with unacceptable conditions was turned down on 4 August by a vote of 147 to 45 with almost the same abstentions. A decision was made to have Kerenskiy form a new cabinet effective 6 August, mainly with a socialist vote. As vice-president of the socialists, he carried his agrarian program directly to a vote without bothering to submit it to the future Constituent Assembly for approval. He did submit it to the Duma, which was powerless but was in accordance with his party's instructions. Some writers have identified Kerenskiy as a dictator from then on. The author doesn't necessarily agree with this assumption, certainly not in that time frame, in view of the prevailing, almost impossible revolutionary and unstable conditions. Chernov, the agriculture minister and a Socialist Revolutionary leader could have interfered more vigorously but decided against disruption and harmony. Was there a possibility that the Constituent Assembly could have solved many of the agrarian problems if it had been convened? It would appear doubtful, in view of the prevailing composition of the Assembly with its diverse views, which would most likely have been stalemated by Chernov's advocacy in behalf of the wealthy landowners and rich peasants. This is, however, only the author's view. On 22 August a decree signed by Kerenskiy postponed the elections to the Constituent Assembly from 30 September to 25 November and the date of the meeting to 11 December. On 25 July a meeting of various groups representing the entire country with 2,500 delegates, met at the Bolshoi Theatre in Moscow, apportioned according to various party groupings. Some party delegates assumed the meeting to be an exchange of views and not binding on any party. Since nothing was accomplished because of extreme divisions between government forces and the opposition, the delegates departed on 25 August, accomplishing nothing.

On 21 July General Alexey Brusilov resigned as commander of the Russian army and was succeeded by General Lavr Kornilov. The new commander demanded immediate restoration of discipline and formal relations between officers and ranks. Shortly before, Kerenskiy had ordered the death penalty restored at the front in order to maintain discipline and continue the war to the end. Kornilov appointed General Krymov, a distinguished corps commander, to take command of special troops from the Caucasus. While his army was reorganizing, an individual by the name of Lvov (no relation to Prince Lvov, the former prime minister) approached General Kornilov on his own initiative on 7 September to mediate strained conditions between the army and the government. Lvov held the position of procurator general, with previous connection to the First Provisional Government, a position of meaningless power in the revolution. He represented himself as an envoy of Kerenskiy and secured an appointment with General Kornilov. At the meeting he put forth three proposals to the general to choose, each based on dictatorship: a new government headed by Kerenskiy; a committee of three or four including Kornilov; Kornilov as both civil and military chief, with Kerenskiy serving under him. Under unsettling wartime and revolutionary conditions, the General preferred the latter.

A day later in Petrograd, Lvov went to see Kerenskiy and stated that Kornilov was backed by several important people and asked Kerenskiy to resign in favor of the general and accept the portfolio of the minister of justice. Kerenskiy was upset and called Kornilov on his direct line to confirm the veracity of the statements by Lvov. Apparently unaware of Lvov's statements to Kerenskiy, the general replied affirmatively and asked when he could be expected at his headquarters. Kerenskiy, disconcerted, stalled with his answer and began to verify Lvov's statements with the people he had mentioned as the supposed partners in the new government. Angered by the entire episode, Kerenskiy issued an order dismissing Kornilov from his command and placed Petrograd under martial law. The general, surprised and hurt by Kerenskiy's order, refused to surrender his post. Kornilov sent General Krymov an order to commence operations against the government. Getting wind of the order, the Central Executive Committee of the Soviet set up a Military Committee and welcomed any forces to fight Kornilov's and Krymov's forces. A quick response by rail and communications workers delayed the advance of Krymov's troops. When Krymov's troops finally entered the capital and saw no uprising, they became doubtful of the situation and deserted. Krymov, after talking to Kerenskiy, realized he was being duped and committed suicide. Kornilov then surrendered to General Alexeyeev on 14 September. This strange episode, a comedy of errors concocted by Lvov—an opportunistic amateur, a schemer, and a fool—was apparently done in hopes of securing a more important position with the new government. Realizing he bungled, he disappeared into the midst of revolutionary convulsions to save his skin, with his whereabouts and fate unknown.

Shortly thereafter the government turned into a five-man directorate, similar to the directorate of the French Revolution, then headed by Fuché. This directorate lasted till 7 November accomplishing practically nothing under the pressure from the Central Committee of the Soviet, which demanded expulsion of the Cadet members in the government. Afraid of being outvoted and untenable in his position without the Cadet votes, placing little confidence in revolutionary type democracy, Kerenskiy secured approval of his colleagues in the directorate to be named supreme commander-in-chief, making General Alexeev his new chief of the general staff. Uncertain of the consequences and probable outcome of the move, the directorate declared Russia a republic—although it was already a de facto republic. Under pressure by the Executive Committee of the Congress of both the Deputies and Peasant Soviets, a meeting was called for 27 September to reconcile their differences in forming a coalition. Not much was accomplished—with vague declarations proposed and none voted on. Efforts to bring other non-revolutionary elements, including industrialists and some minority members, into the coalition failed. Yielding to pressure from provincial soviets, the Soviet Executive Committee ordered elections to be held 2 November in the second All-Russian Congress of Soviets. Protests from the Peasants' Committee cancelled the summons. The Peasants' Committee was worried about the possible seizure of power by the Bolsheviks, which could precipitate a civil war. Some writers have since speculated that perhaps the Bolsheviks could have won a majority of the Peasants' Committee. It would appear that if they had won, the Bolsheviks needn't have used strong-arm methods five days later, on 7 November, to seize power.

Meantime, the western allies experienced a heavy American involvement in the war. This intervention caused Germany to thin out its ranks on the eastern front, throwing all available reserves to the west. The balance of their forces was stationed in static positions against the demoralized Russian army, which turned into rabble and became altogether inactive on the fronts. Fraternization with the enemy became commonplace, particularly in the southwest, along the Austro-Hungarian front. Time was closing in on the second German objective of Russia's nationalities problem, as well as the deterioration and unstable frontline conditions of the Russians.

After the abortive July uprising, Lenin escaped to Finland in September to avoid arrest and remained there until 22 October. During that short period in Finland, he wrote "State and Revolution," a thesis explaining the new tactics of the Bolsheviks. His main change in tactics was his abandonment of "All Power to the Soviets" and "Defense of the Constituent Assembly." He feared Kerenskiy would have enough power to take over without waiting for the Constituent Assembly to convene. He was convinced, as ever, that the time had come to grab power immediately and made that known to his colleagues in his thesis. At first they thought him too rash and objected. When he tendered his resignation, they yielded. On 23 October the members of the Bolshevik Central Committee, with Lenin in attendance, agreed to an armed uprising without setting a date. However, two moderate members, Kamenev and Zinoviev, voted against it. At the same time, the Politburo was established for policy decisions of the top echelon of the Bolshevik party, which included Lenin, Trotsky, Kamenev, Zinoviev, Sokolnikov, Bubnov, and Stalin.

The general consensus was that there was no great desire for an armed uprising, since the masses were for the local Soviets and not the Bolsheviks. Regardless of the consensus, the final decision for an armed uprising by the Bolsheviks was made by Lenin in Finland, and preparations began. Trotsky was the brain behind this preparation, and he is the one who masterminded and controlled the actions of the Military Revolutionary Committee.

On 5 November he single-handedly convinced the troops at Peter and Paul Fortress to switch from support of the Provisional Government in favor of armed insurrection. The fortress was a pivotal point within the city, with its large cache of weapons. It was he who accomplished the seizure of railroad stations and telegraph offices. He also organized the capture of the Winter Palace, the headquarters of the Provisional Government. He convinced the sailors of the cruiser Aurora, berthed on the Neva River, to open fire at his command on the Winter Palace, which was guarded by some Cadets and a women's battalion; this battle was easily won by Trotsky's sailors. The helpless Provisional Government, accomplishing nothing in its final days, abandoned by those who needed it most, finally expired. Kerenskiy and a few others in the government escaped, while other members were imprisoned in the Peter and Paul Fortress. Russia, having had a chance for possible democracy, forfeited its right in the revolution. Lenin, hearing the latest results from Trotsky, was convinced more than ever that his decision for an immediate armed insurrection was correct. He had an uncanny feeling for certain events, which proved to be right. Henceforth the members of the Politburo were careful in opposing his arguments.

**The Second Revolution: The Bolshevik Takeover**

Making sure that most centers of power in Petrograd were under their control, the Bolsheviks called the Second Congress of Soviets into session for 11:00 P.M. on 7 November. It was calculated as a convenient time to exhaust the majority dissenters and drag the session into the early hours of the morning, when they would probably be asleep at their desks. Of the twenty-two members of the Presidium elected, fourteen were Bolsheviks, with Kamenev acting as chairman of the Congress. Martov, the Menshevik leader, took the floor to demand that all bloodshed be stopped in the streets and that an all-socialist coalition be created instead of a Bolshevik dictatorship. Sensing trouble from majority Bolsheviks in the Presidium, with their armed troops milling around and threatening, most of the Social Revolutionary (SR) members, Mensheviks and members of the Jewish Bund withdrew, leaving only the extreme SR members, Menshevik Internationalists and extreme left Jewish group. In the early hours of 8 November, Kamenev announced the overthrow of the Second Provisional Government and proclaimed that the Congress was assuming power. Later in the evening on November 8, the Congress abolished the death penalty—which had been previously done by the Provisional Government—and tackled the problems of peace, land, and government. Lenin himself proclaimed the decree abolishing the rights of landowners without compensation, while the rights of small peasants and Cossack groups were left intact, at least for the time being. Any discussions on the above questions were forbidden, and in the early hours of 8 November, all the above measures were overwhelmingly adopted.

Kamenev proposed a new government, to be known as the Council of People's Commissars, which included Lenin and all the Bolsheviks, pending the first session of the Constituent Assembly. This was challenged by all other parties present, including the rail workers, who threatened to stop delivery of food to the capital. To win over most of those assembled, Trotskiy intransigently stated, "There is a need to have a party which would grab power against counter-revolutionary elements. You, the Congress of Soviets, here is the power, and you must take it." The lateness of the hour prevented a roll call, which was anticipated by the Bolsheviks. The only item left to discuss was the confirmation of the previously selected members of the all-powerful Central Executive Committee, to which the Council of People's Commissars was responsible. Promising cooperation to all, the Second Congress of Soviet of Workers' and Soldiers' Deputies adjourned in the early hours of the morning on 8 November. And who were the members of the all-powerful Central Executive Committee and the Council of People's Commissars? Lenin and his Bolsheviks. The second revolution was accomplished, and Russia was Bolshevised and Communized without the consent of its people. Lenin proceeded to reform the party and the country in his image, and delivered the packaged goods to the Constituent Assembly as a fait accompli when it met 18 January 1918.

All the while he was consolidating his position with his goon squads in the streets of the capital, which had an important and critical effect on the rest of the country. Most of the citizens in the country, particularly the upper classes, felt the Bolsheviks couldn't last more than a few weeks at most and would then be overthrown. But then again, they didn't know who the Bolsheviks were nor did they realize what was happening in the country—living in splendid isolation and detachment—until it was too late. This would prove to be a catastrophic miscalculation in a time of revolutionary turmoil, where Lenin and his utopian exercise was welcomed by the illiterate and hungry masses. Not many citizens were aware of the deadly Bolshevik character and determination to achieve single-mindedly the objective of confiscating power and rule by dictat. All these revolutionary events took place only in Petrograd, and the rest of the country had little, if anything, to say about the turmoil. It was rather obvious to the members of the provisional government, who were aware of the surreptitious nature and methods used by the Bolsheviks but were incapable of stopping them because of their vastly divergent views in objectives for Russia. Those dissenters who knew Bolshevik methods were largely unorganized and mainly objected on moral grounds and argument. Having had no following with the street mobs, they were powerless, while the Bolsheviks used deadly means and tactics suitable to the character of their mission in the streets.

The Constituent Assembly finally met on 18 January 1918, as demanded by most left and Cadet parties prior to adjournment on 8 November. Lenin accommodated them gladly in order to grab the government and legitimize it. The meeting hall was not only packed with delegates but also with Bolshevik thugs and soldiers, armed to the teeth, throughout the hall and entrances. Not withstanding the armed men, the Bolshevik proposal for "Declaration for the Rights of Toiling Masses and Exploited People" was rejected by a vote of 237 to 138. Having heard the rejection after the recess—which meant nothing to them—the Bolsheviks and left-wing Social Revolutionaries withdrew from the hall. The remaining delegates overwhelmingly turned down Bolshevik dictatorship, but approved an armistice with Germany, the land decree, proclaimed Russia a republic for the second time, and called for a socialist conference. In the early morning of 19 January with the Bolsheviks in full control of the chamber, with delegates under threats and intimidation by their thugs, the Constituent Assembly adjourned for twelve hours and never reconvened.

That single act of the Bolsheviks sealed the fate of Russia. On the same day Lenin ordered the dissolution of the Constituent Assembly. The dissolution act was not challenged, since only the Bolsheviks were in the majority, and one of the Bolshevik predicaments was out of the way. It was a simple act without debate and subsequently became normal procedure in the Soviet Union. It was a deadly comedy, played best by communist rules. Because of complications of diversity and compromise, as is common in democratic systems, the Bolsheviks promised immediate salvation to the downtrodden, who tired of hunger and war and in confusion gave in and prepared for the experiment. The author would add that the common people of Russia, particularly the lower classes, were insufficiently educated and too unsophisticated to see the differences in the programs offered and possible consequences. Living under autocracy throughout their history under extremely austere conditions, they fell under the spell of the heavenly gifts promised by the Bolsheviks. In considering the character of the Russian masses as compared to the French revolutionaries, whose political and social consciousness was substantially superior, one must conclude that the Russian lower classes were easily duped. Violence apparently has varying degrees of tolerance, and the French settled their problems with minimal loss of life, yet the Bolsheviks and the masses never quite understood the limits and never knew when to stop.

At last Lenin's lifelong dream had come true—to be rid of his pitiful existence in Europe with nothing to do but theorizing. However, things weren't working out that well yet, since there were other predicaments which confronted him. Russia was still at war with Germany, and in solving that problem and attaining peace, he was convinced that the final revolution at home and in Europe would occur. They found peace difficult to attain, since no warring nation in Europe agreed with their arbitrary seizure of power and radical measures, believing they wouldn't last long enough to attain their goals. Lenin's call for peace and cessation of hostilities among Russia's former allies received a cold shoulder. In view of the rejection by the allies and to spite them and force the allies to comply, the Bolsheviks published secret agreements between the Imperial regime and its allies—the first, known, open-faced blackmail in modern times between allies, yet it didn't work. They also approached the Central Powers on 20 November 1917 for a unilateral and immediate cessation of hostilities. They mounted a propaganda campaign directed against their troops to force the Central Powers to agree. Concurrently Lenin ordered the headquarters of the Russian Army

Command to halt all operations. When no response was received, he ordered General Dukhonin, the commander of the front, to seize all operations. Lenin got on his direct telephone line and ordered him to terminate operations forthwith. When the general refused to comply with the order, basing his decision on the grounds it was a political matter, he was shot, and his place was taken by an epileptic second lieutenant. It was Lenin's theory that any idiot could command an army.

Within a week a thirty-day armistice was signed between Germany and Soviet Russia. On 22 December a peace conference was convened at Brest-Litovsk. The Soviet delegation included not only political and military members but also a worker, a peasant, and a sailor, to emphasize the change in new Russia. It was reported that General Hoffman, the German negotiator, accepted this delegation with a laugh. Nothing was accomplished soon, and the Germans took advantage of the peace talks to reinforce their troop formations in the west. When the question of self-determination began during the talks, it was apparent from the start that it would be a nettlesome problem. The Bolshevik intention was based on stripping colonial powers of the many subjugated nationals they had and allowing workers friendly to their cause to stir up trouble and fight the occupying colonial powers. The Central Powers, saw through the scheme and justified their own position in behalf of the Ukraine, which was then occupied by the Central Powers. Ukraine, a breadbasket not only to Russia but also to the Central Powers, was not negotiable from their point of view. On 7 January 1918 the Ukrainians were invited to the conference and with a dislike for the Bolsheviks, they took advantage of the invitation to speak in behalf of all nationalities of Russia. From the start they demanded the return of Galicia, Bukovina, and Kholm, then under Austrian occupation. The Austrians reluctantly agreed, having internal problems of their own, in exchange for grain. This caused Trotsky, the new chief negotiator, at first to agree to their presence, but as the negotiations progressed, he realized his own negotiating position would be compromised, for fear of a separate peace treaty between the Central Powers and Ukraine. Having no choice, he waited out the Ukrainian demands. The Germans encouraged the Ukrainians and signed a peace treaty with them in February. In exchange Ukraine was to deliver grain and other foodstuffs. When the Ukrainians promised deliveries, the Central Powers saw no need for further negotiations with Trotsky. Taking advantage of the situation the Germans slyly suggested new boundaries for Russia, which caused immediate internal squabbles among the Bolshevik negotiators. Some agreed on drawn-out methods, while still other members of the team suggested termination of the conference, while others were for long delays.

When a decision for delays was agreed to on 10 February, based on Trotsky's famous formula of "no war, no peace" and to underline their disgust, the Bolsheviks walked out of the conference. This gesture was an excellent propaganda ploy but didn't last long because the Germans decided to abandon the cease-fire on 18 February. Responding to their own requirements and to extract compliance with the new suggested boundaries, the Germans launched a new offensive along the entire eastern front. Encountering no resistance in the offensive, Lenin narrowly won the approval in the Central Committee to cease all hostilities. As a result, the Bolsheviks reluctantly trudged back to the negotiating table, only to sign the original German boundary demand. The boundaries were signed on 3 March 1918 in Brest-Litovsk. The terms of the treaty were devastating to Russia. It was a geopolitically strategic advantage wholly in favor of the Germans, nothing less than a humiliation and loss of material and human resources for Russia. Politically, it included diplomatic recognition of each party (a first for the Bolsheviks), exchange of prisoners, withholding all propaganda against each party, and development of economic relations. The Russians also had to agree to recognize Georgia, Ukraine, and Finland as independent states under German influence. Agreement was also reached on German control of Poland, Lithuania, Latvia, and Estonia, and the Russian evacuation of the Aaland Islands in the Baltic. They also agreed to the Turkish occupation of Kars, Ardakhan, and Batum on the Black Sea as well as the ratification of Rumania's seizure of Bessarabia.

To clearly define Russia's devastating losses and to quantify its magnitude, consider the following: Russia lost approximately 1.3 million square miles of territory and 62 million of its inhabitants, although the territories lost were not yet under Bolshevik control. Under the last Imperial regime, these territories contained 30 percent of Russia's arable lands, 25-28 percent of its rail network, 33 percent of its factory production, and close to 75 percent of its coal and iron deposits. In the future, to regain some of these lands and material assets, these republics would have to be won back at a terrible cost. These losses were meaningless to Lenin, so long as he held on to his power. To do so, it was necessary for him to socialize and communize Russia and western Europe, regardless of human and material losses to Russia.

The Bolsheviks had two primary objectives—one of which was the transfer of the capital to Moscow, which was done secretly at night. It was a crucial and important decision, in view of its central location in Russia. The other objective was the creation of a new army; the goal was to replace the rowdy street mobs and the demoralized existing army and make the new army the vanguard of the new regime. In this connection the new army was open to all class-conscious citizens age eighteen to fifty and was compulsory for all peasants and workers. The order excluded all members of the bourgeoisie but included the drafting of 50,000 former Imperial army officers. The Bolshevik government reimposed the death penalty for deserters, eliminated the election of officers by the troops, eased up on the powers of army committees, and introduced political indoctrination workers, known as the politruks. In short, everything they had fought against under the Imperial regime was now reimposed and made legal. The Bolsheviks succeeded in raising a huge army, which became a disciplined force, supplied with large stocks.

They also introduced social changes; one of the most significant changes was the introduction of the western Gregorian calendar on 14 February. They abolished religious and judicial courts and extricated the church from supervision of schools. Economic changes included the confiscation of capital stocks of all private banks, discontinuance of dividend payments, and nationalization of all natural and mineral resources. It further nationalized foreign trade and all major commercial enterprises. Inheritance was abolished forever, and the poor were enrolled to distribute food for the cities. The constitution injected certain propaganda items, including "No exploitation of man by man." It proclaimed the duty of all citizens to perform work on the basis of the maxim, "he who does not work, neither shall he eat." It further authorized "the arming of workers for the honor of bearing arms in the defense of the revolution." It separated the church from the state, and schools from the church. Freedom of assembly was guaranteed under prescribed rules, and so was asylum to all foreign nationals who were persecuted for political or religious reasons. Voting franchise was denied to all persons who employed hired labor, who lived on income not derived from work, and to former members of the police, their informers, and members of the Romanov family. When translated, it meant vengeance against all those who opposed Bolshevism. All administrative and executive power was placed in the reconstituted All-Russian Congress of Soviets. The Congress was to convene twice yearly, and between sessions the Central Executive Committee was designated as the supreme legislative, administrative, and controlling authority, being charged with the general direction of the government. Those who were disenfranchised under the constitution—and there were many—had to make do as best they could. Those not favored in their ranks were confused, unbelieving, left penniless, and were considered non-persons and parasites before the masses. To cap their victory in subjugating the country to their theories, the Bolsheviks expelled Social Revolutionary and Menshevik members from the soviets in order to kill all opposition.

The Bolshevik constitution was not accepted by all, however, as the law of the land. Instability and disruptions began erupting gradually. Some in the lower classes, the common people, the bourgeoisie, the wealthy, and the army rejected it out of hand, yet they could do little since they could not appeal. Those who could left the cities for the countryside and their estates or disappeared into hiding and were considered non-persons. Looting of the wealthy was encouraged as a patriotic duty, with drunken mobs breaking into houses and apartments, looting everything in sight with encouragement from the new regime. Normal life turned into turmoil so severe that most people of all classes (except industrial workers and peasants), were thunderstruck by events happening at lightning speed. When considered as a whole, the world of Russia, as known then, disappeared into thin air, never to recover. Since none of the principal Bolshevik leaders was an economist in the normally accepted terms but rather a theoretical social thinker, consequential economic problems which later overwhelmed the regime were not foreseen or anticipated. Their main dependence on economic transformation was partially based on Karl Marx's *Das Kaptal*, written during European revolutionary convulsions in 1848 in addition to whatever was extracted from the writings of Frederic Engels. Russia was open for an experiment on a mass scale, never before attempted anywhere in society, yet it endured for seventy-four years, largely because of its abundance of natural resources—which were drained to their limits—and the instilled Soviet discipline and terror watched over by the KGB. Gradually, but too slowly, when things were getting unbearable and could no longer be tolerated in a civilized society, various political and civil groups and former Imperial army officers began forming resistance to overthrow the Bolshevik regime. The resistance, while formidable later in the war, started too slowly, allowing the Bolsheviks central control of the country, thus separating the armies of resistance forces. This separation of anti-Bolshevik forces proved to be detrimental to the opposition.


**Recommended Reading**

Dmitryshin, Basil. *Imperial Russia: A Source Book, 1700-1917*. 2d ed. Hinsdale, IL: Dryden Press, 1974.

Florinskiy, Michael T. *Russia: A History and Interpretation*. New York: Macmillan, 1954.

Riazanovskiy, Nicholas V. *Nicholas I and Official Nationality in Russia, 1825-1855*. Berkeley, CA: University of California Press, 1959.

Seton-Watson, Hugh. *The Russian Empire, 1801-1917*. Oxford University Press, 1967.

Yarmolinsk, Avraham. *Road to Revolution: A Century of Russian Radicalism*. Casell, London: 1957.

# CHAPTER VI
# THE CIVIL WAR

Upon withdrawal of Soviet Russia from the war by the Treaty of Brest-Litovsk, the battlefield abruptly changed, with the Allies in the west taking full brunt of German offensive operations. However the United States entered the war in 1917 and further buttressed Allied forces in the west. Prior to events at Brest-Litovsk, the Central Powers, although holding central positions in the war—which helped them split their enemies—had to conduct a two-front war. The Brest-Litovsk Treaty changed the equation for the Central Powers by facing only the western allies. Ammunition stocks left by the Allies in the Russian ports became a serious concern, lest the Bolsheviks (or worse yet, the Germans) get hold of them. To ward off this danger, the Allies were forced to intervene in Soviet Russia to recapture the huge amounts of armaments and other supplies sent to Imperial Russia. These stocks were delivered to the northern ports of Murmansk and Arkhangelsk, in the Barents and White Seas, respectively. Additional supplies were dropped off in Vladivostok, in the Far East on the Sea of Japan. All diplomatic efforts to recover them were turned down by the Soviet government. Afraid that the Germans or Bolsheviks would capture them for their own war efforts, the Allies landed contingents to recover them. In this connection, the British landed in Murmansk in early March 1918, followed by French, Italian, and American troops. The British also landed troops in Baku and other areas of the Caucasus in late 1918 to prevent the Turks or Bolsheviks from capturing oil fields.

Japan's incentives were also satisfied in view of its interests in China, Korea, and particularly south Manchuria and eastern Siberia, with their vast territories and natural resources. The Japanese occupied Vladivostok and the northern part of Sakhalin Island and marched west along the TransSiberian Railway to the eastern shore of Lake Baikal. The aggressive moves of the Japanese caused the Allies to suspect ulterior motives in occupying these territories. The Bolshevik government's reaction to landings in the northern ports at first was unclear, and then they welcomed their intervention, hoping the landings would somehow restrain the Germans; later, however, they opposed these landings by the Allies as well as Japanese. The other serious problem on Soviet territory was the presence of Czech and Slovak prisoners of Austro-Hungarian armies, previously captured by the Russian armies. By the Treaty of Brest-Litovsk, the Bolshevik government was obligated to release them; however, their exit back home was limited by the location and isolation of their camps in Siberia. The Bolsheviks found them to be a danger, having been stranded there. Besides the brawls they caused with the Hungarian prisoners, on their way home—released by the treaty—they posed a danger as loose armed foreigners on Soviet soil. To contain the prisoners, Trotsky, the war commissar, ordered them to disarm. When they refused to comply, the Bolsheviks responded by occupying most of the stations along the TransSiberian Railway to Lake Baikal. The Czech incident, Allied intervention, and Japanese landings, along with the disintegration of the Russian army at home, encouraged and prompted the enemies of the Bolsheviks to unite and resist them, thus resulting in the civil war.

The Russian civil war was the most brutal, fratricidal, and self-destructive conflict by all accounts of the time. No other civil war in the annals of history is recorded to have been equal to the slaughter and vengeance perpetrated on both sides. Although no official figures are available, best estimates from various sources seem to place the figures in the range of six to eight million dead, missing, or unaccounted for. The causes of the war were many and complex, and any conjecture on them even at this writing becomes distorted because of the bias reflected by both the Bolshevik government and the Whites in exile. To add to the confusion, the future Soviet government under Stalin manufactured tales of happenings and situations which either didn't exist or, if they did exist, were strongly tilted in favor of the Bolsheviks. Review of some diaries, memoirs, and notes—after the war's end—in Berlin, Paris, Harbin, Manchuria, reveal a somewhat different picture than the several published versions by the Soviet government. These versions alone show differences in emphasis on some battles, political decisions, and conditions in the country. Particular emphasis is placed by Stalin on the Tsaritsin (Volgograd) battlefront, his troubleshooting at Lenin's request, conditions in the country during the war, as well as the version of his political importance during the war.

The Russian civil war was precipitated by war in Europe in 1914, which was the principal cause in creating a serious schism among Russian classes. Under the Imperial regime the lower classes—the poor peasants and industrial workers—found no sympathy for their plight, while the growing middle class—bourgeoisie—was avoided by the strictures of Imperial rule. The intelligentsia, who were a class by themselves in splendid isolation, had sought change in political and social structure of the country in diverse philosophies since 1825, yet they did nothing but theorize. The nobility and the agricultural and industrial barons were immune to the desperate conditions of the country, both socially and politically. The czar continued to hold on to Alexander III's (his father's) autocratic rule, lest he betray him. He relied on the Imperial bureaucracy and political police for order, disregarding the Duma each time it sought appropriate change. This unstable social-political atmosphere in peace and war precipitated the country into convulsion, yet no one could predict the outcome. The government and the Duma, even in the beginning of the 1914 war, suspected nothing of the unhealthy underlying symptoms in view of nation's enthusiasm for war. Some of the symptoms were there, yet other factors also played a part, which singly and collectively contributed to convulsions.

The Bolsheviks won the civil war, gaining control of all territories in the north-south axis, from Petrograd to Moscow, and further south adjacent to the Volga and some portions of northern Caucasus, which was the most productive part of Russia (of what was left after the Brest-Litovsk Treaty) thereby preventing the opposition from uniting. In most military situations, holding inner positions is an important advantage. They possessed this classic position control, efficient inner communications, abundant military stocks, an industrial base, and an almost-adequate grain supply. The iron discipline combined with terror and a fanatical belief in the outcome of the war—which almost eluded them at times—was the critical and decisive factor in their victory. One might add a good portion of luck and timing.

This much is certainly in favor of the Bolsheviks. The Bolsheviks realized from the beginning that they lacked proper military skills in conducting a war. They pressed former Russian army officers into service, holding their families under threat of death as hostages, and in some cases outright execution on the spot, should the attacks fail. However, political decisions in conducting the war were clearly under the control of the party—a critical and important factor in any war objectives. They constantly used terror as a weapon to reinforce their armies with men who could be coerced under political commissars, whose job it was to enroll workers and peasants into the army. They forced these terrorized troops to attack, even in hopeless cases when the military staff's advice was to hold back. Having control of interior lines, their communication and supply routes were shorter and consequently more efficient than those of the Whites. Under these circumstances they also had full control of food distribution within their enclave. By confiscating grain and produce and enforcing the system of ration cards for various categories of citizens, they succeeded in forcing compliance. In short, the territory they controlled was an enclosed prison from which few civilians could hope to escape. In time the Cheka (political police) was a thoroughly trained force and could deal with the mass population which lived constantly under fear of death or the loss of ration cards.

On the opposition side, several members of the Duma and Provisional Government were present at the war councils of the White Army but had little, if any, say in the conduct of the war. Nevertheless, had the army been properly organized in a unified command, though dispersed on several fronts, with unified political direction, they could have won decisively. If they had won, Russia would have never been the same as it had been before the abdication of the czar. In the far-flung fronts of the opposition White forces, from the extreme north at Murmansk and Ackhangelsk to the south in Ukraine and Crimea, including portions of Caucasus, they harassed and fought the Reds, yet some of their lower rank officers were incompetent and corrupt, acting on their own as warlords. Coordination between them and the senior commanders was scanty at best, yet they were mostly led by competent generals of the Russian army who had commanded troops against Central Powers. The General Staff (Stavka) was considered by military authorities of the time to be well qualified, competent, and aware of the army's strengths and weaknesses. Their use of overwhelming infantry units along with massed artillery techniques—artillery which later in the war became more available—were considered masterful. Food supplies in the south—the Kuban, Caucasus, and the Volga areas—were available from the peasants at reasonable prices and were not subject to expropriation similar to Bolshevik-controlled areas. Coal and iron deposits and natural resources in other occupied areas were more than sufficient to satisfy the requirements of industrial production, which had been short in the beginning.

Had Allied armaments been at their disposal in the beginning of the civil war, it would have carried them over until local production took over. There were enough industrialists, financiers, engineers, and workers available in the south for manufacturing to commence consumer and armaments production. This was confirmed by exiles in western Europe. Notwithstanding this background support, the Whites experienced a critical weakness since they lacked political direction, unified command, and a national program for the masses under revolutionary conditions. Lacking direction at the top, and with no allegiance to any symbolic purpose, most confused troops deserted to their villages while the Bolsheviks with their propaganda fought for soldiers, workers, and peasants. Even with disadvantages, the Whites still held strategic positions and forced the Bolsheviks to fight on several far-flung fronts. There was, however, no unified supreme command, and each front fought separate battles, uncoordinated with other fronts. In the end, it was mostly battles of attack by the Bolsheviks and reaction by the opposing Whites. Too many questions remain unanswered. Even the dairies of General Denikin, the commander in the south; General Yudenich, the commander in Estonia; and General Miller, the commander in Arkhangelsk fail to dispel the confusion. Subsequently the White generals in exile in Paris, Berlin, and Manchuria, after the civil war defeat, tried to justify their actions on individual fronts, again confirming their uncontrolled and uncoordinated efforts.

In their defense, Imperial army officers condemned the Bolshevik peace agreement with Germany, which they mostly used as a basis for lack of cohesion and confusion among their troops, permitting the Reds to incite the army against fighting the Germans. While it is true that Bolshevik propaganda to terminate the war against the Central Powers was an effective deterrent to continue the war, it does not justify their actions in losing the civil war. The memoirs written by the Whites never mention the real causes for the loss. When the officers of the Imperial army finally decided to act to create a Volunteer Army and enlist the Don and Kuban Cossacks, momentum was lost at least in the beginning, when it counted most. Russia's national minorities also played a part in bringing ethnic groups of the empire to the Reds—including Ukrainians, Georgians, Crimean Tatars, and others—to fight for the Bolsheviks, who promised them with double-talk that later they could secede from Russia and form their own independent states.

Some writers assumed most generals and politicians were loyal monarchists; this assumption seems incorrect. Upon Nicholas's abdication of the throne and Grand Duke Mikhail's refusal of the crown, the monarchy died a natural death. Some diaries of the war reveal that some generals at the front didn't even appear to bid him farewell at the railway station at Mogilev and other towns on the way to Gatchina. Some generals and most socially minded politicians later, (mainly Social Revolutionaries in the Samara Government) were members of the Constituent Assembly and concluded that the abdication and the overthrow of the monarchy was a final act. Although they were socialists, they believed in a constitutional and republican form of government. At first they and the military saw a need for a strong military government, but later they intended to convene the Constituent Assembly on democratic principals and had no intention of reinstating the monarchy.

The allies were dumbfounded by the Bolshevik withdrawal from the war and cancellation of their foreign debts, as announced by the Bolsheviks in February 1918. The other irritant was the Bolshevik peace treaty with Germany, signed at Brest-Litovsk, which the Allies would not recognize, although it mattered little to the Bolsheviks. Finland, formerly under Imperial occupation and now free under command of General Mannerheim, a former Russian army colonel, asked for help with their own civil war against the Finnish Bolsheviks. Meantime, the Allies made contact with anti-Bolshevik opposition to see what could be done to help them fight the Reds and in turn to get their help to secure the huge armament stores left in the ports. The Japanese landings and occupation in eastern Siberia with excessive forces was viewed by President Wilson as a danger, in view of possible creation of military bases to endanger China and the Russian Far East. President Wilson's dispatch of American troops there was meant to check any ambitions they had to establish permanent bases. In this connection, the President ordered his troops to stay absolutely neutral in the civil war and instructed them to give assistance only to the Czechs, who were in active opposition to the Bolsheviks. A substantial number of the Czechs served in the Russian army during Kerenskiy's intended offensive in the summer of 1917 against the Central Powers, which eventually fizzled.

Meanwhile, "war communism" commenced during the civil war, which deprived ordinary citizens of decent rations for food. The troops had only enough to keep them going, while the Bolsheviks ate substantially better. The entire system of war communism was based on keeping citizens opposed to the Bolsheviks under conditions of famine, which helped the Bolsheviks to maintain adequate food supplies for themselves. Upon Russia's withdrawal from the war, about forty thousand Czechs requested transfer to the western front to fight against the Central Powers. Unable to be transferred to western Europe directly, they were dispatched by way of Vladivostok, with the first contingent arriving there in May 1918. The balance of the forces following them strung out throughout the length of Siberia. The German ambassador, Count Mirbach, protested to the Bolsheviks that this was a violation of the joint agreement. However, when informed that they would be interned again as prisoners of war, they rose against the Bolsheviks. Being strung out throughout Siberia and portions of eastern Russia, they took possession of the principal urban areas from Samara to Vladivostok. Their presence was soon to ignite additional political revolt against the Bolsheviks in all Russia and Siberia.

While the Allies were involved in the northern ports and eastern Siberia and with the Czechs along the TransSiberian rail line, the German command took advantage of this confusion to occupy the southern regions of Russia. At the request of the emigre Ukrainian government, the Germans ejected remnants of the Ukrainian Bolsheviks and concluded a treaty with the new Ukrainian government for the sole purpose of exploiting its rich natural resources. As the Germans reinstalled the landowners on their estates, grain and produce began arriving in the farmers' markets until the Germans surrendered in the west, and Ukraine was recaptured by the Reds. The Germans also occupied Rostov on the Don in Russia across the border from Ukraine as well as the entire Crimea, which was a violation of their treaty with the Bolsheviks. At this time the Reds were incapable of defending all of the Russian territory. Territory controlled by the Reds had shrunk by then, when counter-revolutionary movements broke out in the south, southeast, and Siberia. In the sectors of Bolshevik control, they extended their iron rule to the rural areas, and with their confiscation of lands, grain, and produce, deliveries promptly stopped.

In order to control the rest of the country, they reorganized the entire army under Trotsky, and in mid-1918, they introduced compulsory military service, disbanding the Soldiers' Committees for which they found no further use. They established Communist cells to induct peasants and other categories into the army and introduced severe discipline and terror. In order to retrain the army, Trotskiy introduced a new element by inducting former Imperial Army line officers, most of whom were in the central part of Russia, under the control of the Reds. In fact, civil war operations against the Whites were conducted by former Imperial Army officers. The Red Army was transformed into a real fighting organization, and by the end of 1918, it was almost four hundred thousand strong.

In the first half of 1918, the Don Basin and north Caucasus were the principal areas of operations by the Whites, commanded by former Imperial generals Alexeyev and Kornilov. In the previous winter during the revolution, they had gone south to organize an army against the Bolsheviks. Alexeyev left Petrograd for the Don basin in the Winter of 1917-18, soon after the revolution began, where he organized an army under control of his friend Ataman Kaledin of the Don Cossacks. General Kornilov, who was imprisoned by Kerenskiy and escaped shortly thereafter, joined Alexeyev. The three formed a command, with Alexeyev as chief of the general staff, Kornilov as commanding general of the army, and Kaledin as head of the Don Cossacks. When the Don Cossacks refused to fight the Red Army, Kaledin committed suicide in February 1918. Without Kaledin's Cossacks, the Volunteer Army was not more than four thousand poorly equipped men. Receiving only minor funds from Moscow by clandestine means, it was forced to retreat from the Don Basin to the Kuban Valley and to the northern slopes of the Caucasian Mountains to the south.

While Alexeyev and Kornilov were building their army on the Don Basin, another group of officers, independent of the first, was building another anti-Bolshevik force behind the Red Army on the Rumanian front. In the early months of 1918, the Volunteer Army commanded by Kornilov began a drive into the

Kuban Valley to join some disaffected and isolated Cossack forces fighting the Bolsheviks. In more than a month of heavy fighting against overwhelmingly superior Red Army forces, Kornilov succeeded in joining with the Cossacks in the Kuban and decided to attack Krasnodar (Ekaterinodar), the headquarters of the Red Army in the Kuban. The first assault failed, and Alexeyev and Kornilov suspected Red forces were being led by professional officers of the former Imperial Army. Having familiarized themselves with the methods used by the Red Army forces, a second assault was scheduled shortly thereafter. Before the second assault commenced, Kornilov was killed by a random artillery shell in the rear area. General Denikin, who had not been thoroughly apprised of the situation, assumed Kornilov's command and promptly lost the battle. This forced the evacuation of Krasnodar and a retreat back to the Don Valley, where Kaledin's Cossacks, who at first refused to fight the Reds and were now disaffected with them, defeated the Reds and captured Novocherkask. This battle was successful in part because of the arrival of some elements of the loyal Russian army from the Rumanian front. Denikin extricated his small army from Krasnodar, but suffered disproportionate losses and retreated to the Don Valley to join the rest of loyal Russian army elements from the Rumanian front and the Don Cossacks. In spite of lack of coordination between the Volunteer, the Kuban, and the Don Armies, they somehow managed to clear the Bolsheviks out of the Don and Kuban areas in 1918. Denikin's army was by then about five thousand strong, vastly inferior to the Red Army, which totaled at least twenty thousand for each major battle.

However, problems cropped up and interfered in the Soviet government's intent to counterattack because of the Czechs, who were beyond the Volga and Siberia. A plan was formulated in February 1918 by White officers and the Social Revolutionary party, which had previously been excluded by the Bolsheviks from the National Assembly, to enter into an alliance with the Czechs and Ural Cossacks. These Cossaks were discontent with the Bolsheviks—the majority of whom were socialists—because of the confiscation of grain from the peasants by the Reds. A fair number of them were employees of the peasant cooperatives, and they entered into a relationship with the Czechs, who were Socialists. In this connection, a new government was formed in Samara (Kuibyshev) composed of members of the Socialist party of the Constituent Assembly under Chernov, who was president of the 1918 Assembly. Known as the Samara Government, it attempted to organize a People's Army to fight the Reds. This effort failed to materialize primarily because of the peasants' fear of Social Revolutionary agrarian policy, which they surmised to be almost similar to the Bolshevik's, whom they were fighting. The People's Army succeeded in cooperating with the Czechs and local Cossack bands in establishing a boundary between the eastern and western Russian areas, running from the Volga to the Kama Rivers. The groups soon fell apart in spite of their capture of some $317,000,000 gold reserve from the State Bank of Russia. No trace of these funds ever surfaced or was accounted for. The People's Army was soon forced to retreat before a Red Army assault.

Meantime, a conservative government named the Siberian Government was formed in Omsk in Siberia, and with the support of peasants' cooperatives, it took over command of all anti-Bolshevik forces in western Siberia, up to Lake Baikal. In September 1918 the Samara Government, which had fallen previously, united with the new Siberian government and formed a five-man Directorate, consisting mostly of Social Revolutionaries. They tried to enlist General Alexeyev to lead the armed forces. Despondent over conditions in the south, Bolshevik betrayal of the allied cause, and Allied refusal to help the Whites, General Alexeyev died—an irreparable and fatal loss for the anti-Bolshevik cause. General Alexeyev, a distinguished soldier and scholar, equally competent as a general staff officer and field commander, was one of two Russian soldiers who consistently won battles against the Central Powers. In the future civil war battles, the death of Alexeyev spelled doom to the anti-Bolshevik cause and resistance and eventual victory by the Bolsheviks.

In September-October 1918 the position of the Soviet government was anything but bright. Bolshevik control was exercised only in the central part of Russia. The rest of Russia was segmented into bits and pieces of various groupings in the Russian motherland.

In the south Ukraine was under German and Austrian occupation; the Don Valley was independent but friendly to the Germans; the Kuban was free from the Bolsheviks but opposed to Germany. The southern Ural region and western half of Siberia came under the Czech-Siberian Directorate. The western allies also controlled eastern Siberia, adjoining China and the Far Eastern Pacific Coast. When Soviet chances of winning the civil war were practically non-existent, WWI ended with the surrender of the Central Powers on 11 November 1918. The Allies found no special reasons to continue to help the Whites after the surrender of the Central Powers and made insignificant efforts to intervene in the conflict. A small British contingent from Iraq occupied Baku, on the Caspian, in late November 1918, and a month later Batum, the terminus of the TransCaucasian pipeline on the Black Sea. The French occupied Odessa with a small force but insufficient to be effective and re-embarked for home as soon as Bolshevik propaganda was directed at their troops. The surrender of the Central Powers and an Allied victory, with their subsequent and early evacuation, actually helped to speed up the Soviet government's own victory in the civil war. However, the conclusion of the war in the west created unforeseen developments in Siberia. In view of termination of hostilities, the Czechs saw no further interest in fighting the Bolsheviks, since their fight was with Austro-Hungary. It took a strong effort to coax them to guard the TransSiberian railway while the Allies tried to settle diplomatically with the Bolsheviks.

In January 1919 President Wilson issued an invitation "to every organized group that is now exercising or attempting to exercise political authority or military control in Russia" to send representatives to the Island of Prinkipo, in the Sea of Marmara. Both parties, the Whites and the Bolsheviks, were invited to attend and to discuss the future of Russia. The Bolsheviks accepted the invitation without any preconditions. In view of their precarious military situation, they had nothing to lose, and it could possibly offer them relief from their opponents on the far-flung fronts. Although the Whites were in somewhat better military position then, they could see no advantage in accepting the offer and turned it down. Had the Whites been guided by political objectives, instead of purely military ones, they may have achieved certain advantages, being in a better bargaining position in view of their military situation and being a legal government. The Whites considered the invitation degrading—to negotiate with the Bolsheviks who betrayed the Allied cause in signing peace with the Central Powers. Military chivalry had disappeared years ago, yet the Whites honored it, and it apparently played a more important part than simple logic. The Allied position under the same circumstances forgot and forgave the Bolshevik peace treaty with the Central Powers. The White military concluded that their presence at the conference was tantamount to recognition of the illegal Soviet government; therefore they could not morally agree. Thus the only possible avenue for legitimacy left to the Whites was mindlessly frittered away. It was possible with the passage of time that the Bolsheviks could have lost power, due to imposition of hunger, terror, and inhumane treatment of the population under their control—especially when compared to the Whites, who could have gained substantial refugees from Red-occupied areas, and whose behavior was somewhat more humane. With this rejection, the final outcome of the civil war in favor of the Reds was a forgone conclusion. Within a few months the desperate political situation the Reds were in changed dramatically in their favor, although they still had to subject the population to their will. The military situation of the Whites in 1919, however, was rather desperate in view of the far-flung fronts and the lack of help from the former Allies.

Eventually the Bolsheviks won the war, principally because of lack of cooperation among White armies and the absence of political and diplomatic direction and skills. Their two principal military leaders, General Denikin, commander in south Russia, and Admiral Kolchak, commander in Siberia, were guilty of non-cooperation and diplomatic skills, which they both lacked. Denikin also had problems with the Ukrainians and the Kuban Cossaks because he limited their autonomy. Here again, the same problem with political guidance and diplomatic skills was absent when precisely these attributes were needed most. The Bolsheviks were eventually able to defeat the Whites, one at a time, even though the Reds were not in the best of conditions, as events subsequently proved.

Admiral Kolchak shortly assumed the leadership of the Siberian Directorate by a coup d'etat on 18 November 1918. He was a capable naval commander but lacked the required knowledge of land battle strategy as well as diplomatic skills in dealing with the Czech contingents and Allied occupation armies. He was also unfamiliar with Siberians, who were primarily pioneers from Russia proper, and their officials who were under his command. His assumption as head of the directorate caused a split with the Social Revolutionary party, which organized a campaign against him among the peasants and Czechs. Despite these difficulties, he rushed into battle against the Reds with the Czechs and succeeded in capturing the city of Perm and then Ufa in March 1919. He chased the Reds in their headlong retreat until he was able to create an arc at Perm to Ufa, Orenburg, and Uralsk, all west of the Ural Mountains.

Because of these successes, on 26 May 1919 the Allied Supreme Council, seat-ed in Paris, informed him that they were willing to supply his government with appropriate supplies, munitions, and food to establish the government of Russia. They were willing to do so on the condition that his new government would summon the Constituent Assembly, allow free elections, disallow special privileges to any class, recognize the independence of Finland and Poland, and acknowledge the autonomous status of the Baltic States and Caucasian territories. Having done so, he was to call a peace conference to settle the question of the status of Bessarabia and Russia's membership in the League of Nations. Admiral Kolchak replied affirmatively to the proposals of the Supreme Council.

The steps taken by the Allies and Kolchak induced General Denikin to submit himself to Admiral Kolchak as the Supreme Ruler of all Russia. Having achieved this great honor, Admiral Kolchak developed a strategic plan to carry out a campaign against the Reds by supporting the Northern Army, commanded by Czech General Gaida. The original intent of the operational plan was to drive through to the British and Russian forces in Arkhangelsk, in the White Sea. In the vast stretches of Russian territories, spanning from the Baltic to the Black Sea and thence to Siberia in the Far East and the Pacific coastline—resembling wide ocean expanses where ships could maneuver almost at leisure—the Admiral felt quite optimistic with his strategy, similar to naval battles on the high seas. Despite grave warnings from Yudenich (in Estonia) and Denikin (in the south) not to advance without achieving full contact with the southern army, the admiral brushed aside such apprehensions. Based on Gaida's assurances he could achieve the plan before the Reds could be ready to counterattack his army, he ordered the advance. The strategic plan in itself made good sense; however the plan suffered from lack of contact and support of General Denikin's southern army to cover his left flank. The admiral assembled 125,000 troops, while the Reds had 110,000, mainly Siberian peasant conscripts serving under duress, with Cheka and *politruks* arresting and shooting laggards. As the attack progressed on schedule with the uncovered left flank, the Reds, sensing the admiral's error, waited for the column to open more distance and then counterattacked. Meanwhile Denikin's southern army was far too distant to affect contact and closure before the Reds closed the gap and launched a full-scale attack earlier than expected. The Reds delivered a very heavy attack precisely in the middle of the line, which achieved a separation of his forces. The Red attack was a stunning success, with heavy casualties to the Whites. The admiral's advance collapsed when the northern wing of his army realized a probable cutoff and retreated back to its starting bases.

Concurrent with the admiral's advance, Denikin's army, composed of approximately 150,000 Volunteer troops, engaged the Reds in the south and captured Kharkov, Yekatinodar (Dniepropretovsk), and Tsaritsin (Stalingrad, now Volgagrad) on the Volga. It was precisely at that time that the Reds delivered a counterattack on the admiral's forces. Freed from the battle against the admiral, they engaged Denikin's forces by a counterattack. The first encounter failed apparently because of insufficient preparation not to lose momentum. In October, the Volunteer army captured Voronezh, Orel, Kiev, and Odessa. Concurrently

General Yudenich advanced with his army from Estonia and captured Gatchina, outside Petrograd, and then launched an assault on the former capital. Fighting on several fronts simultaneously—in Siberia, south Russia, Petrograd, and even Arkhangelsk against General Miller—they took on the Whites with dogged determination and fanatical pursuit of their cause, to victory. Hunger, ration coupons, and terror in their areas actually helped them win. Against Denikin they threw over 200,000 troops and still had over 55,000 reserves. Taking advantage of their interior positions as a supply base, they pecked at his troops from all directions with no letup, until a weak point in the line collapsed, and then they threw a mass of troops to overwhelm the Whites. Casualties were heavy on both sides, with dead exceeding the wounded, and no quarter given. To save whatever was left of his army, Denikin retreated all the way to the Black Sea. Most of the Don and Kuban Cossacks retreated to the Crimea, earlier abandoning their positions at Novorosiysk. Angry and in despair over the admiral's land strategy, Denikin surrendered his command to General Baron Wrangel in Crimea.

Meanwhile, Kolchak's army was disintegrating. The promise of the Allies in June 1919 to support him in every way possible never materialized. At the same time the Social Revolutionaries—who were out of the government—incited the peasants against him which undercut all support to him. The Czechs, in control of the TransSiberian Railway, joined the Bolsheviks, and the admiral was isolated from whatever troops he had had. He was captured with the help of the Czechs and the consent of French General Janin, the plenipotentiary of the Allies to the admiral's headquarters. He was handed over to the Bolshevik Revolutionary Committee in Irkutsk, which executed him a few days later. With the arrival of Bolshevik troops and government bodies, they established themselves in Irkutsk, west of Lake Baikal, facing the Japanese on the eastern shore.

Meanwhile, the Japanese occupation troops on Lake Baikal refused to leave voluntarily by way of Vladivostok, which they had previously occupied. It took two years of fighting and acrimonious negotiations before they left all of Siberia. Upon departure of the Japanese troops, Soviet Russia became free of all foreign troops. With their evacuation, former members of Kolchak's army and their families and hundreds of thousands of Siberian refugees followed the Japanese departure and either crossed over to Manchuria or temporarily settled in Siberian Maritime provinces. Memoirs, notes, and diaries of the civil war in Russia and Siberia flooded Manchuria by the dozens, as well as subsequent writings by higher army officers, politicians, and historians. After being in power for two years, the Allies concluded that the Bolsheviks won the civil war and could not be overthrown with their small contingents and pulled out their troops. In mid-January 1920 the Allied command decided to terminate the blockade of Russia and shortly thereafter evacuated their troops from Arkhangelsk and Murmansk and withdrew.

After the defeat of anti-Bolshevik forces in Russia and Siberia, General Wrangel, still holding out in Crimea, withstood all further Red onslaughts for the time being. His astute political advisor Krivoshein instituted a new agrarian policy by prohibiting outright seizure of grain and other agricultural produce without fair market compensation. Most peasants were skeptical at first, but later they relented, when it was too late. He based his policy on fairness, hoping to gain support of the peasants in the rear areas. In June 1920 he issued a new agrarian reform, confirming the right of peasants to own their own lands. Other peasants to the north, within the Bolshevik occupied areas, never heard of the policy, while those in the Ukraine, most of whom had already appropriated the lands, were tired of unkept promises and failed to cooperate. Krivoshein advised Baron Wrangel that unless something was done soon, he feared for the outcome of the struggle and advised Wrangel to contact the Polish government to persuade it to cooperate against the Bolsheviks. Poland decided to attack the Bolsheviks to regain its former eastern territories adjoining Russia. At first they succeeded, but later the Bolsheviks turned them back and attacked on all fronts, almost reaching the gates of Warsaw. Poland, having had enough problems with the war against the Bolsheviks, advised Krivoshein that they had no interest in widening the conflict and undertaking further burdens.

The French government realized the growing military power of the Bolshevik government, and to prevent possible Bolshevization of Europe and France itself, decided to send General Maxim Weygand to Warsaw to stem the Bolshevik tide. Under Weygand's direction, the Reds were driven back almost to the edge of Minsk, in Belorussia. The Bolshevik government panicked, and fearing serious setbacks, it sued for peace and commenced negotiations for a truce, which was concluded on 12 October 1920. The peace terms for the Bolshevik's were harsh and resulted in surrender of territory almost equal to the German penetration before the armistice in November 1918. The truce caused millions of Ukrainians and Belorussians to come under Polish rule, which would later cause serious repercussions. About the same time, in August 1920, the French government recognized General Wrangel's government as the de facto government of South Russia, probably not realizing that the Bolsheviks still had sufficient power left to conduct at least one major operation.

The cessation of the war with Poland allowed the Reds to throw their full weight against Wrangel in Crimea. In November 1920 a hopeless battle was fought on the Perekop Isthmus, which connects South Russia to Crimea. General Wrangel, the only hold out against the Bolsheviks with no help from the Allies, convinced of probable slaughter, ordered the evacuation of all troops, their families, and thousands of civilians. Estimates of the evacuation range anywhere from 80,000-120,000 troops and civilians who boarded French ships and departed Bosphorus for exile from their homeland.

The Soviet counterattacks against the Poles created patriotic feelings among the Russians, and they even secured the cooperation of its opponents among the Whites. The great proponent of this cooperation was none other than General Brusilov, who had recently resigned from command of the Russian army, the victor of several engagements against the Austro- Hungarian armies. Brusilov volunteered, by urging former Imperial army officers to join and fight the Poles and Wrangel's army. After the Bolshevik victory in Crimea, they dumped Brusilov as useless prerevolutionary garbage.

The Russian civil war was over, and a new chapter in Russian history commenced. The peculiarities of the war make it difficult to assign specific faults to the Whites in general. However, certain incidents and conditions are known to have caused their defeat. The relocation of the Soviet government to Moscow, as the capital and centrally located administrative point of the government, was not at first anticipated as a center for the civil war. Having established themselves there, it turned out to be the most critical decision the Bolsheviks made. This decision sent the opposition Whites to the periphery of the borders, splitting the White forces from direct contact with each other. The Whites could have profited immensely if they had been fully supplied by the Allies and politically guided. The Allies helped very little—only retrieving their own military supplies and some other help usually of token significance—thus seriously weakening the position of the Whites. The separated White army groups had little, if any, direct coordination among each other, allowing the Reds to fight them from the center, mostly on their own terms. Additionally, their late entry into the war was a serious handicap. Their program to the nation was never clearly defined, and even if it had been, it would have been too complex in view of diverse opinions among various parties who couldn't agree among themselves. This, added to lack of political direction, made it adversely decisive in the loss of the civil war.

The Reds, on the other hand, appealed to the masses in a simple program, promising everything to anyone who had nothing. The masses, being poor lower class, had little choice and decided to throw in their lot with the Bolshevik platform. This didn't necessarily mean all the people in the lower classes were simpletons. The Bolsheviks propaganda told them that the new Russia was for them and that they should expropriate from the expropriators. Since life was harsh, they believed them. The fact is, however, that industrial workers were the primary beneficiaries, and the peasants who worked on the land belonging to the government were ruled out as recipients. The agricultural question was purposely never clearly defined, but carefully crafted, and couched in double-talk, and never questioned until later. After all, "The Soviet of Workers', Soldiers', and Peasants' Deputies" implied and included the peasants.

The ration cards and terror used in the civil war actually helped the Bolsheviks win. Hunger is devastating to rich or poor alike, and when applied with terror, is an unmatched combination. Research of memoirs, diaries, and notes in Berlin, Paris and Harbin, Manchuria confirm that the above conclusions apply to campaigns in both Russia proper and Siberia. The notes on campaigns in Russia proper are mainly cryptic in terse military form, except for private notes of some staff officers, which are more illuminating than memoirs and diaries. Siberian campaigns described in diaries and private notes reveal astonishing details by staff officers, journalists, and former government clerks. Private notes include incidents of Japanese battle encounters with Red troops, their withdrawal to Vladivostok, and some two thousand stragglers, who were cut off and strung out in the rear, marching along the TransSiberian tracks. With no weapons or food, they were stripped naked and forced to march back into captivity. The few stragglers who survived the ordeal after their troops withdrew from

Vladivostok showed marks from beatings and torture. After years in captivity these men wouldn't return to Japan for fear of shame and settled among the Chinese, Korean, and Mongol-Buryats in fishing villages in the Maritime Provinces. These notes also recount American and Italian contingents leaving Vladivostok at daybreak, loaded with food and weapons, with Russians on the docks pleading to take them aboard. Generally in White-occupied areas, since no civil government or administration existed, this left the generals in complete command, as an army of occupation in a foreign land.

There may have been other reasons for the loss of the war. Lacking objective analysis in memoirs and diaries of the White generals, one is forced to read Bolshevik literature on the subject for comparison. The Soviet versions were written and rewritten several times to suit Stalin's trumped up inventions for historical reasons. One must balance Soviet versions with available material, personal encounters of White participants, many foreign representatives who were present as witnesses on both sides, and subsequent Western writers in the war in order to properly judge. Officially the Bolshevik government was a dictatorship of the proletariat, in whose behalf they seized the government; it was therefore the proletariat who ruled the country. To further elucidate the point, they organized hundreds of meetings among industrial workers. When questioned, "Why there were no representatives of the proletariat in the government," the answer would come back in Maxist dialectics something like this: "Because if there were, we could not select millions of proletarians to run the government, and there could be no dictatorship. Therefore a small tight group with a mission should run the government for your benefit."

**War Communism**

During the civil war, the Bolshevik areas were transformed into a military camp, and they had to face objective realities of war with an alienated population. Abandoning all pretense to theoretical concepts, they instituted "War Communism." This concept was first expounded as an ideal communist society and was adopted in March 1919. Among other things, it proposed improvements in the lifestyles of women, children, peasants, workers, students, the sick, and non-Russians. Women were to be liberated and relieved of household chores. They never went into any details about who was to cook, clean house, and care for the children. Schools were to be free and transformed from an instrument of class domination of the bourgeoisie into a different instrument, while reworking society into communism. It proposed free adult education in native languages for non-Russians and financial aid to university students. It graciously offered to liberate the masses from religious superstition, to introduce planning in the economy, and to help peasants with all the required knowledge in increasing agricultural yields. Additionally, the Bolsheviks promised to abolish child labor, to improve the housing situation, and to enforce improved standards of working conditions. It also approved new free health clinics. Economic conditions were to be drastically improved, when compared to the Imperial regime. They officially annulled all foreign debts, nationalized all banks, placed industries under worker review and control, and nationalized nearly everything else. Although these objectives were certainly laudatory, it was the means used and the experiments conducted which eventually turned Russia into a prison camp.

After the end of the civil war, the country was devastated with millions dead and wounded, and many families broken up. Many hundreds of thousands were missing and presumed dead. Famine was widespread, with people roaming the streets dazed; some went insane from hunger; others were homeless, roaming the countryside searching for their families. Memoirs, diaries, photographs, and notes flooded the eastern territories of Siberia and eventually found their way to Manchuria. Lenin had to feed millions more people in the former White-occupied areas in addition to those already under his control. Under War Communism, special control of food rations was maintained until conditions became so unbearable that millions more died of hunger. The drought in 1920-21 heaped further misery on the population.

Charitable societies, principally from America, fed starving millions to the disgrace of the Communist government. Permission was granted to feed the hungry under conditions unacceptable to charitable organizations, and it took weeks to convince them that human relief was their only objective. Agreement was finally reached, with the Bolsheviks making a terse comment, "food could be a weapon." While Herbert Hoover was in charge of food distribution, he informed the Communists that not only did they need help, but they also needed soup kitchens. The death toll would have undoubtedly been higher had it not been for the American Relief Administration, which supplied nearly $200,000,000 in food alone, a huge sum considering the time and place. The American Red Cross furnished $8,000,000 in medical supplies, while the U.S. Army furnished blankets, tents, and other needed supplies. Some 10,500,000 adults and children were fed. No thanks were ever received for this help, nor do the Russians officially know about it to this day.

Only when the lower classes and factory workers couldn't take it any more—and production slowed to a trickle, unemployment soared to record heights, and absenteeism became common-only then did these problems get the attention of the Communist government. Outbreaks among the sailors of the Kronstadt Naval Base broke out; they had previously been the main supporters of the revolution. They called upon the government to keep their promises, permitting peasants to own land and sell their produce on the open market. This rebellion was put down by execution of all those taking part. Only then did Lenin finally acknowledge that he had the Russians under his total control. The experiments with human beings continued until the Bolsheviks themselves were affected. Although some illicit food trade was practiced in the urban areas—apparently by those who still had rubles to spend—it was meager by any normal standards.

**New Economic Policy**

Lenin was finally convinced that a counterrevolution could commence and his government could be overthrown by those over whom he would have no control. To this end, he convened the Tenth Congress of the Communist party in

March 1921 and declared, "We are in condition of such poverty, ruin, and exhaustion of the productive powers of workers and peasants that everything must be set aside to increase production." Translated, it meant, "Communism isn't working, at least in the agricultural sector, so let's call it quits and restart it another time." Again, as on previous occasions, the turnabout on utopian politics took place by a simple solution of free agricultural economy, a system practiced from time immemorial, which he had originally condemned as capitalist exploitation. In so doing, he reinvented socialism in a free economic mode previously demanded by other socialist parties. He liked the results and invented a term for this turnaround, "state cooperative socialism." Regardless of the name, it was pure free enterprise. In July 1921, a decree was published permitting free economy in agriculture, light industry, and internal trade, with not more than five employees in each enterprise. Foreign trade however, remained a government monopoly.

It was in the period between Lenin's convalescence and death (1921-27) when the Bolsheviks finally created political and governmental structures. In recalling the Bolshevik slogan, "All power to the Soviets" in 1917, they undertook to substitute Soviets for the Constituent Assembly, which was to exercise power as the legislative assembly. The Third Congress of the Communist party officially confirmed the principle of the "Government of the Council of People's Commissars." Until the formation of the constitution at the Fifth Congress of Soviets in July 1918, they never bothered to define or outline the political structure of the state. In accordance with the adopted constitution, the highest executive power was vested in the All Russian Congress of Soviets. In reality it was nothing more than window dressing to conform to the party's constitutional legality without bothering to ask the people. Actually it was the Council of People's Commissars (cabinet) which wielded all the power through its Politburo. This system subsequently was adopted in the other Soviet socialist republics in December 1922, and a few months later a new constitution of the Union of the Soviet Socialist Republics was passed. In effect the constitution officially adopted dictatorship of the proletariat, which eliminated all opposition. If it was a dictatorship of the proletariat, how many proletarians were consulted in this dictatorship? Not one. In fact to insure compliance, the Cheka (secret police) was renamed OGPU and monitored the show of hands during balloting.

After War Communism, the New Economic Policy was a rude awakening for the intellectual elite of the party. Why then was the policy adopted? As abhorrent as it was to the party's elite, it saved the Communist party and its dictatorship from collapse. Lenin saved his regime, and condemned millions of people to communist experiments. To impose a dictatorial state-controlled system never before tried and call it scientific was tantamount to having a laboratory of 150,000,000 human beings, and treating them subsequently as mere guinea pigs and asking them to perform impossible tricks. This deceit was carried over by every leader of the Communist party until the dissolution of the Soviet Union and its empire in December 1991. Since the dissolution, former Communist diehards throughout the world as well as in present-day Russia became known as the "Democratic Left"—another falsehood to be watched by democracies. The reader must wonder why the Russians permitted this to happen. There is no simple answer. For one thing, their entire history was based on an autocratic *vozhd* (ruler), even in the Imperial period. Although the czars and emperors were autocrats, the economy and lifestyles were free, and the population went about its life and business under normally accepted standards, paying little attention to government, which affected them little, if at all. The only exclusion was the overthrow of the Imperial regime. There was some quasidemocracy under the First Provisional Government when the nation was at war, which lasted a few months until the Bolsheviks overthrew it. Even this changed little under the Bolsheviks, and every citizen was adversely affected, with rules fit for blind automata similar to George Orwell's description in 1984—who correctly perceived Soviet dictatorship for what it was. No wonder they had no economists among them in creating utopian economic dribble. The only one who had any inkling of economics was Nikolai Bukharin, and that was based on Marx and Engels readings—which was an anachronism and didn't apply. Yet Lenin kept on experimenting.

The next step was to turn on the peasants and agricultural lands, which the Communists considered to be state property, to be run and administered by the state. They considered the peasants as workers on government land and not independent. Regardless of the pretense, that peasants had rights to landed estates, which the Bolsheviks had promised them to win their support prior to the November Bolshevik takeover. Taking advantage of War Communism, they quickly ended those rights in mid-April 1918. Not fully cognizant of the meaning of the new program, the peasants at first believed that it affected state and landlord rights. When the government applied the new law to them, it met serious resistance. The government's intent was to gather them into massive collective farms, but they refused to join. Additionally, the government arbitrarily applied a new demand on the peasants by forcing fixed low prices on their produce. When the two sides couldn't agree, the government confiscated their entire produce.

The result was a decree on grain monopoly in May 1918. The government encouraged the poor peasants to go after the rich and confiscate their lands and produce. This decree also permitted the government to use armed force for compliance. In August 1918 it organized food requisition bands to force peasants to sell at fixed prices and, in case of refusal, to use armed force. The peasants reacted in many ways, but most prominently by killing the officials responsible for collections. When these measures didn't work, the peasants planted only enough to feed themselves. This stand-off reduced the sowed area throughout the country to an unbearable subsistence level and lead to the great famine of 1920-22. All these Communist experiments were so utopian that even the workers rebelled. Overworked and underpaid, they resorted to absenteeism and later went on strike. In this period of crisis in agriculture and industrial production, the country was also experiencing a civil war; it never occurred to the Communists that human beings could only bear so much deprivation.

The banking system, as such, was eliminated, and a "People's Bank" was established in 1918. After going through various exercises by amateur Bolshevik economists, it was absorbed into the the Budget Accounting Department. Those who had been private bankers before the revolution left their jobs or escaped the country. Money was reinstituted as the medium of exchange, and the printing presses ran twenty-four hours a day, resulting in rapid inflation never before evidenced in any country at that time. Some measure of the magnitude of inflation may best be illustrated by the following figure: in the beginning of 1918 one dollar was equal to 8.59 rubles, and in 1920 it was equal to 1,200 rubles. When they destroyed the sensitive balance between market exchange and trade, the economy under War Communism collapsed. To resurrect it, a new system of production and distribution was installed, similar to bartering. In transforming the economy, no heed was paid to the delicate balance of supply and demand, in addition to destroying economic incentives which had existed under the Imperial regime. Any product depended on the various categories of consumers with ration coupons, with privileged Bolshevik members having first choice.

With the removal of labor incentives, the government applied force to worker and peasant alike. In 1920 the Decree of Compulsory Labor was confirmed into law. The cooperative societies also came under the same decree, and the country began experiencing more experiments. Translated, it meant, "we'll whip you into shape to make you eat." During this period millions of citizens roamed the countryside in search of food, shelter, and escape. Life was no longer sacred; thousands committed suicide, and many more thousands escaped into exile. Those in the western part of Russia—who were out of reach of the Bolsheviks—escaped to Europe, mostly through Finland or Black Sea ports. Most others fled to Siberia and its Maritime Provinces. Siberian borders were not as densely guarded as those of the Bolshevik-occupied area in Russia proper. Vast refugee throngs crossed over at any point of the twelve-to sixteen-hundred-mile border adjoining Manchuria and Mongolia. Some escaped to search for Kolchak-occupied areas to fight the Bolsheviks, and some left for the vast stretches of Siberian hinterlands to lose themselves forever. Other refugees joined thousands who worked on the TransSiberian Railroad connection to Chinese Eastern Railway in Manchuria—who had previously escaped the revolution in the first exodus after February 1918.

Between December 1920 and January 1921, discontentment rose to a level never before experienced under War Communism, when agricultural production was down to almost 50 percent of prewar levels, which occurred about the same time as the end of the civil war. Bad climatic conditions contributed to the problem, along with the demobilization of army veterans, who were so distressed upon return to their villages that they actually joined rebel forces against the regime. These convulsions also spread to urban areas and affected them even more. On 2 March 1921, sailors at the Kronstadt Naval Base defied and rebelled against the inhumane and arbitrary government rules. Through their Provisional Revolutionary Committee, they called for new elections of the Soviets by secret ballot, promising the peasants control of the lands and produce. Additionally, they demanded freedom of the press and speech, free assembly of workers and parties representing them previously, release of all political prisoners, abolition of the privileged status of the Communist party, and an end to food-rationing privileges. Unprepared for the uprising, Lenin demanded their immediate surrender. When they refused to surrender, he ordered loyal forces to storm the base on 18 March, and they then surrendered. As a peace gesture, they executed almost 1,500 sailors.

This execution caused a serious discussion among Politburo members, who refused to surrender power. Henceforth, it appeared that this sunk deep in Lenin's brain, and he conceded to his colleagues that War Communism didn't work and another solution had to be found, yet he would not surrender his power under any conditions. Cheka or its successor, the GPU (KGB), was always present and ever watchful. Ordinary citizens were continually checked for passports and work status, lest they were anti-revolutionaries. The government provided power and steam at reasonable prices. Most homes were occupied by party functionaries, but not all. The author's family lived in Dr. Nikitin's house; he was employed at the government hospital, and before the revolution he had his own practice. School propaganda never ceased praising the regime or Father Lenin, the genius. Books were rewritten to suit Communist ideology and to slander the church, since God never existed.

These relatively simple conditions of life existed until an announcement on the cold day of 24 January 1924 that Lenin had died. All schoolchildren were required to attend a mock funeral procession, after which warm milk was served. Not much changed till 1927, when life gradually became strangely unpleasant, due to unannounced searches that were made in homes for jewelry, excess money, and documentary proof of no involvement in the civil war on the side of the White Guards. Passports stating reasons and purpose were required to leave or vacate one's place of residence or to go out of town, and upon return one had to report to the GPU headquarters. (While this had also been a requirement under the czarist regime, ordinary citizens had nothing to fear from it.) No exit visas were issued to leave the country under any circumstances. School lunches became austere; prices on most products began rising, and some produce was unavailable. At least one police officer was posted at every street intersection. Children were interrogated in school or homes about their parents' work habits and what they did after work hours. House searches on most occasions were made after midnight, rousing both parents and children. Some people were hauled away with no reasons given. Fear among ordinary citizens increased as conditions became steadily worse, with some people being stopped on the streets and randomly arrested, never to be heard from again. There was no one to complain to, other than the GPU, which eventually became dangerous since anyone could be branded a bourgeoisie or counterrevolutionary.

Dr. Nikitin's house was confiscated, and shortly thereafter we never saw him, his wife, or his two children again, although we lived in the house until fleeing the country. One night after midnight, the GPU knocked on the door, arrested my father, and hauled him away. It took Mother a couple of weeks to find out that he was in the hospital and to get him—since the hospital was overcrowded and definitely not a vacation place. He had been beaten with sandbags to reveal anything he might know about Dr. Nikitin. Convinced that he didn't know anything, they released him with a warning that he may be a guest in the hospital again if he didn't cooperate. It became gradually apparent that they were after the former troops of the White and Kolchak armies, the bourgeoisie, those formerly self-employed, professional people, teachers, and former members of the bureaucracy in Russia proper and Siberia. Practically everyone was suspect. Suddenly friends of the family disappeared overnight without a trace and were never heard from again.

On some occasions, far eastern *Pravda* would announce arrests were made of saboteurs, counterrevolutionaries, and White Guards. These announcements were signed by the Central Committee and the secretary of the Communist party. Prior to these events, rumors spread that Stalin was in Siberia on an inspection trip and that Trotskiy was imprisoned in Alma-Ata. Life was becoming dangerous, and people were desperate to leave the country. Gradually, people became aware of possessing "excess money" (which was illegal), disguised as bribery, with hundreds volunteering to donate it to the party and then disappearing from the country. There were however some rigid diehards within the party structure who would not accept it, and extreme care was exercised in soliciting those for hire.

The call to appear before the Central Registration Commissariat prompted my father to take the fateful step that same night to escape. That cold winter night we left the house in a peasant's horse-drawn coach and drove to the shore of the ice-covered Amur River adjoining Lake Khanka. The peasant gave us directions to another peasant's house, a fisherman who would take us in his sleigh to the other shore by a circuitous route. Avoiding all roads, where the GPU stationed its guards, we finally reached the lake shore by walking to freedom in Manchuria. This trek was traveled by thousands months before and after us, until Soviet border troops were posted along the border in bunkers a few kilometers apart.

## Recommended Reading

Deutscher, Isaac. *The Prophet Unarmed: Trotsky, 1921-1929.* New York: Oxford University Press, 1954.
Florinskiy, Michael T. *The End of the Russian Empire.* New Haven: Yale University Press.
Kennan, George F. *Decision to Intervene.* Princeton: Princeton University Press, 1958.
Kerenskiy, Alexandar. *The Catastrophe.* New York: Appleton-Century-Crofts, 1929.
Pares, Bernard. *The Fall of the Russian Monarchy.* New York: Alfred Knopf, 1939.

# CHAPTER VII
# THE EMIGRES

Confusion prevailed in the country and the headquarters of the army command after the abdication of Czar Nicholas II in March 1917 and the refusal of Grand Duke Mikhail to assume the crown unless the Constituent Assembly requested it. Since the Assembly was to be called in February 1918, the time required to assume the crown would have taken too long. It might have even been the grand duke's desire not to assume the crown.

Various groups were screaming for both cessation of hostilities and elimination of czardom, while others were advocating continuation of the war, feeling honor-bound to the Allies. The First Provisional Government, under Prime Minister Alexander Kerenskiy, tried to persevere and continue the war to honor its obligations to the Allies. Hunger and labor strikes broke out, with the government unable to control the chaos. The Bolsheviks under Lenin forcefully assumed leadership of the government before the Constituent Assembly was called back into session in February 1918 to select a new government from among the various parties. In the meantime, all the parties agreed that the Constituent Assembly would reconvene for elections previously scheduled by the Provisional Government.

Lenin knew the Bolsheviks could not get a majority and would have to hand over the government to less radical parties of the Soviet. To preempt this, he seized the reins of government by intimidation with verbal and physical threats. The legislators were not sure when they left the Assembly if they would ever reach their homes alive. The reader should bear in mind that the majority of the Duma went along with the elimination of czardom, although some opposed it. On 20 January the Central Executive Committee of the Soviet (all left wing parties) issued an order disbanding the Assembly. Kerenskiy was blamed for encouraging the army to continue the war against the Central Powers. The Bolshevik wing of the Soviet demanded a complete cessation of all hostilities and a proclamation of peace at any price. The commander of the Russian army, General Dukhonin, was ordered by Lenin to stop all operations on all fronts; when he refused, claiming it was a political decision, he was tortured and killed on the spot and replaced by an epileptic Second Lieutenant. The resulting peace treaty with Germany was harsh, depriving western Russia of tremendous territory, natural resources, and population.

Opposition to the high-handed tactics of the Bolshevik government was mounting. There was also opposition to the peace treaty, which presented the

Bolsheviks with another crisis. Afraid of losing, Lenin immediately proclaimed socialism and eliminated all other parties in the National Assembly. The Bolsheviks—holding Moscow, Petrograd, and other central territories—prevented the west and east areas held by the Whites from uniting. This precipitated the civil war, which subsequently led to the defeat of the Whites. By the time the civil war ended, literally millions of people roamed the country for safety and food, neither of which was available. Thousands committed suicide and others decided to flee anywhere they could, depending on their location. Generally, the emigres were divided into two groups: western and eastern. Since the central location of the Bolshevik areas was around Moscow spreading out to the north and south, this essentially and effectively cut Russia in half. Those in central and western Russia crossed the borders to Finland, Poland, and the Baltic countries, while those in the east escaped to eastern Siberia to hide from the Bolshevik squads.

**Western Emigres**

The civil war in western Russia lasted until the last remnants of the White Army under General Baron Wrangel were evacuated by French warships from Crimea to exile in western Europe. Meanwhile, in the east, Admiral Kolchak in Siberia was still holding out with his army a bit longer until final defeat.

By the end of the civil war, Russia was devastated, exhausted, splintered, and starving. After the dissolution of the Constituent Assembly in February 1918 and the confinement of the Imperial family and its entourage in Siberia, the plight of royalty, nobility, and generally the upper and middle classes was one of uncertainty and extreme hazard. Even the professional classes, whom the Bolsheviks needed most, were frowned upon and found themselves isolated from the rest of the workers who had worked for them previously. After termination of hostilities with Germany, those in western Russia fled to Finland, Germany, the Baltic states, or other nearby countries. Others not so lucky were stranded and hunted down by Bolshevik squads. The Imperial family was confined incommunicado in its retreat, at first in Czarskoye Selo, an Imperial village retreat a few miles outside Petrograd, uninformed about what was happening in the country and the whereabouts of their relatives.

Meanwhile, the talk of exiling the czar and his family to England by way of Murmansk on the White Sea promised by the Provisional Government came to nothing. The British prime minister, Lloyd George, refused them permission for domicile after months of waiting. The secret intent of the Bolsheviks was to execute the Imperial family at the appropriate time and to leave no traces of martyrdom. There was vicious denunciation by the Soviet left against them leaving the country. Despite Kerenskiy's promise, Lenin issued orders for the family to leave for Tobolsk in Siberia, where they arrived 19 August 1917. The town had a population of twenty thousand. They lived a few months in the governor's house until they were hurriedly relocated west to Ekatirenburg. When Admiral Kolchak's forces were advancing in the area, the local Soviet panicked and asked for directions from Moscow. The reply came to murder the royal family there, having little time to evacuate further west. So the czar and his family were executed in

Ekatirenburg 16 July 1918. Even the czar's entourage was marked for execution—including foreign tutors, a doctor, and other attendants to the family. The town was renamed Sverdlovsk by Stalin in honor of the man who carried out the order to assassinate the entire Imperial family. (Incidentally, Francis Gary Powers was shot down in his U-2 over Sverdlovsk in May 1960. The town now is a highly polluted area with a population of over one million. In 1993 and thereafter, some of their remains were located and submitted for a DNA test in Britain in 1993 and subsequently in Washington in 1995, which confirmed the identity.) Rumors spread of the Imperial family's murder.

Bolshevik control within the country was not yet consolidated, and the civil war was spreading. The czar's relatives, princes, nobles, wealthy merchants, and many others began scrambling to leave the country. Having close contacts in western Europe and with the borders closed, escape became a question of money to gain freedom, and thousands gladly paid to leave. Lenin's orders were quite precise with respect to which people were to be incarcerated and disposed of later. In most cases those wanted were in Bolshevik territory, those outside Bolshevik control faired better. With Admiral Kolchak's army still fighting, most of the relatives of the czar escaped. Since Kolchak was still fighting in Siberia, many merchants, professional classes, intellectuals, and ordinary citizens were able to escape by way of southern and eastern Russia to Manchuria. Some White Army units from south Russia also joined Kolchak, but most people bypassed his headquarters in Omsk and went farther east to Irkutsk, Khabarovsk, and Vladivostok on the Pacific coast.

When Kolchack's army was beaten, the admiral was unexpectedly caught and executed. The remnants of the White Army, along with some civilians, left the country during the Japanese occupation of eastern Siberia. As the Japanese evacuated for home in 1922, some emigres, still stranded in eastern Siberia, followed them and entered Manchuria. The eastern emigrants found it a friendly haven and stayed there for many years until circumstances changed. The Russian population in Manchuria prior to the revolution was approximately 375,000. They were mostly railworkers, administrators, bookkeepers, teachers, engineers, and shopkeepers. The rest of the population was comprised of merchants and small business people supplying their needs. By the end of 1927, when Stalin closed and reinforced the borders permanently, the exodus amounted to approximately 4,500,000.

The majority of people arriving in Manchuria during the civil war period were middle-class professionals—lawyers, doctors, former military officers, teachers, professors, intellectuals, artists, and other literary figures—along with rail workers, merchants, landowners, farmers, and tradesmen. Finding no future in revolutionary Russia, they settled in Manchuria among their compatriots who had already resided there for years. At the time Manchuria was a fief of Chinese warlords, and among the most powerful was Chan-Tso-Lin, who looked forward to Russian veterans enrolling in his army, as well as expanding his civil service and economy. Trade and most professions were also staffed by the newcomers.

Dowager Empress Marie Feodorovna, the former Princess Dagmar of

Denmark and mother of the czar, was in Crimea at the time. As the Red Army approached, she left aboard a British battleship at the insistence of her sister, Queen Alexandra of Britain, the mother of George V of Britain. Refusing to believe that her son and his family were murdered, she was carried reluctantly aboard. Returning to her native Denmark, she lived in a wing of the royal palace of her nephew, King Christian X.

Meantime, false rumors persisted of her seeing various "Anastasia" pretenders; records indicate she never saw any of them. Her younger daughter, Olga, did see them and pronounced them all pretenders. The dowager empress lived unhappily in the king's palace with her miserly nephew and died there in October 1928 at the age of eighty-one. She was beloved by European royalty and aristocracy, as well as Russian emigres the world over, as the gay Danish princess, wife of Alexander III and mother of Nicholas II. Her daughters, Grand Duchesses Xenia and Olga, sisters of Nicholas II, also left Crimea in British ships. Xenia went to England and lived in a manorial house in London provided by the British royal family. She lived there happily with her husband, Grand Duke Alexander, until he died in 1933; she followed him in 1960 at age eighty-five. Grand Duchess Olga never married and lived quietly in Denmark with her mother until October 1928 when her mother, the czarina, died; she then moved to a small farm near Toronto, Canada. She lived there in obscurity until Queen Elizabeth and Prince Philip invited her to lunch in 1959 on their yacht Britannia, surprising her neighbors and Canadian society. She died in November 1960, at age seventy-five, six months after the death of her sister Xenia.

Grand Duke Nicholas, an uncle of the czar and the former commander of the Russian army fighting the Central Powers until Nicholas II took over, also boarded the battleship with the dowager empress, but he went to live in Antibes in southern France where he had a villa, having no wish to burden his sister-in-law whom he greatly admired. He died in 1929, and his funeral was attended by all the Allied commanders of WWI. Another grand duke, Cyril, who was the eldest son of Vladimir, a brother of Alexander III and an uncle to Nicholas II, escaped by clandestine means and settled in Brittany, France. In 1924 he proclaimed himself "Czar of All the Russias." To consolidate his claim to the vacant throne, he visited Paris in 1930 and held a military parade before some former Imperial officers. His claim was not recognized by the dowager empress. He died in Paris in 1938 at age sixty-two. Cyril's son, Vladimir, lived in Madrid and was considered head of the Romanov dynasty since Nicholas II had left no heir.

Grand Duke Dmitry, the youngest grandson of Alexander III and cousin to Nicholas II, was another claimant to the vacant throne. He participated in the murder of Rasputin in 1916, along with Prince Yusupov, and was ordered by Nicholas to report for duty with troops in Persia as punishment, thus escaping execution by the Bolsheviks. He married an American heiress in Biarritz, France in 1926 and died of tuberculosis in 1941 at age fifty in Davos, Switzerland. Prince Felix Yousupov—husband of Irina, daughter of Grand Duchess Xenia, and the actual killer of Rasputin—escaped with his wife and his art to Paris. He was a scion of the wealthiest family in Russia and Europe, helping newly arrived emigres financially.

Many nobles were executed when caught by Bolshevik thugs. Countess Hendrikov, lady-in-waiting to the czarina; Mlle. Schneider, the governess to the czar's daughters; Dr. Botkin; and all officials and servants who shared captivity with the royal family in Czarskoye Selo and later in Tobolsk, were executed in Siberia in 1918. Baroness Buxhoeveden, another lady-in-waiting, and Sydney Gibbs, the English tutor to the children, escaped by crossing Siberia before the execution of the Imperial family and reached England safely. Pierre Gilliard, the French tutor, and his Russian wife escaped to spend three years in Siberia. They embarked from Japan for their home in Lausanne, Switzerland. He kept a diary of his service to the royal family and became a professor of French language in Geneva and died in 1962.

The minister of the interior, Goremikin, age eighty-five, was strangled in St. Petersburg by a Bolshevik mob in 1918. The ministers of the Provisional Government—Alexander Kerenskiy; Prince Lvov, the prime minister of the first Provisional Government; Pavel Miluikov, the foreign minister and historian; and Guchkov, the war minister—went to France where they were active in anti-Bolshevik circles. Kokovtsov, the former prime minister and later finance minister, and Sazonov, the foreign minister, also escaped to France; while the president of the Duma Assembly, Rodzianko, escaped to Crimea and died in Belgrade in 1924. Anna Vyrubova, personal secretary and an intimate friend of the czarina, was imprisoned several times but finally escaped to Finland in 1920. She lived there for forty-four years and died in 1964 at the age of eighty. The two marshals of the court to the czar, Counts Benkendorff and Frederichs, left separately. Benkendorff wanted to escape but waited until he confirmed the disappearance of his stepson, Prince Dolgorukiy, and the murder of the Imperial family. He was held up on the Estonian border by visa problems and died in a bordertown makeshift hospital in 1921. Frederichs, of Finnish descent, lived for a while in Petrograd, and while he was there, he wore his resplendent court uniform for spite on his walks on Nevskiy Prospekt. Later he was permitted to return to his native Finland and died there in 1922, in despair after losing his family, the czar, and his dear friend Benkendorff.

For unknown reasons, only a few senior generals left Russia. General Sukhomlinov, the war minister, fled the country to Finland. General Alexeyev, the most competent chief of the general staff and later commander of the White troops in south Russia, died of natural causes in the field. General Kornilov was killed earlier by a random artillery shell while fighting the Reds. General Denikin, who commanded White army troops in the south and could have succeeded in winning the war had he been politically advised, left his command in Crimea to General Baron Wrangel. After the civil war, Denikin lived in Europe and later came to visit his daughter in Detroit. General Baron Wrangel, who succeeded Denikin as commander in Crimea, was evacuated by Allied warships to Istanbul for western europe and died of exhaustion in Brussels in 1921, helping his veterans resettle.

World-renowned scientist Peter Kapitsa went to England and returned to the

Soviet Union in 1935 to visit relatives and was forbidden to return to England. Among those who escaped after the revolution was prima ballerina Mathilde Kschssinskaya, who married Grand Duke Andrey, cousin to Nicholas II. She opened a ballet studio in Paris and aspiring ballet dancers the world over came knocking on her door for acceptance. She danced in the Paris Opera House at age sixty-three, still active in her studio at ninety-two, and died shortly thereafter.

Some relatives of the czar and the high nobility who were tied by funds or kinship to their European cousins, did rather well in exile. Some relatives of the czarina in Russia of the German house of Hesse-Darmstadt escaped to Germany and rejoined their relatives there. Wealthy merchants, big landowners, and bankers with connections in Europe also did well there, particularly in Switzerland, France, Berlin, and London. Most other emigres who escaped to Europe left their fortunes in Russia; however, a few had huge fortunes in Swiss, London, Paris, and Berlin banks. Others, in escaping Russia to Europe, had no base upon which to build. There were some exceptions, which included outstanding members of the Petrograd Academy of Sciences who managed to be accepted in various higher scientific institutions. In general, the Russian emigres in Europe never fared as well as their compatriots in China. Those without fortunes were forced to drive taxi cabs, become waiters, or work at menial jobs—mostly in Paris. Having no training or talents, they eventually died and left no trace of their existence.

Later, when it was still possible to escape, western emigres again flocked to Paris. French language and the arts were very popular among higher social circles and artists. This attraction for everything French was further cultivated by court circles when Faberge was invited to be the main couturier, jeweler, and perfume supplier to the court. The French ambassador, Maurice Paleologue, was constantly invited to the czar's court and took every opportunity to advance the cause of French goods, artistic achievements, etiquette, cuisine, and manners. After all, ballet came to Russia from France, and Russian ballet dancers were world-renowned, surpassing any of the French, or so the saying goes.

The mass exodus from Russia during the revolution began a chapter in history of "displaced persons" escaping from the land of their origins by the millions, unequaled anywhere, even during the French Revolution when royal and noble exiles left France, mostly for Germany.

These upheavals were originally stirred up by Russian social intellectuals and anarchists who had been in contact with European liberal ideas since 1825. In Russia, however, when revolutionary movements were springing up the intellectuals lost control to the extremists, largely because of their divergent theories and their debates instead of action, thereby forfeiting their rights to lead. They were eventually eliminated by the Bolsheviks as useless garbage and replaced by power-hungry and vengeful Bolshevik thugs and workers who understood nothing of the liberal ideas preached by these intellectuals.

In 1944 during the liberation of Paris on 25 August, the author met some Russian emigres at the Russian Center they had escaped in 1918-22 from Soviet Russia. These were people who worked for a living in various enterprises and described their existence as quite tolerable. They lived huddled in one bedroom apartments with children who spoke only French and displayed no interest in the Russian language or in Russia itself. They congregated at the Russian Center, as a place of the homeless and lonely exiles from their homeland. They were employed as teachers, librarians, writers, social workers, small business owners, and just plain workers. Some were veterans of the French army who were demobilized after the German occupation in WWII. Although they were enjoying French democracy, they never felt at home in their new domicile. They spoke of life by wealthy Russians, who cared little about their own people, enjoying life in French high society, even under German occupation. Even under autocratic and dictatorial rulers for over a thousand years of Russian history, they hungered for a free Russian homeland. The Russian "soul" draws them to their homeland, and that longing never leaves them, wherever they may be in the diaspora.

**Eastern Emigres**

While Admiral Kolchak was fighting the Red Army in Siberia, many Russians fled east to Siberia to escape the Reds. When the Admiral was defeated and executed by the Reds, these people crossed the Manchurian border into China, comprising the largest concentration of emigres in the world up to that time.

The feeling and the environment of the Russian emigres escaping by way of Siberia was substantially different from those in the west. The difference seemed to be in the environment. The newcomers melded into a substantial Russian colony which had been established in Manchuria years before Russian language, newspapers, customs, traditions, and churches existed. All the assets to which they were accustomed by tradition were in place, including the climate, which was similar to Siberia and the Maritime Provinces. With Manchuria leased to Russia for ninety-nine years, prior to the Russo-Japanese War in 1905, many Russians were employed there in railwork and administration. Before the arrival of the emigres, there also existed a significant nucleus of professional classes.

The Chinese Eastern Railway was built by the Imperial Russian government to connect with the TransSiberian Railway and the Maritime Provinces, down to Port Arthur and Dairen (Dalian) on what is today the Gulf of Bo Hai (Gulf of Peitaho). With the cooperation of the Manchu Dynasty, and later the Chinese warlords who ruled Manchuria, the new arrivals flooded in by the hundreds of thousands from all over Russia. The Russian colony expanded into every field of endeavor—from small business owner to farmers, from engineers to librarians, from surveyors to school teachers, from professors to politicians, from performing artists to skilled workers. High schools were opened, performing arts flourished, and several newspapers were published. Chinese students in Manchuria attended some of these high schools, becoming professionals themselves.

The population of Manchuria was at its highest with approximately 32 million people, of whom almost 4.5 million were Russians. With its substantial Fushun and Antung coal mines, iron ore deposits, game, mineral resources, kaoliang (grain), dairy farms, furs, lumber, fruit, timber, and wool industries, it was similar to the Siberian area, and it became an economic haven for them. They flourished in a society of a newly-found domicile and freedom. Manchurian political life was as democratic as any in the Orient, with tolerant Chinese laws and courts. Here was a colony whose children went to universities in Harbin, Shanghai, Hong Kong, Europe, and America, while Lenin and Stalin practiced their Socialist experiments with dictatorship, police terror, and slave labor to the detriment of the entire nation. Russia, which never had a true democratic society under autocracy, was now forced to suffer Communist dictatorial rule, with utopian philosophy never before tried. It is true that life for the poorer classes, particularly small peasants and the untrained, was hard under czardom, but they were reasonably treated, with many philanthropic societies helping. Generally Russians under the czars, who took no part in political disorders, were pretty much left to themselves, particularly those outside St. Petersborg, Moscow, and other urban areas—so long as they didn't conspire to throw off the Imperial regime.

Chang-Tso-Ling and later his son Chang-Hsui-Liang, General Ma, and a few others ran various regions of Manchuria, employing Russian specialists in government administration and the courts. The demand for Russian specialists in engineering, civil service, accounting, bookkeeping, surveying, law, and many other trades were filled by the emigres. The newcomers had several diverse parties and organizations and practiced democracy without being aware of its status. Their children were well educated and in most instances were equal to those in European countries. Many of the students were graduates of European and American colleges, and upon return were employed in Harbin, Mukden, Beijing, Shanghai, Nanking, and Hong Kong foreign trade firms and consular offices. Many of them learned foreign languages, and it was rare to speak only Russian. There also existed an emigre military intelligence unit of the former czarist army, run by the Society of Russian Patriots. It cooperated with the Russian Emigre Bureau in Paris under General Miller, former commander in Murmansk in the civil war. It was quite common for escapees from Soviet Russia to cross the Ussuri and Amur Rivers to Manchuria in the depth of winter. These escapees brought quantities of information on conditions in both Russia proper and Siberia, which was later funneled to Paris and distributed to Deuxieme Bureau of the French Army and MI6 in Britain. Eventually Miller was murdered by Stalin's agents in Paris.

The Russian colony thrived in Manchuria with a reasonable standard of living from the 1890s to 1941, although under the Japanese Kwantung Army occupation, it became more restricted in freedom. The Japanese government in Tokyo, forced by the Kwantung Army Command, installed a puppet regime in 1932 and named it Manchukuo under Emperor Henry Pu Yi, of the *The Last Emperor* movie fame. Although no criticism of Manchukuo or Japan was tolerated, the newcomers were left alone to pursue their daily lives.

Subsequently, when conditions in 1938 became tense, wtih border incidents against the Soviet Far Eastern Army initiated by the Japanese Kwantung Army, the Russian exodus slowly began to Peking, Tientsin, and Shanghai. Even before the Pearl Harbor attack, large foreign colonies had existed in China for many years, with territorial concessions extracted from China after the Boxer Rebellion.

The Japanese occupation of Shanghai in WWII made life for the emigres uncomfortable but still tolerable. There was imprisonment and cruel treatment of citizens of countries at war with Japan. The Russian colony, by and large, was spared this treatment since it was stateless. As conditions in Germany became untenable for German Jews after 1934, some clandestinely escaped by way of Poland, Switzerland, and other countries. Failing to gain permanent status, they petitioned the Chinese Government for entry to Shanghai as stateless citizens and were accorded refugee status. They lived there before and throughout the war among the Russians. After the war they mostly settled in America along with Russians—to be free at last. Russians and Jews were also accepted in some Latin American countries, which welcomed them not only as refugees but also for their professional and trade skills.

WWII was another misfortune for millions of people and nationalities, including former Soviet citizens who constituted second wave of emigres. Soviet Russian prisoners, who had been imprisoned in Germany as captives for slave labor and had no desire to return to their homeland after the war, roamed a ruined Europe seeking shelter and peace as "displaced persons." Finding no solace among strangers in Europe, who had their own problems with survival, they sought refuge elsewhere. The surrender of these refugees by Anglo-American armies on demand from Stalin was shameful, and they were delivered for repatriation. Later however, President Truman ordered a halt to this practice. Others not so lucky were shipped back home to slave labor camps, and when no longer useful, they were executed or left to die.

This saga is another chapter of dark history of WWII to accommodate Stalin. Hitler's genocide (the Holocaust), barbaric and terrible as it was, lasted twelve years and ended with six million dead Jews. In Stalin's case, labor camps, executions, and wholesale banishment of nationalities started years before Hitler and continued right up to Stalin's death. Families were broken up and torn asunder, banished with no hope of reunion, and were denied knowledge of the fate of their loved ones. The unitary nature and fabric of families had been greatly torn apart by events caused by dictators uprooting them from their domicile. Because of the humanitarian traditions of the American, Anglo-Saxon, and Scandinavian nations, the United Nations was able to establish a commission on refugees. As a consequence, there was happily a wide acceptance of displaced persons by nations either affected or unaffected by the turmoil and rigors of war. Their adopted countries had no reason to regret the humanitarian efforts they rendered. With few exceptions, Russian and Jewish emigrants made excellent citizens and enriched the countries to which they migrated—with culture, professional talents, intelligence, business, and pride of citizenship. It was a loss for Europe and the Soviet Union, whose talents were needed more than ever after the war.

**Emigres in the United States**

After the end of WWII, when American industry was converting to consumer production, there was a shortage of engineers, geologists, mathematicians, and other professionals. The recession in 1948 was due in part to the inability of American industry to expand its industrial base because of the shortage of qualified people. Not until the GI Bill of Rights was passed and subsequently applied to educate the great mass of troops coming home did this gap begin to fill in the mid-1950's. In the meantime, the Russian immigrants with their professional skills coming in from China filled this demand admirably. It was said then that had it not been for the emigre Russian engineers, the expanding base of industry would have been delayed for years as it was in Europe.

The beginning of the Russian migration to the United States was to the west coast and began even before WWI, when a religious group of Russian Dukhobors came to practice their religion in freedom, being persecuted at home. Russian settlers had come in 1865 from Alaska when Russian merchants abandoned their efforts to profitably exploit its riches. After its sale to the United States, they settled at first in Northern California, during the gold rush, and later moved to San Francisco Bay area.

On the other hand, the second wave of Russian immigrants after WWII came as products of the Soviet environment, breakneck industrialization, and Hitler's concentration camps. They may be considered as unschooled refugees but were hard-working, blue-collar workers. A few did have higher educational degrees and found work in colleges and universities, as well as technical-professional employment. The difference between the two groups occurred because of the dissimilarity of the Soviet environment, influence, and education. The well-educated middle class from China was fortunate to live in a far freer society than their kin in Russia. The basic Russian educational system before the revolution was similar to German schools. Mathematical sciences were stressed, along with natural sciences, world history, literature, and language arts. This system was continued in China, while it was largely abandoned by the Communist regime. Only years after Stalin's death did school curricula shift away from an emphasis on Communist propaganda and revolutionary history. Recently, Russian institutions of higher learning have improved considerably in the teaching of sciences, professions, and the arts, though none equaled most Western standards. Additionally, it is now taken for granted that Russia and other advanced former autonomous nations have a well-educated workforce after so many years of stagnation under Stalin. Nevertheless, the prevailing culture in the workplace has not yet acquired individual initiative, with the herd instinct still in place. In this respect, the first emigres from revolutionary Russia, after the civil war and subsequent immigration, should be considered fortunate in settling in the land of opportunity. Most children of the emigres in America have acquired a sense of purpose from their parents and have attended colleges and universities to prepare for their future. Most have intermarried and settled into normal life as U.S. citizens, with outstanding capabilities in the professions and various other disciplines. Most of them are now grandparents, and they have imparted that same purpose to their children and grandchildren. Life to them has become precious and worth living. The story of Russian emigres, east and west, after the civil war and WWII, is a more widespread and comprehensive subject than space allows here.

Nevertheless the reader should have a reasonable idea of their numbers, and who they are. Opinions expressed in this chapter are those of the author through personal knowledge and experience, and subsequently supplemented and broadened by several well informed sources present at the scene, who shall not be named by request.

# CHAPTER VIII
# TRANSFORMATION OF SOCIETY

The end of the civil war found the country in economic shambles, with the population dispersed and wandering throughout the land with worthless currency and no food supplies. Occupation and consolidation of former opposition army areas was a difficult problem for the Bolsheviks. The Cheka was arresting and executing people randomly, with more stringent controls under War Communism than in the Bolshevik-occupied areas.

The population increased by almost 60 percent, and no improvement was foreseen to feed, house, and employ people. Most people scrambled to emigrate when they could, not knowing what to do or where to go, with some begging in the streets. Those who escaped after the mass exodus during the war related unrestrained random arrests and shooting of innocent people.

**New Economic Policy**

Even among supporters of the regime—the peasants, workers, and discharged veterans—discontentment mounted daily because of Bolshevik mishandling of agriculture and industry. Most discharged troops, workers, peasants, and some former Whites joined rebellious groups. To add to the misfortune, a drought gripped the land and added to discontentment and culminated in the rebellion of the Kronstadt sailors, the former supporters of the regime.

Faced with these problems, knowing full well there was no solution under War Communism, Lenin prompted the Bolsheviks to reassess their economic policies and get the country back on its feet again, as it had been before the revolution. The Bolshevik principle of iron discipline had never before wavered under adversity, but under these circumstances, they were completely helpless. They were reluctantly forced to change course, having no other alternatives. The Bolshevik theoreticians were never really in contact with the masses; they just issued directives and expected instantaneous compliance, with the Cheka enforcing their theoretical principles. These principles were apparently more important than the condition of the people for whom they claimed the revolution occurred. Here again, Lenin was not prepared to relinquish any power under any circumstances for fear he would lose it all.

It is doubtful that any other civilized country could take this much punishment and still survive. There has never been such exodus from native lands in history. After substantial deliberations and some dissent, it was decided to backtrack and reverse War Communism by transforming the socialist economy into a free market, with some constraints on labor rules, ownership, and employment. In overthrowing the Imperial regime, they inherited power with false promises and didn't know how to execute these theoretical socialist experiments and acted as amateurs. There is a limit to untried theories when applied to millions of human beings. It appears that even the Russians, who are unusually patient and compliant, couldn't take it any more. The new policy in essence permitted free market economy for the peasants and small businesses with not more than five employees. This reversal worked miracles, and the nation gradually got on its feet—at least during Lenin's guiding hand—and subsequently fell back under Stalin.

In the strictest sense, the New Economic Policy (NEP) was a temporary economic concession forced on the Communists by the realities of famine, the probable collapse of the socialist system, and the strains of the civil war. Had it continued, the system would probably have caused the collapse and the overthrow of the Leninist regime. Acting just in time to contain the unbearable strains on the economy, which was almost in its primitive stages and collapsing daily, Lenin reversed himself and decreed the new policy which saved the Bolsheviks and the nation from total collapse. Yet there were other czarist forms left to transform, which had nothing to do with the economy, and they promptly instituted measures to conform to Marxist-Leninist principles.

**Church, State and School**

In prerevolutionary Russia the church played an active role in family life with its ancient customs and traditions and was related to the czar as head of the church. Marriages were legal only through the church; divorce was extremely difficult to obtain; and mixed marriages were prohibited—although the church had no influence over other Christians, the Armenian Church, Judaism, and Islam. The communist government took advantage of this diversity and severed all ties between church, state, and school.

In a changing twentieth century, church doctrines in civil affairs had become anachronistic, without adapting to new realities of separation of church and state. Instead of separating the church from its secular ties, the government embarked on organizing a godless society, "The League of Militant Atheists." Relations between the church and state were never reconciled, and any unofficial contact was based on the church's termination of condemning the government and its atheistic policies. Many patriarchs, bishops, and priests were arrested in the beginning until they recanted. In antagonizing the church and its unity with the family, they succeeded in destroying it. When separation from the church was achieved, the government had control of the children in schools and preached its atheistic propaganda, making communism the official religion. In the beginning, however, the government prohibited officials from interfering with church worship, which could offend devout believers and make fanatics out of them. Subsequently in 1927 when Stalin was already in firm control, relations continued to deteriorate as many priests and devout believers were exiled to Siberia. The influence of the church on the Russian people during Stalin's regime was minimal. Church attendance was limited to older people, whom the Communists considered as dying breed.

Architecturally outstanding church landmarks remained—such cathedrals as Annunciation, Archangel Michael, St. Basil's on Red Square, and the Kremlin—as symbols of historic significance. Other "insignificant" churches were shorn of their decorations and used as horse stables, libraries, atheistic gathering halls, or government meeting places.

Children were taught to spy on parents who attended church or read the Bible to them. Even non-Orthodox churches attended by foreign embassy personnel or journalists were spied upon and photographed, lest they propagate religion. As a result of these policies, communism became a *weltanschauung* of youth and the general masses. A godless society was established, where communism transcended religious worship and became the common standard of the nation. Prior to the revolution, Russians were a devout and religious people.

**Education**

Education was the one area of society the Communists stressed to its limits, particularly since illiteracy was widespread among impressionable youths. The one exemplary and truly worthy experiment of communism was their serious effort to eradicate illiteracy by enrolling every person up to age seventeen in school. The pre-revolutionary schools were almost equal to those in the West but were limited in number and attendance. The communist intent was clearly identified and spelled out as having a basis in scientific Marxism and could only be applicable to educated people. Aside from this philosophy, it was also intended to be mind-remodeling to suit conditions of communist society. The desire of most people in prerevolutionary Russia was to get an education, and the new government was acutely aware of this. While teachers welcomed the revolution in education in principle, most were either indifferent or paid little heed to communist policies in the beginning of the transformation period. Education was free, compulsory, and co-educational. The primary objective of new schooling was based upon eradication of the pre-revolutionary system from kindergarten to university levels. They abolished homework, examinations, and academic degrees. School administration was placed in collectives comprised of teachers, school children, and employees, while the school curricula was turned upside down to fit requirements of the new social order. Additionally, teaching of languages and history was mandatory, instead of practical application for work. The school furnished lunch, pencil, and paper. The new school system was made part of the constitution in 1918, and it commenced only after the implementation of the New Economic Policy. The autonomy of universities was abolished. Since the government guaranteed free education but had no funds to support the program, it delayed implementing the system until the economy improved.

While it was a great achievement, it had disturbing and harmful elements. Courses were not taught to prepare a student for useful work, since the intent was to employ a student for whatever work was available. On the whole, the system was meant to make a student literate in socialism and communism more than anything else. Mathematics and upgraded arithmetic were taught to students who showed promise in the subject; others had to study history, grammar, the new social order, and obedience to the Party. School discipline was rather lax at first, with students, teachers, and employees quite frequently coming in late and leaving early. Teachers were usually bewildered by various regulations and curricula, which changed almost constantly. The employees acted as enforcers of the different regulations. Food was mainly potatoes and radishes, but soup (borsch) was served once or twice a week, which was usually insufficient, and children went home hungry. Not until later, when food was more available for school distribution under the NEP, was it reasonably adequate, but by then farmers' markets were open, and prices were affordable under the free economy. The author attended these schools as a youth in Ussuriysk, Siberian Maritime Provinces and experienced the system and hardships firsthand.

The university system was based on different objectives than the lower grade schools. The intent there was to educate an intelligent body of students, first in scientific Marxism, and later with the special requirements in the fields of electrical and industrial engineering. In this connection, when almost 1.2 million professional people emigrated after the civil war, shortages in these fields became critically apparent and seemed insurmountable. The government appealed to emigre professionals to return to their homeland. Few returned, which caused it to employ foreign engineering professors and firms to construct various enterprises—particularly electrical plants, industrial machinery factories, and implements. It took the better part of eight years to assemble enough of their own experts to teach future engineers. The first batch of native engineers employed in industries was inadequately trained to produce quality products. The early experiments in full use of native talent had to be supplemented with foreign contracts in addition to sending its own engineers abroad for more training. Eventually, native engineers took over and performed adequately. However, industrial engineering never succeeded in perfecting high quality products as long as USSR existed, except in military armament factories, where the most money was invested and the best talent was used.

Commencing approximately in 1935, other scientific disciplines were taught in the universities—physics, chemistry, higher mathematics, medicine, and aeronautics. Among the world-renowned physicists who returned home for a visit was Peter Kapitsa; he was forbidden to return to Britain and was forced to settle in Russia with his own laboratory.

The quality of medicine was particularly inadequate when compared to Western standards, which was probably due to inducting more women (with low pay scales) in to the profession. The free socialized clinics were deplorably inadequate and understaffed in dispensing reasonable health care, although the Kremlin hospital employed foreign doctors and their best native talents. As time went on, the university systems improved but never equaled western European or American standards. Moscow and Leningrad State Universities did have good literature and history departments, in addition to other subjects. After several years of refining the subject matter, some foreign students were enrolled—principally from Asian and African countries.

When it came to autonomous Soviet republics, their universities never equaled those mentioned above because of the shortage of funds allocated by the central government. Brighter students of several nationalities tried to enlist a quota system on Russian institutes of higher learning, although years later, there was improvement in their own schools because of higher grade school standards. A few Soviet republics possessed ancient manuscripts, dating back several hundred or more years, and Western scholars visited them occasionally. Kiev State University archives possess some manuscripts on Kievan Rus. The Matenadaran in Yerevan, in the Armenian Republic, has documents, manuscripts, utensils, and a building dating back to Roman times and even prior to our era, to the ancient Armenian kingdom of Urartu. Foreign history and archeological scholars in particular displayed serious interest in these manuscripts. Occasionally, Kremlin archives on early Kievan Rus and their successors were opened and examined by foreign scholars.

Research institutions associated with universities—similar to western custom did not exist; research institutions existed by themselves under strict directives of the Communist party. Probably the better known research institutions are the Marx-Engels Institute in socialist sciences and the USA and Canada Institute in political science, although later research institutions in sciences and other disciplines were also created. The absence of these institutions in the universities was probably based on the fear of the Party, that too many undesirable discoveries could be made by too many students, which would not be in the best interests of the Party and its citizens in a closed society.

**National Minority Peoples**

The educational systems in the Soviet republics—except Ukraine, Belorussia, Armenia, and Georgia—lagged substantially behind Russia. Subsequently, this caused minority customs and traditions to collide with the intent of the communist programs. Substantial disturbances occurred, particularly among TransCaucasian tribes, Muslims, and people settled in areas of Siberia where illiteracy was predominant. It took years for the government to force elementary school education system to become common. The curricula had somewhat lower standards, at least in the beginning. Subsequently, until minority republics established a base for higher education, qualified students attended Russian or other advanced educational establishments nearby. Eventually some minorities succeeded in establishing their own higher educational systems, though they were mainly in the Russian language since Russification had already been established. Since the Imperial regime never bothered with education for minorities, it is fair to state that the Soviet government bestowed an educational system in backward areas where it hadn't existed, regardless of their intent. On the other hand, they fooled minority nations into thinking they were entitled to autonomy and even separation.

Lenin entrapped national minorities of Russia away from the Provisional Government with his "Declaration of the Rights of the Peoples of Russia." He also condemned the Russification policy of the Imperial government and supported self-determination of all minority nationalities. On 14 November 1917 Lenin implemented this declaration with the statement of equality, sovereignty, and self-determination—even emphasizing it to the point of separation and formation of independent states. To be sure, he couched his declaration with dialectic and semantic double-talk. When these nationalities tried to implement this declaration later, the Bolshevik government balked and threatened to use force to stop them. During the civil war, to ensure their allegiance and subordination, he suggested to national minorities a government with his own advisors at the head of each nation, autonomous area, or region, and reserved for himself the right to separate them from Russia. As if to emphasize their complete independence, each Soviet Socialist Republic established itself as an independent entity with a sovereign constitution. Each eliminated private ownership of land and production, guaranteeing political power to the working class, along with freedom of speech, assembly, and dictatorship of the proletariat. From commencement of this status, each accepted complete solidarity with other Soviet republics. Each was to cooperate with others in a close political union, in its struggle for the triumph of world communism.

In early 1919 the economy, railways, labor, and military elements were politically and categorically unified with the Russian Soviet Federated Socialist Republic in Moscow. The entire program was subtly tailored for transformation to communism and compliance to Moscow directives. Simply translated, it meant complete subordination to Soviet Russia in every field of endeavor. When the status became official, it was not only disappointing to minority nationalities, but they were quite resentful of being fooled by Lenin first and by Stalin later. There wasn't much they could do about it since Lenin and Stalin had the power to enforce compliance with the army and the Cheka. Notwithstanding the language he used, Lenin sent his advisors to each of the supposed autonomous entities to enforce Moscow's dictates. These advisors behaved haughtily and with utter defiance, dictating total compliance with Russification and subordination to the will of Moscow. They let it be known that any language other than Russian, was prerevolutionary and unacceptable. The dictates were so overwhelming and rude that any sympathies left by the minorities for the Russians evaporated quickly into disturbances. Eventually, transformation of minority nationalities to communism and its dictates was completed. While Ukrainians and Belorussians spoke their own version of Slavic, characteristic to their homelands, they could understand Russian; nevertheless they resented this intrusion in the beginning. In so far as TransCaucasian nationalities were concerned, Armenians and Georgians submitted voluntarily to political dictates but not to Russification. The Georgians, previously conquered by Russia in the early nineteenth century, were rather docile. The Armenians welcomed the Russians, to escape genocide and persecution by the Turks. The other nationalities of the mostly Muslim Caucasus included the Abkhzians, Adzharians, Chechens, Circassians, Cherkessians, Ingushetians, North and South Ossetians, Kabardinians, and numerous other tribes. They were fiercely independent, previously conquered and pacified by Russia in centuries past, and resented Russian influence to the point of disobedience. These mountain peoples of the Caucasus never exceeded more than two million in total population. During the Imperial regime, they were left alone, and some even joined the Russian army. Under Stalin's regime, they were considered unreliable, and excessive pressure was used to tame them, although later they saw the wisdom of education (with no written language of their own) and tenuously accepted Russification and dictation by Moscow. Special treatment awaited them all undeservedly during the Nazi-Soviet war in 1941 when Stalin exiled most of them to Siberia. Generally, the entire political structure of the proclaimed minorities as independent states imitated that of R.S.F.S.R., and all directives and orders emanating from Moscow were in Russian. The reader should be made aware that Soviet Russia was not a true federated republic as implied and stated by Lenin; in fact it was the seat of dictatorship imposed from Moscow. From the beginning, Moscow had total control of everything done in these republics. It was a duplicity, defined and justified by Marxist dialectics and double-talk and was unintelligible to most minorities, at least in the beginning.

**Propaganda, Literature, and Performing Arts**

Since everything else underwent transformation, the Communists tackled propaganda in down-to-earth methods, with excellent results. Most lower strata of society couldn't yet read, and in view of this, the educational and propaganda system was employed to enforce literacy and to enhance communism. Once the program was set, they produced literary millions of murals, periodicals, textbooks, and newspapers in plain words to exhort workers and peasants to work harder for socialism. The schools became nurseries of propaganda which was spread to the parents when children came home. Propaganda for hard work never ended, stressed in school to influence parents and to prepare school children for work upon graduation.

The school day began at 8:00 A.M. and ended at 4:00 P.M. Students in the lower grades were young children and teenagers who were illiterate, and most all came from working class or peasant families. The first hour was dedicated to the importance of the group instead of the individual; and as a class, they were children of the proletariat, for whom the country was being transformed to inherit the earth. In each class session thereafter, the first thirty minutes was again dedicated to communism and hatred toward the wealthy and the bourgeoisie who had enslaved the proletariat for centuries. Reading and writing came next. Praise of Lenin the genius, was mandatory and was pounded daily; later the same was true for Stalin. Denunciation of non-working parents, whose names were spelled on blackboards, occurred daily. Since the government possessed all printing presses, books were used as propaganda against the previous regime and capitalist countries. Mention of religion or God was forbidden.

Factories, bakeries, lampposts, and farmers' bazaars had numerous slogans displayed for the glory of communism. Similar slogans were used in university classrooms and dining halls. Atheism was preached before each session, and recruitment to atheistic societies was encouraged. Newspapers used every means to debase pre-revolutionary society, world capitalism, and the bourgeoisie and proclaimed the triumph of communism in the new age. Newspapers and schools proclaimed that other nations throughout the world were held in bondage by the capitalists and bourgeoisie and that the day would come when the enslaved peoples would call upon the great Soviet Union to liberate them. This drumming was so intense that it left an indelible mark on future soviet generations. On the whole, socialist and communist propaganda never ceased, and should be considered a highly successful transformation of society for the blind automatons.

Every child, knowing no better, swallowed it—much like the author who also experienced this drumbeat day in and day out. Returning home from the war in Europe (WWII), the author was amazed to hear some American friends talk of the great Soviet Union in unabashed praise for soviet troops. These troops were clothed in flimsy uniforms and worn-out boots, though they carried good weapons. They ransacked most German homes for booty and anything they could find, and there was plenty. Among other things, they would send home torn silk stockings, watches from deceased German troops, and anything with encouragement of their officers. The officers enriched themselves by commandeering furniture, glassware, rugs, and whatever was available to send home by departing GMC trucks. However, some Soviet POWs whom I encountered in German stalags realized the falsehood of communism for the first time, and afraid of being sent home to concentration camps, defected as displaced persons in Germany, hoping to emigrate to America. These officers confirmed industrialization slogans plastered all over, "Catch up and beat America," had a hollow meaning for them, since tools, supplies, and other necessary means never came on time and were inadequate.

After the civil war, the transformation of society by soviet sociologists accomplished its purposes by brainwashing new generations, irradicating the truth, and instilling in its citizens what might be called a new type of human being, "Homo Sovieticus." It was a life-shattering experience to all Homo Sovieticus when the Soviet Union dissolved. The brains of its citizens will take generations to unscramble just to attain reality. Simply stated, the Soviet Union was never Soviet, nor was it ever a Union. It was a closed club for the privileged *nomenklatura*, which exploited the proletariat with slogans and at their expense supported their luxurious lifestyles.

## Literature

The beginning of the Soviet triumph evidenced a lack of Russian intellectual talent since most prominent writers had left the country for the diaspora. The few who remained were at best second tier. However, some social-minded writers, poets, and other literati remained to expound the cause of the poor working class. Even these writers found it difficult to toe the communist line. Among prominent poets who remained were Osip Mandelstam and Anna Akhmatova, both of whom were ostracized, and the former died in prison. Some Symbolist and anti-Symbolist writers quit or were imprisoned. Among the few who stayed and supported the lower classes was Maxim Gorkiy, the writer and publisher who accused Lenin of being a trickster. He suddenly died in 1936; Stalin is suspected of poisoning him. Symbolists Alexander Blok and Andrey Beliiy committed suicide, and subsequently so did Vladimir Mayakovskiy, who was the soviet futurist and poet. The party under Stalin demanded absolute socialist propaganda from these writers and poets, instead of art. As a result of these decrees, the art of literature disappeared, with few exceptions, never to rise again. Some writers and poets, to escape hunger, joined *Prolekult*, an organ of the Communist party's literary group and did the party's bidding. However, when it got to the point that they were forbidden to express themselves outside the Party's doctrine, they quit, and the Party disbanded the organization. Later, when the economy improved and some contact was permitted with Western writers, the government—left with mediocre writers—pardoned some of the talented ones who returned from self-imposed exile. In any event, with few exceptions, nothing produced after the revolution with straightforward socialist realism ever equaled the age of Russia's enlightenment of the 1800s. Any effort ordered by Stalin and produced under the tutelage of socialist realism never equaled the talents of those who migrated into the diaspora.

Still later a group called Serapion Brothers, whose members desired to produce works free from political content and guidance, were condemned and disbanded. The Central Committee of the Communist party declared on 18 June 1925, "In a classless society there is and can be no neutral art." The group pleaded for understanding from other nonconforming literary writers; for a while recriminations stopped the quarrel between the party and the group, but later they were forced to disband. Those other few who were able to perform superb works under the harsh political system passed Soviet censors.

The herd instinct in artificially imposed socialist realism never succeeded, since no one knew what it meant. Those who did succeed picked the subject of the Patriotic War or breakneck industrialization for the glory of Stalin. Some foreign communist artists and painters were applauded by Stalin and his all-knowing stooges. The transformation of society was intended to whip the population into a collective herd system, depriving individual initiative and squashing any talent—although outstanding musicians, ballet dancers, and others with similarly outstanding talents were encouraged individually, since these artistic achievements were inherited from the old regime and socialist realism couldn't apply. The transformation of Russian society generally succeeded all too well, and the population was whipped into discipline, from generation to generation, until dissolution of the Soviet Union. It will take many years to shed this training—what the common Russian would call *Drisirovka* (animal training). Yet when the Soviet Union dissolved, the Russian government hauled the coup leaders to court, only to set them free, apparently because it was all legal under the Soviet regime. Most satellite eastern European Communist government officials were similarly pardoned. Perhaps this is the wave of the future, to reward the guilty for their criminal behavior.

# CHAPTER IX
# VLADIMIR ILLICH LENIN (ULIANOV):
# 1870-1924

Vladimir Illich Lenin should be considered a phenomenon as a Russian. While there were other revolutionaries, none were equal to him. Revolutionary theoreticians Chernishevskiy, Nechayeev, and Plekhanov, were also intellectuals, but they lacked the organizational skills, iron will, and foresight that Lenin possessed. Other opponents of the regime were individual terrorists, intent on assassination of the czars or their ministers, who were promptly hanged when caught. He was well educated as a lawyer at Kazan University on the Volga. By most reliable accounts, he was substantially different from these characters. He was theoretician, a thinker, and an intellectual, calculating, exacting, and profound, with a stubborn disposition.

He was the son of a minor nobleman who was in charge of a provincial school district in Kazan. His mother was a Volga German whose roots date back to the time of Catherine the Great's invitation to German farmers to migrate to Russia, offering free or low-cost land. Lenin, however, had not a drop of Russian blood in him. His origins were Germanic, Swedish and Chuvash (a tribal nomadic people in the steppes of Russia). From all accounts it seems he and his siblings had a good childhood and loving care from their mother. Later, he entered Kazan University for the study of law, achieving good grades. His rector at the university, was none other than Alexander Kerenskiy's father, who jotted down his comments upon Lenin's graduation that he was an excellent student but lacked logic. While there he got in trouble for fomenting social unrest among students. It took the best efforts of his mother and her dead husband's connections to get him reinstated.

After graduation he entered the practice of law, with not too successful results, and wandered around for a while until entering conspiratorial work against the government. He was promptly arrested, and his mother again intervened in St. Petersburg to have him released. He finally journeyed to Europe to escape further imprisonment. He lived in Switzerland, Germany, France, Poland, and Britain, among other places. He visited other countries for short spells for clandestine meetings with other social revolutionaries. His constant visits to the libraries in Europe became so frequent that clerks called him a "perpetual student." There, among voluminous books, he read a treatise on Hegel's dialectics, finding the subject rather dull and too complex for the Russian proletariat to com-

*Vladimir Illich, Lenin*

prehend.

In time, he couldn't evade the subject since most European social scholars constantly discussed and referred to it. This caused him to review the subject further, and he finally accepted dialectics as a philosophical base for his objectives. His stubborn and uncompromising character was such that only a few revolutionary socialists agreed with him. To convert the Russian working class to his philosophy, he published a pamphlet, "Iskra" ("Spark"), which he and Plekhanov wrote, edited, and smuggled to Russia. He also read up on Marxism while he was a student and again while in exile in Europe. In temper and character he was a lonely person, who only shared his inner thoughts with his common-law wife, Nadezhda Krupskaya, and even she, an intelligent woman and a revolutionary in her own right, found it difficult in the beginning to sort out and articulate his abstract thinking. It is granted that he was a superior intellect, though not personally a creative one although he occasionally possessed an uncanny feeling for certain events. He lived on books and more books in his exhaustive eighteen-hour work day.

It appears that he quickly settled on Marx's utopian theory in *Das Kapital*, as the social-economic theory for the ills in Russia; which could also be easily understood by the Russian proletariat. Meanwhile other European social thinkers believed that Marx's theory was an anachronism, in view of changing conditions in the workplace. After the European convulsions and revolutions in 1848, most European governments adopted social and welfare programs, which considerably improved the lot of the workers, by the same industrialists whom Marx had decried. European governments instituted child labor laws, laws requiring safe working conditions, medical aid, better wages, and holiday observances with pay; thus life became more tolerable and rewarding. Nevertheless, Lenin thought that the theory was admirably suited to the Russian proletariat. No arguments by any thinkers would change his mind. Some intellectuals argued that the European working class was substantially more mature than the Russian and that the introduction of such harsh measures into an undeveloped Russian economy, which had no advanced industrial base, could cause untold hardship. Little did these thinkers know that Lenin had a mean streak in him, and he would use terror, assassination, murder, imprisonment, and starvation as weapons to force his doctrine as a matter of principle on the Russian proletariat, whether it was out of date in Europe or not.

Additionally, he was immensely impressed with the economic theory of "The Wealth of Nations" and believed that a nation's wealth belonged to the state and not to the capitalists and exploiters. Lenin's knowledge of his people and rulers convinced him that the dictatorship of the proletariat, initiated by the intellectuals, was the correct path for Russia's salvation, regardless of the means employed, although initially he disguised the fact that the dictatorship was to be employed by the intellectuals over the proletariat. He disregarded theorists who developed the thesis based on Britain and Germany, the two industrial giants of the time. To confirm his theory, he conferred with Plekhanov about his ideas of dictatorship to achieve the required results. Plekhanov agreed in principle, but declined any discussion of dictatorship. On the contrary, Plekhanov advocated a European-type social democracy for the Russian working class, with a fair balance of free economic enterprise as well as government ownership of certain sections of the economy, which was common in most countries in Europe. This precipitated the final rift between them and the abrupt departure of Lenin from the right wing of the social democratic party.

He created a new left wing party with himself as its head. Some followers of similar thinking trailed along, yet most members doubted dictatorship was the right course. He chose to dismiss the doubters and created a party in his own image and subsequently led it to victory; it later became known as the Bolshevik Party of Russia. The reader should be aware that *Bolshevik* in Russian means "majority"—when in fact it was a minority party when Lenin arbitrarily seized power from the Provisional Government.

Meanwhile his advocacy of the violent overthrow of the czarist regime was spreading among the Russian working class. Several communist cells were clandestinely created in Russia with assassinations, and bank robberies occurring almost daily. Henceforth Lenin worried less about funds to publish pamphlets or to defray personal expenses; still he lived rather frugally. He could not leave for Russia, for fear of being arrested by the secret police (Okhrana) for intent to overthrow the Imperial regime. Meanwhile, the clandestine party became more active, with more members joining daily, although it had substantially fewer members than other legitimate parties. Lenin's propaganda war went on gathering steam with all sorts of people, including the lowest elements of society and the industrial workers in St. Petersburg and Moscow. The violent overthrow of the government became the main theme in smuggled pamphlets, which the police confiscated by the hundreds. The government shut down the presses and arrested or exiled dozens of people to Siberia. Nevertheless communist agitators still infiltrated factories other work places and government offices, to incite workers to strike and kill people in charge. Meanwhile the Duma was being dissolved by the czar, for demanding to be included in discussions on economic appropriations in the forthcoming war effort.

Lenin opposed the war as an Imperialist trick to make more money through manufacture of armaments. World War I was approaching with the government commencing conscription of troops for possible dispatch to the war fronts. Lenin seized the opportunity while still in Europe to advocate disobedience to the officer corps and urge conscripts to return home. This effort at first didn't produce any significant results, and conscription proceeded normally. The Putilov munitions works—the nation's largest—and some others couldn't produce sufficient armaments in time to arm all the troops, and upon the outbreak of the war, shortages quickly developed. Some conscripts were assigned to the rear as medical and supply personnel, others without arms were sent to the front lines and told to acquire rifles from the fallen. Russia entered the war ill-prepared, while the Western Allies bore the brunt of the early German offensive operations head-on.

The czar was beseeched by the Allies to commence an offensive forthwith against the Germans in the east. Having received insufficient intelligence on the

German formations and dispositions, coupled with a sincere desire to adhere to their previously committed obligations and to relieve the pressure on the western front, the Russian command ordered an offensive within sixteen days after Germany attacked. A Russian army under command of General Rennenkampf hurled its troops into East Prussia. From the start Russian troops were superior in number to the Germans and met minor resistance as they rushed headlong into the interior. The Germans, sensing superior numbers of the Russians, slowly fell back to contract their mass against the Russian troops. Having achieved the objective of spreading out Russian ranks advancing head-on, they succeeded in splitting the mass and destroyed the Russians piecemeal. Hindenberg and Ludendorff triumphed, and the battle of Tannenberg was over, avenging an earlier defeat of the German Teutonic knights in earlier centuries by the Russians, Poles, and Lithuanians. Shortly thereafter another army under General Samsonov sustained another defeat by the Germans at the battle of Mazurian swamps in Poland. The two successive and serious defeats subsequently contributed to undermining troop morale by communist agitators, with dire consequences for the war effort and later contributing to the fall of the monarchy.

If these defeats were not enough, Czar Nicholas, against the advice of senior commanders and political advisors, took over the command of the Russian forces from his uncle, Grand Duke Nicholas, a professional soldier, ostensibly to upgrade moral authority in the army. This takeover was a fatal error which caused a breakdown in the Russian command. The communist agitators stepped into the void and weakened morale among the troops, and soon the army began fraternizing with the enemy, resulting in gradual disintegration on most fronts.

With funds furnished by the German government through intermediaries in Switzerland, Lenin's group entrained for Finland, arriving in Petrograd's Finland station shortly thereafter. For pretense it was a secret undertaking between the group and the German government. The train was supposedly sealed, with no communication between the Germans and Lenin's group. Subsequently, after the fall of Berlin in WWII, salvaged German Foreign Office documents confirmed the transaction without specifically naming Lenin.

In view of the defeats suffered and poor morale associated with the war, two high members of the government were dispatched as emissaries to Mogilev, the field headquarters of the Russian command, to ask for the czar's abdication. The czar abdicated instantly on 15 March 15 1917. Shortly thereafter the Black Sea fleet revolted in Sebastopol. Elections were called for party seats in the Assembly. Results for Lenin's party were highly disappointing, receiving only a few seats, while the Cadets and Social Democrats received a majority. This caused a formation of a provisional government with Alexander Kerenskiy, a socialist, assuming the posts of minister of justice and subsequently minister of war and prime minister. Unfortunately, this government lasted only seven months. When the Assembly was convened, Lenin's armed thugs closed all exits in the hall and arrested the deputies. Some, including Kerenskiy, fled with the support of loyal troops to escape imprisonment. Lenin assumed the role of the chief commissar and chairman of the council of ministers; while Trotskiy became commissar of foreign affairs. The Assembly was finally dissolved by the Bolsheviks.

Kerenskiy surfaced at the front and exhorted troops to continue fighting against the Central Powers. His efforts were in vain, while the Bolsheviks were after him for encouraging the army to resume their duty to fight on. Kerenskiy escaped and secretly fled to western Europe, where he urged the Allies to land in Arkhangelsk in northern Russia. He was turned down flat. The army continued to disintegrate when facing the Germans, though it held its own against Austro-Hungarian troops on the Rumanian front. Lenin proposed a truce with the Central Powers at Brest-Litovsk. When the German demands at the conference became excessive, Trotskiy began stalling, thinking the Germans would give in, and declared his famous formula, "No peace, no war." The Germans wouldn't buy it and resumed their offensive. Lenin, realizing the Germans were serious, was forced to give in despite objections from his colleagues. Ukraine, as well as other large chunks of the country, was already occupied by Germany. Lenin tried consolidating his hold on the country by employing terror with the Cheka against counterrevolutionaries (Whites).

The civil war in all its fury commenced shortly between Red power and loyal Imperial forces. It was Lenin's original intent to eliminate all opposition as soon as possible, although he didn't realize the magnitude of the struggle. The Whites opened a front in Arkhangelsk on the White Sea, while other forces advanced from the Ukraine and further north. Admiral Kolchak left the United States to assume command of loyal Siberian forces and to mount an attack from the east. The Bolsheviks held strategic interior positions around Petrograd-Moscow area, the Caspian Sea, and up the Volga River, cutting the country in half. He exploited his interior positions, while the Whites were unable to make contact with each other, being cast to the periphery of the country, thus losing the civil war. Upon termination of the civil war, the country was totally ravaged. Lenin blamed the Whites, and the terror against them began. Felix Dzerzhinskiy, a minor Polish nobleman, assumed control of the Cheka (GPU) and went berserk with killings and executions without let up.

The country was exhausted, and starvation was rampant. The Soviet government asked for help from foreign countries, which was furnished en masse, primarily by the United States. When it became apparent that no amount of help could alleviate the severe problem of starvation, Lenin declared his "New Economic Policy," permitting the peasants to sell directly to the public. This policy, in effect, confirmed the failure of the Bolshevik socialist experiment, and under normal civilized conditions should have been abandoned forthwith. However, dictatorship of the intellectuals over the proletariat would not be abandoned for fear of losing power.

Soviet Russia disavowed all its foreign debts previously accumulated under the Imperial regime. The Allies as well as the rest of the civilized world condemned Russia as an outlaw. By this time Soviets were in full control over Russia. As if having insufficient landmass and desiring to regain its former possessions, they mounted an attack on Poland, which had previously seceded from Russia and become independent. The intent was not only to regain Poland but to enter

Germany, which lay prostrate and was ready for a takeover by the Bolshevik hordes. The French, aware of the consequences and fearful of the probable results, dispatched General Maxim Weygand to repel the attack. The Wegand-planned counterattack forced the Soviet forces to retreat almost to the outskirts of Minsk. Eventually a peace agreement was signed.

Meanwhile an assassination attempt on Lenin's life by Fanny Kaplan (Roitman), a Menshevik, lodged a bullet in his neck, causing serious complications and occasional paralysis. He was ordered to take a complete rest in Gorki. This attempt on Lenin's life had profound consequences for Soviet Russia and its people. During Lenin's recuperation in Gorki and the absence of his guiding hand at the helm, the battle for succession began and became the barometer of future things to come. Intrigues commenced almost immediately for succession in the struggle for the leadership of the Party, soviet style. Since the country didn't bother having a constitution or legitimacy for orderly succession and was being run as a fief of the Communist party, the struggle for the top position began in earnest, at first between Trotsky and Stalin. Stalin secured the position as secretary of the Communist party to take care of Lenin's health. Assured by doctors of no possible cure, the rest of the members of the Politburo began jockeying for power and started lining up sides. Stalin was rewarded with more government and party positions by Lenin than was any other member of the Politburo, and he outmaneuvered the other members and usurped Lenin's authority by placing his cronies in important positions and successfully isolating Lenin from contact with Moscow; and he subsequently got rid of the competition. Telephone contact with Gorki was bugged and interrupted, and contact with Lenin was made by occasional courier.

Stalin triumphed and isolated all rivals. The most incapable and unworthy substitute secured the position, which in the future had profound consequences for the nation and the world. While lying ill in Gorki, Lenin warned his Politburo colleagues to replace Stalin with someone more considerate and compassionate, less rude and better qualified. Alas it was far too late by then. His advice no longer mattered, since Stalin had previously placed his cronies in high positions, and they owed him allegiance under threat of dismissal. In despair, Lenin was quoted as saying, "I believe I'm guilty before the workers of Russia," a late understatement and confession of failure. His health deteriorated rapidly, and he died on 21 January 1924—an occasion the author remembers well by attending his mock funeral in Siberia a few days later.

In his writings and speeches while in exile in Europe, he taught that the salvation of the Russian masses lay in the dictatorship of the proletariat; but in reality the proletariat had nothing to say about its role in the new order and were given orders as actors and blind automatons by dictates of the party. By his actions Lenin admitted to himself that the workers of Russia were not as mature or intelligent as those in western Europe. If he had said so publicly, it would have made his theory of proletarian dictatorship meaningless. This duplicity lived with him throughout his control of the country, while his death revealed the truth of his legacy in Stalin's hands. The possession of ultimate power was his primary goal.

So ended Lenin's life of deceit, leaving to his successors a legacy of torment, murder, slave labor, and lies. No reasonable analysis would be complete without an insight to the Russian revolution, the civil war, and what followed thereafter. It was Lenin who preached dictatorship with terror and Dzerzhinskiy who enforced it. It was Lenin who illegitimately dissolved the National Assembly in February 1918, with negligible representation in it. He taught Stalin the tricks required to overcome opposition, to which later Stalin added his own special treatment and surpassed Lenin several times over. It was simple for Lenin to publicly state, "Now we shall commence the socialist order"—an illegitimacy which escaped him and his heirs. He never stopped to emphasize that the workers of Russia wanted socialism, though he never asked for their approval.

If his premise was true, why was terror used to enforce it? Who were the enemy forces, if all the workers of Russia wanted communism and socialism? Were they composed of deserting troops from the German or Austro-Hungarian fronts? Were they peasant conscripts, who had no reason to defend communism or socialism? Reasons given in declaring terror as the choice of enforcement are not only unconvincing, they are a fraud perpetuated on a simple people of Russia. Under constant threat of execution, the workers and peasants were forced to battle the Whites in the civil war, even in hopeless cases. Most of the population during the civil war within his area of control was originally docile, convinced Lenin's government couldn't last longer than a few weeks. However his rear was always secure, and no uprisings were ever attempted since Dzerzhinskiy's Cheka was always there and ready to kill rather than imprison. It was Lenin who ordered politically unreliable intellectuals, teachers, landowners, the bourgeoisie, and the industrial barons to be terrorized and deprived of food and deported to slave labor camps for fear of opposition to his program.

He found it more important to have power rather than peace and encouraged the civil war to cleanse the population of unreliable elements. Most off the members of the Duma who were opposed to him were either imprisoned or executed en masse, while some who managed to escape went into exile—mostly to western Europe, including the last prime minister, Kerenskiy. Lenin proclaimed "democratic centralism," which meant democracy within the confines of Politburo sessions only. When Menshevik party members, who were given a seat there as a show of democracy, opposed his ideas, he would dismiss them outright without discussion, having his majority in the sessions veto it. At the conclusion of the civil war, after the country was devastated, exhausted, and cleansed of undesirable elements, he was forced to confess that "the country is in such a state of despair and hunger, we have to take two steps forward and one step back." When translated it meant, "We have to revert to a free enterprise system in order to survive." This meant proclaiming a new economic policy or the old capitalist system.

Lenin deviated from the path he proclaimed on so many occasions that his own members of the Politburo and Central Committee opposed him, yet he ignored their advice and threatened to dismiss them or tender his resignation—here again a pathological fear of losing power. It is likewise true that Stalin and Dzerzhinskiy, who were party hacks rather than intellectuals, agreed with him, probably knowing no better. Yet Trotsky, Kamenev, Zinovyev, Radek, Bukharin, Rykov, Piatakov, and some other intellectuals quite often disagreed with him and caused him sleepless nights. Yet in the end, while not agreeing with him, they submitted because of his overwhelming willpower.

European socialists warned him while in exile in Europe that the Marx-Engels theory was a moral thesis of justice for the toiling masses and an awakening of the spirit, rather than a solution. Since Russia had a substandard industrial base and too few industrial workers (as compared to Europe), that the extreme socialist ideal would necessarily fail and cause a serious economic and social hardship on the population, and it did. After all, Britain and Germany were the industrial giants with a basis for grievances in 1848. Since then, conditions had improved there substantially, yet he dismissed these arguments as gutter-sniping gibberish. Not only Plekhanov, but even Paul Lafargue—Marx's son-in-law—and his wife, Laura, saw the futility of Marx's theory as an anachronism after 1848 and committed suicide. Lenin never forgave them for this act. How could he agree, when his entire basis for existence was *Das Kapital*. They also disagreed with his theory of dictatorship, which Marx never even alluded to, and his experiments with human beings. Lafargue warned him that in destroying present institutions, he would be eliminating the basis for the society to transition to a more just order, for which all were striving. Lenin chose to disregard this advice and subsequently paid a price to attain it. Later in Central Committee sessions, he reminded his colleagues not to trust the working class, to apply constant terror without letup, to catch elusive saboteurs, to cleanse the population, and to be on guard. That is exactly what Stalin did.

Lenin was a poor judge of character on many occasions and paid for it in the case of Stalin when it was too late to stop him. He had no use for psychological methods or kindness; made of intellectual iron, he couldn't give in or consent. He was also ill at ease among crowds, unless he lectured them. Although he didn't live opulently and slept on an iron cot, he wielded more power than the czars, who slept on an Imperial bed. An obsessive man in work, his food and drink habits were primitive—perhaps to set an example. This austere lifestyle was totally disregarded by Stalin upon Lenin's death, and he indulged in an opulent lifestyle and excessive banquet giving. Lenin created an order of professional revolutionaries—under Stalin known as the *nomenklatura*—whose members received special rations in the early days of revolutionary upheavals when food was scarce. These revolutionaries were told to teach the workers and peasants what he did for them, lest they forget that they now owned all property, all factories, and all land. He died disillusioned, considering himself betrayed by his colleagues, and left it to Krupskaya to fight for his cause. She was insulted and disregarded and bypassed by Stalin, since she knew him too well. He considered her a nuisance in his perversion of Lenin's teachings. She too died disillusioned in 1938, during the infamous Stalin's mock trials, feeling betrayed by Lenin's colleagues, particularly Trotsky, whom she had asked to protect her. He didn't, and during the early struggles against Stalin, he was exiled from Russia.

In time history and civilization will judge Lenin harshly for his diabolic experiments with a simple people, when a time of human rights and democracy was springing up—which was the wave of the future in the twentieth century, even in third world countries. Attila the Hun, Genghis Khan, Tamerlane, and other barbarians could take a back seat to Lenin's violent upheavals and transformation of society. Russians and their minority nationalities were persecuted and forced into submission by his iron will, with cunning aplomb and deception, until they too suffered his methods. One can't fault Marx and Engels—after all they were social scholars in a time of revolutionary upheavals in Europe when workers were exploited during the Industrial Revolution, though that time had long since passed.

How then does one explain Lenin's obsession with socialist-communist theory? Obviously he believed in it but only as it suited him for Russia at first and subsequently for the entire world. As he attempted to hammer it into Russia, he saw workers in other countries similarly motivated. That was a convenient exaggeration without any proof, since European workers decided to bargain or strike until employers consented and treated them fairly. It didn't take him long to realize his failure when he tried to foster his system on the European working class, particularly in Germany, and they overwhelmingly rejected it in favor of bargaining and strikes. While some national groups tried communism in Hungary, in Bavaria, and Berlin, their workers and citizens turned them out. Unfortunately, Lenin died too early to see his creation plunged into an abyss by his erstwhile pupil, Stalin, who outdid him many times over with a megalomaniac perfection unknown in history. One should also admit that Lenin created free education for all the masses—here again for a specific purpose, to indoctrinate students into scientific Marxism. What was scientific about Marxism is still unknown in the world, except in the Soviet Union. He was also responsible for free health care, (such as it was) equality among people (at least in the beginning) and books, libraries, and work for the laboring class. Subsequently the workers were educated, and it was no longer so simple to defraud them.

In time people realized it was the export of natural resources which supported their mediocre living standards. A land of rich agricultural soil was squandered away by peasants forced into collectives, causing the government to import foreign grain to supplement their meager diets, while the *nomenklatura* enjoyed life like Western millionaires. Lacking any quality manufactured products for export, the stagnating economy floundered in useless quagmire in repetitive work, for which there was no demand. Asked by foreign correspondence about their work conditions and status, their reply was classic: "They pretend to pay us, and we pretend to work." The defense industry was always busy supplying third world countries with weapons for their civil wars and got paid with discount prices on various items. The defense industry employed the best talents in the country, thus robbing other industries of required know-how. On the other hand, the wealthy found an escape in imported products, while the poor working class and pensioners fought for bread and minimum meat rations. The *nomenklatura* helped break the country of its lifestyle by pocketing cash, thereby robbing the country in covering its reserves to pay the workers. Lenin appealed mostly to poor and illiterate workers and peasants of the autocratic regime, who mostly knew poverty and isolation from the rest of the world, clutching at straws which promised them gifts from heaven. In the few years in which he exercised power from November 1917 to the day of his assassination, he caused more social turmoil and remaking of societal harmony to mankind than any other tyrant in history.

In January 1994 Oleg Andrianov, director of the Moscow Brain Institute, reported that "in the anatomical structure of Lenin's brain, there is nothing sensational, but it is undoubtedly the brain of a talented man." Touted as a genius by the communists, apparently he was not even close. If Stalin and the rest of his successors were to rise from their graves and hear this report, they would most probably request instant reburial.

In honor of Lenin's memory in the USSR, his successors placed his mummified body in a sumptuous mausoleum in Red Square, above which their leaders surveyed their demented empire with military parades for blind automatons, reminding their citizens of the greatness of communism and of Lenin, the genius.

It would be fascinating to have an analysis of Stalin's brain, though it is now brain-dead, which would probably reveal how another genius in cowardice, murder, lies, cunning, betrayal, and possibly how deviously his rotten brain operated.

The time finally arrived for the promised utopia to fold and dissolve itself—a Soviet Union which was not Soviet, nor was it ever a union. Historical analysis indicates that Western civilization took centuries to develop and is still developing, while Leninism in Russia came too quickly, accomplished nothing constructive, perhaps ruined the country (even if temporarily), set back Russia for years to come in a predictably destructive sequence, and expired in violent strangulation of its own making. Perhaps the most appropriate epitaph for Lenin lies in one word uttered by Maxim Gorki: "trickster." When the Soviet Union expired in December 1991 and the removal of his body from the mausoleum to a common grave was debated, his surviving niece, a daughter of Lenin's sister, revealed her existence and spoke to have his body lie in peace where it rests in Red Square; though entrance to the mausoleum is locked and the honor guard in special uniforms and soviet-style goose step no longer guards the mausoleum.

**Conclusion**

The Imperial bureaucracy, though cumbersome and slow to react to conditions, nevertheless had some progressive means, most of which were adopted by the Soviets, and claimed as their own brainchild. Lenin stage-managed a revolution to benefit workers, peasants, and soldiers at the expense of a burgeoning middle class. The same class which before WWI and the revolution was the basis of economic growth, with some workers receiving health benefits and gradually improving wages. Child labor laws were already in place, admittedly somewhat later than in western Europe, yet conditions were improving constantly. The same class after the revolution escaped to Manchuria and created a free economic boom until displaced by the Japanese in 1941. Under the Imperial regime, the Duma embraced various parties which dissented among themselves, with the majority vote prevailing after debate and full hearing—though if it displeased the czar, he would not concur, which happened often. Here again, it was a matter of time before the czar stopped interfering, since the question of the constitution for the empire was pending when WWI started. Autocracy as was known then could not continue, since both the German Reichstag and the Austro-Hungarian empire were also intent on revamping their constricted constitution, until the war's commencement.

Except for common government-owned enterprises throughout western Europe (railroads, post office, telegraph and telephone services) the economy was under the private enterprise system. Russia's agricultural production in 1913 was such that it exported its surplus grain to Europe and was repaying its debts in gold currency to several countries from which it had borrowed. Most natural and mineral resources, oil and railroad mileage, were accelerating in production outputs and were run by private companies. The boast of exceeding production quotas by Stalin were exaggerations of his statistical bureaus. The one drawback under the Imperial regime was Nicholas II, the autocrat himself, who refused to see the writing on the wall and interfered into most prerogatives autocratically, including the occupation of Poland, Ukraine, Finland, the Baltic countries, and TransCaucasus. The other drawback from centuries past was the secret police (*Okhrana*), which was paranoid about the possible assassination of the czars and government ministers by assassins trying to attain Western cultural heritage and freedom. One should also remember that the Mongol influence of domination, conquest, and spies had an overriding effect on the military culture of the nation and shut the country off from those outside its borders. Western Europe never had that experience, at least not in recent memory. However, this was also loosening up substantially before WWI, with more and more people permitted to leave the country; and many did. While these were drawbacks, some other Western powers had colonial interests which were also drawbacks. In that sense, Russian domination of adjoining territories was a defensive strategy to insure the safety of its own borders and to keep adjoining countries close to its territories; while not excusable, it was a reason to acquire more territory, which never seemed to be enough.

It is reasonable to assume that the revolution was not only not inevitable but was a tragedy instigated by Lenin. In seeking power at any cost, the Communists applied a strangling yoke on the people and caused the nation's doom. On the other hand, the Imperial regime couldn't adjust to changing conditions. This was required for its survival and to accommodate its people in the changing world and its environment in the beginning of the twentieth century. Autocratic Czardom had outlived its usefulness years before but had no will nor desire to adjust to changing conditions when it held power—a dilemma almost impossible to comprehend.

**Recommended Reading**

Clark, Ronald W. *Lenin*. New York: Harper & Rowe, 1988.
Payne, Robert. *Lenin*. New York: Simon & Schuster, 1964.
Volkogonov, Dmitriy. *Lenin*. New York: Free Press, Simon & Schuster, 1994.

# CHAPTER X
# JOSEF VISARIONOVICH STALIN (DJUGASHVILLI): 1878-1953

Origins

For historical reasons Stalin should be considered a minority national among over one hundred nationalities and races of the huge Russian empire. He was a Georgian by birth, and there was not a drop of Russian blood in him. He was the son of a drunken cobbler, Visarion Djugashvilli, who abused his wife and son vengefully in a drunken stupor for no other reason than for want of anything to do. He was lazy, and the repairs brought to him didn't get done for weeks until customers complained or took the work elsewhere. He died at the early age of thirty. Little is known of his father's origins except that he was born to a peasant family in Didi-Lilo, a village close to Gori, Georgia. Stalin's mother, Yekaterina Geladse, a daughter of peasant serfs, was born in the small village of Gambareuli, close to Gori. She was a humble woman with no schooling who did her chores and complained not at all about her lot in life. After her husband's death, to support her son and herself, she worked in menial jobs for wealthier families. In her later years, she left her native Georgia to visit her son in Moscow—a trip arranged by the Georgian Communist party, unknown to Stalin. She left promptly two days later. She was a devout Christian and wanted her son to be a priest, with hopes for subsequent higher post within the church hierarchy. She put him through school and later arranged for his seminary attendance without payment, although the wealthy Georgian family Ignatoshvili, her patron, helped financially.

Not much is known of her life after Stalin assumed power, other than certain care was taken by the Georgian Communist party to satisfy her daily needs although she was in frail health. While taking his summer vacations on the Black Sea coast of Georgia, it was reported by some Georgian neighbors that he saw her only twice for short visits. Her last two years were spent in the governor's palace in Tiflis, where the Georgian Communist party allocated her two rooms. She died at eighty-one in 1938, during the most frightful years of fake court trials and executions ordered by her son. She was buried in King David's cemetery in accordance with the rites of the Eastern Orthodox Church. As reported by close neighbors, Stalin never attended the funeral, sending two NKVD officers with flowers and a note: J.V. Stalin, General Secretary, CPSU.

The characteristics Stalin inherited from his father were somewhat complex,

*Iosef Visarionovich, Stalin*

a combination of vengeance, hard drinking, a violent temper, laziness, cunning, and stone-cold actions. On his mother's side he inherited patience, an unusual memory, and infrequent talk. When combined with both contradictory personalities, his behavior may be partially explained by his lack of formal education, accented Russian speech, and modest intelligence, coupled with his inferiority complex among superior talents. He was a man of brute force and a complex personality. One may conclude that here is a man of contradictions rolled into one being, capable of paranoiac behavior, cunning in one instance, silence and rare utterance in another. His parental legacy was not much, considering Stalin's reputation in history. It is this complex personality which calls for analysis of his twenty-nine years of absolute and unchallenged supreme power. His power haunted the Soviet Union after his death to its dissolution in December 1991, and to the present day Russia and the newly independent states. Josef Visarionovich Djugashvilli was born 21 December 1879 by Soviet records in Didi-Lilo, Georgia, in the village of his father's birth. Other documents uncovered by historian Anton Antonov-Avseyenko, in researching Stalin's records, show him to be born 6 December 1878, a date which was issued by the Czarist police when he was first arrested. He was born with two toes of his left foot joined, and later when still a child, he was afflicted with small pox, which left him pockmarked for the rest of his life. When only ten, he sustained a left elbow injury causing his arm to be withered and shorter than his right. He was five feet three inches tall. He hated his father for physical abuses and beatings he received, with the inevitable result that he learned to hate people and became hardened and indifferent to cruelty. For consolation in his youth, he sang in the neighborhood church choir and learned liturgical language, which deeply affected him in later life. His ambition then was to become a priest and subsequently to aspire to a higher position in the church hierarchy, which would have pleased his mother. The Orthodox Church has the altar behind the iconostasis, which makes mysteries more profound to the glory of God. It seems this had a deep influence on him, in view of his many manipulations of power behind the Kremlin walls. When considering his many deformities of character, the result would appear to be a demand for deification. Since the school had only four grades, he was prepared to go to the Tiflis (Tbilisi) Theological Seminary on a scholarship offered by the priests and previously arranged by his mother and a wealthy Georgian family, with no expenses paid. Before entering the seminary, he spent his summers in the countryside reading books and singing in the choir.

In September 1894 he took a train to Tiflis to enter the seminary. It was a dour building with barred windows and strict discipline. At the time, the seminary was a breeding ground of forbidden books, which were smuggled in. The police confiscated these books, yet they constantly reappeared. Among the books he read in secret were Darwin's *On the Origins of Species by Natural Selection* and *The Descent of Man* and books by Russian radicals, among which were Chernishevsky's *What Is to Be Done*. Universities did not exist in Georgia, and students desiring to attend would have gone to universities in Russia, since the desire for knowledge wasn't provided by the monks. The students who longed for knowledge smuggled books in and circulated them. Additionally, since nationalism was rampant, students demanded Georgian literature, since none was provided by the rector, who was Russian. Constant rebellions took place, with dire consequences for some students. Josef Djhugashvilli, by then, had changed his mind about entering the priesthood and began reading forbidden literature and composing poetry, showing no particular desire for theology. On at least two occasions he made remarks to some of his colleagues, and one of them remarked that Josef said, "They are fooling us about God. There is no God." When asked how he knew, he answered that he read Darwin. A reading of Darwin's writings does not explicitly reveal the absence of God. This instance begins to expose his early untruths to justify his arguments. He began getting in trouble for fomenting disobedience and reading forbidden literature on many occasions, and yet he was not expelled but reprimanded and disciplined along with other students.

About 1898 he began developing ambitious attitudes, atheistic reasoning, and a ferocious temper; he was filled with sarcasm and hatred for the Imperial regime and his brighter colleagues. He assumed an authoritarian temper with fellow students who disagreed with him and tried compelling them to his views. Occasionally he would disappear from school in the evenings to attend subversive speeches by exiled railway workers who had returned from Siberia. Lastly, after refusing to take his final examinations for fear of failing, he was expelled from the seminary.

He developed a determination to be a revolutionary, with utter vengeance against authority and the bourgeoisie. At the time he was destitute and untrained to earn a living and had to face an uncertain future—without resources and skills and in bad health.

**Unemployed Revolutionary**

One can see that Josef was being transformed from a potential theologian to a revolutionary following his gradual development into manhood. From the prison environment in earlier years when exiled in Siberia, and later still when evading and escaping from the secret police, he learned to deceive and betray his close associates to the Okhrana. He used liturgical style and poetry, which he had learned while in the seminary, throughout his lifetime as a dictator. When combined with all the above traits, his diminutive height, and added deformities, one may detect a warped and tortured personality. He could not bear to be reasoned with, contradicted, or considered inferior to superior intellects, whom he despised and years later deposed or executed at will. Like a master magician, he invented scenarios to implicate his real or imagined opponents, competitors, or witnesses to his sinister deeds and crimes.

An array of documents on Stalin's early life, after expulsion from the seminary to his commencement as a revolutionary, have been made public by Anton Antonov-Avseyenko in the archives of the former czarist police. Previous efforts to secure them were rebuffed by the Gorbachev government. However, documents available for research have been recently examined and show deliberate tampering by Beria, his KGB chief and a fellow Georgian, or Stalin himself.

Documents do not show Stalin to be an astronomy observer or an apprentice bookkeeper in the Tiflis observatory, as he had claimed; neither could these claims be substantiated or confirmed by fellow emigress in Manchuria who were at the observatory with him after the civil war. It took considerable time to secure documents and publicly expose them, since the archives of the czarist regime, and particularly the extensive Soviet archival system, have been recently placed under "The Archives of the President of the Russian Federation" to be examined by General Dmitri Volkogonov. It took almost seven months of deliberate order just to locate Lenin's order to execute Nicholas II, his family, and entourage. Gorbachev would not release these or other critical files for political reasons while he served as general secretary and president of the Soviet Union for six years. Generally, after leaving the seminary in 1899 until about the beginning of the Russo-Japanese war in 1905, there is nothing heard of Stalin. Although he claims to have led a Marxist group at age twenty-one, this appears to be a fantasy of his *Collected Works*. Apparently these years seem to have passed in obscurity, particularly due to his having no trade skills and feeling his way through underground circles.

Some of his colleagues in Georgia, noting his ambitions in revolutionary work, suggested he write an article in a propaganda leaflet to gain recognition and experience. Being extremely cautious, he pondered the idea carefully and concluded that he would wait a while until he better understood socialism and Marxism, the better to appeal to the workers to rebel. Subsequently, he collaborated on an article in the magazine *The Struggle*, printed in Baku and later still wrote an article himself, in the most liturgical style imaginable, showing his entry as a revolutionary writer. Some of the articles later were circulated by the Georgian Mdivani family, who were emigres in Manchuria. Nothing else significant was heard from him until he is requested to leave the newly formed Socialist party in Tiflis when it didn't select him to be its chief. Subsequently he vilified and castigated the party and left for Batum on the Black Sea to oppose it. Some emigres writers suspected, and Anton Antonov-Avseyenko indicates, that for spite he collaborated with the czarist police. Naturally, no proof of that exists in the files. These writers paint a plausible scenario in connecting him to these events, in view of his betrayals, disappearances, jealousy, and conniving methods, with ambitions of grandeur even at that early age. Although coincidences do occur, the historians evidence two different birth certificates, arbitrarily tying him to these scenarios, along with constant absences during certain periods. Subsequently his family connections were such that his two wives and their immediate relatives were disposed of, perhaps for possible fear of exposure, which makes it more plausible.

While at school and seminary, teaching was conducted in the Russian language; and since Georgia was a Russian province, the Russian language was mandatory. Stalin spoke Georgian at home; upon entering Russian school later, he could not shake his Georgian accent, which silently amused his underlings when he attained power. On rare occasions when he had to deliver a short speech at a congress or conference, he spoke in bursts of a few words and tried to avoid making long speeches as much as possible. His Russian was reasonably good but quite ordinary and simple, always liturgical as acquired in the seminary. Some of his notes in Russian have been edited for grammatical errors as well as sentence structure in his published *Collected Works*. He displayed a serious inferiority complex, suspecting his mostly Russian-speaking colleagues were secretly laughing at him when he passed notes in Politburo (later renamed Presidium) meetings.

Stalin led a double life from the beginning of his revolutionary career until his death. When first arrested by the czar's Okhrana for subversive activities, he apparently snitched on his colleagues and got paid for it. This talk was bandied about during the civil war, along with German government funds for Lenin and his group to entrain for Russia. When dispatched to Stockholm for a Marxist conference, he was taken into confidence by his Marxist colleagues and given assignments. After this conference, he appears to have changed his mind about working for the police and joined revolutionary circles. To hide his past, he eliminated those who knew him well, including his relatives and close friends. Both of his wives died under mysterious circumstances. His second wife, Nadezhda Alliluyeva, gave him two children, who under the circumstances turned out to be unfortunate. Svetlana, his daughter, married a Jewish doctor, whom Stalin rejected and made sure she divorced him. Her second marriage was to an Indian Communist, who died later in India. In attending his funeral in India, Svetlana requested permission from American authorities to travel and relocate to the United States. Upon her arrival, she married Wes Peters, an architect, by whom she had a daughter. Subsequently, after his death, she relocated to Britain. At this writing, mother and daughter are in a halfway house in London. Svetlana is the author of a book entitled *Twenty Letters to a Friend*. His son, Vasilliy, a general in the Soviet air force at the age of twenty-five, was a constant source of trouble to Stalin. He was an alcoholic who married several times. He attended his father's funeral in a drunken stupor and died shortly thereafter. Stalin's second wife's niece, Kira Alliluyeva, claims that the family is convinced he shot her with her own revolver after a heated argument. This was recently reported in the *European*, a weekly newspaper in Britain.

There is no proof to the allegation that Stalin poisoned Lenin. However, since Nadezhda Alliluyeva was in Lenin's secretariat in Gorki and reported to Stalin daily concerning Lenin's confidential writings, the comings and goings of people, and was privy to many secrets, it is certainly possible. It is not beyond Stalin's character to have conspired to have him poisoned, since he was already first secretary of the Communist party and was delegated to look after Lenin's well-being. His closest Georgian revolutionary colleague, Ordzhonikidze, was put to death by Stalin in 1936 after a violent quarrel, perhaps threatening to expose his past and for killing too many good Communists.

Perhaps the best description of Stalin was revealed by Khrushchev at the twentieth Party Congress: "What do you expect? We had a madman at the helm." Khrushchev was not then in possession of most documents about Stalin's double life against the Bolsheviks. It took almost forty years after his death (in 1953) for Anton Antonov-Avseyenko and later General Volkogonov to uncover them.

Simple suspicion branded as a saboteur was sufficient for Stalin to send people to slave labor camps in northern Siberia or near the Arctic Circle. Documents and Russian history writers show only fragments of incidents, yet relatives and friends of those lucky enough to escape to the Maritime Provinces, who crossed the Ussuri and Amur rivers into Manchuria almost weekly, told of extreme hardships, executions, slave labor camps, and imposed hunger. The episodes described between 1927 and 1939 in the emigre press in Manchuria, Paris, and Berlin described thousands attempting to escape. From the time of Stalin's assumption of power until World War II, some estimates place the dead from executions, starvation, and overwork as high as seventeen million. This estimate covers people in Russia proper, Ukraine, all regions of Siberia, areas bordering the Arctic Circle, TransCaucasus, the Maritime Provinces, and other slave labor camps, along with regularly ordered executions by the KGB.

It is doubtful that all tyrants combined throughout recorded history even came close to accomplishing such horrendous feats as Stalin. It is surprising, unjust, and somewhat disappointing that Stalin was never branded a war criminal, executioner, or psychopathic killer, as judged under civilized standards of behavior by any judicial bodies similar to the Nuremberg trials of the Nazis. He did, however, hide his past quite successfully while he ruled the USSR and the satellite nations. He successfully fooled Roosevelt during WWII, but not Churchill—who knew him better—at the Teheran and Yalta conferences in 1943 and 1945, respectively. In trying to fool Truman at the Postdam Conference of Victors in 1945, he failed, since the President could see through his schemes. Clement Atlee, the new British prime minister, unfamiliar with Stalin and his tricks, deferred to Truman's better judgment on that score.

Further analysis would show that, in effect, Stalin perverted the Soviet Union as envisioned by Lenin and his colleagues, commencing in 1927. Not that Lenin was innocent, with his own brand of rule and repressions. While the Communist Marxist system was a utopian idea and purely theoretical, at least Lenin endeavored to acknowledge mistakes within the confines of the Politburo. Stalin, on the other hand, could never permit himself to acknowledge making any mistakes. He made so many that it would be a futile to attempt to count them. Lenin's interpretation of industrialization and agriculture was substantially different in principle; in Stalin's hands it was a backbreaking and murderous machine which cost the lives of millions. When Lenin ranted against his colleagues in the Politburo and Central Committee, particularly against Kamenev and Zinoviev and others who objected to dictatorship of the proletariat, there is no record of him personally ordering executions of his colleagues or others. Only on two occasions did he find it necessary to order executions: General Dukhonin, the field commander of the Russian army in late 1917 who refused to order a cease fire, and Nicholas II and his entire family and entourage. This last attempt was based on his fear of possible martyrdom and the first attempt on the fear of counterrevolution.

**The Conspirator**

Sometime in 1903 in London, Lenin brought about a split in the Russian Social Democratic party between the moderate and radical wings. Weeks later

Stalin heard about the split while in exile in Siberia and tried to compare it to his split with the Georgian Party, writing a letter of congratulations to Lenin. Lenin had a habit of writing letters to people, thanking them if they agreed with him, so he sent one to Stalin. Subsequently Stalin claimed to have had his first relations with Lenin from that exchange. No such relations are acknowledged or ever recorded in Lenin's correspondence or archives nor even entered in Stalin's *Collected Works*. He claimed he burned them as an old habit of all conspirators at the time. After Lenin's death Stalin used these supposed letter-writing exchanges as evidence of a long-standing relationship between Lenin and himself, implying that he was a true and faithful follower of Lenin from years back, to further consolidate and justify his leadership. Yet his years in conspiratorial work are shrouded in mystery, at least until 1910, when his prompt appearances and disappearances were never clearly documented. Nevertheless, one would naturally assume that Stalin would have mentioned them in his writings, had there been any significant occasions for this conspiratorial work, yet these mysteries persist. It is true that czarist police files do acknowledge his apprehension, but not to the extent he claimed—hence the suspicions of Western and Russian emigres writers, some of whom were Socialists and knew him in exile in Siberia. The few conspirators with whom he had contact hated his overbearing attitude and extremely rude and rash decisions, bordering on black or white.

His masterminding of bank holdups, murders, and betrayals of his colleagues as well as his blackmailing techniques were legendary. He would justify these actions by claiming that nothing should stand in the way of "expropriating from the expropriators," by whatever means necessary. When Lenin heard of such unsavory methods, he did nothing to stop them. Since Stalin was a simple direct action man, lacking any theoretical basis and intellectual background, his only recourse was brutal force and simplistic language which impressed workers who couldn't distinguish the difference and knew no better.

Most documents available during the czarist regime showed him as a conspirator, and his actions later, when becoming dictator, confirm him to be a pathological liar. Even before becoming dictator, he expressed a violent temper when challenged and was a rumormonger among party members. When he was challenged among knowledgeable comrades, he would answer next to nothing, take out his notebook, and pretend to learn from his colleagues—and all the while, keeping score for future vengeance and retribution. His stay in Batum, according to his biographical records, is exaggerated to the extreme when he claimed that he led a rebellion there. Although enough time has elapsed to dig out the facts, no witnesses or records exist of the incident. Most probably he passed out revolutionary pamphlets to the workers and led clandestine meetings. Records indicate only that he was arrested there and subsequently exiled to Irkutsk in Siberia for three years. Prison in Siberia had a strict regimen, however. Treatment of the prisoners by the guards, by and large, was reasonable if the prisoner behaved but cruel if he didn't. Exile in Siberia under the czarist regime usually meant isolation, with reasonable freedom to roam around and report to the police at designated times. As it turned out, for all the bluster, Stalin was confined to a prison and took no part in the rare beastly outbreaks by other prisoners. He was deathly afraid of beatings by prison guards, lest they cripple him for life, what with the deformities he already had. On the other hand, he was sneaky and deceitful on many occasions. When questioned about troublemakers, he didn't hesitate to betray the culprits. Some of the former prisoners who later escaped to Manchuria revealed his behavior, bearing in mind his double-dealing in the pay of the czarist police earlier.

In Georgia, Lev Borisovich Kamenev (Rosenfeld) was better known and more active and admired in Marxist circles than Stalin. He was an original member of Lenin's close group in exile and later one of the principal members of the Politburo. Subsequently, when reading Stalin's writings, one would never know that Kamenev ever existed. Stalin escaped and returned from exile in Siberia in 1904 and went back to Gori, Georgia. He married Yekaterina Zvanidze of the same village, in June. Little is known of her since he domineered and kept her in the background. Yakov, a son, was born to them, and little was known of him until captured by German troops in July 1941. He was a lieutenant in the army, and after a lengthy interrogation, he admitted to studying machine technology and said nothing more. He was confined in the Oranienbaum concentration camp in Germany for special prisoners and died there on a barbed wire fence trying to escape or find relief in death. Stalin never liked him and saw him only on rare occasions; he refused to recognize him after hearing of his capture.

About 1906 Stalin issued his first acknowledged pamphlet, *Anarchism or Socialism*, under a pseudonym, Koba. In it he theorized that a revolutionary movement of the dictatorship of the proletariat cannot be led by one man or a revolutionary elite—apparently knowing little of Lenin's intent of personal control. He believed in an "emancipated anarchist" before the masses could be emancipated. In Marxist doctrine the individual can only be emancipated when all the masses are emancipated. Stalin, the theorist, couldn't survive this writing and discarded it. He later talked about the Paris Commune as not being a dictatorship but rather a dictatorship in name only. "But if it turns out that it was a dictatorship," he said, "then down with Marxism." Such dribble about the subject has never before been written. Having no intellectual credentials for theory, he was a failure, but as a magician in double-talk, he undoubtedly excelled.

He was above all anti-Semitic and most likely joined the Bolsheviks, rather than the Mensheviks, since there were fewer Jews who considered themselves Russian atheists. These few Jews, however, were the most important collaborators of Lenin. The Mensheviks, on the other hand, had many members who came from the Jewish Pale and Jewish Bund and as a party were more tolerant and democratic. While he knew Kamenev—who was quite a prominent Bolshevik—well in Georgia, Stalin developed his anti-Semitism against all Jews, probably from jealousy of their higher intellectual capabilities and their positions as important collaborators and personal friends of Lenin. Lazar Kaganovich, a Politburo colleague, was a cultural Jew by birth but did not consider himself Jewish, similar to other Jews who didn't come from the Pale or the Jewish Bund. Lazar Kaganovich's sister, a Jewess, was Stalin's mistress for years.

He recognized that funds to run clandestine operations were mandatory, so he took it upon himself to be the initiator of bank robberies; in the end it proved to be a failure. He was later forced to face a party tribunal and was expelled from the party. As usual, he had his comrades steal the documents implicating him in staged robberies and when time came to review the records, none were found. These exploits occurred in Georgia and were of minor significance to the overall picture in revolutionary times. The case was dropped for lack of documentary evidence. While he instigated robberies, riots, labor strikes, and the entire panoply of clandestine activities, he never once participated in them. Between 1910 and 1916 he managed to disappear from sight on many occasions without a trace and to reappear just as suddenly among the revolutionaries. These mysteries have never been traced. It is unlikely that he had a loss of memory, for we know the one thing he inherited from his mother was a lasting and extraordinary memory.

He decided to write a letter to comrade Seameon intended for Lenin's eyes, hoping to gain recognition as a revolutionary. He wrote of the grim conditions of Party members in Russia and the hopelessness which had set in among revolutionary theorists and workers, who had lost hope in their endeavors. Since he was not known at all in Moscow, he was trying to impress Lenin and his exiles in Europe of his importance. In that letter, which eventually wound up in police files, he identified people by name—an unforgivable sin for a revolutionary—and reminded the recipients of the letter about his exploits in Baku and Tiflis (Tbilisi). A few weeks later he wrote to Moscow Bolsheviks, conveying his dislike for Lenin and his gang of theoretical do-nothings who enjoyed life in Europe as tourists. Eventually, Lenin came to recognize Stalin as a party worker who could be useful as a revolutionary among Russian minority nationals, for want of other minority nationals in the Bolshevik party. At a Prague conference of the Bolsheviks in Europe, Lenin created a Central Committee of prominent party colleagues to be elected for membership. Stalin was not elected, but Lenin made him a member anyway as a useful worker in TransCaucasia and as a member of a national minority. The question of minority nationalities of Russia, and what to do with them in the coming revolution, was a problem for Lenin, and he called on Stalin for his opinion since he was from the Caucasus. Stalin never came up with any innovative solutions on the question of nationalities in Russia. Since he didn't have a solution, Lenin used double-talk on the nationalities question and skirted around the problem of independence or autonomous status within the Russian empire. Only then did Stalin commence to form opinions about their status. It turned out to be the same as Lenin's. Subsequently, after Lenin's death, Stalin diverted from their independence and opted for autonomous status into the Soviet Union. Lenin was notorious for being a poor judge of character and Stalin is a prime example.

Stalin spent four years before the revolution in exile in Turukhansk, Siberia, as a member of the Central Committee, apparently unmoved by his membership. Yakov Sverdlov and Suren Spandarian, his fellow party members in exile in Siberia, were better known and ran the exile communities as leaders, yet Stalin kept to himself by fishing. During WWI life was getting worse in exiled camps, though people were rather reasonably free to do as they wished in normal times. Stalin never entertained the thought of volunteering in the armed forces, though it's doubtful he would have been accepted because of his deformities.

At the Eleventh Party Congress, in which he was a non-voting member, the application called for: "To which social category do you belong? Clerk, worker, or peasant." Stalin left it blank. Having had no work experience, he claimed at first to be an observer and then an assistant to a bookkeeper, which was a fabrication. He never knew any workers or mixed with them. Being uncomfortable in social situations, he kept to himself. The probable reasons he stayed away from workers or better-educated people were his inability to give coherent speeches, his accented Russian speech, and his lack of intellectual abilities to convince. In essence, the author concludes that Stalin was a nineteenth-century, uneducated, streetwise wanderer, who was searching for something to do at the time. Having no trade skills, he stumbled upon the easiest outlet—to rave and rant against established authority. Later however, as a member of the Central Committee, having been indoctrinated by Lenin and his colleagues, he acquired certain attributes which he used in the role of commissar of nationalities. Surrounded mainly by fellow Russians and Russian Jews in his circle, Stalin was the only minority national who could be useful in filling that job. He was also rewarded because he staged holdups and secured funds for the party. It is not particularly unusual for a person having no formal education to succeed in a specific field. Stalin did in fact succeed in acquiring a position of high authority, partially because of his extraordinary memory and his penchant to jot down everything on record, regardless of the fact that he was a rude, vengeful, conniving, cheating, lying, rumor-monger. He succeeded in achieving a high position by surrounding himself with people of like intelligence. When he became secretary of the Communist party by Lenin's order, he selected people of his own caliber and staffed them in thousands of positions of authority throughout the country, under threat of expulsion unless they obeyed his orders. By using the newly created bureaucracy during Lenin's illness and after his death, he amassed enormous power and later achieved dictatorial rule over superior intellectuals in the Party.

**Prelude to the Revolution**

The Provisional Government issued an order in late spring of 1917 to release all political prisoners. Stalin was released and traveled to Petrograd, where all the action was taking place in fomenting uprisings by the Bolsheviks. By July it became evident that the Bolsheviks agitated for the overthrow of the Provisional Government. Lenin was afraid of being imprisoned when the Provisional Government issued an order for his arrest, caused by his demand for the overthrow of a legitimate government. Lenin and his comrades deliberated whether he should face a court trial. The decision was finally reached not to surrender Lenin, and he promptly escaped to Finland in disguise. During Lenin's absence, Stalin claimed to have formed a party center, in which he was the principal organizer and head. Research of documents shows no evidence or existence of such a party center; apparently it was aimed to establish himself as a principal follower of Lenin. Yet when Lenin was hiding in Finland, nothing of any importance seems to have occurred with Stalin, other than he was one of several editors of the party paper, *Rabochiy Put* (*Pravda*) and acted as a messenger. In fact, his whereabouts in this time frame are clouded in mystery. Stalin had little to do as commissar of nationalities at that time. When Lenin returned from Finland and dissolved the Second Provisional Government, he clamored for secession of hostilities against the Central Powers. When operations were continued, Lenin called General Dukhonin, the commander at the front, on the direct line and ordered him to cease operations immediately. When the general refused on the grounds that it was a political decision, Lenin ordered him shot. He was accompanied by Stalin and an epileptic Lieutenant Krylenko, whom Lenin made commander-in-chief of the army. This prompt and ultimate decision by Lenin made an immense impression on Stalin for its sheer gall, which he subsequently used just as effectively against his enemies. The learning of arbitrary and prompt decisions had begun, and he used it often in the civil war and thereafter until his death in 1953.

**Stalin and the Civil War**

At the commencement of the civil war, Stalin was still commissar of nationalities, with little or nothing to do. Lenin realized that Stalin could be used as his eyes and ears at the lagging Volga front. He was ordered to the Tsaritsin, (Stalingrad, Volgagrad) front to investigate why food supplies were lagging from the Volga Basin, and to secure shipments of grain, vegetables, and meat to the Moscow and Petrograd areas. Stalin knew nothing of supply problems and took Voroshilov, a former army sergeant, along with him. In a few days he informed Lenin that the supplies of grain, vegetables, and meat would be forthcoming shortly by rail. As it happened, supplies sent by rail were minimal, and Lenin complained of being deceived. However, Stalin took the occasion to blame the incompetence of the military commander at the Tsaritsin front as a reason. He later blamed Trotskiy's leadership and his use of former White officers in the Red Army. Gradually he began sniping at Trotskiy and other appointed leaders in the battlefield area. He informed Lenin that food supplies were directly related to the army's poor military command. In effect he was telling Lenin to appoint him military commander and send him artillery and airplanes. He reminded Lenin of his previous request to do just that, but since he heard nothing from him, he intended to disregard Trotskiy and take matters in his own hands. Records indicate that Trotskiy's leadership as war commissar was remarkably effective, resulting in extensive gains on various fronts. Trotskiy was intelligent and wise enough to leave purely military affairs, command, and control to professional army officers. He knew his role as political commissar of the entire battlefront. He was all over the frontlines, supplying the armies with men, weapons, ammunition, food, and propaganda.

In his letters to Lenin, Stalin does not mention that he had already dismissed several commanders without authority and unknown to Trotskiy. This appeared to be the first instance where Stalin showed jealousy against Trotskiy and his ability to command. He hoped to be given authority and direct military command of the Tsaritsin front while disregarding pleas from Lenin for delivery of food supplies, which was his assignment in the first place—not replacement of military commanders. The author finds it puzzling why Lenin showed more patience with Stalin than he usually did with his other close comrades, particularly since Stalin knew next to nothing of military strategy or tactics. Stalin's writings were limited to criticism, rather than proof of his military command capabilities. Perhaps he thought Stalin was as ruthless as himself and could serve a useful purpose. Another reason could be that perhaps he considered Stalin as the representative of minority nationalities and thought that he could bring about their active military participation among the Bolsheviks. At any rate, Lenin had enough problems of his own; he didn't have time, energy, or desire to bother with military problems, which were Trotskiy's responsibility. Nevertheless Lenin sent Sverdlov, the president of the republic, to ameliorate relations between Trotskiy and Stalin, but this proved unsuccessful. Conditions on the Tsaritsin front the first week of October 1918 were going from bad to worse, and Trotskiy sent a telegram to Lenin, requesting Stalin's recall from the front for stirring up trouble when there was none. Apparently Stalin got wind of the contents of the telegram and left for Moscow, hoping to have Trotskiy relieved as war commissar and get Lenin to appoint him as a member of the Military Revolutionary Committee. Amazingly, Lenin again approved his request, and Stalin left for Tsaritsin immediately with new powers. Trotskiy was not impressed and insisted that Stalin and his friends must go. At this point, Lenin sent Sverdlov again to Tsaritsin to patch up their differences before a new offensive was launched against the Whites.

Concurrent with these events, Lenin was wounded in the neck, prompting Sverdlov to issue an order for mass terror throughout Bolshevik occupied areas. Subsequently Sverdlov decided to hear them both at a conference. Stalin, being junior to Trotskiy and in Sverdlov's presence, was afraid to tip his hand and amicably asked Trotskiy, "Do you really want to dismiss them all? They are fine boys." Trotskiy retorted, "These fine boys will ruin the revolution, which can't wait for them to grow up." After hearing the exchange for hours, Sverdlov telegraphed Lenin his opinion on their exchange by concluding that Stalin must immediately be relieved from the Tsaritsin front and stripped as a member of the Military Revolutionary Committee. Lenin consented, and Sverdlov brought Stalin back to Moscow with his boys. The Tsaritsin battle was lost in view of the complete disorganization in the ranks and poor planning, for which Stalin was wholly responsible. Stalin remained adamant and never forgave Trotskiy for this humiliation.

The battle against Admiral Kolchak in Perm, west of the Urals, which was going badly for the Bolsheviks, was another of Stalin's doings. Stalin again used the same indirect sniping tactics against Trotskiy. He was ordered to the battle area to report the problem and reason for its loss. Instead Stalin bitterly attacked Trotskiy for poor leadership. Here again records of Kolchak's command and the Bolshevik's investigation confirmed Perm's loss was an unexpected surprise attack by the Whites. Upset with personal infighting instead of answers, Lenin demanded answers to specific questions and made it plain to Stalin that he was angry about involvement in military decisions instead of direct answers to questions requested.

Eventually Lenin got exasperated with Stalin, and to get him out of the way of military affairs (on advice from Trotskiy), he assigned him to the newly created position of chief of the Inspection and Control Commission, where he could execute people in the rear without any questions asked. Stalin seems to have found his most desirable additional power base, where he could threaten people under questioning, without interference from anyone, making the commission an instrument of his power and terror. Having acquired three positions—Commissar of Nationalities, Secretary of the Communist party, and Chairman of the Control Commission—Stalin become the second most powerful Bolshevik functionary in the party. This was apparently too much for some members of the Politburo and the Central Committee, who complained that Stalin had his hands full already. Nevertheless Lenin defended Stalin as acting decisively with authority when called upon. In fact Molotov and Kuiybishev were demoted as secretaries, and Stalin took over the position, with Molotov under him. These last two positions were acquired by Stalin in the last days of March 1922. The original assignment of the secretary of the Communist party was that of high administrative clerk in preparing the agenda and keeping records of the meetings of the Politburo and Central Committee. Acquiring more positions than any other member of the party or government made Stalin more powerful by the back door, where he eventually succeeded Lenin as the absolute dictator of the USSR. Trotskiy was offered higher positions, including vice-chairman of the Council of Ministers, but he declined the honor. It seems he didn't think much of the job, since Lenin himself was chairman. It appeared that Lenin offered this position as a reward to Trotskiy for his services during the civil war and as a possible successor to himself, although it is rather speculative, in view of Lenin's inconclusive *Last Will and Testament*. As previously mentioned in another chapter, Lenin was a poor judge of character, and this fault remained with him until he died.

Who was Trotskiy, from where did he come, and what made him war commissar? Lev Trotskiy (Bronstein) was born in the Ukraine and lived in New York. Upon commencement of uprisings he left for Russia. He was without a doubt a self-taught intellectual and should be classified a Menshevik in his original beliefs, at least before the revolution. The reader should be careful in considering him a pure Leninist Communist, since he often questioned Lenin's decisions. On the other hand, he was devoted and loyal to Lenin once a decision was made. He was a high intellectual in his own right and considered all decisions on his own before adopting a stand. Stalin expelled him from the Soviet Union, and in his final exile in Mexico, he wrote his memories with hatred and emotional condemnation of Stalin; although biased, everything he wrote was true.

Lenin's *Last Will and Testament* seems to acknowledge Trotskiy as superior among his colleagues, yet withheld judgment on who should succeed him in view of Trotskiy's questionable commitment to true communism. Lenin gave high praise to Nikolay Bukharin as a theoretician but faulted him for lack of understanding dialectics. He described Stalin as being rude, acquiring enormous power, and unsure of how to handle this power properly. After Lenin's death, it was decided to read his Testament at a special Politburo session, to which Stalin objected. Trotskiy demanded it be read, and it was seconded. Trotskiy listened carefully, without any comment on the document. Stalin's comment was brief and to the point, "It's too late to worry about it now," and was backed by his minions in the Politburo. Stalin waited thirteen years to take his revenge to get rid of Trotskiy in Mexico in 1940 by having him murdered. This paranoia, suspicion, and vengeance never left him.

Years after Lenin's death, Stalin invented various skirmishes against the Whites in the civil war, masquerading them as serious and important battles. Most of them were written with Stalin's guidance by his puppet, Voroshilov. As an example of his military genius, long after important witnesses in battles were either shot by him or died naturally, Marx-Engels Institute published and edited *Josef Stalin: A Political Biography*. The language used therein is liturgically Stalinesque and was written to advance the theory of a military genius in civil war campaigns. A most inventive mind couldn't surpass Stalin's imagination. Stalin's "cult of personality," his megalomania, and paranoia reinforced with alcohol commenced early in his life and progressed in later years to a degree that the simple people of the Soviet Union believed all in view of the previous transformation of society. His public appearances were rare, except on Revolution Day, when no speeches were made.

After Stalin's death Khrushchev exposed some of Stalin's falsehoods and his cult of personality in 1956 but withheld some critical issues. Yet strangely enough, some people in the Soviet Union still refuse to believe Stalin's falsehoods and murders even at this writing.

**The Great Purges**

Having control of the main sources of power—the party, the government, the KGB, and his puppets—Stalin unwittingly created divisions of the left and right in the Politburo. His arbitrary decisions on collectivized agriculture and excessive speed in industrial production, sometimes over the authority of his Politburo colleagues, aggravated the grain supply and industrial goals to a point which caused great hardship to the country. Famine began spreading, with the peasants refusing to join collectives, destroying cattle, and growing only enough grain for their own consumption. The speed and acceleration of industrial output which he demanded began falling due to poor supply deliveries, slow extraction of natural resources for lack of proper equipment, exhaustion of industrial workers, and false reports of established goals.

The right faction consisted of people who desired Stalin's removal, and some even contemplated his execution. They felt compassion for the peasants, wishing them to be free as in the days of NEP; they also wanted to relax the severe requirements and subordination of the KGB to the Party. Sometime in mid-1932 a document was circulated among Party members wanting to get rid of Stalin immediately, as opposed to those who wanted to wait for the right moment. The document was penned by a second-tier old Bolshevik, Ryutin, and was supported by another, Slepkov. It was coined the "Ryutin Platform." While the contents are somewhat sketchy, it was purported to have demanded his resignation from all his positions. The document may be paraphrased thus: the right wing was correct in criticizing the prevailing economic conditions and Trotskiy's opinion from afar in exile, with respect to arbitrary rule of Stalin's methods in the Politburo. It was to be brought up before the Control Commission, instead of the Politburo, where matters were not yet consolidated to Stalin's liking. The chairman of the Commission decided it was not a disciplinary but a political question, and referred it back to the Politburo. At that meeting, Stalin called for the death penalty for sabotaging the unity of the party. In the end Stalin was turned down by Kirov's initiative—the Leningrad party chief—who appealed for moderation and led the fight against death sentences. He even succeeded in converting some of Stalin's and other adherents to his cause. Subsequently Stalin never forgave Kirov's unacceptable behavior at that meeting, and at the appropriate time had him killed.

Stalin still had plenty of power since he was the secretary of the Communist party, which gave him the luxury of time, threats, patience, and arbitrary decisions to get rid of his enemies. Additionally, his control of the hand-picked Central Committee and the Secretariat was an asset he used to exercise his arbitrary rule, regardless of the opposition, which began wavering and weakening with time. Stalin's memory and vengeance never left him, and he waited for the opportune time to start his bloodbath, which would commence shortly.

On 1 December 1934 in the evening, Leonid Nikolayev entered Kirov's Leningrad party office and shot Kirov in the back. This assassination was the beginning of a bloodbath without letup until all of Stalin's enemies were dead by 1938. Hundreds of his enemies were executed for his drummed-up assassination charges of Kirov, engineered by Stalin. In subsequent purges, most of the prominent party, government, and military leaders perished. The killings continued until millions of innocent citizens perished in slave labor camps, were left to wander in desolate frozen Arctic and Siberian snows, or were executed under trumped-up charges. Stalin's complicity in the assassination is no longer in doubt; in fact he was the originator of the murders, purposely creating a terroristic atmosphere in his new order. He took his time for some fifteen months to prepare and fabricate his case in 1938, with the complicity of Yezhov, the new head of the NKVD (forerunner of the KGB). The massacres perpetrated amounted to unprecedented numbers, where eventually millions died by execution, in slave labor camps, or through torture. In the bloodbath of old Bolsheviks, Lenin's original comrades were executed after forced preparation of self-incrimination in open court proceedings with the foreign press in attendance. Among those accused in this group were the top echelon of the Politburo and Central Committee, whom Lenin personally selected for these bodies. The list reads like the Who's Who of Communism: Zinovieev, Kamenev, Smirnov, Mrachkovskiy, Yevdokimov, Ter-Vaganian, Ordzhonikidze, Bakayev, the Lurye brothers, and several others. Perhaps these are names which the reader may not recognize since these were old Bolsheviks of prior years, yet they were the original backbone of Lenin's party and government. Suffice it to say the top echelon was almost decimated, but not quite yet, since he had others in mind. While the trials were going on, Stalin was in Moscow monitoring the proceedings with his observers in court. Upon completion of the trials and verdicts, Stalin left for his usual vacation. During the forced preparation of the trials, the accused were led to believe that they would not be executed and could appeal for leniency directly to Stalin. Subsequently all were executed while Stalin enjoyed his vacation and was not available for appeals. By the end of 1938, Stalin succeeded in having the Party, all organs of government, and every person in the USSR under his control.

However, before the murders in 1935, the enforced collectivization of agriculture, particularly in Ukraine and other agricultural districts, was another distinct chapter in Stalin's resume. When the pogrom commenced to enforce supply of grain and other food staples in Ukraine—the likes of which has never been before experienced even by Hitler's massacres—he sent his vassal, Lazar Kaganovich, to exterminate all peasants who refused to join the collectives and surrender the grain. When Kaganovich completed the massacre, Ukraine lost over four million of its population. In reporting the results to Stalin, he was told to kill an additional 30,000 to 35,000 for good measure. Kaganovich inquired which group to murder, and was told it didn't matter—you choose anyone you wanted as long as he killed them.

In 1936 other killings were ordered of second and third tier Communists as a lesson. In 1937 a show trial was held against Karl Radek, a prominent member of the Party and Lenin's close colleague, who was editor of the communist paper in Moscow. As preparation for a typical case in trying a defendant by self-incrimination, Karl Radek incriminated himself. After beatings and torture, he was shot. The Red Army's turn came a few weeks later when it was announced in June that the top echelon of the Red Army was accused of treason; they were executed the next day. The line-up of the military command included some of the most responsible commanders of districts, general staff officers, and others: Marshal Tukhachevskiy, deputy commissar of defense; army commander Uborevich; army commander Kork; army commander Yakir; and corps commanders Eideman, Putna, Feldman, and Primakov. Yan Gamarnick, first deputy commissar of defense/political committed suicide a few days before. In addition to the above, hundreds of lower rank generals and colonels, some from the general staff corps, were executed en masse. At the end of the massacres, the army's four million men were left almost leaderless, and the morale of the lower rank officers was hopelessly adrift. While there were a few marshals left, they were mostly Stalin's political appointees who came out of the civil war and the Polish campaign. For some unexplained reasons Generals Shaposhnikov, (a former czarist colonel) Zhukov, and Vassilevskiy were spared. One wonders why Hitler waited four years to attack the USSR when he could have overwhelmed it in shortshrift in 1939 with the country already in turmoil and with the top command decimated. Yet Hitler chose the Western Allies for conquest. The bloodshed of the army was a serious blow to its morale, and it took all of four years under the above-named generals to buildup the army's officer command almost from scratch to withstand the upcoming German assault divisions in 1942.

If this debacle were not enough, Stalin decided to take time out for the preparation and final solution against the last remnants of the political opposition. After all, there were still other old Bolshevik comrades and colleagues of Lenin left to complete his master plan and become absolute dictator. In this connection, in March 1938 the trail of the so-called Rightist group opened, consisting of Nikolai Bukharin, Rykov, and Krestinskiy (the members of Lenin's Politburo), Rakovskiy (Central Committee member), Yagoda (the deposed NKVD chief), and several others. To add color to the trials, three doctors were introduced: Pletnev, Levin, and Kazakov, accused of administering poison to Kuibyshev and Maxim Gorkiy. All were accused of the same Trotskiy connection as in other previous trials. All were executed, except for Drs. Pletnev and Rakovskiy, who got long prison sentences. In Lenin's last testament, Bukharin, an intellectual, was identified as the darling of the entire Party. Bukharin's widow was recently quoted by Itar-Tass in Moscow that she was fully aware of the trumped-up charges against her husband. At the completion of the murder trials in Moscow, Stalin was in his glory and settled down to rule his flock of blind automatons.

Only one other former member of Lenin's Politburo, hero of the revolution and the civil war remained alive, and that was Lev Trotskiy, who was in exile in Mexico. A couple of years later in 1940, Stalin caught up with him by planting an assassin as a guest of his female secretary, who axed him to death. Stalin was now free of all his imaginary enemies in the USSR and abroad. Stalin's fear for his own life knew no bounds, and he surrounded himself with over three thousand body guards in the Kremlin and his dachas—who were themselves under suspicion. The Russian tradition of absolute obedience to the head of government, acquired earlier from the Mongols and the autocracies of the czars, prevented his own assassination, for which the Russian people and their minority nationalities paid a horrible price and loss of dignity as a people and nation.

**Hitler-Stalin Pact**

Hitler occupied the demilitarized Saarland on the French border by plebiscite and annexed it to Germany in 1935. He then occupied Rhineland without a fight with the French and shortly demanded Danzig from Poland in 1937. Poland refused to give it up. He annexed Sudetenland, a largely German-settled area in western Czechoslovakia as part of his Anschluss of German-speaking people. By the end of 1939 all of Czechoslovakia fell to him in the Munich Pact. The world sat and waited for him to annex other areas without a fight. Deathly afraid of being dragged into conflict with Hitler, Stalin began negotiating with a Franco-British military mission in Moscow for an agreement against Hitler while playing for time. In the midst of these negotiations, Hitler's intelligence informed him of its progress.

To disrupt them, Hitler proposed a pact with Stalin, who accepted it in August 1939. Armed with a secret treaty agreement, Hitler invaded western Poland while Stalin took eastern Poland. Within a few weeks Poland disappeared.

To defend and honor their obligations to Poland, Britain and France declared war on Germany. Hitler then decided to invade Norway, Denmark, the Netherlands, and Belgium, which capitulated quickly, and in a lightning campaign against France, he overran it in mid-1940. By a secret agreement with Hitler, Stalin occupied not only eastern Poland, but also western Ukraine and Belorussia, extending the western border by some three hundred seventy-five miles. Stalin wasn't quite satisfied with these measly acquisitions, and in violation of the Riga Agreement of 1921, Soviet troops occupied all three Baltic countries. By the end of 1940, Hitler had full control of western Europe and its continental shoreline, except for Britain, though the air war with her continued. It was rather simple for Stalin to flip-flop in choosing sides between the Western Allies and Hitler. There is no honor among thieves. The rewards to Hitler for permitting Stalin to occupy the above countries were raw materials, oil, grain, and other goods in short supply in Germany, which Hitler badly needed, and to which deliveries Stalin strictly and meticulously adhered. For some unknown reason, while Stalin was always suspicious of Hitler, he trusted him to keep his part of the bargain, although he was convinced that eventually Hitler's intent was to invade the USSR. What other country was a breadbasket and had natural resources equal to the USSR? Soviet intelligence tracked Hitler's infiltration and reinforcements in East Prussia, Poland, the Balkans, Rumania, and Bulgaria. Yet when inquiring from the German government for the reasons for troop reinforcements in the east, he was assured they were troop rotations and peaceful intentions. Soviet troops on their western frontiers were not placed on alert, for fear of possible miscalculations by their own troops.

When Hitler launched his overwhelming blitzkrieg, Operation Barbarossa, against the USSR, it achieved a total surprise. At first the Soviet troops were forbidden to shoot back to defend themselves. These orders were issued personally by Stalin to front commanders. When Wehrmacht penetrations along the entire western Soviet border became obviously in depth, only then were troops ordered to resist. By then it was too late, and the USSR was forced to fight its "Great Patriotic War" against Hitler. It took until early May 1945 for the combined Allies to crush Hitler and win the war.

**The Cold War**

After the conclusion of the war, at the Potsdam Conference of victors in 1945, Stalin demanded twenty billion dollars in reparations from Germany. The Allies turned him down, not desiring another future war with Germany, who had caused the first World War. As a result and in revenge, Stalin refused to pull out his troops from all of his Eastern European occupied territories including East Germany, the Baltic States, Poland, Czechoslovakia, Hungary, Rumania, Bulgaria, and portions of Yugoslavia. Since his troops took full possession there, native Communist party chiefs were installed as heads of communist governments. He had no problem collecting all the reparations he needed from the satellite countries until he bled them dry. What's more, he started threatening the Allies with unprovoked incidents by creating a blockade of west Berlin. He had Tito, the new communist Yugoslav president, shoot down American and Allied planes on the way to repel and re-supply progovernment forces against communist insurgents in Greece. When Berlin and Greece wouldn't buckle to his threats, he stopped creating incidents for a while. President Truman informed the world that the Allies would defend Greece and Turkey no matter what it took. Stalin's intent to capture Greece and bypass neutral Turkey was based on the old Russian dream of a warm water port in the Mediterranean; he would also threaten Turkey from the west and south. In addition he wanted to pose a threat in the Mediterranean to the Allies.

Meanwhile Winston Churchill, by now no longer British prime minister, though a member of the British Parliament, delivered a speech in Fulton, Missouri, identifying Stalin, his regime, and his satellite countries as an "Iron Curtain" descended upon Europe from Stettin to the Adriatic. The war left the USSR hungry and devastated, with millions dead and incapacitated veterans lay in understaffed hospitals lacking proper medicines. The country was in ruins, and industry was hardly on its feet. Slave labor camps worked overtime to rebuild the infrastructure of the country; agriculture was in ruins in the western portions; women were driven fifteen to eighteen hours a day doing menial work. By then it appeared Stalin was going mad and out of control. Reports reaching the West showed the country was in a terribly chaotic shape, with Stalin issuing unbelievable demands for production goals. The Soviet propaganda machine was echoing tremendous achievements in all economic fields. In fact it was just the opposite—achievements were attained in munitions factories, which were bartered for reparations with satellite countries. The damage inflicted on the USSR by the German invasion, as well as the scorched earth policy of the Russians themselves, was of catastrophic nature, and it was impossible for Stalin to resurrect the country to normal peacetime conditions within the short period before his death, even by slave labor. Yet his propaganda echoed that production and economy were almost equal to prewar days.

On the other hand, it is true that relocation of war industries during the war to Siberia was accomplished in the shortest time frame. One must consider these relocated facilities as primitive, since weapons factories to produce tanks and artillery pieces, except for firing mechanisms, were a roughly hewn product and were promptly sent by rail to battlefronts only haphazardly inspected. Nevertheless, by superhuman efforts they succeeded, having had no other alternatives. To mobilize the country for his Patriotic War, initially Stalin proclaimed and appealed in radio broadcasts that the "Russian Motherland" was in great peril and that it was the duty of all Russians to save it. On another occasion to boost morale, he gathered the top echelon of Party members in the Mayakovskiy subway station in Moscow during the war and appealed to them for help against the German beast. He never appealed to the people before or after the war. He also made peace with the church to have its many believers fight for Holy Russia's cause, thereby allowing the church freedom to propagate its Orthodoxy. He was later quoted as saying, "Russians won't fight for us Communists but will fight for socialism."

After the war, Stalin played a deadly geopolitical game throughout the world with his Cold War, while Russia and its minority nationalities were bleeding. Since Stalin's devious and furtive mind never rested in creating turmoil throughout the world, he decided to try a blockade of Berlin. Although Berlin was fully isolated and divided among the four allied powers within communist East Germany, he cut road and rail traffic for food supplies and oil to west Berlin. When Allied planes defeated that effort in 1949 by the Berlin Airlift, he lifted the blockade and gave in, afraid of losing face. Subsequently when things were getting out of hand, the free nations of Europe, the United States, and Canada created NATO, the North Atlantic Treaty Organization, to counteract the Soviet threat. The "Cold War" which Stalin unleashed eventually broke the back of the Soviet economy to the extent that the communist empire couldn't survive its economic chaos, and it fell of its own weight in 1991. Stalin's successors continued the Cold War, threatening and brandishing their might on Red Square parades and the satellite countries, and all the while going gradually, but inexorably, broke until the downfall of the USSR.

Stalin's orders to accomplish impossible socialist economic goals to fulfill his demands were never attained, nor did they ever come close. He assumed his demands would be met just because he was the enforcer. All the so-called communist economists in charge lied to him about statistics, though he never knew otherwise. Since he never left his offices in the Kremlin or his dachas to review the accomplishments in the country being the dictator, he naturally took it for granted that his goals were met or else. It was rare when he summoned a responsible official like Voznesenskiy, the minister in charge of economic goals, to verify the attained goals. When he found out the goals weren't met, Voznesenskiy paid with his life. The war was over, and women were at work along with slave labor, rebuilding the country with primitive tools to satisfy Stalin's needs. The male population available for work was down precipitously, causing most women to do menial work instead of men.

The author analyzed Stalin's five-year plans prior to the war and concludes that substantial gains in industrialization were achieved—although it was Imperial Prime Minister Sergey Witte who started industrialization in 1890 which formed the basis for the Soviet five-year plans. The quality of products suffered under the breakneck speed imposed by Stalin and his successors, and it never recovered. Stalin's quotas for production and deliveries after the war were hollow paper figures, though he never knew it, even after Voznesenskiy's open admissions.

This quota system of the five-year plans was continued after his death, with the armaments industry leading the quotas, while the consumer and agricultural industries were, for all practical purposes, dying. For years absenteeism of workers due to alcohol, was commonplace. Subsequently, workers showed up for work and were told to go home; eventually most stayed home for want of any work, getting paid the same wages, while inflation soared. The saying was, "We pretend to work, and they pretend to pay us." The unraveling of the Soviet economy started sometime in the early 1970s and accelerated thereafter, until the time arrived to close the books on utopia.

The destruction of German industry in the east by the Soviets, while severe, never compared to Hitler's ruin heaped on Russia. Russia's self-inflicted and punishing socialist economy in industry and collective agriculture never succeeded and was bound to run out of steam when the shortage of capital and consumer demand collided. The USSR was forced to import grain from free economic countries and imported most desirable consumer goods from the West, all with hard currency obtained through sale of their natural resources abroad. Ironically, Germany gained by the total destruction of its outmoded industrial plants and equipment and joined the Western nations as a true democracy with its free economic system, to become one of the great economic states of our day.

On 25 June 1950 Stalin started another conflict, this time with a war on the Korean Peninsula by remote control, involving the North Korean dictator, Kim Il Sung, against South Korea. Stalin furnished all the required weaponry. At first North Korean surprise attacks succeeded in overrunning most of South Korea, capturing Seoul, and almost reaching the gates of Taegu. American troops stopped them on their march down the peninsula on 15 September 1950 and counterattacked. An Allied landing at Inchon threatened to cut off the mass of the entire North Korean army in the south. MacArthur went on the offensive with Allied contingents, threatening to overrun most of North Korea. By approaching the Chonjin Reservoir close to the North Korean border with Manchuria, MacArthur threatened water resources to northern China. Stalin panicked and got Mao-Tse-Tung involved to relieve the North Koreans. The Chinese succeeded with terrible losses in wave after wave of infantry attacks in the dead of winter, causing the Allies to pull back to the prewar border. Some political analysts, even at this writing, claim the U.S. and its Allies lost the war. The basis for this conclusion is puzzling to the author. I do not believe, it was the United States or UN objective to conquer North Korea, which would have been another financial burden for the United States and United Nations to bear with nothing to gain. Since each warring party got to reoccupy its own territory after the war's end, with the North Koreans back at their starting line, how did the United States and the UN lose the war? Had the United States intended to conquer North Korea, it could have done so, with or without Chinese or Soviet help to North Korea.

Before the end of the war in 1953, Stalin the executioner, torturer, and barbarian died. Not fully apprised of the new leadership's position in USSR, it was prudent of Chinese and North Koreans to settle the problem as soon as possible. In this connection, an armistice was signed in the village of Panmunjong with the North Koreans, who pretended and behaved like the victors. However, the Cold War continued under Stalin and everyone of his successors. While Stalin won the Patriotic War at the cost of millions, Hitler lost the entire war with only two million dead.

Hitler died by suicide, while Stalin died a horrible death in bed in the presence of some of his minions and his own daughter, who described his death as agony. The Patriotic War was a catastrophe for the USSR, and when added to the insane policies of Stalin's driven socialist economy and barbarian rule, the nation will need decades—at least—to recover. In analyzing Stalin objectively as a leader of the Russian nation, one must see his achievements as well as his faults. It must be conceded that Stalin introduced industrialization to the Soviet Union at breakneck speed, though it was achieved at the expense of quality and millions of lives. Is that an achievement? He could not have achieved industrialization without being a slave labor owner and killer. What were his accomplishments in the Cold War? He created the Cold War, convinced of conquering all of the Eurasian continent, having made inroads in Eastern Europe with his satellites. He started a war in East Asia and began insurrections with his communist sycophants in democratic countries. What legacy did he leave to the Russian nation and minority nationalities? He left them lies, underhanded rule, slave labor camps, murder, terror, intrigue, hunger, and ironclad borders. He also left a ruined country embraced by terror—a militarized, impenetrable, surgically isolated prison.

In transforming Soviet society, communism succeeded in brainwashing its people, and upon his death, in most Russian eyes, Stalin was a god. At his funeral a million Russians thronged to Red Square to send him off to Communist Valhalla with tears in their eyes. The larger question still looms ahead. Why did the Russians tolerate him? He was not even a Russian but an uneducated Georgian, with accented Russian speech, a boor, and everything else attributed to him. He was the ultimate barbarian in the annals of history. Yet those Russians who were alive after his death loved him as Father Stalin. They had been previously bound by historical chains to Mongol-type rule and their own autocratic rulers and subsequently their own brand of special dictators. The chain has yet to be broken, if ever. The self-styled god was going to be the greatest conqueror on earth, yet he died like all human flesh, although it was an especially horrible death—without a doubt fully deserved. It would be prudent to identify self-taught intellects among the original comrades of Lenin who helped him attain power and who as individuals left a mark of distinction, contributing to the history of Russia under communism.

### Lev Trotskiy

Trotskiy was born in the Ukraine, but left Russia for United States, and lived in New York among socialist intellectuals. When the revolution commenced, he promptly left for Russia to take part. Without a doubt he was a natural-born leader and a fiery speaker who possessed a certain aura among crowds which few could match. His intellectual capacity was derived from a deep review of any subject and was based on his own conclusions, regardless of the opinions of other colleagues in his tight circle. It was that quality which disturbed Lenin, who described him in his last testament as an intellectually superior to his colleagues, yet withheld judgment who should succeed him in view of Trotskiy's questionable commitment to true communism. Yet none was more qualified to succeed Lenin. He was the great propagandist, organizer of the revolution, and the mastermind of the civil war—an achievement of monumental proportions in the revolution. After being exiled in Mexico, he wrote his memoirs, full of hatred and condemnation of Stalin, although everything he wrote was true. Stalin, who could not compare favorably with Trotskiy, sought vengeance against him and succeeded. Sylvia Ageloff, an American Trotskiyite who knew Trotskiy well, acted as his part-time secretary. Her lover was Ramon Mercader, who wrote some articles for Trotskiy to review and was an occasional visitor in Trotskiy's house. One day in 1940 while Trotskiy was reviewing one of Mercader's articles, apparently with no one else present, he plunged an ice pick into Trotskiy's skull and within twenty-four hours Trotskiy was dead. Mercader received a twenty-year sentence and was released in 1960. Thus passed one of the luminaries of the Russian revolution.

## Zinoviev & Kamenev

Two of Stalin's colleagues, Zinoviev and Kamenev, were cultural Jews but considered themselves Russians and communists. They were intellectuals in every sense and did not believe in dictatorship; on several critical occasions, they objected to participating in various meetings under Lenin unless Mensheviks and Social Revolutionaries were heard and took part in discussions. Eventually both deferred to Lenin's wishes, whom they highly regarded. Both of them were in mortal danger under Stalin, since they would have caused him to accommodate the opinions of others, rather than permit him personal dictatorship. The fact that they were members of Lenin's original circle was sufficient reason for Stalin to mark them for elimination.

## Nikolai Bukharin

Bukharin was the youngest of Lenin's colleagues and the most congenial member of the inner circle. Among the Bolsheviks he was considered an authority on any aspect of Marxist economics. Lenin described him as the darling of the party but he lacked in Hegelian dialectics. Although he was no threat to Stalin, Stalin murdered him because he was a member of Lenin's original inner circle.

There were of course other members of the inner circle, such as Piatakov, Rykov, and dozens of others whom Stalin eliminated. The four important collaborators of Lenin mentioned above were true theoreticians and intellectuals among the Bolsheviks. Although Stalin was a member of the inner circle, Lenin selected him for want of another member of minority nationalities.

The reader should bear in mind that Stalin was not an intellectual or a thinker. He was not more than a streetwise conniver, a boor, and a total misfit within the inner circle. He was substantially inferior to all of them, yet he eventually triumphed by splitting the groups within the circle. His strength lay in being the secretary of the Communist party, the Commissar of Nationalities, and the chairman of the Control Commission, the disciplinary organ of the Party, with no one to account or watch over him. He accumulated more arbitrary power than any member of the inner circle, which enabled him to run indiscriminately over all organs of the Party and the government during Lenin's illness and after his death. These three departments enabled him to choose any of his enemies for elimination. He picked them, one by one, until there were no more. As a sadist, he enjoyed having his former colleagues (enemies) questioned and tortured, while peeking from behind a curtain. When he died, millions paid him homage and wept his passing. The Russians have a saying—*narod drisirovaniiy* (animal-trained nation)—that was precisely what happened to the Russian people beginning in 1927 when the great taskmaster officially took over. On his death bed, he uttered prophetically to his Politburo circle gathered around him, "You will not survive without me." Probably for the first time in his life he spoke the truth, which escaped him and his successors. His successors pursued the same murderless course with dissenters but invented so-called humane treatment with insane asylums and gulags until the dissolution of the Soviet empire.

Historically it would be fair to say that Stalin was a cowardly terror specialist in sheep's clothing and a betrayer of the revolution, commencing with the civil war. Stalin, like Lenin before him, must have attained immortality in the holy of holies in the communist valhalla. In this connection the author requested a psychiatric analysis of Stalin by a competent psychologist, and his report is presented below.

**Psychiatric Diagnonis of Josef Stalin**

I enjoyed reading your historical account of the life of Josef Stalin, and as per your request, have considered his behavior within the framework of modern day psychiatric nosology.

More specifically, the diagnosis below is from the American Psychiatric Association's *Diagnostic and Statistical Manual*, Fourth Edition (DSM-4). Furthermore, the diagnosis is by nature somewhat speculative in that it's based on historical record and third party accounts of his life and behavior, and not, of course, on direct examination of Stalin. Stalin would be characterized in the main as having a mixed and severe personality disorder. His most prominent personality disorders are of the paranoid and sociopathic type. Regarding the former, his behavior included to an extreme degree the following traits: suspiciousness, mistrustfulness, vengefulness following insults and slights, quickness to angrily react or to counterattack against perceived attacks, and pathological jealousy. Stalin's behavior is fully consistent with the following sociopathic qualities: a history of criminal conduct (including his adolescence), indifference to cruelty, absence of remorse regarding harmful behavior towards others, deceitfulness and pathological lying, impulsive, rash, overly aggressive behavior, and vengeance against authority. There are also indications of strong narcissistic features in his personality including his grandiosity and preoccupation with power, interpersonal exploitiveness and nonexistent empathic capacity. These personal developments are highly correlated with a history of profound physical and emotional abuse of Stalin by his father and the absence of a strong attachment and bonding with his mother. It appears further evident that Stalin was a serious and chronic alcoholic. Stalin's abuse of alcohol likely grossly exacerbated many of the above described personality traits.

Regarding Stalin's intelligence, it is likely that, despite being undereducated, he was of at least average or better innate potential, in that he was so successful in using his personality features to attain such a position of power.

Respectfully submitted,
Andrew Sweet, PhD, Clinical Psychologist, PSY 8934, December 9, 1994

## Recommended Reading

Conquest, Robert. *Stalin, Breaker of Nations*. New York: Viking, 1991.
Conquest, Robert. *The Great Terror*. London: Macmillan, 1968.
Deutcher, Issac. *The Prophet Armed*. New York and London: Oxford University Press, 1954.
Laquer, Walter. *Stalin*. New York: Charles Scribner & Sons, 1990.
Payne, Robert. *Stalin*. New York: Simon & Schuster, 1964.
Payne, Robert. *Life and Death of Trotskiy*. McGraw-Hill, 1977.
Tucker, Robert C. *Stalin in Power*. New York: W.W. Norton & Co., 1990.
Volkogonov, Dmitri. *Trotskiy*. New York: The Free Press, a div. of Simon & Schuster, 1996.
Volkogonov, Dmitri. *Stalin*. Free Press, 1994.

# CHAPTER XI
# THE GREAT PATRIOTIC WAR

After a spectacularly successful Blitzkrieg campaign in 1940 against the French and British forces and a short five-day battle against the Belgians, the occupation of Denmark without a fight, and a quick campaign in Norway, Hitler took time out to demobilize some of his forces. He deliberated whether to attack Britain or Russia, and sometime in August or September 1940, he abandoned his intention to invade Britain, although he didn't prevent any further preparations for its invasion.

It is not known to this day why he decided not to attack Britain. German foreign office records give no clues, and the chancellery's records were destroyed during the Russian attack on Berlin. Since most of Hitler's records relative to the possible invasion of Britain are not at hand, it may be assumed that he could not attain air superiority over Britain and therefore decided to invade Russia. He had full control over the Atlantic coastline of western Europe, except for Britain. Hitler was quite secretive about many decisions he made and gave few, if any, reasons to the *Obercommando Wehrmacht* (armed forces) for his decisions.

He finally decided to launch a campaign against the Soviet Union. In this connection, he ordered an operational plan for campaign Barbarossa. What made him invade the Soviet Union is a matter of speculation even to this day. Perhaps he thought he could gain Russian oil for free and in abundance, as well as other natural resources, by conquest. Some of the principal reasons assumed and speculated were his desire for traditional German *Liebenstraum* (living space), which would provide all the amenities and Russian slave labor. Other reasons given were his hatred for Slavs, Stalin, and communism, and his belief that Russians would not fight for Stalin and communism. In this he was right, although they fought for Mother Russia instead.

He refused to heed his generals' warnings about historical reasons for Napoleon's defeat. They also warned him about Russia's territorial expanses, their mass population, and their willingness to die for their soil, which was the cause of Napoleon's defeat. Additionally they reminded him of the desire to avoid a two-front war, which was the cornerstone of Bismarck's foreign policy and proved correct in WWI. They also insisted he review the reasons for the loss of WWI and the lessons gained therefrom.

German officers on secret maneuvers in Russia during the time of the Weimar republic in the 1920s observed Russian troop maneuvers. They concluded the Russian troops were not as well trained or updated, but attacked and counterattacked in mass formations regardless of casualties, then reached a consensus that their retreat into the hinterlands and open spaces would prevent total destruction of their military power, as evidenced in WWI. Some of the same German officers who took part in these maneuvers were to head Wehrmacht armies in the Russian campaign.

Hitler instructed the chief of the Wehrmacht general staff, Col. General Franz Halder, to prepare plans for him. Halder took a few weeks to complete a cursory review, discussed it with his general staff members and leading field commanders, and advised Hitler that the great majority of his staff and field commanders were against the campaign. Hitler reminded Halder of his oath and told him to confine himself to planning the campaign and not to meddle in political decisions. Halder saw no prospect of changing Hitler's mind and resigned himself to preparing the plan. Within a matter of six months, Halder produced a masterpiece and again advised Hitler not to execute it—this time from a purely military point of view. The strategic aim of the plan was to secure all of Russia proper—in the north from the Barents Sea at Murmansk and Arkhangelsk on the White Sea, to Astrakhan in the south on the Volga delta, to the north shore of the Caspian Sea, and envelop all of the Caucasus because of its oil.

After the conquest, the center was to be held as defensive area, to withstand any attacks from Soviet troops. Halder warned of heavy casualties, should the offensive plan be put into operation. Furthermore it would take at least three million troops to defend the conquered zone since the land had no natural barriers. Hitler retorted that casualties would be no greater than in the western campaign, and in any event, it was a political decision. The arguments between them were stormy, and at one point Halder threatened to resign, accusing Hitler of throwing troops into the meat grinder.

The offensive plan envisioned distribution of the armies based on a three-pronged simultaneous attack, to confuse Russian forces by breakthroughs and bypassing pockets of encirclement, destroying them later, and racing to the main objectives with Panzer units. Army Group North was to attack northern Russia pointing toward Leningrad, under the command of Field Marshal von Leeb, an outstanding professional soldier and siege specialist, fresh from victories in the western campaign. Army Group Center was to attack central Russia in the direction of Moscow under the command of Field Marshal von Bock, who had a distinguished command of an army group in the western campaign. Army Group South was to attack in the direction of Ukraine, Caucasus, and its oilfields under the command of an outstanding soldier, Field Marshal von Rundstedt, who was called from retirement for the western campaign to command the group. Field Marshal von Brauhitsch, as commander of the Wehrmacht, was in overall command of the army and field operations. Colonel General Franz Halder, as chief of the Wehrmacht general staff, was responsible for the operational plan. All the above generals had taken part in WWI as junior officers as had some in the 100,000-man army under Colonel General von Seckt, permitted by the Versailles Treaty after WWI.

When the Wehrmacht hurled its mass in the invasion of the Soviet Union on

22 June 1941, the breakthrough was so complete in western Russia that millions of troops and civilians were encircled and captured. Most civilians were unexpectedly surprised at the speed and welcomed the Germans, believing them to be liberators. This could have been accomplished, particularly among the peasantry, had Hitler listened to Josef Goebbels, the propaganda minister, instead of Alfred Rosenberg, the Nazi theoretician. The pocketed Russian troops were badly treated by rear echelon commands in regard to food, shelter, and ruthless behavior. As a consequence of this behavior, Hitler further compounded the error by ordering Himmler to introduce Algemeine SS and the dreaded *Einsatzgruppen*, (similar to KGB units) for the extermination of the race. Some civilians at first believed the SS were after the KGB elements, political commissars, and communist cadres. In fact, when the German troops occupied Belorussia and Ukraine, the people found the troops more tolerant than when they advanced farther into Russia proper with Gestapo elements behind them. Yet some of the Russian troops put up a courageous fight. The majority of the people and troops hated Stalin and his regime, but when treatment under the Gestapo became intolerable, resistance stiffened. When it came time to defend their country, they gave their all, even when they were cut off and surrounded, and stood up to put up a hopeless defense. Without appropriate warning from their own government, the troops defended themselves as best they could, although it was a hopeless fight.

Conditions in western areas were so confusing by this time that the Soviet commanders lost control of the situation. It was finally decided to relieve Voroshilov and Budennyi, the commanders in the western area. They were old Party hacks of Stalin's during the civil war. Stalin was still meddling in military affairs, as he had done in the civil war, against the mightiest military machine ever assembled.

As it happened, a professional soldier, Marshal Timoshenko was in command of the Kiev military district encompassing Ukraine in the southwest—a survivor of Stalin's 1938 executions of military commanders. He gave von Rundstedt considerable trouble with seesaw battles in some areas, even without air support and with insufficient armor, though he had good artillery support. The battle with Timoshenko carried over into 1942, when he retreated and sustained heavy casualties, yet he saved whatever was left of his army.

Political and social conditions in Moscow became untenable for the Soviet government during the invasion, causing it to evacuate to Kuibyshev—lock, stock, and barrel. Meanwhile, Moscow defenses were heavily reinforced with fresh Siberian contingents, well armed, and supplied with winter clothing, held in reserve for the upcoming battles for Moscow.

Leningrad was isolated almost completely, with occasional supplies coming in covertly by way of Lake Ladoga, Murmansk, and Arkhangelsk, even though threatened by Finnish troops. Moscow was surrounded on three sides. Ukraine and Belorussia were behind German lines, with military conditions becoming unbearable and seemingly hopeless.

Panic broke out in Moscow, with civilians leaving by the thousands. Gangs of looters and speculators roamed the streets, with no order and no police in sight.

Foreign agents and embassies, prior to leaving for Kuibyshev, reported unbelievable loss of order and control; and reports circulated that some KGB agents were changing into civilian clothes and escaping the city. The American ambassador, before leaving for Kuibyshev, reported to the State Department that he could see from every window in Spasso House, the American embassy compound, and that no buses or streetcars were running. Looters were operating in the open, and people by the thousands were fleeing on foot with their meager belongings. He did, however, report massive military formations on foot and in trucks on their way to the frontlines to stem the tide and panic. Stalin was no where to be found or heard from.

Moscow Radio reported that Stalin was in the capital to direct its defenses. He may have been there but was reported drunk for the first eleven days of the invasion—as was secretly attested to by Khrushchev at the twentieth Party Congress in 1956 and later leaked by eastern satellite puppets to the West. It was left to Molotov to address the people on the radio. What's more, all the members of his Politburo and some members of the Central Committee demanded his return from his dacha. In despair and in a drunken stupor, he was quoted as saying, "Everything Lenin created has been destroyed." The great invincible Stalin lost his nerve and had to be brought back to Moscow to sober up and face the immense problem of rallying the people to fight back. Finally, on 3 July Moscow radio announced Stalin's speech in Mayakovskiy subway station, where most of the Politburo members and other officials were gathered and heard him addressing the people as "brothers and sisters," to defend "Holy Russia" against German invaders. No mention of the Soviet Union was uttered, but he reminded them of their past history, with names of their great heroes, writers, and thinkers. He conveniently ignored how he butchered thousands upon thousands, sending them to slave labor camps and decimating almost the entire military command only to discover that he was powerless, and so he begged his "brothers and sisters" for help.

His sycophants couldn't believe the mighty Stalin was helpless at the moment of the gravest need, with the very existence of the country at stake. It was so easy for him to execute innocent people and opponents of his rule when no one was threatening him. But at the subway station that day, he publicly showed his insecurity, helplessness, and fear. Records indicate some six million troops were captured before the German troops reached the outskirts of Moscow.

In June 1941 the reason given for Russia's frightful losses was the element of surprise. The reasons were not very convincing in view of the *Draft Field Regulations*, published in 1939, and later quoted in *The History of the War*, which stated that the Red Army would not wait for the enemy to attack and would go on the offensive before being struck. In fact, these regulations had nothing to say with regard to defensive tactics or lack of appropriate weapons. No mention was made of Stalin's decimation of field commanders and general staff corps before the war. He alone was responsible for the horrendous casualties which the troops suffered and the destruction caused in the country, yet it wasn't in him to ever admit it.

Stalin's involvement and intimidation when the military doctrine was being written stymied all military thinking and proved to have been a useless paper in war. The failure of appropriate defense and the use of inferior equipment in the beginning of the war was clearly due to Stalin's "military genius," as Khrushchev characterized it later. In the meantime, the progress of the war was proceeding at an alarming pace—too fast for German formations approaching and facing Moscow because of the disintegration of the Russian armies in western Russia.

The commander of the German Fourth Army, von Kluge, facing Moscow, talked to frontline troops and their line commanders and decided to abandon the attack because of the exhaustion of the troops, which by then were only at half their strength. The German advance positions were in the suburbs of the capital, and field commanders could clearly see the church steeples of the Kremlin.

With only summer clothing on and winter fast approaching, with insufficient supplies and unreliable roadwork, they weren't prepared for static defense. But they dug in, in their hedgehog positions, and withstood all Russian attacks. However the northern and southern sectors of the Moscow front gave in, with the loss of some two hundred miles in each sector. Von Kluge's order to withdraw was based on tactical considerations for the safety of his troops and was not authorized by Hitler, who upon discovery, ordered rear positions to prepare to defend every inch of soil, with von Kluge strenuously objecting.

It so happened that digging in prevented a rout. The suspension of that attack was disappointing to Hitler's Obercommando, in view of some frontline positions close to the capital. In late October Zhukov, the Russian commander of the Moscow front launched massive attacks on the north and south flanks against the Germans, gaining considerable ground. The Germans dug in and held their ground in hedgehog positions, with Hitler refusing a request to retreat, being afraid on this occasion of a full rout. In fact, this order did prevent a rout and panic among ill-clad troops at half strength.

Zhukov learned that the Germans were a tough foe and prepared to overcome them with superior numbers and overwhelming massed artillery techniques, having gained previous knowledge of German tactics and their shortage of artillery while on maneuvers in Russia before Hitler came to power. The Moscow front was continually engaged by the Russian command with a ratio of three to one against the Germans. Although the German troops were exhausted and had scant replacements, they nevertheless held their positions due to strict discipline and training. The Russian attacks helped to relieve the pressures in the north and south, as well as in the Kiev and Odessa enclaves, by slowing down the Wehrmacht on the way to Moscow and the Caucasus before the onset of full winter weather.

By the end of 1941, the Germans controlled all of the Baltic states, Belorussia, most of the Ukraine, a big chunk of western Russia, and were on their way to Crimea. Leningrad was isolated and blockaded.

The evacuation of Soviet industry was ordered shortly after the German invasion and should be considered one of the great achievements in the war by the Soviet regime—a stupendous effort under the most desperate conditions. All elements of the population participated in this tremendous undertaking, from industrial managers to workers, from women to railroad administration, from eastern Russians to Siberians; this was something Hitler never counted on, with calamitous consequences to follow. Few examples in history have shown such feats of accomplishments. The relocation of industry to the east was done by the free will of the people, under the most primitive conditions imaginable, to save their homeland from the enemy. The fact that Russian territory, population, and natural resources were of such great magnitude that Hitler didn't even conceive of the possibility of relocation when he launched his attack. His general staff warned him, yet his intuition was that his German troops were superior to the Russians, and they were. The Russians were prepared to die to save their land, and they succeeded because of the reservoir of manpower and natural resources, which no other nation in Europe possessed. The German military machine was a superb creation but had its limits in manpower, natural resources, and territorial mass.

Thus the general staff realized it had to administer a quick knockout blow before the Russians recovered, but Hitler disregarded it. By the end of 1941, with Moscow battles lasting to 5 December, it became apparent to the Germans that they couldn't break through to take Moscow, although they had captured the most productive and populous part of western Russia, which was a serious blow to the Soviet Union. In 1941 the estimated Russian losses were somewhere between 3,750,000 and 4,000,000 troops taken prisoner and almost 1,550,000 dead; these numbers are not easy to comprehend, and the ratio of dead to wounded was not easy to come by because of the secret Soviet records on dead and wounded might cause a psychological fear of defeatism. Few nations could afford such catastrophic losses, equaling genocide. The military prisoners sent back to the Reich were treated as *untermenschen* (subhumans), and their treatment was cruel, to say the least. The capable ones with specialized trades were sent to the rear to work in factories on minimum rations, while the great majority were sent to slave labor camps under inhumane conditions, where great numbers eventually died of deliberate starvation, a fate similar to the Jews of Europe.

The civilians were treated somewhat better, with some driven into labor camps, and after the war they were liberated by the Allied armies. Refusing to return to the Soviet Union, they became "displaced persons," roaming a ruined Europe as refugees, a legacy left over by Stalin's and Hitler's barbaric deeds and inhumane conditions.

UN Commission for Refugees and various religious groups were created to help resettle these unfortunate people in foreign lands. A great majority settled in United States, Canada, Latin America, and Europe. Complaints from the Soviet government in not returning them to Russia were later disregarded due to Stalin's view of the prisoners and refugees as traitors.

By the end of 1941 it became clear that the German Command failed to achieve its main objective in the Blitzkrieg, although it still possessed tremendous capability to achieve certain victories. In this connection, Chief of the Wehrmacht General Staff General Halder, who accurately predicted the outcome, was fired by the end of 1941. What went wrong?

Hitler's demobilization order after the western campaign, slashing tank and aircraft production, and reverting to peacetime conditions helped Russia, coupled with its industrial potential, manpower reserves, and its territorial mass. Supplies from the United States and Britain, while small at first, became a flood in the months ahead. Russia's abundance of natural resources, even with loss of territory in western Russia in the beginning, was also a critical factor. Hitler's dogged interference into purely military affairs, his erroneous belief that Russia could be easily conquered because Russians wouldn't fight for Stalin, and his disregard of purely military advice of his commanders were also contributing factors. Britain's air and land battles overseas, which also drained Hitler's manpower and resources, and the entry of the United States in the war hurt Germany considerably.

Hitler, still not convinced of his defeat before Moscow, blamed most of his senior commanders and sacked them. Thereafter, the army's general staff and command was placed second in importance to the newly empowered personal OKW (*Oberkommando Wehrmacht,*) with Hitler as supreme commander. Field Marshal Keitel, Hitler's useless tool, became chief of OKW under him, and Col. General Jodl became chief operations officer. General Jodl was considered a highly competent general staff officer and loyal to Hitler, but having to perform under Hitler's directives without freedom in exercising his talents seriously undermined his true capabilities.

Stalin's spy, Richard Sorge, a German journalist in Tokyo, informed his contacts in Russia that Japan decided to launch a war in the Pacific against United States. Stalin had serious doubts about the accuracy of this report and held back his Siberian reserves until the battle for Moscow. When on 7 December 1941 Japan launched its pre-emptive Pearl Harbor attack, Stalin hesitated, in view of manpower losses in western Russia and finally ordered Siberian contingents to the Moscow front. The demands of the military for additional reserves and armaments never ceased. Sorge's information came to Stalin around August or September of 1941, although he didn't act on it for some time, not trusting the report. Nevertheless, he deliberately withheld this information from the Allies, for fear it would cause them to concentrate in the Pacific area, thus depriving the Soviet Union of much needed supplies and the hoped-for second front in Europe. Stalin's expertise in duplicity was by then well-known. He was a master at this game, and it is now common knowledge that he never revealed it to the Allies until it became known after the conclusion of the war with Japan. After Japan's defeat, a Japanese counterintelligence colonel interrogated by General Willowby, MacArthur's intelligence chief, and confirmed that he had tracked Sorge meticulously for months. In addition to bits of communications from the German embassy, the press office, and hideouts, he finally caught him and had him tried and executed prior to the Pearl Harbor attack. Until Sorge's discovery was acted upon, Stalin kept a powerful far eastern command in Siberian Maritime Provinces and along the TranSiberian Railroad adjoining Japanese-occupied Manchukuo with its Kwantung Army of 500,000 men.

In the meantime, Leningrad and its three million residents had been isolated since September, with only scant rations supplied by water, ice, and air. A story of this hardship deserved an entire book, as written by Harrison Salisbury in his *Nine Hundred Days*. The heroism, hunger, and death are adequately described therein.

When the Finns declared war on the Soviet Union, all they wanted was to get back the territory they lost in the Finno-Soviet war, and they rejected all Hitler's requests to push from the north against the Russians. Meanwhile, Soviet operational plans for the encirclement of German troops between Smolensk and Moscow and the recapture of Bryansk and Orel did not materialize, apparently due to failure to accumulate sufficient troops, armor, and aircraft, and more importantly, the lack of offensive operational experience by Soviet field command (*stavka*).

In early 1942 the Germans had control of enormous areas of western Russia, while the battle for Moscow continued with the German hold on Rshev, Gatsk, and Vyazma spearhead fronting Moscow. It was the beginning of 1943 before the Germans were driven out of the area. Crimea was still occupied, however, and remained in German hands after an ill-fated attempt to relieve it.

A counterattack by the Soviets to relieve Kharkov in May 1942 also failed to dislodge the Germans. This was a subject of severe recriminations against Stalin by Khrushchev at the twentieth Party Congress in 1956 for demanding to hold the city to the last man and interfering with operations, as he had done in the civil war days. The Kharkov operation was an amateur effort to hold on, which resulted in extremely heavy losses, when logic dictated an immediate pullback. By spring and summer 1942, the Germans were rushing to the northern Caucasus at breakneck speed with von Kleist's Panzer group, Heeresgruppe A, headed to Kuban and thence south to the Caucasus after capturing Krasnodar.

Kleist's Panzer Group broke through with such speed that the Russians didn't have time to evacuate their industries or the majority of the population. Failure to stop the Germans on the Don caused the Russians to lose territories, offering only minor resistance to the German advance. The Russians succeeded in blowing up Maikop and Grozny oilfields in Chechnya, northern Caucasus, which prevented Hitler from using them. Hitler's plan to conquer the Caucasus was too ambitious in view of the loose northern flank at the edge of the Don. He was unable to move quickly to the Black Sea coast, by way of Grozny, to touch Turkey's border, and influence it to join his coalition. His intent was to cut off the northern Caucasus and its oil fields, which eventually failed. As the fighting in the mountains was difficult and progress slow, the weather intervened, and by October snow swept the mountaintops and roads, making mountain fighting and Panzer operations practically impossible. Yet they could see the Black Sea from nine thousand feet up. Another attempt to break through by way of Mozdok also failed.

Hitler's Directive 41 called for the capture of Crimea and Voronezh to create a double threat southeast of Moscow and Stalingrad and to eliminate the Russian hold on the Don bend. He intended to clear the way to Stalingrad and then turn south to the Caucasus. Hitler thought the Russians were too weak to defend the

Caucasus but was forced to change his plans when the Russians counterattacked at Voronezh. The Germans headed south and thinned out their forces. By superhuman efforts, the Russians and the minority nationalities of the Caucasus built obstacles over the mountain passes, slowing the German advances. Hitler's hope for mass desertions by the Muslim peoples of the area didn't materialize, and he got bogged down.

The Russians brought in reinforcements across the Caspian Sea to defend the Caucasus. By then they had also reinforced the Stalingrad area with Siberian reserves. As a result of overwhelming Russian reserves, the German command lost the required momentum in the mountains of the Caucasus and in the Stalingrad area. Sensing danger of being cut off, von Kleist requested permission from OKW to abandon the attack on the Caucasus and fall back on the Rostov bridgehead on the Don and Krasnodar. This request was acted on much too late by Hitler to become effective, and it took more time than allocated by Kleist, with subsequently fatal results. In January 1942 with temperatures of zero to fifteen degrees Fahrenheit and their reserves on line, the Russians achieved parity in troop strength and superiority in tanks and aircraft. They achieved some successes north of Moscow, but got bogged down on the Moscow front in trying to encircle the Germans.

The Russian offensive operations from January to March 1942 proved a failure. It appeared that the Soviet army had not yet mastered operational organization and experience for offensive action. Actually the weather hampered them more than the Germans, since the roads were icy and snowbound, making it impossible for armored warfare and truck convoys, while the Germans were dug in without movement, picking out Russian infantry and armor. The first half of 1942 may be characterized as disastrous for the Russians, while it was full of great successes for the Germans. On the other hand, the last half of the year should be considered the beginning of the end of major German offensive operations and the commencement of small Russian successes. As the supreme warlord, Hitler relieved von Leeb as commander of Army Group North encircling Leningrad and replaced him with Colonel General Kuhler, a former army commander. He relieved von Bock, commander of Army Group Center, and promised him another assignment shortly. He replaced him with a highly skilled commander of the Fourth Army, Field Marshal von Kluge. He also replaced von Rundstedt, this time appointing von Bock to take over as commander of Army Group South. He was displeased with von Rundstedt's inability to take Kharkov quickly while he was fighting Timoshenko. The new commanders didn't fare too well in the north or center but did advance rapidly in eastern Ukraine, Crimea, and the Rostov region on the way to the Caucasus, although Army Group South's east flank was hanging loose, facing the Volga and Stalingrad some distance away.

Suffice it to say that the failure of the southern offensive operations to seal off the Caucasus and their inability to capture and break through at Voronezh on their way to the Volga caused the Germans to lose momentum, on which they had pinned their hopes to split Russia in half. Hitler's constant interference in military operations—taking his time, not acting promptly, and thinning out his forces to reach too many objectives simultaneously with scant reserves—made operations difficult. It should be admitted that Hitler had an uncanny feeling for tactical operations and close combat conditions, as attested to by many German field commanders who were genuinely surprised at his intimate close combat knowledge. Apparently, lack of coordination within Army Group South, particularly between the Caucasus operations and the troops on the Don bend, caused the Russians to counterattack and slow the German advance toward the Volga in the direction of Stalingrad. Nevertheless, they reached the Don bend and struck out for Stalingrad from the south—primarily at Kotelnikovo, southwest of the city—and from the west and northwest. The Germans finally broke through to the Volga, north and south of Stalingrad but not on schedule, because of the shortage of reserves and troop strength.

The German command decided to launch its Sixth Army from the south under the command of Col. General von Paulus, a former vice-chief of the general staff, supported by von Hoth's Panzer group, and to avoid encirclement by the north and south German forces. The sixty-second Soviet Army and other echelons became isolated from the rest of the forces and retreated to Stalingrad proper. By that time, Richtofen's Fourth Air Fleet unleashed continual air attacks on the city, killing thousands of people. In a frantic effort to save the sixty-second army from destruction, Col. General Chuikov took over command of this army.

The battle for Stalingrad was being fought within the city in mid-October, with the Russians holding three small bridgeheads on the west bank of the Volga, supported by heavy artillery on the east bank. The Germans, outnumbered many times over, were unable to capture these bridgeheads, which later formed the basis of Russian counterattacks and subsequently isolated and destroyed the German Sixth Army. Under compulsion of the general staff on 12 December, Hitler gave orders to extricate the Sixth Army from encirclement; alas it was too late. Field Marshal von Manstein, a master strategist commanding Army Group Don, was ordered to relieve the troops inside the cauldron. Manstein discussed the operation with von Hoth, commander of his Panzer group, and both agreed that the forces at their disposal were insufficient, and the order to relieve the troops was given much too late to affect the outcome. Manstein requested an additional three infantry divisions and several Panzer formations, which Hitler refused. Had this request been granted on time, the outcome could have been different, and the Sixth Army could have been relieved and rejoined Army Group Don.

Although the distance between the encircled troops and von Hoth's relieving force was only a few kilometers, successful relief depended upon the encircled troops breaking out of the cauldron, since von Hoth's Panzers were insufficient. Hoth found it impossible to penetrate the distance against Russian troop concentrations, which amounted to over one-and-a-half million by that time. The Soviet command amassed 2150 tanks, nine artillery regiments, and almost four hundred guns across the Volga; von Hoth's strength was two understrength Panzer divisions of 225-240 tanks and one full infantry division which had just arrived from France—it was hardly a relieving force.

Since Manstein's Group Don was unable to relieve the Sixth Army within the Stalingrad cauldron, Hitler ordered von Paulus to holdout with his army. It turned out to be an impossible task against three Soviet army groups attacking Stalingrad from the north, west, and south with an overwhelming mass of troops, tanks, artillery, and aircraft, sometimes at a ratio of 5:1 in every category against the Germans. Isolated and doomed, the Sixth Army fought on from November to January 1943 and finally surrendered, against Hitler's orders.

The German casualty figures in this one battle in Russia were the highest they had ever been. The battle lasted two hundred days, and it was the bloodiest battle of WWII—290,000 German and German-allied troops fought in the war; 77,000 died; 197,000 were wounded; 13,000 surrendered during the battle; and 77,000 were missing. These cumulative figures are from von Paulus's daily record, quoted by Walter Goerlitz in his book, *Paulus and Stalingrad*, and adjusted since publication.

In 1993, after the dissolution of the Soviet Union, the Russian Federation released secret documents of Soviet losses from the former Soviet Defense Ministry Archives on the 200-day battle for Stalingrad. Russian casualty figures are overwhelming: 1,940 tanks destroyed; 1,791 planes shot down; 1,100,000 people died; 2,300,000 people were wounded; 86,000 people were missing; 13,500 people were executed for cowardice.

The Russian and subsequently the Soviet general staff's use of massed artillery techniques, and more critically the use of overwhelming manpower in any war to wear down the enemy with uninterrupted attacks, regardless of losses, was decisive in the battle. Although to sustain such casualties, even based on Russian military strategy, required Stalin's "killer instinct" and obvious disregard for human life. After all, it was Stalingrad which bore his name, therefore it was justified.

The Stalingrad battle could have been fought and won to a standstill by the USSR on the east bank of the Volga when the Russians shot down a plane in August 1991 carrying a German staff major, Reichel, with documents and plans showing the extent of Hitler's intentions in Russia, albeit to reach the Volga at Astrakhan on the Caspian Sea, and stay put for the duration of the war. Attrition alone would have worn down Hitler's armies because he never expected such ferocious defense by the Russians. Most knowledgeable military authorities agree that Hitler exhausted his manpower in his Russian campaigns combined with Allied aerial bombings, the invasion of North Africa, his Balkan and Greek campaigns, his troops were overextended, and his victories were over. He still had to wait eighteen more months before facing the Normandy invasion and the campaigns in the west. He could not have accumulated enough reserves to bolster his troops.

On the other hand, Stalin couldn't afford to wait, or he would have lost face and perhaps political power if Stalingrad had fallen to the Germans. That was his main concern, regardless of casualties sustained. On this assumption, he threw in manpower recklessly, regardless of losses, which must be considered totally unacceptable in military terms. Was this a victory, when he could have waited a few weeks for Major Reichel's document to come to fruition, and to settle the battle on his own terms? He killed millions in peacetime. Why should it matter to kill more in Stalingrad? It was, after all, his symbol of survival. After the conclusion of the battle, it should be accepted that Stalin had a 5:1 advantage in manpower superiority but suffered substantially greater ratio in casualties. When it came to Hitler's decision to conquer Stalingrad, he is said to have been mesmerized by its name and his hatred for Stalin, although he has been known to have admired him for his ruthlessness and his control of the military.

When on 16 October 1941, the Russian command ordered a counterattack against German forces facing Moscow, causing the Germans to fall back to north and south by about 150-200 miles, respectively, Halder, and the general staff recommended immediate withdrawal to the starting line; Hitler rejected this outright.

By September 1942, even when major victories were attained by Army Group South in the Ukraine, Crimea, and the Caucasus, Halder demanded a withdrawal, due to shortage of reserves, exhaustion, and lack of armor. Hitler's refusal to confront objective reality prompted him to replace Halder and appoint Col. General Zeitzler, a logistics specialist, who was out of place as a general staff chief.

Simultaneous attacks in different directions were ordered by Hitler's revised Directive 45. This called for sealing the land gap between the Don bend and the Volga elbow, with no available reserves for casualties and contingencies. No amount of argument was permitted to be entered in the general staff's diaries for objections to illogical tactics. Analysis by military scholars apparently established that clandestine records were kept in addition to the publication of diaries and books by several German generals (and others) after the war. It should be emphasized again that von Paulus assumed command of the Sixth Army in January 1942, having vacated the position of deputy chief of the Wehrmacht general staff under Halder. Furthermore, whatever independence he had as a member of the general staff in assuming the new command evaporated by adhering to Hitler's dictated OKW plans, prepared by General Jodl.

About that time Rommel's Afrika Corps was retreating from El Alamein to Lybia. On 8 November American forces landed in Morocco and Algeria and defeated French Vichy forces. To counteract these moves, German and Italian troops were flown to Tunisia. On 11 November Hitler ordered the occupation of most of France.

Concurrently, the Soviet Twenty-First Army and Fifth Tank Army began an offensive and broke through the Third Rumanian Army on the Don, and the Soviet Fifty-First and Fifty-Seventh armies broke through the understaffed Fourth Panzer and Fourth Rumanian armies to the south of Stalingrad. Commander of Army Group B, von Weichs, realized the consequences of the breakthrough and ordered all attacks to cease in the Stalingrad area. Army Group Don absorbed the remnants of the Sixth Army, Fourth Panzer, and Rumanian Third and Fourth armies in the Don-Volga sector. With insufficient manpower reserves, armor, ammunition, and food stocks, he endeavored to extricate the Sixth Army from the Stalingrad area—an impossible task with heavy Soviet forces surrounding

Stalingrad from the north, west, and south, with over 1,500,000 troops and 3,100 tanks.

Hitler paid a catastrophic penalty for interfering in strategic planning, as well as procrastinating—as was his habit—until it was too late. Suffice it to say that when ten Russian armies converged on Stalingrad and broke through from the west against the Third Rumanian Army and Sixth Rumanian Corps in the south, having had no contact with understrength fourth Panzers, it became necessary for the Fourth Panzer Army to extricate itself immediately for fear of being trapped. As conditions developed, the Sixth Army was trapped. The agony and death of the Sixth Army continued, until surrender in the northern cauldron by the Eleventh Corps on 2 February 1943.

Numerous versions of the Battle of Stalingrad are available from Soviet and German sources and independent analysts. The author chose to analyze an eminent and objective German military historian, Walter Goerlitz, as well as General Chuikov's account, though highly colored, it covers some battle engagements objectively. The battle of Stalingrad may be considered the bloodiest single battle in history of WWII, and should be conclusive evidence that Halder's prediction that Hitler would be throwing troops into the meat grinder was prophetic and accurate. Thereafter, Hitler's war in Russia was a routine retreat back home, although skillfully executed, to save lives. Anglo-American help on various fronts against Hitler in the air and with supplies were substantial intervention and serious help to Stalin, yet one would never know it from Stalin's communiques.

As previously stated, Russia was too large for Germany, whether communist or free. Germany's chance of localized victories lay in a blitzkrieg as planned by Halder without Hitler's interference. Germany's lack of population, its own meager natural resources and its dependence on them from conquered territories, its geography, and its own size were against it from the very beginning. The blitzkrieg was intended for quick knockout blows against limited targets, like France and small countries, but not against large geographic masses with heavy opposing reserves.

His involvement in minor tactical operations were sound in some instances, in view of his experiences in WWI. However his strategic sense in purely military matters had no basis since it was politically-motivated, and it should have been left to top professionals, who were extremely able. While his geopolitical vision was generally correct, he committed the same errors he accused World War I leaders of committing in indulging on a two-front war and being stabbed in the back by the homefront.

On the other hand, Stalin, who was not as intelligent nor as perceptive as Hitler, knew when to stop after learning a lesson in interfering in the civil war. He also learned a lesson when Marshal Timoshenko was conducting skillful operations in 1942, being almost surrounded in the south. He tried to tell his commanders what to do but eventually realized his incapacity and left the conduct of military operations to professional commanders to do their work, and guiding the war politically, though after the war he claimed all credit for the victory.

Germany's limitations were obvious, and the general staff knew it when they invaded and conquered western Europe. While it may be unpopular to admit it,

Germany's cause after WWI was just, in view of the harsh peace terms of the Versailles Treaty, with its heavy and unbearable vengeful penalties. This observation is not intended to justify Hitler's deeds or actions. Fortunately, this error was not repeated after WWII, and the results were fully justified, with Germany becoming a model of democracy and a healthy economic giant.

The German military standards demanded obedience to political authority, but since Hitler demanded a personal oath to himself only, rather than to the constitution, the question became moot. The attempted assassination of Hitler on 20 July 1944 failed, and it was too late when it came, with dire consequences to the conspirators. More than fifty years after the battle for Stalingrad, it may be compared with certain other limitations, including the battle for Moscow in 1812, which Napoleon entered into during the invasion of Russia. The Russians evacuated Moscow after setting it afire. Napoleon sat in the Kremlin, waiting for Alexander I to sign a peace treaty; he never showed up, but instead hurled his troops against Napoleon and caught him in Borodino, where he inflicted catastrophic losses on Napoleon. The battle at Borodino subsequently cost Napoleon his throne and resulted in exile to St. Helena. After returning to France with Napoleon, his aide General Caulaincourt retired to his estate in France and wrote a book about the battles in Russia. This book subsequently became classic reading for most German generals in Russia. It described the vast expanses of Russia, their acetic acceptance of punishment, and their fierce retaliation against the aggressor. Hitler never entered Moscow; he may have been lucky by being pursued only, and he retreated in orderly and masterful manner.

In World War II, Soviet troops were not as well trained as the Germans, yet they still had their population, their great landmass, industrialization and natural resources in their backyard, and fierce determination to help them achieve victory. They sacrificed an inordinate amount of troops in battle but won the war.

After the war's end, there was a serious shortage of manpower in Russia since so many men had died. Women performed heavy work with bare hands and elementary tools to rebuild the country. Progress in rebuilding was slow due to vast destruction, yet not much appeared in Stalin's press for several years concerning the women workers; apparently it was a state secret. Had it not been for the Russian women and slave labor, it is doubtful the country could have survived the war in good enough shape to rebuild the country, such as it was. Some of the war's destruction is still visible in substantial areas of both urban and rural areas at this writing.

Destruction in Germany was also severe, but slave labor during the war kept most industries working at high levels almost to the end of the war, even under heavy air raids, according to memoirs of Albert Speer, the minister of armaments. In 1943 the Germans still had a stronghold in Kursk, about 150 miles south of Moscow. They managed to recapture Kharkov from the Russians and were ensconced in the Caucasus.

The loss of Stalingrad caused Hitler to dismiss several distinguished senior commanders, among them Field Marshal Eric von Manstein, considered by most military experts to be the most brilliant tactician and strategist of World War II;

Col. General Heinz Guderian, the great Panzer leader; von Kleist; von Bock; von Weichs; von Leib; von Runstedt; and many other generals, including Franz Halder, the great chief of the general staff. In effect, he fired the brains of the regular army and assembled mostly the brawn of the party, the fanatical SS, to carry on the war with him as the great warlord.

He increased Waffen SS formations from five divisions to fourteen and appointed generals (like Sepp Dieterich), whose "expertise" in warfare was based commanding SS formations in peacetime parades and secret police work. Fanatically loyal to Hitler, they obeyed his orders. SS troops fought for every inch, but with incompetent commanders, they were sacrificed in unnecessary battles to the last man.

Despite Stalingrad's surrender, the German armies were still a formidable foe in mid-1942 and managed to launch serious attacks and captures, with several seesaw battles for Kharkov and points farther east. The Russians subsequently recaptured Kharkov again, but at great cost. In view of the undefined and chaotic frontline positions in the Ukraine, the Caucasus, and Crimea, it became apparent that a probable encirclement of depleted German formations would be attempted by the Russians. At this point, sensing probable and immediate encirclement in the Caucasus, frontline commanders advised Zeitzler, the new chief of the general staff, to abandon the Caucasus and speed up evacuation to the Ukraine. Hitler vetoed the idea and instead ordered an offensive to avenge Stalingrad.

He ordered an attack on the Russian positions in the Kursk salient between Orel and Belgorod against the advice of the army's general staff and von Manstein, who was to conduct the operation. Concurrently in 1943 the Russians had their own plans for the same sector and concentrated tremendous amounts of tanks, artillery, aircraft, and manpower—substantially greater than the Germans. General Model, the German commander to the north of the salient, advised Hitler that the battle could not be won without heavy tanks equal to at least half the Russian armor, and equal to at least three-quarters of Russian infantry. Although Hitler usually refused his generals' requests, he ordered a delay until numbers recommended by Model were met. Troops were assembled, but Panzers and heavy artillery had to be brought in from factories in Germany, which further delayed the element of surprise. Additionally, other delays were involved, including Hitler's apprehension of the Italians staying in the war, the failure of Rommel's Tunisian campaign, and Allied landings in Sicily. This necessarily delayed all preparations for the campaign, in addition to rerouting equipment to Sicily for a probable campaign in Italy.

Hitler had his hands full with fewer weapons and personnel, nevertheless he decided to go through with Operation Citadel, as he named it. The generals restated their objections and waited until all numbers were met and in place. According to the accounts of German generals after the war, General Hoth, commander of the Fourth Panzer army, was to attack from the south of the salient, and General von Kleist was to attack with his Panzer divisions from north of the salient. Both declared that 2,000 Tiger and Panther tanks and Ferdinand mobile guns were required to break through formidable Russian concentrations. The generals doubted a victory even with 400 tanks in reserve. Hitler promised that they would be rushed straight from German factories to the front. This promise was never kept, and he kept some for his own reserve—although most German generals interviewed after the war acknowledged 1050 tanks were delivered, wholly inadequate. The balance was sent for the Sicilian campaign and the northern Italy reserve, where Hitler expected a new Allied attack. Although the Russians were able to secure the plan of attack, it was not in itself a serious problem, since it was almost common practice to capture officers who knew some part of the plan, and later fill in the gaps with information from others who were captured by special commando raids.

Lacking the required strength in each of the Panzer divisions, the German commanders were dismayed and doubtful of success. The Luftwaffe was to furnish 900 planes but only 540 were delivered. Intelligence information received by the Germans accounted for more than 2,500 Russian heavy and 1,600 medium tanks in addition to 1,200 heavy and medium artillery pieces and 1,500 aircraft. Hitler intended to commence the offensive simultaneously from the north and south of the salient, not later than 1 June; however, the attacks commenced in early July.

The delays gave the Russians more time to collect troops and armor, with an overwhelming concentration of manpower and weaponry already in place. Five Soviet army groups were ready for the German attack and for the follow-up counteroffensive immediately thereafter. Soviet army groups amounted to 1.5 million troops and ranged from Orel in the north of the salient to Stalino in the south—a distance of some 450 miles in an arc, a mass concentration not common for a set piece battle.

At the commencement of the battle, the north and south Panzer armies of the salient made substantial penetrations deep into Soviet defenses; however, the German and Russian losses were exceptionally heavy, and the intensity of the battle increased as they advanced. The German momentum was lost because of a shortage of armor and infantry reserves. In the first engagement, the Germans losses were 276 tanks destroyed; 87 aircraft lost; 29,500 dead; 61,000 wounded; over 900 missing. The Russian losses in this battle, estimated by the Germans (who were more truthful with their numbers then Stalin was) were over 90,000 dead; at least 110,000 wounded; 4,500 captured; 171 aircraft downed.

The German army group commanders, von Kluge in the north and von Manstein in the south, conferred as to the probable outcome of the engagement and decided to order immediate disengagement from the battlefield to the starting positions without consulting Hitler. They were afraid of the outcome in view of the heavy Russian superiority in manpower, armor, artillery, and aircraft and feared a probable bloodbath in the end. Hitler reprimanded them both severely. Von Manstein was relieved of all duties in the Wehrmacht and discharged from the army, while von Kluge was placed in reserve.

Since Rommel had wounds inflicted by Allied aircraft during the campaign in France, Hitler dispatched von Kluge there to report on conditions—where he could enjoy the scenery without encountering the enemy. Eventually Hitler made him commander in the west against Anglo-American forces. Under severe constraints, von Kluge retreated as best he could with his armies in France, which displeased Hitler, who replaced him with Field Marshal Model. VonKluge's name was then linked with the 20 July 1944 plot against Hitler's life. Realizing the hopelessness of his armies in northern France and the linkage of his name to the plot, he wrote a letter to Hitler in which he stated his opinion of a hopeless battle and advised him to save Germany by negotiating a peace treaty with the Allies. Upon completion of the letter, he ordered his adjutant to drive him to nearby woods; there he committed suicide. Hitler lost one of the best military brains and field commanders in the Wehrmacht.

A few German junior officers reassigned from this battle to the western front and captured in a bloody battle at Coutance-Perrier road (inland from the Contenin Peninsula) in the presence of the author revealed some details of the massacres on both sides at the battle of Kursk salient. In the first five days of the attack, one of them said "No quarter was given by either side in the battle, and more iron was strewn on the battlefield than they have ever seen before." He continued, "We never had enough oil for tanks and trucks. Captured horses were used in the offensive. We never had enough tanks against the Russians, whose tanks were very good." Finally he admitted, "We never had a chance at Kursk against the Russians. They had many times more of everything than we, so we broke off engagements and went into defensive positions."

Von Manstein's memoirs give no credence to the commander of Soviet forces, Marshal Konev, who stated after the battle, "It was the swan song of the German Panzers." Von Manstein clearly states that the Tunisian campaign and the expected Sicilian invasion were responsible for the removal of several tank formations and that he and Kluge mutually agreed to terminate the battle after the first heavy encounter, in view of severe battle losses, shortage of armor, air support, and oil, and the removal of some elite SS divisions for Hitler's reserve.

On 7 July a Soviet counterattack began with overwhelming infantry formations, armor, troops, and aircraft. The slaughter on both sides was repeated. Nevertheless, Hitler ordered a counterattack on 10 July. As previously stated, both army group commanders refused and were relieved of their commands. In discharging von Manstein, Hitler lost the brains of his army. Hitler assumed it was von Manstein who convinced von Kluge to suspend the attack, while von Manstein's memoirs strenuously contradict that.

Meanwhile, the Allies landed in Sicily on the same day the Soviet offensive commenced. On 12 July the Soviet command ordered an attack north of the salient toward Orel and in the back of von Kleist's Panzers which had previously penetrated Soviet defenses. Fearing encirclement of his Ninth Army, Model persuaded Hitler to withdraw. Coupled with the Italian failure to defend Sicily and with conditions in the Kursk salient extremely critical, Hitler officially gave the order to discontinue the entire operation 13 July.

In reality, the battle for the Kursk salient was over about 5 July when neither von Kleist's nor Hoth's Panzers could exploit the penetration of Soviet defenses in sufficient depth, lacking power to affect a juncture, which still separated the Panzers by about 160 kilometers. By that time, German losses were proportionately higher in armor, infantry, and aircraft (and could not be replaced); additionally, they lacked sufficient oil. The Russian losses were staggering in armor, infantry, and aircraft, but they were replaced.

With the invasion of Sicily and constant Allied shipments for Soviet command requirements, the Russians continued their offensive until 5 August, when Orel and Belgorod were recaptured. Records of the battle for the Kursk salient were destroyed by OKW, Hitler's supreme command but survived in the entries of the army's general staff archives. Records of the Russian stavka are not available at this writing. Any Soviet comments made were those spoken or written by individual commanders in notes, with line by line censorship—much like Marshal Chuikov's account of the battle for Stalingrad, after the war, under Khrushchev's leadership.

The German records up to 5 August for the battle in the Kursk salient indicate the following: 67,000 infantry slain; 90,000 wounded; 16,500 unaccounted; 7 general officers killed; 419 other officers killed; 43 unaccounted for; 404 tanks destroyed; 146 tanks damaged but mobile; 406 aircraft missing and presumed downed; 141 aircraft damaged and reusable; 567 pilots killed or missing. German estimates of Soviet losses, subject to intelligence reassessment: 1501 tanks destroyed; 400-550 tanks damaged; 108,00 infantry killed; 7,000 captured; 18 general officers killed; 582 other officers killed; 71 officers captured; 678 aircraft shot down; 280 aircraft damaged; 786 pilots killed; 241 pilots captured; 1,505 horses killed.

After the war, several German generals participating in command positions in the Kursk salient were interrogated by various Allied intelligence personnel, including military historians, who confirmed cumulative German and Russian losses on both sides. Additionally, it was confirmed that Russian troops, although not as well trained, performed callously in infantry attacks, sustaining unusually heavy losses. German estimates, while not strictly accurate, were not out of line.

It was confirmed by von Manstein, commander of Army Group South, that he and von Kluge agreed to their own losses and were responsible for the loss assessments of the Soviets. In his book, *Lost Victories*, (von Manstein 1955), he confirms the reasons for terminating the engagements in the Kursk salient. General von Tippelkirch, commanding a corps in the battle, also confirmed German losses. The OKH records were examined thoroughly by allied intelligence and confirmed German losses to be reasonably accurate. The Soviet command's claim for German losses in the battle for the Kursk salient are shown at a rate impossible to accept and are considered propaganda to encourage their troops and impress the allies to commence the Second Front in Europe. The German command never assembled as much equipment or personnel as the Soviets claimed. Some of the claims made by the Soviet Command for particular engagements were outrageous:

The Soviet claim for German losses in this battle, were published in July 1943. On the first day they claim that they destroyed: 586 tanks and shot down 203 planes. On 6 July they claim to have destroyed an additional 433 tanks and 111 planes. On the following two days, the Soviets claim 520 and 304 tanks and 141 and 161 aircrafts, respectively, were destroyed. The total German losses for the battle of Kursk salient were estimated by the Soviets to be: 97,000 killed; 1,443 tanks destroyed; 195 mobile and 844 field guns destroyed; 1,092 planes shot down; over 5,000 vehicles destroyed. These figures are exaggerated propaganda.

Nevertheless, this battle was the last major armored attack Germany could mount on the Eastern Front, and from then on, they only counterattacked to gain favorable positions to avoid destructive encirclements and retreated all the way to Berlin. While their retreats to Berlin were masterfully conducted later by General Heinrici, with as few casualties as possible, the agony of slow defeat on the Eastern Front was at hand.

Meanwhile, Stalin assumed a position that the Soviet Union was the only one fighting the Germans and that the allied intention was to bleed it to death. He conveniently forgot the Allied effort to supply him with assistance he had so desperately needed. He ignored the fact that they had their own battles in Tunisia, Sicily, Italy, and the Pacific in addition to bombing Germany. The Allied efforts were exceptionally strenuous in view of the diverse battlefronts, and they worked diligently to keep the battlefronts fully supplied and operational by oceans and seas.

To that end, a summit of the three Allied leaders was to be held to ascertain the basic strategy for the progress of the war. To accommodate Stalin, a conference of foreign ministers was held in Moscow for preparation of the summit. Stalin was adamant that he could not leave the Soviet Union for the conference, claiming his direction of the war didn't permit him to leave the country. Eventually he agreed, when reminded that Roosevelt and Churchill had the same responsibilities and traveled thousands of miles to meet their obligations. He knew that President Roosevelt was crippled, yet he wouldn't budge, due to his fear of flying and probably suspicions of a military coup in Russia. A conference of the three was decided to be held in Teheran.

A significant decision was reached relative to the Second Front; however, certain deliberate hints about the status of Poland were dropped by the Soviet side to sound out the Allied position. The Western leaders took a dim view of the USSR's intentions, especially considering that Britain went to war against Germany because of Polish independence and violation of its borders. A decision was extracted by Stalin that "Overlord," the Second Front in Europe, was to commence in May 1944. About this time, certain rumors spread throughout neutral countries in Europe that a possible accommodation could be arranged between Germany and the Soviet Union.

After the battle for Stalingrad and Kursk, with huge losses in manpower, it was becoming apparent that Russian manpower losses were of such magnitude that conscripts from Soviet Central Asia in Siberia and the Caucasus could greatly outnumber Slav conscripts. Most, but not all, of these peoples spoke Russian, and they were not relied upon or trusted. In the early part of the war, Stalin banished the Crimean Tatars to Siberia, and he never trusted his Moslem peoples, many of whom had gladly surrendered to the Germans earlier. It was also known that Hitler trusted Caucasian tribes and Siberian Asians more than the Slavs to oppose Soviet power. Hitler's original intent to kill and enslave Slavs as *untermenschen* was beginning to happen.

According to Soviet demographic statistics, the population of the Soviet Union was 174 million; about 60 million Slavs were behind the German lines, and about 50 million Central Asians and Caucasian peoples were still free in his rear. As a result, the non-Slavs came dangerously close to Slav population. With so many people in captivity and behind the German lines, Stalin was afraid of possible consequences to his rule and loss of the war. In this connection, rumors persisted that an elaborate scheme was afoot to contact Hitler's intermediaries in Sweden to arrange an accommodation. The scheme entailed sufficient leeway for the Soviets to back out in the event it leaked to the Allies prematurely. This "accommodation" was couched in terms so that the Germans would retreat to their own borders (or their starting line in Poland), without being pursued by the Soviet army. While these rumors persisted, there is no evidence that Hitler accepted or rejected it. Most records of the German foreign ministry and Hitler's chancellery were bombed and set afire. Apparently, during the Nuremberg trials of war criminals, where Ribbentrop was one of the criminals, this subject never came up. When one considers Stalin's repeated demands for a Second Front, with no positive response in the beginning from the allies, these rumors sound plausible; yet there is no proof of this, although Stalin was capable of betraying the Allies as easily as he betrayed his revolutionary friends during the mock trials in 1937-38. However, after the Kursk battle, although sustaining heavy losses, the Germans never launched any serious attacks on the Soviet Union. More Asian conscripts were then inducted and did as well as the Slavs.

Conversely, a couple of months after the Teheran Conference, *Pravda*, Stalin's party organ, published an article, "Cairo Rumors," purporting that Britain and Germany were seeking an accommodation themselves, apparently to hide Stalin's possible chicanery with accommodation with Hitler, if true. There never was an end to Stalin's nineteenth century intriguingly dark brain. One should not consider this to be strange, considering who Stalin was and what he had done.

By the end of 1943, things began to look better for the Soviets; they commenced their advance to the western part of Russia and the Ukraine, and south to Crimea. Meanwhile the Allies were bombing Germany and its occupied areas around the clock, some with thousand-bomber raids, and advancing up the Italian boot. This effort was of monumental help to Stalin's armies. The Soviet command took considerable time to prepare for offensive operations, which helped the Germans to prepare for the onslaught. A young German general, Hasso von Manteufel, developed a system of defense in retreat after the Kursk battle. This tactic became the usual operational procedure employed by the Germans. It consisted of waiting for the Soviet attack to begin and then falling back a short distance to have the Soviets lose momentum and hit air. These tactics were forced on them after the Kursk battle when they ceased offensive operations and reverted to defense. Although Hitler insisted on offensive operations to the last, by then it was a thing of the past. In using these tactics they conserved life and bled the Russians, while their own retreats were orderly with much fewer casualties.

By then, also, Hitler had lost touch with reality. The commanders in the field displayed more initiative in sparing lives. However, in that time frame of the war, they were outmatched in manpower four or five to one and outguessed in every category in the field. When the troops fell back and approached a major urban area, Hitler took control and ordered it held to the last. For political and propaganda reasons, which became meaningless in time, Hitler wanted main urban areas held, which inevitably multiplied personnel losses fivefold. Yet this was precisely what Soviet tactics were based on—crowding the Germans back to urban areas, for their own military and political reasons, which permitted them to use massed artillery techniques, throwing in heavy tank attacks, air, and manpower, in addition to propaganda reasons.

By the end of 1943, the Soviets captured Kiev, Kremenchug, Krivoi Rog, Zaporozhie, Nikopol, and Kherson and were able to isolate Crimea. In mid-January 1944 they advanced west 45 miles deep on a front 250 miles long. By the end of February thru mid-April, they crossed natural barriers—the rivers Bug, Dniester, and Pruth—and captured Czernowitz and Botosani in Rumania, as well as Odessa, and attacked Sebastopol down the Crimean Peninsula. In this campaign alone, the Soviets lost more than a million troops. The German frontline commanders encouraged their troops to put up a fight, but also advised them to retreat or surrender when there was no hope. They managed to evade Hitler's orders as much as was prudent under the circumstances, thus saving lives.

By mid-1944 there was relative quiet on the various fronts, with the Germans in control of a Belorussian salient about 250 miles deep into Soviet-held territory. The front ran from the Gulf of Finland down to northern Rumania and Bessarabia. The Baltic republics were still behind the German lines, but all of the Ukraine was liberated by the Soviets. However, the losses sustained by the Soviet troops began hurting again, and Stalin could hardly wait for the Second Front to begin. He used every trick at his command, including insults to persuade the Allies to shorten their time for the invasion. Stalin used propaganda and pressure by involving local communist parties, the press, and intrigues.

Until the Allies were ready for a knockout blow, they didn't intend to move. It was difficult to reason with Stalin about life being precious because it meant virtually nothing to him. He didn't even bother to thank the Allies for the tremendous amount of help they gave him, without which he couldn't possibly win the war against Hitler. His main theme was "Russian blood is being spilled," yet he insisted, like Hitler, to fight to the last man and not take one step back. He didn't care that Germany was being horrifically bombed by the Allies, which indirectly helped him more than he would admit. He cared nothing for the losses suffered by the British running the German blockade to Murmansk for supplies to Russia, nor did he care about all the panoply of material, food, clothing, aluminum, tanks, trucks, jeeps, planes, medical supplies, and just about everything else which Britain had already committed to him. The United States furnished him with a tremendous volume of supplies, by way of the Pacific and Atlantic, from the very beginning—which he desperately needed.

On 6 June 1944, the Allied cross-channel invasion into Normandy began, Stalin was informed ahead of time. Stalin's chief of the general staff, Marshal Vassilevskiy, was informed of the details by U.S. General Deane, the American military attache. Vassilevsky refused to believe the magnitude of the attack with the mass of troops, ships, tanks, and planes involved in the operation. He thought only the Soviet Union was capable of such assemblage, and even they couldn't match Deane's inferred figures.

The Normandy invasion was a welcome sign to Stalin, who continued to demand other invasions, such as one originally proposed by Churchill for the Balkans instead of "Overlord." The invasion of Normandy did not immediately affect Hitler's eastern campaign, but it did arrest his reserves in France for the eastern front. Some insignificant German reinforcements of troops and armaments were diverted to France by rail, instead of to the eastern front. In the meantime, efforts to coordinate Soviet and Allied plans, the interchange of military staffs, and aerial shuttle bombing with landings in the Soviet Union were stalled by Stalin until later in the campaign, inferring that Germany was already beaten, and he preferred to have it done by Soviet armies, rather than with Allied help. He could then determine the outcome in Eastern Europe, as well as Germany, by belittling the Allied effort in the Italy and Normandy invasions. The German command was well aware of how slowly the Soviets mobilized for an offensive and ascribed it to poor communications and logistical problems among echelons of Soviet formations; thus the Germans were fully aware the Soviets were preparing for an assault and prepared accordingly. It finally dawned on Stalin that some of his territory was still in German hands and that it would take substantial time to regain it. Stalin was acutely aware of his manpower shortages, yet he frittered away unusually large formations on his "not one step back" directives.

By then Stalin had begun interfering with his high command's directives, thereby prolonging the war by months. He finally agreed to permit Poltava airbase in Ukraine to be used for Allied landings. Some of the Allied airmen stationed there to service the planes found themselves isolated, without permission to leave the base. These cross-shuttle bombing raids directly affected the eastern campaign, with almost daily raids on Ploesti oil fields in Rumania by the U.S. Ninth Air Force. Hitler depended on these oil fields to supply oil to his engines, as well as targets in East Germany.

In mid-May the Soviets were again on the offensive and cleared Crimea of all German troops. Stalin's losses in Crimea were heavy and he took a respite until he could scrape the barrel for more troops. He toyed with the idea of creating battalions of unmarried women between the ages of seventeen and forty but was strongly dissuaded by his chief of the general staff, Marshal Vassilevsky, and he never brought it up again. One would have to assume that the reasoning was against Russian psyche, in general, and manhood, in particular. He got over that hurdle after the war by employing women in backbreaking work to the clean up and rebuild the country, because of the extreme shortage of men. After the war's end, no credit was given these women for their work in armaments factories, repairs of war damage, and feeding the country, except in general terms in the press and medals for work in armament factories during the war.

A new Soviet offensive was launched 23 June 1944, which crossed the Bug river and cleared all Soviet territory. Leningrad had previously been liberated in January 1944 after nine hundred days of isolation, horror, and hunger. The Soviets entered Poland and rested before Warsaw on the right bank of the Vistula River, capturing some portions of the Baltic states. Their casualties at this point were surprisingly low, placed at 325,000 dead by Stalin's reckoning and estimated about 500,000 by the German command.

They had not yet entered Germany proper. A renewed offensive began in September to clear all of the Baltic states and trap the German Baltic Army Group of thirty understrength divisions north of East Prussia and south of the Latvian border. This succeeded when the Soviets broke through to the Baltic coast at Memel. German army group divisions by then were less than half strength. By the end of the year, the Soviets were on the eastern border of East Prussia, exhausted, recuperating, and re-equipping their stores and manpower.

The Polish underground army in Warsaw under the command of Polish General Bor-Komarovski, allied with the London Poles, staged an uprising against German garrison troops in Warsaw in anticipation of Soviet help. The Germans brought in Waffen SS troops and tanks to reinforce the garrison and extract retribution. It took the Germans two months to quell the uprising, which took the lives of some 300,000 people. The Polish army requested assistance from the soviets, who were across on the east bank of the Vistula, overlooking Warsaw. The Soviet corps requested permission from higher command to intervene; this permission was denied with no explanation. Stalin wanted to make sure that the Polish army was annihilated by the Germans, so that he could seize Poland without opposition. He would later install a puppet communist government known as the "Lublin Committee." Instead of fighting the Germans, he took a political solution by having the Germans defeat them.

The German command quickly realized Stalin's intent, and they used extreme measures with some Waffen SS troops and Panzers, taking no prisoners. A few Poles who escaped told the story to the outside world. It was revealed later that the Polish field commander, Bor-Komarovski, sent an open radio message to the London Poles,(which was also picked up by Swedish monitoring stations), accusing Stalin of treachery. This was based on four primary reasons. It was known that Moscow Radio sent out a message in July, calling upon the people of Warsaw to fight against the Germans. This message was also picked up in Sweden. Secondly, the Soviets refused permission to Allied planes to land on Soviet airfields to deliver supplies to help the Poles. Also, the lack of support for Polish General Berling's troops to force the Vistula adjoining Warsaw. And finally, disciplinary action was taken by the Soviets against General Berling for attempting to hold a bridgehead for Soviet help. Lt. Gen. Berling was deputy commander of the Soviet-appointed "Lublin Committee."

On hearing this, Churchill communicated his disbelief to Stalin for his attitude and inactions and asked for an explanation. As usual, Stalin lied and defended his action by accusing the Poles of not coordinating the action with the Soviet command. Churchill begged Roosevelt to send a joint protest. Roosevelt was not much help, however, when it came to dealing with Stalin and his devious methods.

After weeks of Polish agony and defeat, Stalin's Polish communist forces fought their way into minor portions of the eastern suburbs. A few days later the Soviet air force dropped supplies to them by parachute, some of which opened and smashed upon hitting the ground. The next day the Soviets occupied Praga, a suburb of Warsaw, but were ejected by Germans a few days later. Stalin's intent was to have Bor-Komarovski's troops destroyed and, at the same time, have them think the Soviets were on their way to help him. Due to this treachery, Bor-Komarovski surrendered to the Germans three weeks later. Various reasons have been advanced to either justify Soviet behavior in this incident or to condemn it.

The author researched Gen. Rokosovskiy's reasons—who commanded the First Belorussian Front—in refusing to help the Poles capture Warsaw; they sounded plausible. Yet Soviet commanders can easily justify reasons for not mounting an attack since every commander had to get permission for all decisions from Stalin. However, Rokosovskiy's reasons contradict the Moscow Radio broadcast in July, instructing the people of Warsaw to commence fighting within Warsaw. Gen. Guderian, the chief of Panzer troops, and subsequently the new chief of OKH general staff, in reporting to Hitler, felt the Russian command probably exhausted itself, due to heavy casualties inflicted on the Russians by Panzers in recent battles east of the Vistula. He also referred to his staff records on the two adjoining Soviet fronts as extremely active with unusually aggressive attacks, concurrently with a lull opposite Warsaw, on the right bank of the Vistula. However, he defers to certain political decisions not to cross the Vistula to relieve Warsaw. In view of the above, and in further research on this question, the author is convinced that Churchill's complaints were fully justified because of the strange inactivity on the Warsaw front, based on political, rather than military, decisions. The front adjoining Rokosovskiy's, were the Second Belorussian and First Ukrainian fronts, which were both launching ferocious attacks. This is further evidence to show that it is reasonable to assume that the Soviet decision was politically based.

By the end of December 1944, the Soviet troops were on the eastern and southern borders of East Prussia and had crossed the Vistula, seventy miles south of Warsaw. The German command expected the Soviets to launch an attack in the southern sector of the front; however they launched their attack on a broad front in the direction of the Baltic coast, northeast of Berlin, and isolated East Prussia. They reached the east bank of the Oder River opposite Frankfurt-on-Oder at Kustrin by January 1945. Having outrun their supplies and communications, they rested as usual—this time on the east bank of the Oder at Furstenberg, until fully ready for the assault on Berlin. Enroute, opposite Breslau, they had also captured Cracow. They also entered eastern portions of Germany after liberating Poland. Also by February, most of Hungary, including Budapest was taken. The northern portions of Rumania were also in Soviet hands.

As they approached Germany proper, fighting had become desperate on both sides. Hitler threw in some Waffen SS troops sparingly. These troops gave the Soviets a bad time, inflicting heavy casualties on the Russians because they would rather die then retreat. Most of them were lightly armed, but they fought fanatically for every inch of soil and held up the eastern border two months, to the surprise of the Soviet command, which thought it would be rather easy. Hitler promised to stop the Red Army at the gates of Berlin by assembling all the diehard SS units on the outskirts of and inside Berlin. No mention was made of the Volkssturm, a people's home guard, with men in their sixties and children aged twelve to fifteen. In his daydreaming down in the Reichskanzlei, the chancellery's bunker, safe from Russian planes and artillery, Hitler commanded an imaginary mighty Ninth Army under General Busse and Twelfth Army under General Wenk, as if they were up to full strength as they had been in 1942. General Gotthard Heinrici, the commander of Army Group Vistula, tried to stall the Russians with his meager infantry troops before they reached Berlin. In the end, the approaches to the city for the Battle for Berlin sustained horrendous casualties on both sides. The SS outdid itself—and in most cases died fighting, even when wounded, rather than surrender.

Unexpectedly, Hitler, in a desperate frenzy, ordered General Weidling, commander the Fifty-Sixth Panzer Corps, to take charge of Berlin defenses, although Weidling had no more Panzers left and only a scattering of troops. At the very end, he ordered General Wenk, the commander of the Twelfth Army, to mount a counterattack, even though his army was down to a few hundred men. There is no official accounting of German casualties, which should be considered heavy. However, casualties on the Soviet side, had to be horrendous especially since the Soviets acknowledge the battle as being heavy and bloody. In view of Stalin's demands for immediate conquest of Berlin, whatever casualties it took with three army groups (north, center, and south of Berlin), losses undoubtedly were extremely heavy, whether they admitted or not.

With British troops rushing into north Germany to Hamburg and the Baltic coast, U.S. troops were advancing in southeastern direction to Nurnberg, Regensburg, and Munich, entered western Czechoslovakia in Karlsbad and Pilsen, and then proceeded to Austria. Meanwhile, by the end of April, Zhukov's first Belorussian Front, immediately north and opposite Berlin, turned south to join Rokossovskiy's second Belorussian Front, which was heading west. Konev's first Ukrainian Front, in the south, was also heading up to Berlin. All three made progress toward Berlin by way of a juncture, west of Potsdam, thus encircling Berlin. On the same day the last German stronghold in East Prussia fell.

On 2 May all operations in the west halted, except for minor sporadic fighting, and the wholesale surrender of German troops in various areas of Germany—encouraged by their commanders—to the Western Allies. Five days later the entire German army, or whatever was left of it, officially surrendered at Rheims. Col. General Jodl, chief of operations of OKW, Hitler's supreme command, signed capitulation documents with Anglo-Americans. Field Marshal Keitel, nominal chief of Hitler's staff, signed capitulation the next day in Berlin, with Marshal Zhukov representing the Soviet command and General Hans Krebs the German army. The war in Germany was over with devastation, ruin, and hopelessness overtook the German population and troops as they began streaming west by the millions to escape Soviet hordes.

Stalin demanded the return of all Soviet prisoners and civilians behind the Allied lines. At first the Allies complied with the demand but subsequently refused to give them up. According to Stalin, victory day was achieved in the early hours of 8 May, though Prague had not been liberated, Field Marshal Shoerner was holding out there, but he eventually surrendered it untouched, refusing Hitler's demand to blow it up.

Whatever was left of General Wenck's Twelfth Army gave up in the west to the American Ninth Army of General Simpson, who hoped to get to Berlin before the Russians but was stopped by a telephone call from General Bradley—an unforeseen strategic error which subsequently inflicted dire consequences for the Allies and peaceful Germany. Col. General von Mantueffel, the very competent young Panzer commander of German troops at the Battle of the Bulge, marched west with his third Panzer Group, less panzers, and surrendered to the Americans as on parade.

It is not in the range of this chapter to delve into every detail of the battles for Stalingrad and Berlin, or of the so-called "Great Patriotic War." Only the two major ferocious and decisive battles were reviewed, and sufficient conclusions may be derived about the killer instincts of both dictators. The ferocious nature of battles between two dictators and the disregard of lives on either side, with unacceptable loss of life, meant nothing to both of them.

Hitler rewarded his marshals and generals by firing and blaming them for Germany's defeat before he committed suicide in his Berlin bunker.

Stalin rewarded his most successful generals only as marshals. They supposedly demanded that Stalin deserved more, and so he was honored with the highest honor for a military man, Generalissimo. Thus ended the "Great Patriotic War," coined by Stalin the Generalissimo. Stalin alone won the war, but the ruin inflicted by Hitler as vengeance still exists to this day.

**Recommended Reading**

*History of the Great Patriotic War of the USSR.* The Russian version for English readers; it is however highly biased. USSR Defense MInistry Publication, 1956. English translation by IVOVSS.

*Beginning of the Road.* Marchal Chuikov's, published in Russian, 1963. Description of the Battle of Stalingrad, translated by Harold Silver, published in 1964 by Holt, Rinehart & Winston, New York. It is more objective than standard Soviet publications, but again somewhat biased, written by a Russian Marshal, a favorite of Khrushchev.

*Second World War, 1939-1945.* Schematic Album, Russian edition, Moscow, 1958 USSR Defense Ministry Publication.

*Paulus and Stalingrad.* by Walter Goerlitz, 1963, by Methuen & Co., Ltd. English translation.

*Lost Victories.* by Field Marshal Erich von Manstein, 1955, Verlag, German edition. English edition, 1956. (unable to locate the publisher, at this time)

*Stalingrad Cauldron.* by Phillipi and Heim., German edition, 1955 (unable to locate English translation, publisher, and date at this time)

*Panzer Leader.* by Col. General Heinz Guderian, English translation by Constantine Fitzgibbon, 1965, E.P. Dutton & Co.

*The German Generals Talk.* B.H. Lidell Hart, 1967. William Morrow & Co.

*History of the German General Staff.* Walter Goerlitz, Frederick A. Preager, New York, 1957.

# CHAPTER XII
# THE SUCCESSORS

The Politburo decided to have Stalin's body mummified like Lenin's body and placed it next to his in Red Square Mausoleum. It took up to ten days after Stalin's death on 5 March 1953 for a member of Stalin's close circle of colleagues to grab power, typical of Stalin's own methods. On 12 March *Pravda* and Moscow Radio announced that Georgy Malenkov would succeed Comrade Stalin. However, a few days later on 15 March, the Supreme Soviet of the USSR announced a new government: Moscow Radio and *Pravda* carried the news.

**The Rise of Khrushchev: 1953-64**

Voroshilov was named chairman of the Presidium of the USSR. Malenkov was made chairman of the Council of Ministers, while Beria, Molotov, and Kaganovich became first deputies, and Bulganin and Mikoyan became Deputies. Nikita Khruschev became first secretary of the Central Committee, a position from which Stalin accumulated his power.

Shortly after Stalin's death various disturbances occurred in Soviet labor camps as well as in the satellite countries, including East Germany, Hungary, and Poland. At the demand of the Soviet Politburo, to keep peace and quiet in those countries, some relaxation in production quotas were implemented, which also caused some of their leaders to lose their high posts. Suddenly in July 1953 Moscow Radio and *Pravda* announced the arrest of Lavrentiy Beria, the KGB chief. His trial and execution occurred previously but was announced later in December, by *Izvestia*. Subsequently, Beria's underlings were also dispatched. By 1955 some sixteen thousand prisoners in slave labor camps were released, but this was miniscule compared to the millions still held. At the twentieth Party Congress in February 1956, thousands more were rehabilitated. Incidently during this rehabilitation period, Lenin's old and trusted colleagues—Bukharin, Zinoviev, Kamenev, and Rykov—whom Stalin dispatched in 1938, were posthumously cleared of any charges in trying to kill Lenin, as fabricated by Stalin. However, they were not cleared for opposition to the Party. Apparently, Stalin still had a grip on his comrades, even after his death.

On 25 February 1956, the last day of the Party Congress, Khrushchev delivered a secret speech in which he denounced Stalin's excesses in no uncertain terms. Since his speech was secret, it was never divulged in the USSR, but it was leaked and made available to Western countries almost immediately. It was apparently leaked by the satellite party members or Western communist party chiefs. Rehabilitation, as such, affected the mood in the country against unlawful and arbitrary incarceration, trials, imprisonment, and execution. Khuruschev, as secretary of the Central Committee, was able to isolate the Malenkov-Beria-Molotov clique after Beria's death, although Molotov never aspired to any leadership role. This left Khruschev supreme among Stalin's successors. Shortly thereafter, Mikoyan and Bulganin became members of Khrushchev's inner circle.

The Eastern European satellite countries began erupting in demonstrations to ease unbearable production goals, desiring more freedom from Moscow's domination and autonomy for themselves. Since the Soviet Union had begun experiencing turmoil on its borders some measure of relaxation was granted by Khrushchev in order to pacify them. Nevertheless, the relaxation permitted was apparently insufficient, and serious disturbances began in Poland and Hungary. Polish workers, whose wages were meager, rebelled and called for the ouster of Soviet troops. Polish authorities rushed their regular troops to quell the riots, but they refused to fire on the workers. This confusing condition brought about a review by the Politburo. Khrushchev, accompanied by Mikoyan, Kaganovich, and Molotov, arrived in Poland. At a conference with the Polish leaders, who suggested use of the Polish army, the Khrushchev group stated that they believed the reliability of the troops was doubtful. In this connection, he ordered Soviet troops to march on Warsaw; the head of the Polish committee of the Workers party, Wladislav Gomulka, requested Khrushchev to order a stop to the march. At this point, Khrushchev denied such rumors. In the end Gomulka prevailed, with assurances that his policies toward the Soviet Union would be conciliatory. Soviet troops were ordered to their bases, and the Soviet party left for home.

Hungary's problem was rather different because it was an internal political problem, not caused by wages. Rakosi, the head of the Communist party in Hungary, instituted measures against rivals of his leadership, which caused him to execute Rajk and his colleagues. This irked both the leadership and the people for some three years, and Rakosi's resignation was demanded. To clear up these problems, Mikoyan arrived in Budapest to review the situation and forced Rakosi's resignation. After Rakosi's removal, his entire state security apparatus was arrested, and the reburial of innocent victims was ordered. At this public demonstration 200,000 citizens were present. Later, Mikoyan recommended reinstalling Nagy as head of the Hungarian government. This uprising was a grassroots movement, with most workers participating. Soviet tanks and troops were in Budapest and were stationed just out of town, remaining in close vicinity, which posed a threat. Demonstrators demanded removal of Soviet troops from Hungary. Another demonstration, at least equal to the first in number, took place in front of the Parliament building. Some of the rebel leaders created a National Guard of approximately 20,000 so-called freedom fighters.

It was later confirmed that the Soviet Central Committee adopted a resolution to militarily suppress the uprising, although it was kept secret until the appropriate time. Chinese, Yugoslav, and other socialist countries were queried about the invasion of Hungary, and the Chinese suggested the use of loyal local troops, if possible. Having received approval from the so-called fraternal socialist countries, Soviet troops and tanks reinvaded Hungary on a mass scale on 1 November. When Imre Nagy, the new premier, inquired about Soviet troop movements, Yuriy Andropov, the Soviet ambassador—and later general secretary of the Communist party—lied, saying they were the same troops previously withdrawn. When Nagy confirmed that they were not, he emphasized the Warsaw Pact requirement for entry of troops into a country being received by the host countries. That same evening, Nagy withdrew Hungary from the Warsaw Pact and appealed to UN for help. As a ruse, Andropov suggested that discussions proceed on reentry of Soviet troops. All the while the troops were overrunning the country and setting up occupation of Budapest. Janos Kadar, the secretary of the Hungarian Communist party, was selected by Khrushchev to be the head of the new Hungarian government on 4 November. There is some reason to believe that the Kadar government had been previously formed in Moscow. Soviet artillery and tanks commenced bombardment of Budapest, which lasted some three days, and the hopeless battle was essentially over, although it continued for a few more days in the countryside.

Concurrently, French, British, and Israeli troops were invading Egypt, which the Eisenhower administration condemned. Taking advantage of this chaos and diversion, the Soviets had no problem dealing with the Hungarian crisis. At the UN, more than fifty nations condemned the invasion, but this meant nothing to the Soviet Union; thus Hungary was brought down. Nagy and his colleagues sought refuge in the Yugoslav embassy, unaware of Tito's consent of the invasion. The Soviets finally caught up with them on their way to the Yugoslav embassy and took them to Romania, where they were dealt with in the usual Soviet style—prompt execution. In view of distorted Soviet propaganda at home, it is difficult even now to assess the opinion, if any, of the average Soviet citizen's view of the incident.

To improve conditions at home, Khrushchev deeply desired to make life easier for the average Soviet citizen under communist rule. He embarked upon an agricultural program to increase output in the rural areas. To this end, it was decided to backtrack from issuing quotas and demands from the government in Moscow. The Central Committee permitted the districts—not the collective farms—to decide for themselves what to plant. Collective farms were being transformed into state farms and the peasant farmers into wage earners; thus improving income in both categories. In order to multiply the supply of grain, the fallow virgin lands of Kazakstan and the Ural areas were selected. All preparations were made, except for organization, equipment, silos, and the weather. As it turned out this effort was wasteful, expensive, and not sufficiently productive to warrant more investment. The Central Committee was against the concept from the beginning based on advice from agronomists.

In 1963 a serious drought overtook the areas, wiping out the majority of the corn crop and resulting in grain shortages. For the first time in Soviet history, grain had to be imported from abroad—not that there had ever been enough—and repeated from then on, until the fall of the Soviet Union. Khrushchev's stubborn insistence undid even the minimum requirements of former quotas of crop production. He persisted in other adventures which created strong opposition in both the Politburo and the Central Committee. His declaration that the USSR would surpass American agricultural production, when added to his eastern European rebellions, caused a serious rift in the Central Committee, where he was challenged. The committee voted seven to four to oust him from his position of secretary of the party. Khrushchev decided to oppose his ouster, and with the support of Marshal Zhukov, he won the contest. Later however, Khrushchev felt like he being surpassed in popularity by Zhukov. In October 1957, when the marshal was on a trip abroad, Khrushchev convened the seven members of the Presidium of the Central Committee to discuss Zhukov's Bonapartist attitude. When some Presidium members suggested it wait until the marshal returned, Khrushchev retorted that seven members don't wait for one. As a result of this meeting Zhukov was removed from the Central Committee and retired as defense minister. Khrushchev then assumed the post of premier. Those whom he ousted were not imprisoned or executed—a first in Soviet history.

Eventually eastern European convulsions, disagreements with China and Yugoslavia, the Cuban missile crisis, and peremptory replacements of party and ministerial positions caused the party to be divided. In the fall of 1964, a majority of the leadership, past and present, decided to unseat him for revisionism. He was called back from his vacation for a special session of the Central Committee. At the session a report by Suslov, the Communist party theoretician, of Khrushchev's revisionism was read, and he was peremptorily stripped of all positions and retired as a pensioner. Thereafter, the society's hierarchical system was more careful to secure its privileged position by selecting a general secretary of the Communist party, who was to rule by consensus.

The reader should consider the hoped-for and earnest efforts by Khrushchev for the great mass of Soviet citizens. His unmasking of Stalin's crimes and the cult of personality may have been somewhat premature—just three years after Stalin's death—and risky at best. Stalin's unmasking prepared the way for the release of hundreds of thousands of innocent inmates from Stalin's slave labor camps. Additionally, Khrushchev's agricultural schemes were meant to be beneficial to the entire population, despite its failure. One other tradition instituted by Stalin, eliminating the opposition by execution, was reversed by Khrushchev in a civil manner, replacing the opposition. Khrushchev's leadership paved the way for easing the conditions of life throughout the Soviet Union even under the Soviet dictatorship. It was Khrushchev who introduced a rotation system, where one third of the committees in the party's hierarchy was replaced.

Khrushchev's rule lasted eleven years, and he died 11 September 1971. He was buried in Novodevichi Cemetery—a private plot—by the family, instead of by the Kremlin wall with a public funeral, as all other communist heroes. His main weaknesses were his boastfulness, stubbornness, jealousy, and untimely exposure of Stalin's excesses, which eventually were his undoing. On the other hand, his feelings for his countrymen to ease their burdens were genuine.

Khrushchev made notes of his career during his retirement, which was later published in two volumes as *Khrushchev Remembers*. In the books he outlines his rise as a Bolshevik worker in the beginning and then his years as secretary of the Ukrainian Communist Party. He also outlines his political control over military operations during the "Patriotic War" and relates Stalin's demands for continual counterattacks in hopeless cases, sacrificing troops needlessly. His coverage of special assignments with Kaganovich for Stalin in Ukraine and his rise to the Politburo covers a significant part of his career. He tries to justify himself as the first general secretary of the Communist party for ten years. He explains the virgin lands experiment and, finally, his ouster. When in retirement, he was called to account for the contents of his book, published in the West, which apparently was a violation of basic communist principles (unless special permission was granted). He denied all knowledge of writing it or how it got to the West. He was the last of the first generation of Soviet rulers after Lenin and Stalin.

**Leonid Brezhnev: 1964-82**

On 14 October 1964 Leonid Brezhnev was selected by consensus to be general secretary of the Communist party, replacing the deposed Nikita Khrushchev. The first act of the new group was to revoke the rotation system established by Khrushchev. To protect their interests, the higher echelons of the party preferred a conservative, mild-mannered nonentity in order to maintain their privileged positions. After a search among a few candidates, they chose one Leonid Brezhnev by consensus.

Brezhnev was born in 1906 in a small provincial Russian town, Kamenskoe, close to Dnepropetrovsk, the provincial capital. In 1938 he was assigned to Agitprop, the propaganda section, which turned out to be the future path to the Kremlin and to general secretary. It was Khrushchev who recommended him for the assignment when he was Party secretary in the Ukraine. During the "Great Patriotic War" under Khrushchev, he was appointed, among other assignments, as deputy chief of political directorate of the Ukrainian front. By the time the war ended, not only was he its head, but he also became a major general. In 1950 when Khrushchev became secretary of the Central Committee, he brought Brezhnev with him to Moscow. In mid-1950 he was sent to Moldavia to be first secretary of the Moldavian Central Committee—one of fifteen semiautonomous republics. He remained there till 1964, when he was chosen as the general secretary of the Communist Party to replace his former superior and benefactor by the same men who were in Khushchev's Politburo and the Central Committee. On becoming general secretary, he promised collective leadership, all the while bringing his closest colleagues from Moldavia to occupy important posts in order to firmly consolidate his power rather than build consensus. From 1964 to the 1970s, his rule experienced dozens of clandestine writers, meetings, and propaganda leaflets denouncing socialism, communism, censorship, and imprisonment. Self-published clandestine literature, known as *samisdat*, also proliferated most national autonomous republics of the Soviet Union.

Prominent writers were hauled to court on false charges or were forcibly exiled, either to labor camps for internal exile or put on a plane to foreign exile.

Alexander Sozhenitsyn, the writer and Nobel Laureate who (among other novels) wrote *One Day in the Life of Ivan Denisovich*, was expelled to foreign exile in United States. Andrey Sakharov, the academician-physicist involved with the nuclear weapons program, received internal exile in Gorkiy. Well-known historians and brothers Roy and Zoresh Medvedev, who wrote on the existence of the privileged *nomenklatura*, were constantly under threat and surveillance, and the latter was forced into exile in Britain. Many Moscow State University students, lesser-known poets, writers, and human rights activists were jailed. Psychiatric hospitals were opened specifically for dissidents. Most trials were held behind closed doors in view of the seriousness of accusations against the writers and speakers, who called the communist system a living lie.

Suslov, a former member of Khrushchev's Central Committee and now a member of Brezhnev's Politburo, constituted himself the chief theoretician of the Communist party and played a significant role in condemning people in violation of the so-called "socialist legality." Ukrainian intellectuals expressed dissent due to Russification. Lithuanians were forbidden to practice Catholicism and were forced to stop criticism; Moscow sent several advisors to crack down. In 1968 a crisis developed in Czechoslovakia because of the economic, social, and particularly censorship conditions. Novotny, the former head of the Party, was replaced by a young Communist, Alexander Dubchek, who strongly believed in "socialism with a human face," along with Joseph Smrkovskiy, a Politburo member and theoretician, both of whom wished to lift censorship. At the meeting of communist parties in Warsaw, Gomulka demanded immediate reinstatement of censorship in Czechoslovakia with armed intervention if necessary; all other Warsaw Pact members agreed. In this connection, military contingents from the Soviet Union, Poland, Bulgaria, Hungary, and East Germany mobilized troops for the invasion of Czechoslovakia. By surprise attack, Chechoslovak leaders were captured and flown to Moscow to sign a document permitting Soviet troops on their territory and renewing censorship. That was the end of Czechoslovakia's quasi-independent status and its "socialism with a human face."

About that time, "detente" was proclaimed between the West and the Soviet block. Kissinger convinced a skeptical President Nixon that it was in the best interests of the United States and western Europe. In reality it was not, since it gave the Soviet block breathing space to consolidate its political gains. It also confirmed Soviet occupation of central Europe, within striking distance of West Germany for Warsaw Pact troops close to the North German Plain and the Fulda Gap. Meanwhile, the Soviet economy was in shambles again due to agricultural and industrial production. Most Western economists were aware of the existence of a "second economy" within the USSR, but didn't know its magnitude or its base sources. Subsequently, after tracking dollar reserves and shortages of natural resource materials consigned for production and export, it became evident that some significant people were involved in siphoning them off. It has been confirmed by several dissidents and escapees to the West that without the second economy, Soviet industry (other than armaments) would have probably come to a grinding halt, at least in consumer production. The author heard several repatriates confirm this, and in addition to agricultural imports, the possibility existed of importing consumer goods to satisfy the fledgling middle class. Import of consumer goods by way of Stokman's Department Store in Finland was apparently insufficient to satisfy the demand. The government and Party were apparently aware of this but did nothing, pretending not to know. By that time, corruption became big business—not petty as before—with hundreds of high Party members involved, not only in the economy but also in granting favors of rank and titles.

At about this time also, the Soviet-Chinese conflict erupted, with Soviet propaganda lambasting the Chinese as "yellow peril." The Soviets used detente to shield themselves and enlisted United States for support. Several battles between China and the USSR erupted on an unclaimed minor island on the Ussuri River and on the borders at Sinkiang. The Soviets secretly inquired whether the United States had any objections to using nuclear weapons against China. The United States balked at that suggestion, and the inquiry died a natural death. Brinkmanship was a Soviet trait, and they practiced it as conditions arose.

The decade of the 1970s showed some signs of lessening propaganda vitriol with the signing of detente at the Helsinki conference. Concurrently, the Soviet Union reached parity in nuclear weapons with the United States. From the point of view of government economics, huge losses were repaid by selling off natural resources. The huge loans from foreign banks for grain purchases and the defense expenditures to beat and surpass the United States in nuclear weapons during detente were the principal reasons for the sale of natural resources on the open market. Translated, it meant the country was going broke, and the Politburo and the *nomenklatura* knew it. They did, however, fool their people by withholding this information and securing huge loans from the West. Yet private workshops existed, along with foreign currency exchange business, where huge sums were made by mafia-type gangs.

The United States and the Soviet Union also signed arms limitation agreements. SALT I was signed in 1973, rather quickly, since it was apparent that the Soviet Union had achieved nuclear parity with the United States, SALT II was signed in 1979, but it took almost seven years to complete. Some nuclear scientists in United States thought the reason for the delay was based on new laser weapons and other sophisticated technology on both sides. These arms limitation agreements and funds furnished by Western banks also helped the Soviet Union build a new navy. However, it was generally believed that they never matched Western technology, with the possible exception of the submarine fleet.

While the economy was stagnating, Brezhnev cited rosy economic statistics at the Twenty-fifth Party Congress in 1976. He was contradicted by various Soviet sources in actual statistical analysis, including the economist Khachaturov, who stated figures quite different from Brezhnev's. Khachaturov's and Agabengian's statistical analysis showed that labor productivity in the USSR was 50 percent lower, and agriculture was 70-80 percent lower than in the United States. Their analysis is fascinating reading, even for a person knowing little of economics. For instance an article appeared in *Trud* and *Literaturnaya Gazeta* in July 1979 which read, "There is a threshold in labor productivity, that enterprises have no interest in exceeding planned growth, since that would result in enormous increase in planned targets the next year." Further, "the majority of machine building plants in USSR have 1.4 -1.5 times more workers than similar industries in other countries." Actually, these figures were rather low, which later became apparent. This accounts for their claims that there is no unemployment in the USSR, and also for the substantially lower wage rates. In the total calculation of economic statistics, the introduction of retirement at age fifty-five, further reduced capital outlays, to insure jobs for the coming generations. The author encountered ruble trade in Leningrad in 1991, where even the local people refused to deal in rubles, knowing the group was American. It is quite obvious that the socialist ruble economy didn't work, since there were no incentives—only tricks to delay its demise.

Not satisfied with puny eastern European conquests as satellites, Brezhnev embarked on an expedition, based on the former czarist formula. It was the Imperial regime's dream to have a warm water port, to break through to the Mediterranean Sea at Istanbul (Constantinople), which was not available now in view of the British and French threat. Besides, Turkey and Greece were NATO members, thus closing this opportunity. The time had arrived to find another place to circumvent NATO and resurrect the idea in another location. It may have been a vodka session one evening in December 1979 when a bright idea came up among a few of Brezhnev's drinking buddies, without consulting any other members of the Central Committee. Looking at a map, they discovered Afghanistan, whose government was dominated by local Communists, who were losing the war against the Muslim tribes. It may have been decided at that party to send a couple of Soviet divisions to help out the communist government. This contingent proved insufficient and grew to 100,000 troops under the command of Soviet General Gramov. The Afghan president, Babrak Karmal, supposedly invited them in, having had enough of guerrillas fighting against his own army. Karmal apparently was not suitable to lead the communist government and troops. In this connection, they chose Mohammad Najibullah, as their president. Brezhnev's group decided that the glorious Soviet army of Warsaw Pact fame could overrun Afghanistan and enter Kabul. The strategic intent was to work through the country and then push through Pakistan—perhaps with some help from India by stirring trouble with Pakistan—and reach the Indian Ocean, thus achieving a greater objective than one on the enclosed Mediterranean. It was a masterpiece of geopolitical considerations, with Britain no longer capable of stopping them, having given up its colonial possessions after WWII.

While all this was going on, other tribes united against the Soviet army, and the battle was joined. The population by that time was down to 18 million people. The Unites States sent thousands of shoulder-fired antiaircraft missiles and other weaponry by way of Pakistan to counteract soviet aircraft domination in the rural areas. The peasant exodus from Afghanistan amounted to 2.8 million to Pakistan and 1.5 million to Iran, from a population of approximately 22 million. The Soviet army couldn't take the punishment it received from anti-Soviet tribes, who mastered the technique of avoiding concentrations and stalking the enemy by surprise. In early 1992 the Mujaheddin—native guerrilla groups—and other groups stormed the besieged capital of Kabul. Najibullah escaped to a foreign embassy for protection and refuge. When Afghanistan was first invaded, President Carter had called for a boycott of the Moscow Olympics and canceled a projected economic agreement. At the UN, 104 nations condemned the invasion of Afghanistan. This invasion caused tensions in the Soviet Union, with dissidents gathering steam throughout the country. The heavy losses in manpower, the drain on the economy, and the loss of foreign loans for agricultural subsidies caused Brezhnev to revise his thinking. The Soviet army finally pulled out, with heavy losses in equipment and personnel. The Soviet command decided to withdraw its troops between May 1988 and February 1989.

Meanwhile dissident groups sprang up again by the dozens, and psychiatric hospitals accommodated more of them than ever before. Apparently, transformation of society had worn itself out for a second time when in contact with Western ideals and democracy. The system lasted too long and became an anachronism in the latter part of the twentieth century. It should be assumed that the Afghan war was the beginning of serious dissent in the country, which eventually grew to unmanageable proportions. After 1972 the economic condition of the country was in a state of stagnation and chaos, except for the military industrial complex, which received an enormous amount of capital investment, to the exclusion of other sectors of the economy. Other heavy and consumer industries, agriculture and extraction of natural resources never succeeded in this socialist motherland; in fact it went down precipitously, despite huge capital subsidies. The stranglehold of communism, with socialist self-contradictory economic doctrines, actually helped to imprison and diminish the economic sector, which never recovered as long as the Soviet Union lasted.

Stagnation and decline had begun under Brezhnev's rule years before. After ruling from 1964 to 1982, Leonid Brezhnev died on 10 November 1982. He left a legacy of excessive corruption and incompetence by the ruling class at the expense of the proletariat. He must have known that they were ruining the country, but all the while he sat behind a military shield, pretending that it would last forever. The U.S. involvement in the Afghan war has been compared to its involvement in Vietnam, but this is a dubious comparison since United States involvement was based on saving a legitimate government against communist hordes. Brezhnev was the first of the second generation of rulers to be buried by the Kremlin wall—a dubious honor reserved for Lenin's comrades.

## Yuriy Andropov: 1982-84

Typical Soviet style maneuvering occurred after Leonid Brezhnev's death, except on this occasion, it was behind the scenes. No major disagreements surfaced, and the succession proceeded peacefully. The day after Brezhnev's death, Yuriy Andropov was selected general secretary of the Central Committee. He was proposed by Konstantin Chernenko, his rival, whom Brezhnev had intended to succeed himself.

Andropov's career began in late 1930s, filling a vacancy created by Stalin's great purges. At first he was secretary of Yaroslav region of the Komsomol, subsequently a leader of the Komsomol of the Karelo-Finnish republic, after the Finnish-Soviet war in 1939-40. He took part in organizing partisan group movements in the "Patriotic War." During the 1956 revolution in Hungary, he was an ambassador (1954-57), and took major role in deceiving Imre Nagy, the Hungarian prime minister, about Soviet intentions and troop formations. As a reward for his deceit and manipulations during the Hungarian revolution, Khrushchev appointed him to take charge of the CPSU of fraternal (foreign) socialist parties. By 1962 he succeeded in being appointed as one of the secretaries of the Central Committee, the inner sanctum of communism's power. In 1967 Brezhnev appointed him chairman of KGB and a member of the Politburo. He held this assignment until 1982, when Brezhnev died. In this position, he repressed dissident groups and increased foreign espionage operations.

He assumed the new position of general secretary of the Communist party—previously held by Brezhnev—on 10 November 1982. Rumors were purposely spread of his like for Scotch, his liberal attitude towards dissidents, his enjoyment of foreign novels, his love for French cognac, and his unending liberal ideas. All these turned out to be untrue. However, to his credit, he gathered around him a substantial collection of intellectuals to rid the system of corruption, as well as implement more freedom for the masses under the soviet constitution. In that sense, he may be considered the father of *perestroyka*. Subsequently, in June 1983, he became chairman of the Presidium of the Supreme Soviet. In assuming the new position, he intended to change the order of discipline. Social political needs were to take precedence over material needs, so government and Party came first, and material goods came second. To enforce the government's discipline, he ordered strengthening discipline in industry and agriculture and expanded the authority of the industrial managers. He also emphasized that he had no special solutions for any problems other than this and said that he would welcome a collective opinion of the Central Committee.

He made it clear, though, that he would take measures against corruption. Apparently aware of gross violations, he first embarked on cleansing the Ministry of the Interior, where most bribes and all forms of corruption occurred. During the sessions of the Central Committee in June 1983, several high party members of the Central Committee were disciplined and purged from the Party. To ensure further compliance to discipline, he staffed some of the offices of the Interior Ministry with former members of the KGB and appointed a new minister of the interior. Some undisciplined members were put on trial and convicted. To further press his program, he dispatched his people around towns to observe if any of the people skipped work to shop or abstained from working. Various agencies were interlocked to screen out the violators. After several months of this, discipline seems to have broken down, and things went on as before. It was finally announced that implementation of communism would be postponed to another day, until "real socialism" was totally developed. Most people on the street knew better, and they did not expect life to be abundant under communism. Henceforth this term disappeared from slogans. Russification, however, supposedly for a common language in military formations among national minorities, became obligatory. To further curtail the corruption, which was rampant in the military, he appointed Russian agents to oversee various government agencies, to enforce discipline, and to root out the offenders.

Did Andropov make any difference in the Soviet Union with his discipline of priorities? After reviewing some of the literature about him, in both the Soviet press and written by Western writers, the author concludes that no significant change happened under Andropov, except his health deteriorated rapidly. His intent for the Soviet Union may be considered laudatory within the context of the Soviet system, though it is doubtful he could have succeeded, since the country was stagnating and unruly, and too late for reforms of any kind. The Soviet Union was heading socially and economically downward, regardless of minor measures to resurrect it, with its strict adherence to peculiar socialist dogmas and corruption; it was incapable of changing itself. Andropov did, however, intend to institute measures to relax the strict regimen of existing iron rule and proposed reforms which were to go into effect shortly. Andropov, being in poor health from kidney disease, could not survive to see his new discipline and progressive reforms take shape. He brought Gorbachev to the Central Committee and Politburo to carry on these reforms. It was left to Tass news agency, to announce that Yuriy Vladimirovich Andropov, general secretary of the Central Committee of the Communist Party Soviet Union, died after a serious illness on 9 February 1984.

**Konstantin Chernenko: 1984-85**

Chernenko was elected general secretary of the CPSU Central Committee on 13 February 1984 and elected chairman of the Supreme Soviet of the USSR 11 April 1984. He was a Siberian by birth, though he was Russian. He never served in the "Great Patriotic War." During the war, his biography states that he worked in the Central Committee of the Moldavian Communist party and got acquainted with Brezhnev in 1950. Under Brezhnev's wing, the loyal Party member became head of a department of the Central Committee. Subsequently, he was assigned as secretary of the Central Committee. By 1978 he was elected member of the Politburo—a phenomenal rise to the top without even working for it. The geriatric brotherhood system survived long enough to fill musical chairs.

During Cherneko's first few weeks in office, a law was published and adopted confirming the special curricula for education in schools previously outlined under Andropov's rule. The intent was to commence schooling for children at age six (instead of seven), instill in them the Marxist- Leninist worldview, and give them vocational training. Apparently it was intended to supplement a shortage in the labor force which had been caused by early retirements.

Subsequently, he came up with another "wonder drug" for agriculture. He intended a long-term plan of reclamation and irrigation of land. His intent was to divert some Siberian rivers, reduce further water flow to the Arctic Ocean, and to irrigate parched lands. Previously, such political (rather than scientific) experiments in disturbing nature—attempted in lakes Sevan, Aral, and Baikal—caused horrible environmental and pollution damage, as well as causing water levels to drop precipitously and dangerously. Fortunately it was a lot of talk, with no means to back it. Had the program been adopted, environmental and physical catastrophe could have occurred. Nothing constructive was done under his rule, and he hung around uselessly until 10 March 1985 when he died. He was the last of the second generation of Soviet rulers, and the most useless and ineffective.

## Mikhail Sergeevich Gorbachev: 1985-91

Mikhail Gorbachev was born 2 March 1931, in Privolnoye, Stavrapol region north of TransCaucasus. He was well educated and received his law degree from Moscow State University in 1955. A few years later he attended an agricultural institute, becoming an agricultural economist. His parents were from an agricultural working family in the Stavrapol region. He was engaged in party work since 1962 and achieved rapid promotions until he attained the position of first secretary of Stavrapol region. At the twenty-fourth Party Congress in March 1971, he was elected a member of the Central Committee of the CPSU, and by 1978 he was selected to be secretary of the Central Committee. In 1980 he became a member of the Politburo, which was a startling achievement in so short a time.

After Chernenko's death in 1985, he was elected to the position of General Secretary of the CPSU, thus making him the leader of the Soviet Union. In the April 1985 plenary meeting of the CPSU, he delivered a report on the status of the Party and its citizens. The report envisioned a spectrum of issues which were to change and affect the nation's economy. He toured the country to obtain firsthand knowledge from workers and apprised them of the decisions arrived at the plenary session. He advised them of the necessity to improve the national economy in scientific and technological fields. He considered this to be the first priority of the regime—to discard previous economic and technical models, which were anachronistic and useless. Furthermore, he outlined several areas in foreign relations which were to be fundamentally changed. He was prepared to tackle the difficult problems of the arms race and the threat of nuclear war. To prove his goodwill to other nuclear powers, he ordered termination of all Soviet nuclear explosions a few months later. These were high-minded, ideal intentions for a peaceful coexistence with the West. He named his program "perestroika"—a restructuring and transformation of his envisioned society.

He personally traveled throughout the country to talk to various working groups, including miners, metal workers, and *kolkhoznicks* (farm workers). In his discussions with them, he became aware of the workers' pay and health, which he found unsatisfactory. Stalin's *Short Course*, a schoolbook course of the regime's accomplishments and its intent for the soviet masses, was now discarded for good.

Gorbachev's principal advisor—some say his mentor—was Alexander Yakovlev, former ambassador to Canada. The more Gorbachev inquired, the more convinced he was that his thinking on restructuring was not only right, but was mandatory and should be implemented as soon as possible. He was, however, a dedicated Communist and a believer in real socialism. In order to impress the west with his sincerity, he arranged a trip to see Margaret Thatcher, the prime minister of Britain. It appears, she was both surprised and convinced of his sincerity in *perestroika* and *glaznost*, by commenting when he departed, "We can do business with Mr. Gorbachev." Ambassador Yakovlev and Gorbachev got better acquainted when Gorbachev went to Canada and learned the prerequisites of true democracy and free enterprise economy. The ambassador introduced him to various segments of the population, including farmers. Shortly thereafter, Gorbachev sent for him as his personal advisor, until Gorbachev changed sides and aligned himself with extreme conservatives. Yakovlev's introduction to democracy began when he was sent to Columbia University, apparently to take a refresher course in history and philosophy. His book on the subject, *On the Edge of an Abyss*, reveals him to be an intellectual in search of answers. Gorbachev selected Eduard Shevarnadze former head of the Georgian KGB, to be his foreign minister, and the three set about restructuring and applying *Glaznost* (openness). The curious thing about the triumvirate was their starting position, not knowing proper timing, when or where to start with democratic reforms, and how it would end. This in the end, was probably their downfall, once the genie was out of the bottle.

The first manifestations of *perestroika* were felt in 1989 in the Baltic and eastern satellite countries—which became restless, having experienced freedom before WWII—which were swallowed by Stalin in the Ribbentrop-Molotov Pact as a gift from Hitler. This is not to say that some conservatives still in the Central Committee and the Politburo agreed with the new democrats, their *perestroika*, or their *glaznost*. They considered it an extremely radical departure from normal political structure, and its speed concerned them. Some of these conservatives were Yegor Ligachev, the second position in the Politburo; Ryzhkov, the prime minister; Pugo, minister of the interior; Yazov, the defense minister; Kruichkov, the KGB chief; Lyukyanov, the chair of the Supreme Soviet; and Yanaev, the vice-president. The program of the conservatives was based on improving and refining the existing communist system, while Gorbachev and his reformers wanted to quickly revamp and reinvent a new system under communism. At a Party Congress in February 1986, Ligachev delivered a protest against attacks on the Party's power and privileges when questioned by Boris Yeltsin, who lashed out at Ligachev for defending power and privileges. This was reported in the press as a highly controversial matter, pitting Yeltsin against Ligachev. Open disagreements had never been exposed before. Gorbachev, the arbitrator, sided with Ligachev, apparently for political reasons, and in October of the same year, Yeltsin resigned from the Politburo. However, the opposing philosophies regarding *perestroika* and *glaznost* continued unabated between Gorbachev and Ligachev's comrades, whose disagreement was not only the speed of enactment of the new system but also the turnaround of the discipline itself. The group worried about the population, should all the measures be adopted too fast, and feared internal economic collapse, chaos, and the demise of existing institutions, which could depress and usher in unforeseen difficulties and convulsions. They were also apprehensive about total elimination of censorship; with the one-party system in place, they questioned pluralistic candidacy to the Supreme Soviet and its functioning at such phenomenal speed. Most of all they worried about their own future and their privileged positions.

While Ligachev was a conservative and a communist, his point was well borne out in the not-too distant future proving him to be right. From all indications and reports of his behavior, he was one Communist who was beyond reproach in corruption although he had his faults. Prime Minister Ryzhkov, a mild conservative, was recruited by the Gorbachev government to run day to day government affairs. He was later relieved of his position and faded into obscurity.

Meanwhile, not only the Baltic states, but all other national autonomous states of the empire, were in turmoil for more freedom. To add to Gorbachev's troubles, the satellite countries commenced their own clamor for independence, demanding from Gorbachev's government the removal of Soviet army elements from their territories. The Baltic states, Poland, Czechoslovakia, and Hungary demanded immediate recall of Soviet troops who had been stationed there as part of Warsaw Pact. At the time it began to appear that Gorbachev was in a rather shaky position with his reforms, and he began losing control of the situation. Gorbachev sent his emissaries to each of the captive capitals to cool things down, at least for a while, but not one of the countries concurred. In this connection, he sent his troops to the Baltic states to calm the situation, which turned out to be a tragic encounter with loss of life. Gradually, some measure of independent enterprises was permitted, although some entrepreneurs went independent by themselves.

The economy was improving in some segments of agriculture and small business, while the political chaos and the government's consumer and heavy industries continued to deteriorate. Gorbachev and his reformers found Ligachev to be an obstructionist, and he was asked to resign from all his positions in the government and party, and he left for his beloved Siberia, to write his memoirs. A few months later, Ryzhkov was also asked to leave the government. In early summer 1987 Gorbachev wrote a speech on history, for delivery on the seventieth anniversary of the revolution. His speech, was similar in tempo to Khrushchev's, except he was more tactful with words and double-meanings. When one bears in mind the structure and composition of the Politburo and the Central Committee, which were overwhelmingly stacked with dedicated communist conservatives, it is not surprising that it was received coolly. In October 1987, at the plenary session of the Central Committee, he aired his speech, covering the entire spectrum of Stalin's reign and his "criminal" misdeeds. He described Stalin's 1936-38 terror and purges, when millions of citizens and thousands of Soviet high commanders were executed and 70 percent of the Central Committee disappeared. He further went into the details of the Ribbentrop- Molotov Pact, in which Hitler gave the Baltic states to the Soviet Union—which was unknown at the time—being in the secret vaults of the Kremlin. Among other things, he topped off his speech with Stalin's ineptness and interference in the conduct of the "Great Patriotic War," in spite of Stalin's boastful leadership of the war. The screening of *Repentance*, was also mentioned, with which the Congress mostly agreed, though most of the members weren't around when these things occurred, because they were too young. Gorbachev cautioned them that the entire speech would not be mentioned at the anniversary but was being aired only for the Central Committee. In November 1987 he delivered basically the same speech on national television but prefaced it in moderate philosophical terms until he got down to the crux of his speech. The audience included all the heads of the satellite countries in the Palace of Congresses in the Kremlin. Moscow radio commented that it received a thunderous applause.

Meanwhile, serious disturbances occurred in Georgia, Ukraine, some Soviet Central Asian republics, in addition to the satellite countries of Eastern Europe, where local national forces disavowed communism and set up their own quasi-liberation movements. Unstable conditions in the country, ambiguity of direction of the Party and government were by now so disruptive that some citizens believed in *perestroika* and *glaznost*, while others didn't. These unexpected convulsions were a first in Soviet history. Although some citizens welcomed *perestroika* and *glaznost*, they were not aware of the infighting in the Politburo and the Central Committee. The time arrived in 1989 for democratic elections, with rules rigged by the Communist party to insure their supremacy in the Congress of Peoples Deputies.

In reviewing my (almost daily) notes of occurrences in the American press, journals, and TV, and the Soviet publication *Argumenti* & *Factii* and the other publications, reporting on conditions of the players in the USSR from 1989 on, I conclude that Gorbachev was desperately trying to hold on to power. He gradually began to tilt in the direction of the majority hardliners to contain the chaos and retain his hold on power. By then, the satellite countries were in complete turmoil; his own Soviet Empire was crumbling; and the Berlin Wall was being torn down. Losing control, he cast about aimlessly looking for scapegoats in the Politburo and the Central Committee. Previously, he had abandoned Yakovlev's advice, and Shevarnadze resigned, claiming Gorbachev abandoned the original *perestroika* and *glaznost* in favor of the hardliners. With Sakharov, the formerly imprisoned nuclear scientist and dissident, now living in Moscow, more people looked for his leadership instead of Gorbachev's to get them out of this morass. By then, Sakharov was in poor health and could do little except for his previous moral qualities. Miners from Ukraine to Sakhalin Island went on strike, spontaneously—a first in the USSR—for higher wages to support their families from starving. Moscow promised relief, but in the end nothing came of it. Gorbachev tried to justify chaotic conditions by blaming people from Stalin to Brezhnev and eventually admitted the Soviet falsehood that the Soviet republics and the Baltic states never voluntarily joined the union. He never mentioned the Ribbentrop-Molotov Pact of 1939.

The Baltic countries, facing the mighty Soviet Union, demanded and obtained their independence by their own national efforts. And what of the Russian population living there, which Stalin had forced on the Baltic states? Few of them wished to return to Russia, even under the most stringent conditions imposed by the Baltic states for citizenship. The Soviet Union gradually but inexorably was falling apart. Gorbachev visited East Germany to celebrate its national existence and advised its Communist party bureaucracy to soften up its home rule. They categorically refused and apparently thought the regime would outlast the disturbances. About a month after Gorbachev's departure, in November, the Berlin Wall fell. Czechoslovakia was next, Wancelas Square was jammed with thousands of demonstrators, demanding freedom. Vaclav Havel, the playwright, who had been imprisoned as a dissenter became President, and that was the end of Communist Czechoslovakia. Poland and Lech Walesa's Solidarity had already gone the way of independence previously. Walesa, and electrician at the Gdansk shipyards, outmaneuvered General Yaruselskiy, the Communist party chief, to become President of free Poland. Hungary went the same way, disavowing communism and establishing a free society, ridding itself of its satellite status.

When it came to their own minority nationalities, Gorbachev felt he could control them from the center in Moscow. However, turbulences in these territories were also enhanced by the previous nuclear disaster at Chernobyl, in the Ukraine. The accident was not admitted at first, until most of Europe felt the fallout, and only then did it occur to Gorbachev to admit it. His nuclear power plants were of early vintage, and his engineers and scientists reassured him that it was a minor problem. When it got out of hand, thousands were affected by radiation, and the site was evacuated, with the area cordoned off. To find at least a temporary solution, a concrete sarcophagus entombed the second reactor, while dozens of high rise apartments stood vacant in the ghost town. At this writing, thousands of people, including children, are seriously disfigured, with no cure in sight, awaiting death. The government was helpless and offered no medical help, since it didn't have a cure. Gorbachev flew to Chernobyl and promised all the help his government could give. No help of any kind arrived from Moscow, and Ukraine itself had to feed, house, and clothe its people. Soviet engineers, doctors, and nuclear scientists flew in for a quick look, reviewed the disaster, and reported to the government. That was the help the proletariat received. It took Gorbachev more than two weeks to get on television to calm the people about Chernobyl—a useless effort when the catastrophic results had already taken place. This was a typical Soviet reaction—wait and we'll see after the fact.

The 1988 earthquake in Armenia caused the deaths of more than 25,000 people, with an additional 75,000 people crippled. Were it not for American and western European help, the disaster would have been compounded many times over. Armenian communities throughout the world helped with money, food, shelter, medicines, and medical care. Almost 3 percent of the population of Armenia either died or were left crippled. The government in Moscow was not only unable to help, but it never even had any disaster preparations for relief, or medicines, shelter, or food. The Soviet government never did have proper methods of disaster measurement or preparations. Human losses were usually measured by the press, a hospital count, and demographic specialists who rounded off the numbers, for minimum effect on the population by the propaganda organs.

Added to the above, hunger and starvation was rampant among much of the population scattered throughout the union, but mostly in Siberia. Visitors to the USSR in 1990 described miseries in districts outside Moscow as evidenced by peddlers of few vegetables and prostitutes in almost all the towns along the

TransSiberian railway, all the way to Vladivostok. It appears the *nomenklatura* did well, while the rest of the population went to work, with nothing to do, and got paid with money which had lost its value long ago. The strike of the miners in Siberia shut down almost all industries, except the military industrial plants, which supplied some African countries, Syria, Iraq, Iran, a few other small countries, and its satellite nations.

Meanwhile, the satellite countries, prior to the breakout, didn't do too badly economically, since the USSR was getting little from them for reparations, although subsidies were paid. However, the satellite countries were a serious drain on the Soviet economy. The armament plants were overproducing for nonexisting customers. Yet the Soviet Union—whatever was left of it—had more nuclear weapons than the United States. The revenues from gasoline to western Europe, leaking oil pipe exports, and their natural resources were totally inadequate to feed the 292,000,000 people of the USSR. Meanwhile, Gorbachev made it known to Western countries that the USSR could not survive without their economic help. The above disasters, hunger, and inflation were a prelude to the upcoming disintegration of the union, which should have never seen the light of day.

In February 1990 the biggest demonstration ever was held at Manezh Square, with banners warning the Party not to prevent multiparty elections at the upcoming Central Committee meeting. A few days later, the Central Committee gave in and approved a multiparty system of government. Demonstrations commenced in most major urban areas, with speeches denouncing communism, socialism, *nomenklatura*, and the rest of the bureaucracy. The Central Committee's approval of the multiparty system was no longer meaningful, nor did the citizens pay any attention to it. The population went about its business of desperately trying to survive. Meanwhile, all national minority states conducted business as if there was no longer a Communist party, no central government, no ponderous bureaucracy. The schism between Gorbachev and Yakovlev widened sharply, nevertheless it appeared on the surface that it was kept under wraps. Gorbachev tried hopelessly to keep the union intact, and like a journalist, ran around to find answers from his close associates, instead of facing objective reality in the country. He reiterated his commitment to socialism and communism, as if it mattered any more. Since whatever power there existed with the Central Committee and the Politburo, it was important for him to keep the faith and declare himself.

Yeltsin ran for president of the RSFSR, (Russian Federation) and won the election by a landslide. The Russian tricolor, instead of the hammer and sickle, suddenly appeared spontaneously throughout Moscow, Leningrad, and other urban centers. It must have been a highly interesting time for foreign journalists—who had normally been stonewalled before, but now everyone wanted to talk to them. Tass and Novosty, the foreign news agency, pretended as if nothing unusual was happening. Free market began with various get-rich-quick young entrepreneurs, making millions of rubles and converting them into hard currency. Most of their profit came from hard-to-get items—VCRs, television sets, and so on. These entrepreneurs also paid off gangsters to protect their businesses. Mafia gangs had multiplied, with murders multiplying to an extent never practiced anywhere in the world. Although still a member of the Central Committee, Yeltsin's victory presaged the beginning of the end of the USSR, and it was only a matter of time until communism took its last breath. The Communist party press unleashed an avalanche of hatred against the democratic reformers, accusing them of fomenting trouble and chaos. When the Congress convened in July, Yakovlev was forced to defend himself, and with devastating attacks, he quoted an article from *Russkiy Golos* (Russian Voice), a newspaper denouncing reform, which stated in part, "We badly need a military coup. There is still a lot of space in Siberia waiting for reformers who have buried *perestroika*. The apparent intent was to pretend that there was enough *perestroika* as it was. He made other devastating revelations of the past trials—self-incrimination, murder, slave labor camps—not to the liking of most Congress members. When in August 1990 Gorbachev issued an order rehabilitating all those who had been stripped of their citizenship, Yakovlev took issue with this and called it, "repentance." I believe it was the same evening, that Yakovlev appeared on "Vremya," an evening television news program and made a statement difficult for most Russians to forget. A taped recording of this repentance speech was issued throughout the world:

> "When we say we are rehabilitating someone, as if we are mercifully forgiving him for the sins of the past, it smells of cunning and hypocrisy. We are not forgiving him but ourselves. It is we who are to blame, that others lived for years both slandered and oppressed. It is we who are rehabilitating ourselves, not those who had other thoughts and convictions. They only wanted good and freedom for us, and the leadership answered with evil, prison, and camps. As we breathe the air of freedom, it is already becoming difficult for us to remember the past. There were hundreds of thousands of brutish trials, with people who were shot and killed and people who committed suicide. People who didn't know what they were charged for but were destroyed. For us who are living, they are not an admonition but a cruel reminder, who still have a longing for the past, for those who turn all to fear. I wish to give special attention to the tragic destiny of our peasantry, which paid a price in blood for Stalin's criminal regime. This was not only a vengeful act against them, disrupting the flow of our society, but it too, threw the state into a crisis. History has never before known such focus of hatred toward man."

This speech, gave the clearest and the most sincere clarion call for washing one's soul, and millions were shocked and dismayed by all the communist propaganda for decades, of the rubble of lies, corruption, and decay. Information gathered by foreign journalists began to appear that the bureaucracy was completely bewildered and astonished by prevailing conditions and referred all inquiries to the press bureaus and any agencies they could think of, except themselves. Tourists in Moscow began finding it difficult to use their passes for special events and hotel restaurants for which they had previously paid, unless dollars were used to reimburse their previous purchases.

Rumors began spreading that the military was preparing a coup. The armed forces denied it. Only the military, the KGB, and the diehards of the Communist party were confident that nothing was wrong. Things were going as well as could be expected under *perestroika*, or so they said. Marshal Akhromeyev, Gorbachev's military advisor, and Defense Minister Yazov assured all that no coup was contemplated or intended. After Shevarnadze resigned in December 1990, he warned that "a dictatorship is coming," yet not too many took him seriously. By now Gorbachev's cabinet included Bessmertnykh as foreign minister, replacing Shevarnadze, Yanayev as vice-president, and Lyukyanov as chairman of the Supreme Soviet. Yanayev and Lyukyanov were strong Communists but pretended to be reformers. Concurrent with the United States Desert Storm campaign against Iraq, Soviet tanks rolled over Lithuania and tried to overpower both the capital, Kaunas, and Vilnius. The Lithuanian crowds were so numerous that after causing some deaths, the tanks withdrew, and the Soviet maneuver failed. Soon the strikes spread to machine works, heavy and light industry, alarming all the diehards and the KGB, who tried dispersing the crowds. At first rumors spread that the hardliners were actually preparing a coup, about which Yeltsin warned Gorbachev and cautioned him about his friends, Yazov, Pugo, Kruichkov and Luykianov, Gorbachev disregarded Yeltsin's advice. Subsequently, it became clear that the military—the final authority with power—was intent on doing so, and hints and menacing troop movements occurred.

Amid all the turbulence in the country, Gorbachev left with his family 6 August 1991 for his vacation in the Crimea. Taking advantage of his absence, some of the hardline Politburo and Central Committee members and others decided to take action against him. Previously on 17 June, Gavril Pavlov, the hardline prime minister, appeared before the parliament, the Supreme Soviet, requesting the transfer of some of Gorbachev's powers, claiming that the president was overwhelmed with too much work, however he didn't inform Gorbachev—an obvious effort to seize the reigns of the Party and the government. When Gorbachev finally appeared at the session with Yazov, Pugo, and Kruichkov, he was quoted as saying the "coup" was over. A few days later, Kruichkov, the KGB chief, called the group of conspirators together to work on documents for a state emergency. He also ordered all telephone lines cut to Gorbachev's villa in the Crimea. Kruichkov was also instrumental in gathering the conspirators to inform Gorbachev of the facts of emergency: resign or else. It was a secret conference, with no time to waste. Gorbachev was planning to return to Moscow to sign a new Union Treaty on 20 August. It was necessary to act quickly, before the treaty was signed, disbanding the union of republics. It appeared that there was really no plan to carry out the coup.

On the spur of the moment, it occurred to Yazov to alert various army contingents to march on Moscow, warning commanders that he wanted no bloodshed. Yeltsin gathered his forces at the parliament building on the Moscow River and had his allies convene a session of the Russian parliament. The crowds swelled to 100,000, and more were on the way. The more the crowds increased, the more support for Yeltsin's democratic forces increased. No one present knew whether they would have to fight Yazov's troops and tanks, but they stood their ground, armed with anything available, inside the White House (parliament building) and outside, waiting for a fight. When the tanks arrived in front of the parliament building, Yeltsin waited for them and talked them down. No tank or trooper ever fired a shot, and that ended the rebellion and the coup. It was a stunning victory for democracy—especially in view of the history of the USSR.

Back in Crimea, Gorbachev packed up his family and left for Moscow. Upon arrival, he was not aware of the changed conditions in the country and called up the members of G-7 and informed them of his freedom from the coup; he then called a press conference and discussed the coup. Strangely unaware of the new status in the country, he proclaimed that the Communist party was now more than ever a progressive force of *perestroika*. When he faced the parliament to deliver his pronouncement, most deputies laughed or registered outright opposition. Yeltsin insisted he read the document approving the coup by the Soviet Council of Ministers. This session was broadcast worldwide on radio and television. At first it was difficult to judge the results of this reading, later, however, it became evident that it left Gorbachev suspended in confusion and ambiguity. As president of the Soviet Union, it no longer made sense without realizing that it was not just *perestroika*, but an actual revolution.

Yeltsin proceeded to name his group for the most powerful positions in the country. He appointed the KGB chief and the minister of defense. In addition, the economy was placed in the hands of the prime minister of Russia. These commands, dictated by Yeltsin, left Gorbachev powerless. He finally dissolved the Central Committee and resigned as general secretary of the Communist party. It was the reformers under Yeltsin who forced him to dissolve the Central Committee and the Congress of Peoples Deputies. Sometime in October, Yeltsin decreed a ban on the Communist party in Russia. Yet the Soviet Union still existed, even if on paper, and Gorbachev was still its president. Some of the republics were somewhat hesitant, having been taken by surprise with free market economy and mechanism for independence. By then all Soviet modes and institutions were liquidated, including the primary seat of power, the Party and the armed forces. Russia, Ukraine, and Belarus declared independence. Subsequently Armenia, Georgia, and Azerbaijan did the same. The Baltic states had done so previously but later refused to be part of Commonwealth of Independent States. With no official position left, on 25 December 1991, Mikhail Gorbachev declared the Soviet Union dissolved. Gorbachev was the third generation of Soviet supreme leaders, the seventh secretary of the Communist party and the only president who presided at the funeral of the Soviet Union.

One must, at least in the beginning, applaud him for trying Alexander Yakovlev's formula for a free human conscience, a free economy, and true democracy. By holding on to power under any circumstances and abandoning his closest colleagues when it was time to leave, he discredited himself in the eyes of his own people and most of the world. The Bolshevik Revolution was won on the body of a decaying monarchy by surreptitious and illegal means, and to stay in power, the Bolsheviks fought a three-year civil war, with millions dying for the promised cause. Yet the fall of the Soviet Union happened quietly and without a whimper. A more corrupt and deceptive regime never existed—which served the party's *nomenklatura* and not the proletariat, for which they swore to the nation that they were transforming. The Soviet rule was a cruel hoax perpetrated on a people who genuinely believed in utopian promises, even under dictatorship, not knowing any better. In the aftermath of the downfall of the USSR, the *nomenklatura* recovered quickly from the shock, since they were the only ones left to manage industries and all other important positions. They not only kept their positions, privileges, salaries, and dachas, they also assured themselves of the status quo by securing a substantial communist block in the ostensibly representative parliament. Other members, who called themselves nationalists, also assured themselves seats in parliament, based on pathological fear of capitalism and the supposed American takeover of the country. Between these two parties, they manage well to keep Yeltsin, his government, and democratic Russia on edge. However, the spirit among the young and those who genuinely believe in freedom under democracy will prevail, regardless of the outcome of new elections in 1996.

# CHAPTER XIII
# DISSOLUTION OF THE SOVIET UNION

The dissolution of the Soviet Union, like some other historic events of the past, is not easily perceptible even at this writing, although some certain elements contributed to its demise. Western historians and political scientists attribute their opinions to various elements for the root causes of its demise. Some of the elements, or combinations of them, include the following:

- The economic system and its evolvement into communism was bound to fail, being too utopian to be ever attainable

- The USSR spent itself into bankruptcy

- The burden of being a global power was unbearable

- The burden of support for its internal national minority republics and its external empire was too great

- Western containment policy eventually got into the innards of the system

- President Reagan's rearmament policy and Strategic Defense Initiative sufficiently intimidated the USSR

- A superpower with the most unproductive workforce, only exporting military hardware, which could not survive the strains

- A superpower with no export potential to trade with other nations and gain hard currency on the open market.

- A poorly paid and badly treated working class, envious of Western lifestyles, wanted reform

- Lagging technologically in the information and communication age could have also been a contributory cause

- Socialist command economy inherently flawed

The author tends to agree with several writers that unworkable and stagnant economic policies were the primary cause, along with some of the contributory factors mentioned above, probably caused its dissolution. It was after all, Russia's severe battlefield losses in WWI, along with the promise of peace and propaganda for socialist economic policy, which prompted Russia's withdrawal from WWI and subsequently caused the Bolshevik revolution in 1917. However, some other factors may have also contributed, perhaps to a lesser degree. Its excessive bureaucratic structure, financial incapability of supporting itself as a global power, its external empire, and its union republics caused significant trouble.

The rigidity of the socialist economy, directed from the top in Moscow down to hamlets at the personal level, allowed for no deviation from directives, regardless of conditions or localities. Additionally, since quotas to fulfill five-year plans were mandatory, it prompted enterprise managers to bargain with each other for supplies and deliveries with bribes. Quotas were seldom fulfilled unless extraordinary measures were applied by the Central Committee or the Politburo directly. The gas pipeline to Europe and BAM (the Baikal-Amur rail line) are good examples. Apparently everything could not have been accomplished, as examples above show.

The author doubts that Russian scholars even now can outline the causes, in view of the composition and representation of the present Russian parliament, the Duma. Several principal parties in the Duma and several others not represented in parliament have their own distinct agendas, which reflect conflicting views on the economy, political order, social welfare, military might, and its former world status, which collide with existing realities. The Communist party, at this writing, is riding high in the Duma, yet it couldn't prevent dissolution. The country is still unaware of the causes. It would appear from the composition of the Duma that they may be too close to the scene and represent daily survival of their constituents, large industrial enterprises, proponents of free economy, uniqueness and greatness of Russia and other personal interests; thus they are not objective in the wider context. In fact the Communist party has a greater representation in the Duma than any other, at least at this writing, yet due to the constitution cannot prevail.

The author reviewed several Russian journals and publications and found them all lacking in their objective analyses of the root causes of the dissolution. Their analyses are principally based on conditions of paralysis at the highest echelons of party and government, yet insufficient thought is given to the system of their faulty economy. In another sense, they speak of political consequences, not economic. They also accuse Gorbachev's *perestroika* and *glaznost* of undermining the discipline and order of the Soviet regime. In fact, their conclusions tend to fall along the entire spectrum. Undoubtedly, there is some validity in this reasoning, yet it is not a basis for the root causes. The various opinions expressed depend on some privileged classes, pensioners, workers, and others. The Soviet economy was a social-political instrument rather than one that was market oriented, and therein lay the basic flaw of its economic structure and most probably the main cause of its downfall. Even now that the system has expired, it is not too simple to analyze its flaws after seventy-four years of dictatorial socialist experiments.

These experiments cost Russia, the union republics, and their disbanded external empire dearly in the aftermath of dissolution. Millions upon millions are facing economic chaos, poor lifestyles, and a cruel new beginning, yet those who caused and enforced it are either dead or free, in their opulent lifestyles, at the expense of the working class. Although, it's true that Russia possesses untold natural resources for exploitation, it is equally true that it was misused and exploited for the benefit of the few, and after satisfying them, the rest of the population received what was left. The natural resources are still there, and so is the system, though it never had to account to public scrutiny for its budget, which appears to have exhausted itself. Its chances of success were, at best, dubious from the start, defying logical theories and practices of sound and proven market-driven economics. It was therefore only a matter of time before it exhausted itself into oblivion as a system by corruption, bribery, mismanagement, waste, ineptness, lack of competition, raw material export only, instead of home manufactured goods for export also. The extraction of natural resources couldn't keep up with the pace of inflation, salaries, health demands, retirement pay, and decent lifestyle of the people, and in some cases people died of actual starvation.

When the Imperial government was overthrown, it left the Bolsheviks with economic policies based on government's ownership of some public entities, similar to most European governments at the time, though Europe's basic economy was free and market driven. In 1913 Russia was a net exporter of grain to Europe and benefited by repayment of its debts. The Soviet Union was always broke and had to import grain from overseas. In order to transform the Soviet economy into a socialist base, the Bolsheviks confiscated all personal property and businesses, without compensation to owners, restructuring it to government ownership for the benefit of the proletariat. In so doing, it eliminated all personal initiative and pride of individual ownership. In fact, Lenin's economic doctrine was based on total control and manipulation of the economy as a political tool, which deprived the population of any power of choice, forcing them to either comply or face starvation.

Other causes described by Western scholars are varied and substantially consistent with normal economic theories and practices. As a political-economic system, most competent economic scholars were convinced for years the system was flawed, and the unattainable goals of promised rewards were baseless. Since revenues received by the government were usually short, they relied on export of raw materials—gas and oil—to balance the shortage. The goods, with the exception of military hardware, weren't good enough for export, which is the principal basis of economic growth and gross national product. When it decided to compete with the West in African and Asian countries, it undercut Western bids to acquire capital, which in the end proved too costly for them, yet it kept employment going in armaments factories. In effect the USSR spent itself into bankruptcy by competing with the West and NATO countries. They instituted a retirement age of fifty-five to save money yet claimed they were social rewards. The unbearably heavy burden of its armed forces, its economic support of the satellite countries, and its overseas armaments and cash subsidies were an excessive burden. Trying to compete as a global power with United States, NATO's containment policies, and new applied technologies were burdens they could no longer afford. Some Western scholars also attribute its demise to President Reagan's SDI, the Strategic Defense Initiative ("Star Wars"). When the Soviets were convinced SDI would fail, they nevertheless undertook their own experiments to be sure, which cost them billions upon billions of rubles. All the above reasons may be sufficient to point out that they received insufficient revenues to balance their expenditures, and thus went bankrupt.

It is, however, acknowledged that under Stalin's bloody regime in 1927-41, and after the end of WWII until his death in March 1953, a high degree of industrialization was achieved by barbaric methods—although its product quality, except for conventional armaments, was generally shoddy, and its goals of five-year plans were mostly never met. After the war and through the Cold War period, its successes were based on the production of armaments and export, to gain hard currency at any price, to undercut Western prices and secure repeat orders. This effort kept employment going, whether the products manufactured were in demand or not. Industrialization to suit the demands of consumer industry was never substantially satisfied on most levels. After the war, when consumer demands should have been met as a reward for privations in the war, the Soviet people were left to their own devices and driven even harder to rebuild the country. No major civilized country could have lived under the hardship standards of life which then prevailed in the USSR. It is also true that when Lenin was still the leader, enthusiasm for labor among industrial workers was high, and since there were never enough experienced workers, there was no unemployment.

The days of the NEP in the early twenties, when food and consumer production was at its height, never surfaced after Stalin took over. Subsequently, the rigid economic directives coupled with outmoded plants and equipment, lack of maintenance, unhealthy worker environment, and production lags caused the government to call on the Fiat Group of Milan, to construct and complete an automobile assembly plant in Togliatti, on the Volga. To satisfy the minimum requirements of its auto buyers, who waited for years to purchase one, it was necessary for the buyers to secure connections and a bribe. There were no upgrades or catalytic converters, and leaded gas was the normal standard; all this, after seven full decades of Soviet power and experiments. After 1972, when economic stagnation began under Brezhnev, the economy continued its downward trend and never recovered again. During his leadership, psychiatric wards were opened to squelch all dissenters against the regime. The borders were successfully isolated and secured, and the KGB was on the alert internally against dissenters more than ever until Gorbachev's imprisonment in Crimea in August 1991. Even after that, thousands were incarcerated.

So successfully did they hide economic stagnation, unemployment, complaints, and starvation that no serious Western scholars suspected the downfall of the Soviet Union. Not until the 1989 Berlin Wall incident and the desire of the Baltic countries and eastern European satellites to free themselves and gain independence were there indications of things gone wrong. It was only a few months later, when the coal miners and other industrial workers struck and were joined by hundreds of thousands of workers from other industries, that the problems leaked out. The government couldn't pay the workers to combat inflation because they lacked the funds. The wonder is that it took so long for the Soviet Union to collapse. It was the Soviet discipline and order with KGB surveillance that prevented an eruption, until the workers could take it no longer and unraveled the entire edifice, bringing it down to its knees. The true beneficiaries of the socialist economy, while it lasted, were the upper echelon of the party, the *nomenklatura*. This class consisted of more than seven thousand people during the takeover by the Bolsheviks and the civil war; it was first created for its members to be "professional revolutionaries" under Lenin. Subsequently, the same class multiplied to almost two million and was called *nomenklatura*, under Stalin. They skimmed the top and milked the country dry.

It is fair to assume that some, if not all, of the opinions of Western writers concerning the fall of the Soviet empire have fully contributed or were partially responsible for the dissolution.

The reader should bear in mind the abundant, if not inexhaustible, natural resources Russia possesses in Siberia alone—which are still almost intact for exploitation. It is equally reasonable to assume that it was the inexhaustible wealth of natural resources that supported the existence of the communist regime and its socialist economy. Eventually even natural resources couldn't keep up with the extravagant socialist system, inflation, waste, outmoded equipment, and lack of funds to pay the workers. These resources were used indiscriminately, in a manner unsustainable by most normal standards for demands of industry or consumers. Their extremely careless extraction methods, using elementary tools and processing factories, caused excessive waste and losses and were so out of step with environmental standards that Russia and their former republics will pay for it for decades to come. Their pollution of the soil, rivers, and lakes is astounding. The Bolsheviks depended on the wealth of the country in natural resources and counted on them to carry over for centuries. This wealth required no imports to sustain them, until they squandered it and destroyed the country. The bureaucratic machine and its huge state-owned enterprises were so large that the inertially driven system ran out of control.

To this system should be added the performance of the *nomenklatura* with its exorbitant life style, which helped corner the currency by robbing the country, thus causing inflation and shortage of capital. It is doubtful that any comparably similar class in other countries equaled the systematically amassed treasure and opulent lifestyle of the *nomenklatura*. It was this class, not the proletariat, which enjoyed the workers' paradise for whom the country was created. Only grudgingly, as airtight as the borders were, when it became known worldwide of the conditions of the Soviet workers, did they make any effort to give their people some consumer goods, which were continually in short supply.

In 1956 Khrushchev boasted of the advancement of true socialism and that communism should be achieved shortly. Subsequently, this pronouncement was even denied by his own colleagues. It must be conceded that although Khrushchev was a dedicated Communist, he genuinely believed in the welfare of the workers and made sincere and serious efforts in innovation to boost production. As desirable as these efforts were, in the end they failed. Forced to retire, he had his secret memoirs published. Henceforth it mattered little who the leader was, since the Soviet economy was on political-military control system, inertially driven and too large to control, even if they wanted to contain it. Had they slowed down, the result would have been catastrophic unemployment, since all worked for the government, which guaranteed jobs for life.

Following WWII, the Cold War—a geopolitical instrument of Stalin's imagination—created a state of constant friction with the Western Allies in Europe and worldwide to gain influence and supremacy. It was a doctrine of continual and uninterrupted war economy with occasional military crisis encounters, which they believed would intimidate and communize Europe and eventually the world. It was Lenin who theorized that Russia needed Germany and its industrial might in order for Russia to survive as a communist state. However, Stalin, who industrialized Russia, was no longer interested in conquering all of Germany; he wanted all Europe and whatever else he could get. The reader is advised to review the map of the Eurasian continent to compare the size of western Europe with Russia and its eastern satellites. Western Europe appears rather puny, yet NATO held the Warsaw Pact at bay. This constant war footing, which was carried on until the dissolution, was a heavy drain on its economy (though it allowed for mass employment), hence no priority was given to consumer production, and this eventually helped to bankrupt the country. When overproduction of weaponry was reached, workers were sent home for two or three days a week. The joke around Moscow and Leningrad was repeated over and over that "they pretend to pay us, and we pretend to work."

The most fascinating of all were the communist economists. Where did they get their practical economic training other than from the theoretical Marx-Engels Institute? The Soviet government sent some of these economists to London School of Economics and Harvard Business School to study free market economics and compare. What good did it do? The consumer industry, the backbone of most of the economy in free enterprise nations, is the barometer of all gross national product, yet in the Soviet Union it never had any place as a serious factor. Lacking the most elementary distribution system and living under a single source of supply must have caused serious disruptions within the general economy. Agricultural supplies, in most instances were totally inadequate to feed the population—except for potatoes. Yearly imports of wheat, barley, cereals, and other foodstuffs were imported from foreign countries and quickly consumed the short supply of hard currency. They promised agricultural and industrial workers lifetime work since the revolution was created for them. Instead they experimented and betrayed them, from the beginning to the end, until the Soviet Union dissolved.

In the final analysis, agriculture was a complete disaster, even in areas of best yields, as in Ukraine and north Caucasus. As for nonarmaments industrial workers, they toiled with the most elementary tools, machinery, and methods, with only a pittance as reward. In fact, the Soviet Union may be characterized as a late nineteenth century giant, yet it advanced little from the Imperial regime that was displaced—except in military weaponry. Its collectives and kolkhozes never produced enough grain, even under Stalin's bloody regime—although he was informed otherwise. Stalin's and Khrushchev's experiments with the quack agroscientist Lysenko worsened agriculture to a state of poverty, thus forcing imports of grain from United States, Canada, Argentina, and Australia. With no incentives for hard work, some fields lay fallow; though tractors and combines were used, often they waited in the fields rusting, for want of spare parts. Yearly statistics based on five year plans consistently showed great strides and goals ahead of schedule, though consumers never believed it nor did they experience sufficient foodstuffs. The peasants labored for the government and received pittance for their labors. Peasant housing consisted of dilapidated old huts, built years before the revolution. Instead of an agricultural supply of plenty, it was a constantly diminishing output, and it cost the country billions for imports. In 1973 even their own economic planners were beginning to worry about the coming troubles, yet the economic rigidity was too deeply set to reverse direction and save itself from disaster. It was a huge inertially propelled machine, and even if they had desired to redirect it, they feared the economy would have come to a grinding halt. After all, Lenin, the genius, had ordained the system but wasn't there to redirect it.

In industry, there was a lack of any organized maintenance of worn-out machinery and a lack of worker productivity and safety precautions in any of their factories—including oil and gas extraction. This was the one source of hard currency earnings which never reached its potential. Some foreign oil industry sources, however, doubt Soviet statistics of twelve million barrels per day production, in view of breakdowns in machinery, pipe leakages, and unsafe working conditions. Waste alone cost the country billions, not to mention pollution. They polluted rivers, lakes, and soil to a degree that some sweet water rivers and lakes in northern Russia and substantial areas throughout the pristine Siberian landscape are polluted and unusable. In fact, the inland Aral Sea, bordering Kazakhstan and Uzbekistan, no longer exists. The sweet water Lake Baikal in eastern Siberia had an abundance of trout and other species that are no longer edible. It is an ecological disaster of monumental proportions. In an effort to increase exports and gain hard currency to stave off unemployment, they disregarded all elemental rules of reasonable care and safety.

The most overlooked free labor movement took hold after the war under Stalin and proliferated throughout the regime to an uncontrollable degree, defying the official labor unions. The free labor movement was the real consumer industry and furnished almost everything, either stolen, exchanged, or repaired, according to reports from various sources. After Brezhnev's economic stagnation in the 1970s, letters to Europe and America asked former expatriates and relatives for food parcels and money to prevent starvation. Health care, though free, was appalling—with primitive public hospitals, reused unsanitary bedsheets, inadequate medicines, and incompetent and underpaid doctors. The best hospitals were reserved for the *nomenklatura*, and the practice of medicine was more advanced, but never equaled western standards. The specially designated Kremlin hospital and infirmaries, were reserved for the top echelon of the Party.

While the country was going bankrupt, the *nomenklatura* was getting rich, and ordinary citizens were helpless to do anything about it. Most of the capital was allocated to armaments and heavy industry, whose managers were accustomed to continual production and bargained for certain supplies among themselves, disregarding official rules. They recruited huge ranks of the best educated university students, thus robbing the rest of the economy of the best talents. No special talent was known to have been allocated for any consumer production. In summarizing the promises made by the Bolsheviks to the workers of the Soviet Union in its seventy-four years of existence, the author concludes that only one major accomplishment was ever fulfilled. The one true achievement was to educate their entire population. It succeeded due to compulsory Russification of the different nationalities in the union, with uniform textbooks throughout schools, although the schooling was mostly politically motivated. Higher education in universities was subject to competition among the best and most qualified students. Entrance to universities was a mandatory prerequisite for success in almost all major fields. Most applicants were assigned by the Ministry of Education and were subject to demands in various disciplines of industry, agriculture, sciences, and other disciplines, which had priority requirements. The *nomenklatura* usually succeeded in having their offspring enrolled, although some other students who excelled were admitted. The reader should bear in mind that Russian educational standards were always high, even in Imperial times, though it never had sufficient universities to accommodate them. In this respect the Soviet Union achieved a high percentage of educated classes through several universities, among which Moscow State University was the best. The original intent of educating the masses was Marxism, the better to be disciplined in compliance with elementary knowledge of communism, its slogans, and work rules.

The workers, however, never received the benefits they were promised by the Bolsheviks and had to survive on low wages to support their families. Housing was always poor in quality and insufficient, and workers had to wait years to secure housing. In the end unemployment, insufficient wages, broken promises, and in some instances starvation were more than they could take. With no future in sight for them and their families, the proletariat had had enough of communism and sought salvation. The dissolution of the Soviet Union became inevitable after seventy four years of experiments with lies, broken promises, deceit, labor camps, murder, and isolated borders. Yet at this writing, some citizens (pensioners and dedicated former Party workers who are no longer employed), yearn for the happy days of communism. Do they really know what caused the breakup of the Soviet Union, this quickly and in a flicker? One feels sorry for these people, since pensioners also got pittance or delayed wages. It is certainly true that some segments of the population are undergoing hardships among several classes—due to the gradual transition to a free enterprise economy—which apparently is inevitable coming from the rigid socialist economy. Although the huge enterprises are still run by the government, nevertheless, a beginning had been made. Will this beginning flower to a fully open economy, or will it fold ? Russia, being what it is—complex, large, multinational, and Russified—at least shed its most grievous burden, the support of its semi-autonomous republics and its external empire, the support of international communism, and its huge sums for enormous armed forces. This much is helpful economically, even with large enterprises under government control.

One wonders why dissolution took so long, with the common people taking the brunt of punishment for seventy-four years. The Russian character for punishment is unlimited and may yet change, should true democracy and openness become common. Perhaps dissolution was inevitable and the only solution to all the people of Russia.

# CHAPTER XIV
# ARTS AND SCIENCES

Most Western historians, scientists and, art critics concur with official Russian assumptions that the period between 1820 and 1860 was the Golden Age of Russian Arts and Sciences. Yet today most Russians feel the period didn't end in 1860 but extended into the twentieth century. They base their conclusions on the uninterrupted tradition of accomplishments of their classical composers, artists, novelists, poets, and scientists well into the twentieth century. The author feels there is some justification for this claim, based on the uninterrupted build up on past and present talents in their respective fields.

Commencing in the 1820s, a great intellectual awakening took place, surprising most countries in the breadth and variety of disciplines. In their musical compositions and innovative methods, the Russian composers and their unique orchestral forms gave the world a plethora of outstanding compositions, astounding the world of classical music in both form and composition. At first their works were based on nationalist forms for acceptance by their public, and subsequently through experimentation and maturity, into cosmopolitan forms acknowledged the world over as compositions of outstanding character and admired for uniqueness in themes and experimentation. In literature, astonishingly creative works were written by writers and poets, depicting conditions of Russian life and the mood of the people. In performing arts, the ballet took center stage with unsurpassed perfection. The theater was transformed into a realistic form of acting, never before experienced. Painting took varied forms, in traditional expression and abstract forms, and sciences advanced rapidly in both volume and content.

### THE CLASSICAL COMPOSERS

#### Miliiy Alexeyevich Balakirev: 1837-1910

At first a pianist and subsequently a composer of nationalist forms, Balakirev is the acknowledged founder of the Free Music School and collector of Russian folk music. His compositions include: *Tamara*, *King Lear*, *Islamey*, and *En Boheme*.

#### Cesar Antonovich Cui (Quee:) 1835-1918

A musical historian and writer of the national group, Cui was a descendent of a French officer who settled in Russia after Napoleon's defeat. He composed *Orientale*, the operas *Mandarin's Son*, and *Prisoner of the Caucasus* after a poem by Pushkin; *William Ratcliff*, produced in 1869; *Angelo* from Victor Hugo's play; and

*Saracen* based on Dumas's book, *Charles VII Chez Ses Grands Vasseaux*. He also wrote several symphonies, orchestral scherzos, choruses, songs, and piano pieces.

**Alexander Porfirievich Borodin: 1834-87**

He joined Balakirev's group in 1862, and composed *La Princesse Endormie*, *La Vieille Chanson*, and *Mlada*, a work in collaboration with Cui, Moussorgskiy, and Rimskiy-Korsakov. He also wrote *On the Steppes of Central Asia*; *Prince Igor with Polovtsian Dances* was his great achievement and was written between his medical lectures, (he was also a well-known chemist) eventually finished by friends in his circle, Glazunov and Rimskiy-Korsakov.

**Modest Petrovich Mussorgskiy: 1839-81**

Mussorgskiy was definitely different from the others of the national group because of its originality. His works showed deep emotions and strong passions with savage overtones, characteristic of the Slavs. His formless style didn't hide originality in character, and he was known as a born poet of orchestral music. His compositions for piano, orchestra, and stage reveal a kind of raw strength in his *Intermezzo*, *Night in Calvary*, *The Defeat of Sennacherib* (shows which strong and decisive expressions with its Hebrew choruses). Perhaps his most outstanding works are his piano pieces, such as "Tableaux d'une Exposition," which show a vivid and forceful work. He is well known for his operas, including *The Match-Maker*, and some comic scenes in *The Fair at Soroschini*. But his greatest achievements were *Boris Godunov*, based on Pushkin's drama; *Khovanchina*, based on the early and incorrect Scriptural version of the Old Believers and completed by Rimskiy-Korsakov; *Pictures at an Exhibition*; and *St. John's Night on the Bald Mountain*. He is presently being rediscovered by most musicologists as one of the greats in originality of classical music. He died as an alcoholic at a young age of forty-two.

**Nicholai Andreyevich Rimskiy-Korsakov: 1844-1908**

Rimskiy-Korsakov considered the great nationalist in the group of Blakirev's circle, which he joined in 1865. He composed a symphonic picture, *Sadko*, and a programmatic symphony, *Antar*. His first opera, *The Maid of Pskov* is a drama of Ivan the Terrible. *A May Night* is a comedy of village love and intrigue by writer Gogol. When he accepted a position in the St. Petersburg Conservatory, he apparently outgrew the narrow circle of nationalists, yet he never deserted them. Among his more famous compositions are *Scheherazade* from the *Arabian Nights*; *The Snow Maiden*, based on a poem by Ostrovskiy of the Slav legend of spring; *Mozart and Salieri*, a short dramatic scene; *The Czar's Betrothed*; *The Czar Saltan*; *Servilia*; *The Immortal Kastchei*; *Pan Voyevode*; *The Invisible City*; *The Golden Cockerel*; and *Le Coq D'Or*. He was a musical teacher of outstanding ability who taught many famous students. A prolific inventor of historical and legendary scenes into classical music, he stands as an outstanding example of dedicated service to lovers of classical music the world over.

### Alexander Constantinoch Glazunov: 1865-1936

Glazunov studied under Rimskiy-Korsakov and became a leader of later generation of composers. At the age of eighteen, he wrote a symphony, which was given by Liszt in Weimar, Germany. His *Sixth Symphony* is remembered for melodious and exceptionally pleasing tonal qualities. He also composed Violin Concerto in A Minor op. 82; several symphonic poems echoing the joy of spring, the charm of the forest, the spell of the sea, the attraction of the Orient, and the majestic opulence of the Kremlin; and *Stenka Razin*, the Volga pirate. He wrote the *Triumphant March* for the Chicago Exposition and *Coronation Contata for the Czar*. Other orchestral works are *Greek, Carnival Overtures, The Middle Ages*, and the glowing *Overture Solennelle*. His 100 opus numbers include several large compositions, including suites and orchestral contatas. He wrote two ballets, *Raymonda* and *The Seasons*, and a sacred drama, *The King of the Jews*.

### Anton Stepanovich Arenskiy: 1861-1906

A pupil of Rimskiy-Korsakov, Arenskiy produced an opera, *A Dream on the Volga*; a ballet; *A Night in Egypt*; and his best work, *Nal and Damajanti*.

### Sergei Vasilievich Rachmaninoff: 1873-1943

Rachmaninoff was a great pianist and composer with fire and strength and considered one of the best in the world in piano. He was also one of the great composers of this century with three operas, *Aleko*; *Miserly Knight*; *Francesca da Rimini*. Other works were symphonic pieces, *Prelude in C-Sharp Minor*; *Second Concerto for Piano and Orchestra*; *Third Concerto for Piano and Orchestra* as well as several concertos for piano and several preludes. He also composed *Moments Musical*; *Vesper Mass*; *Etudes Tableaux*; a choral symphony, *The Bells*; songs, *Christ is Risen, How Fair this Spot, Floods of Spring*; and *Lilacs*; *Symphony No 2*; *Piano Concerto No 2*; *The Isle of the Dead*; and *Piano Concerto No 3*. He wrote several more minor works which are admired by classic music lovers the world over. In Hollywood, where he settled, he wrote some serious music for the studios. Rachmaninoff, in addition to his excellence as a pianist, is considered one of the great composers of the twentieth century. He died in Hollywood in 1943 and was buried in Venice, Italy, as his dearest wish was to be interred among his many fellow Russian artists.

### Mikhail Mikhailovich Ippolitov-Ivanov: 1859-1935

A professor and later director of Moscow Conservatory, Ippolitov-Ivanov became conductor of the Moscow Opera in 1925. He wrote many compositions in various forms, most of which were about the Caucasus, where he spent the better part of his life. His most popular orchestral suite was *Caucasian Sketches*. He also composed *National Songs of Georgia*; his memoirs, *Fifty Years of Russian Music in My Memories*; the opera *Ruth*, where he used Hebrew melodies; and the opera *Assya*, using tender expression. He also produced several suites and choruses.

## Anton Grigoricvich Rubenstein: 1829-1894

Rubenstein's works include the *Ocean Symphony*; operas *Nero* and *Demon*; oratorios *Paradise Lost, Tower of Babel* and *Moses*; piano compositions *Kammeniy Ostrov, Melody in F,* and *Valse Caprice*. He also composed a multitude of songs. In 1859 he became director of the Royal Russian Musical Society, and in 1863 he founded St. Petersburg Conservatory. A prolific composer with never ending ideas, his work is admired throughout the world. He was an unparalleled teacher to some of the great Russian composers of his time.

## Mikhail Ivanovich Glinka: 1803-57

Glinka was the composer who started the Russian national music tradition. He wrote patriotic operas, *A Life for the Czar* and *Russlan and Ludmila*. Thereafter the tradition lapsed until new experimental forms took over. In Russia he is revered as a keeper of Russian tradition in musical form.

## Alexander Nicholayevich Scryabin: 1872-1915

Scryabin was a pianist and composer. His piano playing was compared to Frederic Chopin. His orchestral works—*Poem of Ecstacy* (Symphony no. 3 in C Major), *The Divine Poem,* and *Prometheus* are his best-known poetic works. As a pianist he appeared with Sergei Kousevitskiy's symphony orchestra in Russia. His piano compositions are exceptionally beautiful poetic works exploring musical symbolism. Trained as a cadet for six years at the Moscow Cadet School, he left to pursue a musical career at the Moscow Conservatory. By 1892 he had composed piano pieces in opuses 1, 2, 3, 5, and 7. He decided to settle in Switzerland in 1904. In his Symphony no. 1, he introduced a choral finale and completed his *Third Symphony, Le Divin Poeme* in which he tried to represent evolution of the human spirit from pantheism to unity with the universe. He introduced his *Poeme de d'extase* in 1908 in New York. He next wrote *Prometheus* in 1911. He toured the United States in 1906-07. Encouraged by Koussevitzkiy on his *Mystery*, he wrote a poem for preliminary action but left only sketches for music. He composed ten sonatas after 1892. His composition of *Piano Concerto* in F-sharp Minor, op. 20 and preludes for piano brought him an impressive international following. His orchestral works create the impression of orchestral piano music. In spirit and by nature, he was a hopeless mystic.

## Igor Feodorovich Stravinskiy: 1882-1943

Composer and creator of a new kind of symphonic music, Stravinskiy developed and influenced modern musical composition. A student of Rimskiy-Korsakov, in the beginning he wrote music in the accepted traditional style. When he wrote his first ballet, *The Fire Bird*, which was introduced in Paris in 1910, it was a work of discordant tones. From then on, he wrote and introduced more experimental tones in harmony and orchestration in *Petrushka* and *The Rite of Spring*. He further experimented with instruments and voices in *Les Noces, Symphony of Palms, Histoire du Soldat, Oedipus Rex, Appolon Musagete,* and *Le Rossignol*. Later in 1945, to celebrate his American citizenship, he wrote *Scenes de*

*Ballet*. He was a composer of unusual and innovative talents and is considered a true experimental musicologist of the twentieth century. To date no other composer has captivated more audiences with his work.

**Sergei Sergeyevich Prokofieff: 1891-1953**

A pianist and composer of revolutionary style, Prokofieff was also a student of Rimskiy-Korsakov. At first damned by critics, his compositional style and skill in orchestration was later accepted as a new treatise in experimentation. His first pieces were *Classical Symphony* and *Peter and the Wolf*, where a narrator tells the story while instruments describe various characters—a delightful work for people of all ages. He also wrote *Madallena*, *The Gambler*, *Love for Three Oranges*, *The Flaming Angel*, and *The Rake's Progress*. Subsequently, he wrote Concerto no. 1, in D Major for Violin and Orchestra, op. 19, and Concerto no. 2 for Piano and Orchestra, op. 16. His ballets, *Buffoon*, (which Sergei Diaghilev produced), *Romeo and Juliet*, and *Cinderella* were stunning successes. His *Age of Steel*, written in 1924, shows his thematic conquest of the industrial might in motion. He left Russia for United States in 1918, feeling the new Bolshevik regime would not approve of his work. The economic depression caused him severe agony and he returned to the Soviet Union, where at first he found it difficult to adjust and compromise his style. Nevertheless, in the Soviet period he wrote *Semeon Kotko*; *War and Peace*; a cantata, *Alexander Nevskiy*; Symphony no. 5; and a suite, *Lieutenant Kije*—were all equally successful. His *Scythian Suite*, which he wrote in 1915, shows primitive and barbaric polytonal dissonances to vividly illustrate the powerful character of the theme. After WWII he wrote *Ode to the End of War* and *Balad of Unknown Boy*. He had the great misfortune of dying the same day as Stalin; as a result, few people attended his funeral. He left a mighty legacy as a prolific composer and artistic intellectual in various musical forms.

**Peter Illich Tchaikovskiy: 1840-93**

Tchaikovskiy was a composer of unusual talents, recognized throughout the world as a master of melodic inspiration and orchestration. Without a doubt he was a master composer of classical ballet. His mother was half-French, and when she died of cholera in 1854, it apparently affected him the rest of his life. He studied law in St. Petersburg and in three years became a minor official in the Ministry of Justice. He found the work distasteful and switched from law to music. He studied music at St. Petersburg Conservatory, where one of his principal teachers was Anton Rubenstein. In 1866 he became professor of harmony at the Moscow Conservatory. A brief unhappy marriage in 1877 affected him deeply and may have been the cause of his melancholy behavior and despair. It was recently revealed, when his memoirs were reexamined, that he was probably a homosexual. It it also suggested that he was in love with his sister's fourteen-year-old son. Whether these are rumors or facts are of no consequence to the astounding quality of his music. His first orchestral score was an overture of the play *The Storm*. This was followed by an unending array of compositions—Symphony no. 1 in G Minor, op. 13; *Winter Day Dreams*, in 1866; *Romeo and Juliet* in 1869; and *Vakuta the*

Smith, in 1874. A short love affair with Desire Artot, was a saddening experience. He then married a former student, who turned out to be a nymphomaniac, and she left him shortly thereafter. Nadezhda von Meck, a devoted benefactress, issued him annual subsidies to support him. They both agreed not to meet, lest they be disappointed. To repay her for generosity, he composed Piano Sonata in G Major and Suite no. 1 in D Minor, op. 43. Eventually she terminated these gifts, but by then he didn't need them anymore. He composed and dedicated Symphony no. 4, in F Minor, op. 36 to Nadezhda von Meck in 1877 and wrote an opera *Evgeniy Onegin* in 1877-78. He wrote Violin Concerto in D Major, op. 45 in 1878 and Serenade for Strings in C Major, op. 48 in 1880. In 1880 he also wrote *1812 Overture*. *Manfred* Symphony, op. 58 was written in 1885. For an important foreign tour in Leipzig, he wrote Symphony no. 5 in E Minor. In 1891 he conducted some of his own compositions at the dedication of Carnegie Hall in New York. In 1892 he composed the delightful ballet *Nutcracker Suite* in eight parts. In 1893 he composed and conducted his Symphony no. 6 in B Minor, the *Pathetique*. This work expressed all the misfortunes and drama in Tchaikovskiy's life, and he breathed his last nine days later. In addition to the above works, he composed symphonic pieces: *The Tempest, Francesca da Rimini, Capriccio Italian*, Quartet in D Major, (with its renowned second movement), and *Andante Cantabile*. Between 1875 and 1880 he completed his overture *Romeo and Juliet, March Slav*, the ballet *Swan Lake*, and Violin Concerto in D Major; this concerto made Tchaikovskiy a grandmaster in piano music. The choral pieces he wrote include *In Church* and three heart-rending songs, *None but the Lonely Heart, Pilgrim's Song*, and *Only You*. His death was mourned by millions throughout the world. A true music master to the end, he left a legacy of undying music. He and his music will live forever.

**Reinhold Moritsevich Gliere: 1875-1956**

Gliere was of Belgian descent and was born in Kiev in 1875. He composed several outstanding pieces such as *The Sirens*; an opera, *Shah Senam*; the ballets *The Red Poppy* and *The Bronze Horseman*; and Symphony no. 3 (*Illya Muromets*). His pupils were the outstanding young composers Prokofiev, Myaskovskiy, and Khachaturian.

There are of course many other Russian composers, who contributed to Russian musical tradition, including the great tutor Sergei Taneyev, Pavel Blaramberg, Nicholai Soloviev, Segei Vassilenko, Kazatchenko, Korestchenko, Kochetov, Lissenko, Schenk, Famintsin, Lischin, Yuriy von Arnold, Kabalevskiy, and others. All those mentioned, with the exception of Sergei Prokofieff, were composers in the era of the Imperial regime.

THE SOVIET ERA COMPOSERS

**Dmitriy Dmitrevich Shostakovich: 1906-75**

Although a product of the Soviet environment, Shostakovich preferred individual expression but was forced to change his programmatic themes to conform to Stalin's and general Soviet requirements. He was publicly condemned twice for deviation; he nevertheless produced works of outstanding character on communist themes. His music is distinguished by rhythmic vitality and rich melodic expressions. He wrote eleven symphonies, twenty-four preludes and fugues, two operas, a piano concerto, Sonata for Cello and Piano, a string quartet, piano quartet, and the ballet *The Golden Age*. For his work he won the Stalin Prize in 1950 and the Lenin Prize in 1951. For his opera *Lady Macbeth of Mtsensk*, written in 1934, he was severely condemned publicly by the critics of the regime as a neurotic and vulgar counterrevolutionary. In turn he publicly admitted his errors. The title and non-Soviet theme were sufficient grounds for such condemnation, yet it was an outstanding work. He was again condemned for another piece he wrote for which he again publicly recanted. He was a composer of outstanding quality though he was usually constrained by critics; nevertheless, even in this propagandistic work he succeeded remarkably well. His works are constantly played all over the world, and he is considered an outstanding and prolific composer.

**Aram Khachaturian: 1903-78**

An Armenian-Soviet composer, some of Khachaturian's works represent Caucasian dances, although he has other compositions. His ballet, *Gayne*, is where the well-known and celebrated Sabre Dance is ceremonially featured. He also wrote Concerto for Piano and Orchestra, Concerto D Minor for Violin and Orchestra, *Spartacus*, and the orchestral suite *Masquerade*. All his works are of harmonic complexity. He attended Moscow Conservatory of Music and never deviated from the normally accepted standards set by Soviet critics—being involved mostly with music of minority nationalities may have been the primary reason. His *Gayne* Suite was introduced in the United States by conductor Efrem Kurtz; this earned the composer several lucrative copyright contracts in foreign countries.

One of the most amazing things about most of the early composers was their original vocation prior to being involved with music. Tchaikovskiy was a law student and an official in the Ministry of Justice. Cesar was a military engineering officer. Borodin was a professor of medicine and chemistry. Rimskiy-Korsakov was an admiral. Mussorgskiy was a soldier.

Under the Soviet regime, when some of the critics were guided by propaganda directives of the Party, it was no longer possible for composers to choose their own themes. They were directed to produce works mostly for the glory of communism and the proletariat. Conductors were commissioned to play music of past Russian composers since Western compositions were considered decadent and bourgeoisie. After Stalin's death and as time went on, it became somewhat easier for composers to choose their own subjects. It is amazing that composers such as Shostakovich, Khachaturian, and Prokofieff were able to pass censorship under such difficult conditions. Yet their works are considered some of the finest compositions of the twentieth century. No wonder those few who strictly adhered and composed under compulsion never saw the light of day.

Many other talented musicians achieved notoriety during the nineteenth and twentieth century. Among world-renowned pianists and violinists trained in St. Petersburg and Moscow were Vladimir Horowitz, Efrem Zimbalist, Misha Elman, and Yasha Heifetz. Fyodor Chalyapin was probably the greatest basso of his time and dominated the world opera scene. Sergei Koussevitzkiy, the late conductor of the Boston Symphony, first conducted the Moscow Symphony at age twenty-nine. People throughout Russia flocked to hear classical music and opera, which had an eight to nine month season. In 1901 Nicholas II built the People's Palace, a huge building which contained theaters, concert halls, and restaurants, with a twenty kopek admission fee. He dreamed of having his people enjoying their national culture in music and the performing arts. This stands as the one outstanding effort of his reign, where he truly benefited his people.

## BALLET

The Russian Imperial School of Ballet was founded about 1735. At first it had well known French choreographers train its Russian dancers. Later, however, when the Russians learned this art form, they succeeded in establishing their own instructors and eventually excelled all others. The ballet under the Imperial regime was considered a purely Russian art form, in spite of its Italian and French origins. This is perhaps justified by its Russian refinements and substantial endowments by the Imperial and Soviet governments. The Russian ballet dance ensembles were considered the finest in the world under the Imperial and Soviet regimes. The Bolshoi and Moiseyev, and later the Kirov Ballet in Leningrad, were envied for their worldwide performances. Under the Imperial regime such ballerinas as Mathilde Kseshinskaya, Tamara Karsavina, and Anna Pavlova were considered the finest prima ballerinas in the world. Their bookings in Paris, London, Berlin, and New York were sold out for months in advance. Mikhail Fokin, the ballet master, and Diaghilev, the ballet manager, left for Europe and established themselves in Paris as Ballet Russe de Paris. After Diaghilev's death, another group, known as Ballet Russe de Monte Carlo, was founded. The greatest ballet dancer ever, Nizhinskiy, performed there to standing room audiences. George Balanchine, who left after the revolution, was one of the great choreographers; he settled in New York, and organized the New York City Ballet with great acclaim throughout the world. His recent death was marked by American and European ballet lovers. After the revolution, it took some time to organize ballet teams. Once established, the Soviet ballet teams practiced to the highest degree and maintained it to perfection. However, their repertoires were based on old classical forms, by refining the same methods, and disregarding new dance forms. This refinement made Soviet ballet teams the finest in the world, though lacking in innovative forms. Western ballet dancers tended to experiment with new forms. Some of the finest Soviet dancers defected to the West, bored with the government imposed repetition. Nureyev and Barishnikov are examples of two who defected and became ballet dancer and dancer-master, respectively, with great success. No experiments were permitted in Soviet Russia, and if any existed, they never saw the light of day. As a result western ballet companies are beginning to excel and overtake Soviet talents.

**PERFORMING ARTS**

The living theater was particularly enhanced in the early 1900s, by a palace theater built by Czar Nicholas II. All well-known novelists, poets and playwrights were represented, including Dostoyevskiy, Turgenev, Tolstoy, Gorkiy, Chekhov, Gogol, Pushkin, Lermontov, Soloviev, Blok, and Krylov, the fable storyteller. Russian literary talents are world renowned and have mostly portrayed the social and cultural conditions of the country in the form of novels based on reality under both the Imperial and Soviet regimes.

**WRITERS AND NOVELISTS**

### Ivan Andeyevich Krylov: 1768-1844

Krylov translated Jean de la Fontaine's fables into Russian. He also published several of his own and is constantly quoted in Russia.

### Fydor Mikhailovich Dostoyevskiy: 1821-81

Dostoyevsky primarily wrote psychological novels, though his works lack refinement because of his rapid writing. He nevertheless clearly shows sympathy for human suffering and has an uncanny ability to find good in the most hopeless of humankind. His ability to do so elevated his novels to greatness, not only in Russia, but throughout the world. *Crime and Punishment* and *Brothers Karamazov*, are his masterpieces. These novels truly represent social conditions of the human spirit in all its frailties. At twenty-five he wrote his first novel, the *Poor People*, and it was an instant success. He was sentenced to be shot in 1849 for being a member of a revolutionary group, but the sentence was commuted to ten years in exile. He was forced to work in hard labor in Siberia, gathering material for his future novel, *The House of the Dead*. Other novels soon followed: *Insulted and the Injured*, *Memoirs from Underground*, *The Idiot* and *The Possessed*. His life was a constant struggle against poverty and ill health. He remains one of the giants in literature.

### Count Lev Nicholaevich Tolstoy: 1828-1910

Tolstoy was the great Russian writer—a novelist, an essayist, and above all a moral philosopher. He gave up his wealth and riches and lived a life of poverty. He had followers who devoted their entire lives to religious asceticism and poverty. Without doubt he was one of the great writers of our time. His greatest works were his two novels, *War and Peace* and *Anna Karenina*. His other works include *The Kreutzer Sonata*, probably the most graphic story of grubby life ever written. He also wrote *The Story of Yesterday*, *Two Hussars*, *The Memoirs of a Madman*, *Father Sergius*, *The False Coupon*, *The Devil*, and *What is Art?*, as well as the plays *The Living Corpse* and *The Fruits of Enlightenment*. In all his works, he portrays social conditions of life and human suffering. Reading Tolstoy's works and the story of his own life, which represent a heart-rending description of the underclass, gives understanding of Tolstoy's own humanity and suffering. No other works of literature have ever been written as vividly as Tolstoy's. His own life is the apotheosis of personal suffering and human compassion, which he describes of himself and of humankind. The Nobel Prize was not yet issued at that time, or he would have received it many times.

**Ivan Sergeyevich Turgenev: 1818-83**

Turgenev was a novelist and a remarkable person who at first spoke German and French better than Russian, unlike other Russian writers. The son of a wealthy mother who trained him for the landed gentry, he was educated in the universities of Moscow and St. Petersburg. Since the custom in Russia among the gentry was to speak French and German rather than Russian, his writings in the beginning were well-read in France and Germany, unlike those of his Russian compatriots. His novels reflect the suffering of the peasants and serfs whom he helped to free. Upon his mothers death, he freed all his serfs and described their freedom in his novel *A Sportsman's Sketches*, published in 1852. In his novel *Fathers and Sons*, he rages against bowing to any authority and accepts no unproven principle. In his clarity of language, he coined the term "nihilist" upon such persons. The term has become common in many languages ever since. His fine style, strong descriptions, sympathy, and thought-out plots help to relieve the melancholic tone in his stories. His works were popular not only in France and Germany, but also in other European countries as well as the United States. His early novel *A Sportsman's Notebook*, became popular and clearly outlined his position on serfdom. In a later work, *A Nest of Nobles*, he compares aristocratic life with those of the workers. His play *A Month in the Country* and his novels *Virgin Soil* and *Smoke* have become very popular all over the world. He subsequently learned and admired the Russian language and became a stylist in it. Unfortunately, his further talents in writing were not put to use after he left for France to mingle among their intellectuals; he died there in 1893. He is considered a social-intellectual novelist among Russian writers.

**Anton Pavlovich Chekhov: 1860-1904**

A writer of plays and short stories, Chekhov emphasizes a character's thinking and feeling rather than their actions. His short stories are masterful in the brevity of expression in writing. His plays include *Seagull, The Three Sisters, The Cherry Orchard*, and his world renowned play, *Uncle Vanya*. His short stories were "The Bishop", "In the Ravine", "Peasants", and "The Duel." He studied medicine, but soon turned to writing. His *Uncle Vanya* and *The Cherry Orchard* are staged in theaters all over Europe and America. Always in ill health, he died at the young age at forty-four.

**Maxim Gorkiy (Alexey Maximovich Peshkov): 1868-1936**

Gorkiy was a novelist and playwright who wrote realistically social works, mainly on the downtrodden. He had an unfortunate childhood, and his parents abandoned him when he was a small boy. When he commenced writing, he changed his last name to Gorkiy (bitter). His life's experiences as a wanderer among the poor gave him insight in human suffering and misery. He worked as an apprentice shoemaker, street peddler, baker's helper, and other nondescript jobs that taught him about human nature. He learned to read and write from a Volga steamship captain. Considered a revolutionary writer, he was exiled by the czarist police in 1905. After his release, he lived in Italy and returned to Russia in 1914. He supported the revolution because of the Soviet government's support of the working class. Disillusioned with Lenin, whom he called a "trickster," he retired to a village to publish his own paper until it was outlawed by Stalin. He championed the cause of the poor and the working class. There are substantial reasons to believe that violent quarrels with Stalin about executions and slave labor camps caused him to be poisoned or otherwise disposed of in 1936. The author agrees with published reports that in the beginning Gorkiy was a propagandist for the Communists, believing that the regime was helping the working class, whose cause he championed his entire life until he saw the facts for himself and protested. Among his better-known works is the drama *The Lower Depths*, which is often staged in Europe and America. His short stories are his best works and include, "The Outcasts," "Three Men," "The Magnet," and "On Guard for the Soviet Union." His autobiographical works include *Childhood* and *Fragments from a Diary*. He, as well as several other writers, championed the cause of the poor in graphic terms. He stands out among realistic and descriptive writers before and after the revolution as an author of his own childhood legacy.

### Nikolai Vasilievich Gogol: 1809-52

Gogol was born in the Ukraine of Russian descent, and he became both a humorist and novelist. In the beginning he wrote short stories about color, life, and laughter of his people of Little Russia (Ukraine). His friendship with Pushkin, the giant of poetry, gave him inspiration to write. In 1835 he published his historical novel, *Taras Bulba*, about Ukrainian Cossacks. This novel was an immediate success. A year later he wrote his most important work, *The Inspector General*, a comedy ridiculing Russian officialdom. He and his friends were worried that it would be banned. It was taken to Czar Nicholas I for review, and to the surprise of all the czar ordered it to be published immediately. In 1842 he wrote another novel about serfs in Russia named *Dead Souls*. Its humor and realistic depiction has ben compared to Charles Dickens, although he never knew or read Dickens. During the last years of his life he lived in Europe, ill and unhappy. Before his death he burned many of his manuscripts, including the second and concluding part of the *Dead Souls*. He is considered a great novelist who died too early in life, one who could have produced more enlightened works. This opinion is based on Russian critics, who stated that his works were progressively better over time.

### Mikhail Yuryevich Lermontov: 1814-41

A romantic poet, author, writer, and student of painting, Lermontov attended Moscow University but was asked to leave because he disagreed with his professors. In 1840, a year before his death, he wrote *A Hero of Our Time*, a highly admired work which had a profound influence on most Russian writers. He wrote *Problems of Circassians* and *Prisoner of the Caucasus*. His first verse was "Spring," and he followed it up with a drama, *A Strange Man*. Another work dedicated to his beloved is entitled *Duchess Ligovskaya*. He also wrote a play *Masquerade*, *The Song of the Merchant Kalashnikov*, *The Demon*, and *Mtsyri*. In Russia he is considered one of the outstanding writers and painters. He was the son of an army officer.

### Sholom Alechem: 1859-1916

Alechem spent latter part of his life in Kiev, and from 1900 to 1905, he wrote scores of Yiddish short stories, making him one of the greats of Yiddish literature.

### Vladimir Vladimirovich Nabokov: 1899-1977

Nabokov is considered the most outstanding novelist and poet among emigre authors. He wrote in both Russian and English. His writings include such works as *Speak* and the revised version of *Memory*. Two collections of verse, *Poems* and *Two Paths* were published in 1916 and 1918, respectively. He left Russia in 1919 in the middle of the civil war to go to Britain, where he attended Trinity College. In 1923 he wrote two poems, *Cluster* and *Empyrean Path*. In 1925 he decided to change his style to prose and wrote his first novel, *Mashenka*, in 1926; in 1957 he wrote *Pnin*; in 1958 *King, Queen, Knave*; *The Defense*; and *Despair and Invitation to a Beheading*. By 1938 he had written *Sobytie* and *Waltz Invention*. The same year he wrote the novel *The Gift*; *The Real Life of Sebastian Knight* followed in 1941; and *Bend Sinister* in 1947. In 1962 he wrote *Pale Fire* and *Solus Rex*. His most successful novel, *Lolita*, was published in 1955, and his last novel, *Ada*, appeared in 1969. He left for Switzerland and died there in 1977.

### Boris Leonidovich Pasternak: 1890-1960

Brought up as a cultural Jew by birth, Pasternak was an outstanding Russian poet whose novel *Dr. Zhivago* gained him a Nobel Prize for Literature in 1958—a novel of unusual sensitivity in an era of Soviet dictatorship. Opposition to his novel in the USSR caused him to decline the honor. *Dr. Zhivago* received worldwide acclaim and was made into a movie. He wrote other short poems and stories. After his death, he was posthumously rehabilitated and reinstated by Gorbachev's government in 1987.

### Mikhail Aleksandrovich Sholokhov: 1905-84

Sholokhov was a novelist, a winner of the Nobel Prize in 1965 for *And Quiet Flows the Don*, written in 1934. He also wrote a sequel, *The Don Flows Home to the Sea* in 1940, as well as *Safe Conduct* in 1931, and several other novels. Among Soviet writers he was unquestionably one of their finest.

### Aleksander Isaevich Solzhenitsyn: 1918-

Solzhenitsyn won the Nobel Prize for Literature in 1970. He wrote *One Day in the Life of Ivan Denisovich*, *The Gulag Archipelago* in three volumes, *The Cancer Ward*, and *The First Circle*—all of them critical of the Soviet regime. As punishment he was exiled from the USSR. He lived in Vermont until the dissolution of the USSR, when he returned to Russia with his wife. His two sons live in the United States. He achieved fame in writing about slave labor camps in the Soviet Union when it was forbidden even to mention that they existed.

## POETS AND PHILOSOPHERS

### Alexander Sergeyevich Pushkin: 1799-1837

Pushkin is considered by the Russians as their greatest poet, but he was also a playwright. Literature prior to Pushkin was patterned after the classical French style. Pushkin is considered the father of Russian literature because he first introduced a typical Russian style—realistic and simple. He was influenced by the works of William Shakespeare and Lord Byron. His most popular work was a novel in verse, *Evgeniy Onegin*. It is the first Russian work that depicts a realistic Russian scene. He also wrote novels and short stories. The best of his novels is *The Captain's Daughter*; the historical basis of the novel was his *History of the Revolt of Pugachev of 1773*. His background was somewhat different than those of most Russian literati. He was born in Moscow to a distinguished noble family. His mother's grandfather was a captured Negro slave who became an important figure in the court of Peter the Great. Pushkin was educated in St. Petersburg. Before graduating school, he was already known as a poet. He wrote his first long poem, *Russlan and Ludmilla*, based on the early epics. Subsequently, he began to write revolutionary verses, for which he was exiled from Moscow—first to Bessarabia, then to his estates in central Russia. Having achieved high acclaim for his work, he was recalled back to Moscow to assume a position in the Foreign Ministry. A love affair embroiled him in a duel in which he was killed. The author had the pleasure of reading his works as a young child in the Soviet Union.

### Vladimir Sergeyevich Soloviev: 1853-1900

A great religious poet and philosopher, Soloviev began publishing his works in 1894 and touched the illusive soul of every Russian reader. A philosopher and mystic, he originally believed in universal Christianity and the unity of the Eastern Orthodox Church with Roman Catholicism. He leaned heavily on the philosophers Spinoza and Hegel, regarding life as a dialectical process which included interaction of knowledge and reality through constant tension. Some later philosophers regarded him as the original symbolist. He was the son of a history professor.

### Alexander Alexandrovich Blok: 1880-1921

Blok was a disciple of Soloviev, a poet, a dramatist, and the ultimate symbolist. He was imbued with Orthodox religious and mystical elements. His work represents his own exhaustion and despair. His works include *The Twelve*, *Vozmezdye*, and the unfinished *Retribution*, a narrative poem. He at first embraced Bolshevism as a chance to redeem the Russian people. His writings didn't suit the Bolshevik regime, who debased his work and aesthetic aspirations. Extremely disappointed with Bolshevism, he fell into a melancholy state and died soon after. He was a highly esteemed poet and philosopher.

**Vladimir Vladimirovich Mayakovskiy: 1893-1930**

Mayakovskiy was a Soviet-era committed Communist, a futurist, and a leading poet of the revolution. He wrote several poems, among them *Love* in 1922; *About This* in 1923; *The Bedbug*, which was performed in 1929; and *Bath*, performed the year of his death. He fell in love numerous times but was always hopelessly disappointed. He was denied a visa to go abroad and committed suicide in Moscow. Stalin considered him the best poet in the Soviet epoch. Regardless of Stalin's praise, his poetry and topics are considered worthy of a true poet.

**Osip Emilevich Mandelstam: 1891-1938**

Mandelstam was born in Warsaw, Poland when it was part of the Russian empire. A Russian cultural Jew, poet, and literary critic, he remained unpublished during the Stalin era. He was well educated from the universities of St. Petersburg, Sorbonne, and Heidelberg. His poems appeared in the journal *Apolon* in 1910; and in 1913 his well-known *Stone* was published. When in 1922 his poem *Tristia* appeared, he was shunned by the Soviet regime. Thereafter, he wrote children's tales and autobiographic stories. In 1925 he wrote *The Noise of Time*, in 1928, *Egyptian Stamp*, and a collection of poems in *Poems*. He was arrested in 1934 when he called Stalin a "murderer and peasant slayer." Released from prison in 1937, he was rearrested in 1938 and was never again heard from. His two memoirs, *Hope Against Hope* and *Hope Abandoned*, were published in the West in 1970s. His last two poems represent a heart-rending description of human hope and despair.

**Anna Akhmatova (Anna Andreyevna Gorenko): 1889-1966**

The most prominent Russian female poetess, Akhmatova was born near Kiev. Her poetry is about women and deals mostly with unsuccessful love. She was married to Nicholas Gumilyov, a literary acmeist, whose style of writing she acquired; however her use of words was rather minimalist but rhythmic. One critic compared it to Debussy, the French composer. Her first book of verse was *Evening*, published in 1912; thereafter she wrote *The Rosary*, published in 1914. In 1917 she wrote *The White Flock* and *The Buckhorn* followed in 1921. In 1922 she wrote *Anno Domini MCMXXI*, in which the theme changes from unhappy love to hate, apparently due to her divorce from Gumilyov. At first she didn't accept the revolution, finding it coarse and brutal, so she stopped writing and publishing. In 1940 she wrote *The Willow*; then followed a selection of poems in *From Six Books*. Her verse was outlawed by the Central Committee in 1946, though in 1959 when the great critic Stalin was dead, her poems appeared in Soviet periodicals. It appears that her best work in poetry was *Poem Without Heroes*. This work took her twenty-two years to accomplish and although she finished it in 1962, it was not published until 1976, in *Apolon*. It rejected acmeist symbolism and replaced it with beautiful clarity. She also wrote some outstanding essays on Pushkin. She is recognized as the greatest woman poet in Russian literature.

**Ilya Grigorievich Ehrenburg: 1891-1967**

Ehrenburg was born in Kiev of a cultural Jewish family and left Russia for Paris in 1910 to write poetry. Returning back to Russia in 1917, he wavered until 1921, trying to decide whether he preferred to stay in Soviet Russia or return to Paris. In 1921 he wrote *Extraordinary Adventures of Julio Jurenito and His Disciples* and received no accolades for his work from the Bolsheviks. However, since he had been to Paris previously, Stalin sent him back—this time as a journalist, to report on Hitler's conquest of France. Returning to the USSR, he wrote a thesis on *The Fall of Paris*. In 1951-52 he wrote *Ninth Wave*, and in 1954, after Stalin's death, he wrote *The Thaw*. Leaving his journalistic experience, he settled to write *People, Years, Life* and his *Memoirs: 1921-1941*, a self-laudatory account. Some journalists and writers consider him a Soviet opportunist and apologist rather than a poet and writer.

**Yevgeniy Aleksandrovich Yevtushenko: 1933-**

Yevtushenko marks a new breed of poets in the Soviet era. He seems never to have lost that characteristic deep feeling for the Russian soul—even under communism. His poems are deeply felt convictions with rhythmic overtones. He wrote his first poem, "The Prospectors of the Future," in 1952, when he was only nineteen. His next effort was in 1955, "The Third Snow," and "Winter Station" followed in 1956. The first English translation of *Selected Poems* was published in 1962. His *Babiy Yar*, an outstanding work, was written in 1961. In 1962 he published a translation in Paris of *Precocious Autobiography*. In 1965 he published *Bratsk Station*, an academic institute in Siberia. He wrote his first novel, *Wild Berries*, and had it published in 1982. He wrote a different poem, *Fuku*, in his collection entitled *Almost at the End* and had it translated in English in 1987.

The names of people and their work identified herein are necessarily confined to those of worldwide fame and exceptional characteristics. Those who never read Russian novels or poetry are missing a potentially important experience. The author highly recommends such reading to really understand the deep feelings expressed in them, since most people who read them clearly express an unforgettable experience, much like lovers of Russian classical music.

## THE VISUAL ARTS

Stanislavskiy, artistic director of stage plays, ushered in a new era in 1902 in the history of realistic theater with naturalistic style. He achieved his greatest realism in directing Maxim Gorkiy's *The Lower Depths*, and since then the theater has changed to his style of acting in interpretive novels of realistic theater. One of his best and outstanding pupils was Ruben Mamoulian, the Hollywood director of the 1930s.

Russians painters Repin and Aivazovskiy are admired for the realistic depictions, while Kandinskiy and Chagall are well known for their abstract works. Ivan Repin, professor at the Academy of Fine Arts in St. Petersburg, painted historical scenes from Russia's past. Ivan Aivazovskiy, an Armenian-Russian, painted numerous realistic scenes of the Black Sea and its violence, then the most vivid expression of stormy seas. In 1896 Vladimir Kandinskiy, a former Moscow mayor turned painter, executed thematic compositional paintings, admired and displayed in the most prominent museums and galleries throughout the world. He was unable to continue his art in Russia, due to his unconventional painting style and left for Europe, where he was acclaimed throughout the world as an avant-garde painter in his medium. His later evolution from figurative to abstract work earned unusual accolades from critics and became the precursor of modernist painting. Marc Chagall, another Russian cultural Jew, is considered one of the greats in abstract painting of the twentieth century. He studied in St. Petersburg under Lev Bakst. He also left Russia because of his cutting-edge style.

## SCIENCES

The first Academy of Sciences was established in St. Petersburg by Peter the Great in the early 1700s. He engaged several Western science professors, mathematicians, naval scientists, and specialists in other disciplines. Russia began its attempt to catch up with western Europe by gathering under one roof some of the best talents available.

Many Russians received scientific acclaim for their work in the nineteenth and twentieth centuries. In 1904 Ivan Pavlov, the great Russian scientist of experimental chemistry and medicine, received the coveted Nobel Prize for his study on conditioned reflexes. In 1895 Constantine Isiolkovskiy formulated the principal of rocket reaction propulsion. Nicholai Lobachevskiy founded non-Euclidean geometry. F.M. Sechenov, a neurophysicist, first discovered psychic phenomena. Dmitriy Mendeleev, the chemist, formulated the periodic law for the classification of the elements.

Peter Leonidovich Kapitsa (1894-1984) was one of the great scientists of the twentieth century. He left Russia for Britain after the revolution and returned to Soviet Russia for a conference but was forbidden by Stalin to return to Britain. A physicist, he shared the Nobel Prize in Physics in 1978 in research on magnetism and low temperature physics. He discovered that helium 2 has almost no viscosity, which is known as superfluity. He lost his wife and two children during the civil war in Russia. Educated at Petrograd Polytechnic Institute, he left for Britain, where he studied further at Cambridge University. He became a fellow at Trinity College in Cambridge in 1925—a rare honor for a foreigner. He refused to work in the Soviet Union on nuclear weapons.

Igor Vasilievich Kurchatov (1903-60) was a soviet physicist; a science institute in Moscow bears his name. One of the great scientists of the twentieth century, he headed a laboratory of experimental science in atomic power. By 1933 he was conducting studies for an atomic power station. He was the director of nuclear physics laboratory at Physico-Technical Institute and directed the construction of the first atomic reactor and cyclotron in 1944 in fusion energy.

Andrey Dmitrievich Sakharov (1921-1989) was an outspoken advocate of human rights and reform in the Soviet Union and rapprochement with noncommunist nations. The developer of controlled thermonuclear reaction, he wrote a thesis entitled, "Thought on Progress of Peaceful Coexistence and Intellectual Freedom." He denounced the Soviet invasion of Afghanistan and boycotted the Moscow Olympics. Gorbachev released him from exile and isolation in 1986. He was elected to the Congress of Peoples Deputies in 1989. After his death, his memoirs were published by his wife.

The Soviet space program's achievements in the sixties were motivated by political considerations and propaganda incentives by Khrushchev when Sputnik was the first launched spacecraft in orbit. It was scientifically an elementary globe which lacked a matching sophistication and instrumentation. Its launching was intended as a showpiece of Soviet science and was sent up to beat the first American space launch. The next major effort focused on the race to the moon, which the United States won by landing its astronauts on the moon first, causing a Soviet withdrawal from the moon program. To summarize Russian achievements in science, one has to give Russia high marks for their early efforts—although Western science (particularly American), is substantially ahead, with no political strings attached. Russian poets, novelists, musical composers, and other artistic people have carried on the tradition of excellence into the twentieth century, from their beginnings and achievements in the early nineteenth century through the collapse of the Soviet Union. The reader is free to conclude—bearing in mind Russia's isolation from the Western world—whether the Golden Age of Russian ended in 1860 or continues to this day.

# CHAPTER XV
# RUSSIA REDUX

On 19 May 1990 Boris Nikolayevich Yeltsin was elected president of the Supreme Soviet of the Russian Soviet Federated Socialist Republic. He resigned from the Communist party on 12 July of the same year and decreed the Russian Federation's control over all its natural resources. On 24 October he further decreed that no laws of the USSR would have effect in the Russian Federation unless first approved by Russia. He then ran for president of the Russian Federation and won the election on 12 June 1991. Prior to these events, Yeltsin had been a member of Gorbachev's Politburo, but they asked him to leave the post for criticizing certain arbitrary methods used by members and not paying attention to solving serious problems confronting the USSR. In August of 1991, an attempted coup was mounted against Gorbachev in Crimea, where he was vacationing with his family. The coup leaders were opposed to his reformist democratic measures and claimed the country was being driven into chaos. The principal coup leaders were all hardliners and members of Gorbachev's Politburo. They were KGB Chief Kruichkov, Defense Minister Yazov, Interior Minister Pugo, Chairman of the Supreme Soviet Luikianov, and Prime Minister Gavril Pavlov. The attempted coup fizzled due to the ineptness of the plotters, who acted on their own and were out of touch with reality. Political and social conditions in the country to support a coup without consent of the Central Committee were tenuous at best. Subsequently these men were arrested, tried, and then released after the dissolution of the USSR on the grounds they had acted legally under the country's prevailing constitution.

Meanwhile, returning to Moscow, Gorbachev found himself alone and powerless, thrusting about the country as a figurehead, trying to mend fences with hardliners and reformist democratic forces. On 29 August all national Communist party activities were banned in the Russian Federation. Between 30 August and 25 November several former union republics declared independence and rejected a proposed union treaty by Gorbachev. The USSR was finally forced to recognize the independence of the Baltic States as an accomplished fact. Yeltsin, as president of the RSFSR, took control of all former Soviet economy in the Russian Federation. By 25 December, Russia, Ukraine, and Belarus declared the formation of the Commonwealth of Independent States, and all five central Asian republics, as well as the three TransCaucasian republics joined the CIS.

Faced with this dilemma and deprived of any meaningful role as president of a now-defunct Soviet Union, Gorbachev was forced to resign as president and declared the USSR dissolved, effective 25 December 1991. From 19 August through 25 December 1991—in a matter of a few months—the ill-conceived Soviet Union with its 292 million captive people expired.

Russia was reborn after seventy-four years of unmitigated failure of Soviet socialist dictatorship with its experiments, slave labor, murder, and hermetically sealed borders. Never in recorded history has there been a system of rule similar to that of the USSR. After leaving the so-called Union totally bankrupt, corrupt, and exhausted, it evaporated in a flash. The confusion created by this void was so stunning that it is still reverberating at this writing and perhaps it will for years to come because of the many unkept utopian promises. Various proposals were submitted to get the government-run large and small enterprises converted into free economy. While this method was the most preferable, it soon became evident that it was an impossible task. It was abandoned as unrealistic and impractical. Had it been seriously attempted, it would have caused unbearable unemployment of proportions never before experienced by any major nation. The depression years in the United States would have looked childish in comparison. Under original schemes proposed with "quick fix, shock-therapy" methods, soon became evident that the socialist economy as practiced in the Soviet Union was so enmeshed in government bureaucracy and guaranteed birth to death employment and benefits, regardless of poor labor performance, that most enterprises would probably had to fire 75 percent of non-required employees, and they would have been on the public dole.

At first the government experimented with bond issues in small agricultural tracts which could benefit small farmers and achieved partial success until inflation took over and squashed the experiment. Grigoriy Yavlinskiy, Russia's most astute free enterprise economist, and Yegor Gaidar tried, but unfortunately it failed under severe inflation. Small business entrepreneurs have succeeded in electronics goods, restaurants, street bazaars, automobile agencies, selected banking enterprises, and businesses which cater to more affluent consumers. The great majority of the retired people are receiving scant, delayed retirement pay. Some workers at this writing haven't been paid for months, which constrains mass market buying.

The author is convinced that the general conversion of major industries to private ownership is years away, if ever in the foreseeable future. A partial solution could be accomplished with foreign capital and management, with severe reduction in manpower, with updated equipment, and by retraining employees in the concept of the work ethic. With Communist and Nationalist party members in the majority in the Duma—who detest cheaply selling out these enterprises to Americans and foreigners—this prospect is highly unlikely, at least for now, due to the the command economy, although foreign management of enterprises could be accomplished successfully without a buyout, if quality products were sold for export with lower prices to gain hard currency and reduce inflation. It is reasonable to assume free enterprise consumer industry for the home market will eventually succeed. The demand for consumer goods during the Soviet regime was overwhelming and it is more so now. Unless some measure in this direction is taken soon, inflation will keep rising and leave a substantial void in filling this area. Since Mafia gangs are rampant and corruption is inbred, consumer industry will suffer for some time to come, unless the consumers reject bribery—an unlikely scenario in the short run. At this writing, the command economy still exists in all principal industries and collective farming left over from the old regime. The former communist managers of industrial enterprises changed uniforms and are still running all the major government enterprises. No one else has the expertise to take their places, even considering how bad they are. Deals between these managers continue as before. Industrial organizations have a powerful lobby in the Duma to promote their interests and survive intact. The socialist political-economic system was so intertwined into a massive command economy that had these principal industries been converted immediately under a free economic system, they would have most probably collapsed, with mass unemployment ensuing. All heavy industry—including armaments plants, natural resource extraction, and gas and oil industries—are of such magnitude that no amount of capital could possibly be raised for conversion at this writing.

At present, the only solution seems to leave things alone until further developments take their course. The fledgling stock market may yet play a significant role in days to come. Since the infrastructure of breakneck industrialization was the original goal of the former regime, equipment breakdowns are still common and outworn machineries are still in place, according to the reports from observers. The government would do well to export raw goods to gain currency, which still attracts foreign buyers. Even under the Imperial regime, which had mostly private ownership, Russia was always in debt and was forced to borrow funds to meet its internal debt obligations. In the abstract sense, it is impossible to correct and transform a system, as was originally intended after the dissolution, by free enterprise experts. It was rather easy for Lenin and his Bolsheviks to confiscate all assets from the capitalists of the Imperial regime and nationalize the entire economy, which was there for the taking. It's quite a different thing to convert it back from the socialized takeover and untangle the artificially created economic mess, intermingled as it is. In order to succeed and attain a normal business enterprise, workers and management would have to change their entire attitudes and psyches, from reliance on unacceptable work habits—after years of habitual absenteeism, alcoholism, and lack of dedication—to hard work. Therein lies the critical problem. Old habits apparently die hard. The author doubts the present generation of workers could change and accept conversion so easily, particularly with meager rewards for their efforts.

The social problem will be solved much sooner, since they breathe easier now, what with the freedom of speech and press, and no arbitrary arrests—but not the habits inherited in their work ethic; these will last for a lifetime. The problems in free Russia are overwhelmingly difficult at best. The Western democracies will have to live with this dilemma for years to come and learn to accept it. The economic problems in Russia make the future bleak. No amount of foreign capital infused into the economy could change the system and its psyche. With all the resources available for exploitation, they couldn't even feed their population properly. Antiquated equipment, machinery, and methods are no longer competitive in the world markets—except for armaments, but there are too few outlaw nations presently buying them. When added to the lack of advanced technology and maintenance, as in oil and gas pipe leaks, perhaps these losses alone could have made the difference between decent livelihood and starvation.

The Yeltsin government is reduced to depend on the IMF, the World Bank, and G-7 handouts and private loans from foreign banks just to pay workers and pensioners back wages. The communist regime perpetuated itself on the backs of the proletariat and refined its lifestyle by milking dry the proletariat and peasantry. Where did all the capital go? It may be a dilemma on the surface, but it is mostly explainable since *nomenklatura* had full control of the funds at their disposal, yet no one ever asked them. While most of the world's free economies, large and small, thrived economically, the Soviet economy ran out of steam years before. Their armaments industries, with their precision instruments, got the lion's share of capital, but it doesn't necessarily follow that other enterprises could have benefited the same, since no capital was available for such luxuries to the working proletariat. From the point of view of world economy, presently Russia is an abundant land of second world economy, dependent on handouts to correct its communist past. While the rest of the world's industrialized countries are converting to information technology, Russia is still battling with outdated and noncompetitive methods. With regard to agriculture, with its combines, tractors, and silos, its accomplishments should be considered not better than a mid-nineteenth-century effort, at best—when tractors and combines didn't even exist. Yet under the Imperial regime in the early twentieth century, Russia had a surplus of grain for export to Europe. It fed its people adequately and depressed its foreign debt, even though most peasants were illiterate. If this is not a condemnation of the Bolshevist economic endeavor, what is it?

In essence, when one analyzes Russia's superpower status, it should be concluded that there is an advanced segment in scientific production with an intellectual class feeding its chauvinistic military and third world countries, while the rest of the country is still second world. Just before its dissolution in 1991, the Soviet Union should have been classified as a leader among second world nations, with abundant natural resources, excessive military force with nuclear weapons, and a bleak future. The Pacific rim countries of East Asia are so technologically and economically advanced, it is doubtful Russia can catch up in the foreseeable future. Yet its intellectual potential is wasted on the production of weapons of mass destruction. Japan, South Korea, China, Philippines, Singapore, Hong Kong, Malaysia, Indonesia, Taiwan, and some other smaller countries are thriving intellectually and economically, yet thirty-five years earlier, some of them had practically nothing to speak of other than exporting of tin, rubber, oil, and sundry items. Russia—with its wealth of natural resources, an educated workforce, and a base of institutions of higher learning—should have been a truly first-rate nation, almost equal to any in the West, yet it was ground down by an economic system which, at best, was utopian, anachronistic, a hoax, and lost its usefulness years ago. Yet it couldn't get rid of it, due to inner and outer layers of *nomenklatura*, with its pervasive dictatorship guarding its privileges to the end of its days and living luxuriously today. A nation of history, with outstanding artists, scientists, thinkers, and philosophers, subjected to an unworkable experiment, while the rest of the world progressed and advanced. The reader should remember that there isn't a nation or combination of nations in the world which has more natural resources than the former Soviet Union, yet they couldn't feed or clothe their workers properly and held them in bondage.

The 1989 revolution in the satellite countries clearly demonstrated the failure of forty-five years of occupation, dictation, and social bankruptcy of the entire structure. The fall of the Berlin Wall in 1989 was not an accident, and though we never thought it would happen in our lifetime, clearly it was exhaustion under a compressed system of total dictatorship in all facets of life. Though the satellite countries ate and lived better than their socialist compatriots in the USSR, Soviet troops were in East Germany, pretending to confront NATO and provide protection against the capitalist exploiters. The Berlin Wall symbolized insecurity and lack of credibility of East Germany's existence. The domino effect on bolshevized Europe was so rapid that in Poland, Czechoslovakia, Hungary, Yugoslavia, Bulgaria, Rumania, and Albania, communism expired almost instantaneously. Similarly, the Baltic countries couldn't wait for the dissolution of the USSR and left the Union as fast as they could. By the end of 1991, not only they, but all other so-called minority nations of the former USSR, separated at dissolution. At first these minority nations were nothing more than satellites to be exploited, but they later turned out to be a heavy economic burden.

Soviet maps and data in possession of the author, show the glowing picture of the Soviet Union's wealth, demographics, natural resources, production goals, and other miscellaneous data were figments of Soviet imagination. The ecological damage created by roughshod methods is of such magnitude it should be considered a catastrophe which would take billions and billions to correct, if ever. It was a legacy left for the Russian Federation and the former republics. These calamities never bothered the commissars in Moscow, who enjoyed life with only car pollution emissions. The health of its citizens has never been good; with declining birth rates and high death rates, the country's future looks bleak indeed.

What then is the future of free Russia at peace with itself? This question plagues many Russian and Western scholars alike, with no historic precedent in the recent past to guide them. The Soviet Union was a militaristic nation similar to Hitler's Germany, yet Germany was defeated in the last war and shed its image by rejuvenating itself into a civilized society in pursuit of tranquillity, a model of democracy, and an economic powerhouse. The 1993 constitution written by Yeltsin gives strong power to the chief executive over the Duma, yet the Communists and Nationalists hold a majority in it, enjoying full democracy. When will the Russians learn? However, the author contends that democratization will continue since Russians are enjoying its advantages, but not yet its economic benefits.

Paranoiac fear of encirclement by NATO haunts the legislators as well as the government leaders, afraid of NATO's encirclement by incorporating former satellite countries at their own requests. This fear seems to have an overriding effect on foreign policy objectives; why don't they join NATO if they are so afraid? Their abstention and their use of the veto in the UN and the contact group in the Balkan quagmire are also controlled by fear. Another fear is their conviction that a free economy will buy out their industries. All these inherited complications confront Russia with an unknown future. The solution to these dilemmas and fears should be collectively decided by the people themselves by the exercise of their hard-won democratic rights with their legislators. In either event, the decisions should not be left to legislators, which is happening at this writing. It no longer matters who wins the election—Yeltsin or the opposition—in the June and July elections because the die was cast for democracy after Yeltsin was elected in 1992. Thus far their eleven-hundred-year history has been mostly written in blood. Why shouldn't a suffering, patient, and deserving people have a chance to their own future?

**Assessment on Russia**

Should the Kremlin archives ever be available for review, as a few documents have already been, they could shed substantial light on Soviet secrets and pretensions—much more than are available at this writing. A substantial amount is already known, even before Hoover Institution's contract to microfilm them. This contract was to be canceled in July 1996. Whether it is or not canceled, one suspects a substantial amount is already known by Western scholars. Perhaps the only exception may be numbers of people who died in slave labor camps or executions by Stalin, his other cruelties, and confirmation of his direct orders to the KGB execution squads. One other place of possible revelation is the Brezhnev era and its military, social-economic, and political thinking. Some important data on the Stalingrad battle and its horrible casualty list has already been revealed. Nevertheless, even without all the archives, the Soviet Union turned out to be a murder machine and the greatest hoax which ever existed, causing turmoil throughout the world for seventy-four years. It was at first Lenin whom Maxim Gorkiy characterized as a "trickster" with his diabolic experiments. Subsequently, the system was fine-tuned and perfected by the self-perpetuating Stalin, the pathological killer and liar. It was left to his successors, who practiced without open murder through psychiatric clinics accommodating the dissenters. His successors perpetuated a fiefdom unknown in history. It took unprecedented courage of a people who had finally had enough of cruel dictatorship to finally wrest power from the hardliners, who contested it by intimidation to the last.

In retrospect, one should review the entire history of Russian nationhood and question whether the Imperial regime had any prospects of constitutional monarchical rule through evolutionary stages. The author believes that given a chance, it would have been possible through the pre-revolutionary Duma. The Russian leaders will have to finally accept the simple code of human behavior and realize the greatest asset they possess. Although Nicholas II's uncles warned him to accommodate the Duma, he wouldn't. He was only human, and his successor undoubtedly would have assumed constitutional monarchy.

Now that the decision has been made, they will have to accept outright democracy in a republic. Why should the Russian people who suffered through constant wars, revolutions, convulsions, collectivization, famines, purges, executions, slave labor, serfdom, autocracy, and dictatorship again suffer and be subjected to further punishment? The Russians, a long suffering, complacent, patient, and kind people, deserve better. The leaders would do well to steer them in the direction of the future of true democracy. They should also remember that the greatest asset they have is their people, whose lives are precious. Will they remember who elected them and why?

"The nature of the state has yet to be defined by the Yelzin government."